FAMILY LAW AND CUSTOMARY LAW IN ASIA: A CONTEMPORARY LEGAL PERSPECTIVE

FAMILY LAW AND CUSTOMARY LAW IN ASIA:

A CONTEMPORARY LEGAL PERSPECTIVE

Editor,

DAVID C. BUXBAUM

Springer-Science+Business Media, B.V. 1968

Originally published by Martinus Nijhoff, The Hague, Netherlands in 1968
Softcover reprint of the hardcover 1st edition 1968

ISBN 978-94-017-5794-2 *ISBN 978-94-017-6216-8 (eBook)*
DOI 10.1007/978-94-017-6216-8

TO SHEILA BUXBAUM BIER

But there was no breeze in the air, no cloud in the sky.... There was only a presence.

André Schwarz-Bart,
The Last of the Just

The Conference on Family Law and Customary Law in Asia
of which this volume is a result
was sponsored by

THE ASSOCIATION OF SOUTHEAST ASIAN INSTITUTIONS
OF HIGHER LEARNING

Singapore, April, 1964

PREFACE

The Conference on Family Law and Customary Law in Asia, which was held in Singapore in April, 1964, was sponsored by the Association of Southeast Asian Institutions of Higher Learning (A.S.A.I.H.L.). This organization, founded in 1957, "...has the objective of promoting the economic, social, cultural and civic welfare of the people of the Southeast Asian region by the exchange of information, teachers and students among the institutions of higher learning of the region and by suggestions for cooperative action in the development of educational and research programmes by such institutions."

The Administrative Board of A.S.A.I.H.L. includes: Col. Dr. Sjarif Thajeb, Rector, University of Indonesia (President): Prof. Sir Lindsay Ride, Vice-Chancellor, University of Hong Kong (Vice-President); Dato Sir Alexander Oppenheim, Vice-Chancellor, University of Malaya; Miss Helena Z. Benitez, Executive Vice-President, Philippine Women's University; Prof. Huang Ying Jung, Nanyang University (Singapore); Prof. Dr. Svasti Daengsvang, Rector, University of Medical Science (Thailand); Prof. Le Van Lam, University of Saigon (Vietnam).

The very able Secretariat located at Chulalongkorn University in Bangkok is composed of Prof. Prince Prem Purachatra, Executive Secretary; Dr. Prachoom Chomchai, Secretary; Dr. Kusuma Sanitwongse, Assistant Secretary; and Dr. Lydia na Ranong, Administrative Assistant.

A.S.A.I.H.L. has been extremely active since its inception, and, for example, since December 18, 1965, has sponsored or will sponsor the following conferences: Fourteenth Meeting of the Administrative Board (Thammasat University, Bangkok); Seminar on the Role of Universities in Human Resource Development (University of Malaya, Kuala Lumpur); Seminar on the Role of Universities in Economic and Social Development (University of Singapore, Singapore); Seminar on Mathematics and Natural and Physical Sciences (Saigon); Seminar on Agriculture and Veterinary Science (Bogor); Seminar on Language Problems in Southeast Asian Universities (Philippine Women's University, Manila); and Sixth General Conference (Bangkok).

The Asia Foundation was most generous in supporting the conference both financially and administratively. Particular thanks must go to Lindley S. Sloan, the Asia Foundation Representative in Singapore during the conference, who was of substantial assistance in eliminating obstacles and expediting administrative procedures so that delegates from all over the world might be brought to Singapore for the conference.

The Lee Foundation also helped to support some of the delegates, and its help is sincerely appreciated.

The Far Eastern Department of the University of Washington was most generous in supporting me both financially and otherwise so that I had the opportunity to edit these papers. Particular thanks must be expressed to Professor Hellmut Wilhelm who has withstood my continual requests with equanimity and guided and assisted me. Eileen Dillon not only helped to type the manuscript, but also made numerous helpful suggestions.

Finally my wife, Dvorah Buxbaum, who proofread the manuscript on several occasions with care and diligence must be thanked for her patience and forebearance as well as her help.

Unfortunately the papers of all the delegates to the conference could not be published at this time for technical reasons. The delegates to the conference of course are the ones who made the conference a success and made this book possible. Particular thanks to Dr. George Kurian, Head of the Far Eastern Department of Victoria University of Wellington, and to Professor Huang Yin Jung, Head of the Department of Political Science, Nanyang University, Singapore, whose papers are not included but who played a substantial role in the conference.

D. C. Buxbaum
Hongkong, 1966

CONFERENCE PARTICIPANTS

Professor S. Takdir Alisjabbana, Head, Department of Malay Studies, University of Malaya, Kuala Lumpur, Malaysia

Dr. Joseph Minattur, Professor of Law, Nanyang University, Singapore

Mr. Benedict Sandin, Sarawak Museum, Kuching, Sarawak, Malaysia

Dr. Vermier Yanatak Chiu, University of Hong Kong (Deceased)

U Hla Aung, Esquire, Faculty of Law, University of Singapore, Singapore

Professor Luang Chamroon Netisastra, Faculty of Law, Thammasat University, Thailand; Former President of the Supreme Court of Thailand

Professor Adul Wichiencharoen, Dean, Faculty of Liberal Arts, Thammasat University, Thailand

Inche Ahmad bin Mohamed Ibrahim, State Advocate-General, Singapore

Inche Haji Mohamed Din bin Ali, Municipal Secretary, Kuala Lumpur, Malaysia

Dr. S. P. Khetarpal, Faculty of Law, University of Singapore, Singapore

Dr. K. Ishwaran, Department of Sociology, York University, Toronto, Canada; Editor, Journal of Asian and African Studies

Professor Nguyen Xuan Chanh, Faculty of Law, University of Saigon, Vietnam

Professor Hassanally A. Rahman, Principal, Sind Muslim Law College, Karachi, West Pakistan

Dr. Syed Hussein Alatas, Department of Malay Studies, University of Malaya, Kuala Lumpur, Malaysia

Dr. Victor M. Fic, Professor of International Relations, Nanyang University, Singapore

Dr. Voon-Kai Foo, Professor of Commercial Law; Head, Department of Banking and Finance, Nanyang University, Singapore

Professor Huang Yin Jung, Head, Department of Political Science, Nanyang University, Singapore

Professor T. C. Hwang, Executive Secretary, Law Research Institute, Taipei, Taiwan, Republic of China

Dr. George Kurian, Head, Department of Asian Studies, Victoria University of Wellington, Wellington, New Zealand

Dr. Pablo Tangco, Graduate School, University of Santo Tomas, Philippines

Mrs. Ann Wee, Social Studies Department, University of Singapore, Singapore

David C. Buxbaum,
Conference Chairman and Organizer
University of Washington
Seattle, Washington

TABLE OF CONTENTS

INTRODUCTION

The Conference on Family Law and Customary Law in Asia, of which this book is a product, was initiated in the hope that scholars and law practitioners in Asia could—with the help of social scientists—begin a theoretical and practical analysis of some of the problems involved in administering law in communities where custom and customary law exert important influences upon dispute resolution. The conference focused primarily upon problems of family law in view of the particular perseverance of customary influences in this area of the law.

The problem of the interrelationship between the formal legal organs and indigenous customary law is of course only a small portion of a larger problem, i.e., the role of law in modernizing societies.

One result of the conference was a classification of some of the legal problems which are common to most modernizing societies, both in Asia and elsewhere, where the formal legal institutions are often modeled after European institutions while the social institutions reflect patterns quite different from those that gave birth to the common law or civil law.

During the colonial period, all of the countries of Asia were subject to the impact of Western law. Not only did the Asian peoples come to know of the workings of Western law through study at home and abroad, but also the Western-dominated governments of Asia established courts and promulgated codes and statutes that were based upon Western law—and in fact were often duplicates of such laws. Despite the enactment of these law codes, the traditional customary law of the Asian societies was, and generally is, the primary legal force for dispute resolution in most Asian countries. Westernization and Western law only affected a relatively small group of people in most Asian countries, to the extent that they found the Western style law courts and codes a congenial arena for settling legal disputes. This is not to suggest that traditional customary law remained static. It too was undergoing change, particularly as the result of modernization and the Western intrusion into Asia—but the change was and is not so extensive that the „Western" law codes have come to fill the hiatus between law and society comfortably. This particular problem, i.e., the hiatus that exists between Asian society, and the family law and legal institutions promulgated by the government, is one that was made obvious and elucidated by the conferees. The conference focussed particularly on the manner in which the legal institutions have addressed themselves to this question.

The conference was concerned initially with the nature of customary law, thereafter dealt with the interaction and conflict between the formal legal institutions and customary law, and finally dealt with some specific problems of customary law and the family in a modernizing society.

I. The Nature of Customary Law in Diverse Asian Societies

Eugene Ehrlich said: "At the present as well as at any other time, the center of gravity of legal development lies not in legislation, nor in juristic science, nor in judicial decision, but in society itself."[1] Ehrlich, however, recognized the element of command or "state norms" although he did not foresee the extensive role this aspect of the law was to play in industrialized society. Nevertheless he helped to show that the norms, or "customary law," observed by the family, commercial institutions and religious bodies are of substantial importance in determining people's behavior, and in fact in determining what he called law. In pre-industrial society, where political power and authority are generally relatively weak, Maine has shown that there was heavy reliance upon customary and religious law and institutions.[2]

Most Asian societies (with the possible exception of Japan),[3] although in stages of rapid social change, retain strong characteristics of simpler technological societies, i.e., pre-literate societies, and peasant societies of the pre-modern tradition. A major distinction between these preliterate societies and peasant societies is that the latter have for centuries been in "constant contact with the centers of intellectual thought

[1] Ehrlich, Eugene, *Fundamental Principles of the Sociology of Law* (Cambridge, 1936), Walter Moll, translator, Foreword.

[2] H. Maine, *Early History of Institutions* (1888) 26, 38–40. See also Julius Stone, *The Province and Function of Law* (Cambridge, 1961) p. 457 ff.

[3] But see von Mehren, A. T., "The Legal Order in Japan's Changing Society: Some Observations," 76 *Harvard Law Review* 1170 (1963) at p. 1193-4, and related literature which indicates that despite the fact that "...postwar Japanese family law destroys much of the legal structure that supported the hierarchical and collectivist concept of the family..." nevertheless, "[t]he collectivist tendency—the emphasis on the group's good—still remains strong...."

and development...."[1] Thus Redfield noted that in peasant societies two interdependent traditions, i.e., that of the reflective few and that of the unreflective many, are constantly interacting.[2] Of course both pre-literate societies and peasant societies have some common characteristics, but this general distinction is useful for our discussion. In the legal field we can, for purposes of convenience, identify the "great tradition" with the august religious-ethical codes and the secular legal codes often formed under the influence of these religious ethical codes. The customary law of the common people might properly be identified with the "little tradition." Yet it must be borne in mind, as Redfield states, that there was continuous contact between the "great" and "little" traditions, and thus mutual influences; "The two traditions are interdependent."

In the institutional field it is possible, although perhaps less precise, to identify the formal law courts—at least at the highest levels of traditional Asian peasant society—with the "great tradition"; while identifying the social institutions such as lineages and clans, which also administered the law, with the "little tradition." Perhaps the lowest courts and/or the gentry (who performed legal services such as conciliation), as Redfield suggests, form the hinge between the local institutions of the people and those of the state in the legal arena. Both these traditions are of course presently in contact with Western technological society.

Customary law is of substantial importance in both pre-literate and peasant societies, but it has certain differentiable characteristics in each.[3]

In the pre-literate societies, groups tend to be smaller, there is generally less contact with wider groupings, and thus "...a greater degree of conformity is psychologically necessary."[4] Thus in Sarawak, customary law is the basis for settling many disputes.[5] The headmen of

[1] Robert Redfield, *Peasant Society and Culture: An Anthropological Approach to Civilization* (Chicago, 1956) at p. 69, where he quotes George M. Foster, above, with approval. Redfield tentatively defined peasant society as characterized by: "an intense attachment to native soil, a reverent disposition toward habitual and ancestral ways, a restraint on individual self-seeking in favor of family and community, a certain suspiciousness, mixed with appreciation of town life, a sober and earthy ethic." at p. 140.

[2] *Ibid.*, at p. 70–72.

[3] This is not to discount its importance in modern legal systems where as H. S. Morris noted, in a personal correspondence, modern factories are small social systems having a whole array of norms or customs, some of which may become incorporated into rules and regulations and others of which are examined by the courts.

[4] Edward Sapir, "Custom," III *Encyclopedia of the Social Sciences* (New York, 11th printing, 1954) E. R. A. Seligman, editor; p. 658, at p. 661.

[5] Benedict Sandin, "Some Iban (Sea Dyak) Customary Law in Sarawak," *infra*.

the long-houses, farm-chiefs and other leaders settle disputes in accord with animistic beliefs. The long-house is "...an independent unit relying for its continued existence upon the creation and maintenance of a relationship with the 'unseen powers'.... By the proper conduct of ritual, from the major and minor 'festivals' (gawai) to the provision of offerings, the exercise of 'magic' and utterance of words of power, the people and their possessions must be kept in a satisfactory state of balance among themselves and in relation to the 'unseen powers.'"[1] The farms, houses, property, and people in their families all have their own spiritual balance which must be maintained. "Any disturbance of the balance be corrected without delay."[2] "Restoration of the balance..." is accomplished "...by furnishing a 'fine'... [i.e.] by making good the loss with something of equal ritual value."[3] These customary fines are generally enforced by "public opinion."[4]

Thus in the pre-literate societies the institutions for administering law are generally less formal and less "rationalized" or "rational." Perhaps R. Schmidt's and Weber's terminology is useful here in that we can associate "Kadi-justice" predominantly with pre-literate society; while "empirical" and even perhaps on occasion "rational" justice may be more readily associated with certain aspects of peasant society.[5] "Kadi-justice" is "primarily bound by sacred traditions," or "revelation" in its system for settling cases. It employs techniques such as divination, ordeal, prophetic dicta and other religious, magical crafts as adjudicatory techniques. Weber also suggests that in "Kadi-justice" there may also be "...informal judgments rendered in terms of concrete ethical or other practical valuations." However, I would suggest that this latter aspect of justice can be more properly associated with "empirical" justice. At any rate, "Kadi-justice" tends to be predominant in the legal systems of pre-literate society, which may also have aspects of "empirical" and perhaps even a little "rational" justice.

In peasant society, "empirical" justice, i.e., "...formal judgments... rendered, though not by subsumption under rational concepts, but by drawing on 'analogies' and by depending upon and interpreting concrete 'precedents'" is of substantial significance especially in the

[1] A. J. N. Richards, *Dyak Adat Law in the Second Division* (Sarawak, 1963) at p. 1.
[2] *Ibid.*, at p. 2.
[3] *Ibid.*
[4] These customary fines must be distinguished from laws imposed by authorities outside the longhouse.
[5] See *From Max Weber: Essays in Sociology* (ed. and trans. by H. H. Gerth and C. Wright Mills) (New York, 1958) at p. 216. See also *Max Weber on Law in Economy and Society*, ed. by Max Rheinstein, trans. by M. Rheinstein and E. Shils (Cambridge, 1954).

"great tradition." As Weber notes, this "empirical" justice is not unknown in industrial societies.[1] Weber attempts to separate "empirical" justice from "rational" justice. He associates the latter with the feature that "...in principle a system of rationally debatable 'reasons' stands behind every act of bureaucratic administration, that is, either subsumption under norms or a weighing of ends and means." He associates rational administration in law and government with bureaucratization, experts and scientific administration.[2] Conceptually systematized rational law is associated with bureaucracy and modern society. While Weber's knowledge, and thus understanding, of certain aspects of traditional Asian law was seriously incomplete,[3] and his categories not always as relevant as one might wish, they are nevertheless of substantial use for our purposes, for they help us classify certain aspects of law in different types of society.

In summary, "Kadi-justice" especially as being bound by sacred tradition is particularly characteristic of adjudication in pre-literate society. The second feature of "Kadi-justice," i.e., informal judgments rendered in terms of concrete ethical or practical values, is quite characteristic of the conciliation so predominant in the "little tradition" of peasant societies as well as in pre-literate societies.[4] The "great tradition" is characterized by "empirical justice," i.e., formal judgments rendered by drawing on analogies and interpreting concrete precedents. "Rational justice" can be primarily associated with contemporary Westernized legal institutions and some aspects of the legal institutions of the "great tradition" of peasant society.

Not only is the nature of legal administration different, but explicit in the above classifications of law are certain institutional characteristics for administering law. Thus "empirical" or "rational" justice would generally require formal legal machinery of a complicated nature to administer the law.

[1] *Essays in Sociology, op. cit.*, p. 217.

[2] For example, one of the qualities which he rightfully attributes to the bureaucracy is: "The management of the office follows general rules, which are more or less stable, more or less exhaustive, and which can be learned. Knowledge of these rules represents a special technical learning which the officials possess. It involves jurisprudence, or administrative or business management." *Ibid.*, p. 198.

[3] For example he states re: traditional Chinese law, "...in spite of the traditionalism, there was no official collection of precedents because legal formalism was rejected and, above all, because there was no central court as in England,"—which are two largely erroneous assumptions. Max Weber, *The Religion of China, Confucianism and Taoism*; Hans H. Gerth, translator and editor (New York, 1951) at p. 102.

[4] Conciliation of a sort is also an important legal procedure in pre-literate society. See for example Lucy Mair, *Primitive Government* (Maryland, 1962) at p. 41, where she describes a "professional mediator" with "special ritual powers" who can perform the "rite of reconciliation" in Nuer society.

In Ch'ing China (1644–1911) for example, local customary law (which we may associate primarily with the "little tradition") operated within an idealized framework of rites (*li*) and under a code that was national in scope. The *li* and code, along with the collection of cases and the hierarchy of official courts—all of which were part of the "greater tradition"—administered what we may primarily designate "empirical" and in part "rational" justice. The lineages, clans, elders, gentry, *pao-chia* and *li-chia* leaders may be said to have generally administered "Kadi-justice." In Sarawak on the other hand, it was predominantly "Kadi-justice" administered by the heads of the long-house that prevailed. Leaders of lineages and clans, tribal chieftans, family elders, etc., are generally the administrators of "Kadi-justice" in peasant or pre-literate society.

The legal machinery in Ch'ing times was extensive, the bureaucracy complicated and elaborate, and the body of precedents, statutory material, ethical codes, collected cases, handbooks, etc., were imposing. Traditional Chinese peasant society, with its elaborate bureaucracy, may represent one extreme of peasant society, while Sarawak is a more typical pre-literate society. Malay society may be said to lie somewhere between traditional Chinese society and the society of the Dyaks of Sarawak insofar as legal institutions are concerned.

The traditional society of the Malays was composed of the "...individual, the family, then the tribes, who constitute the components of the State."[1] In the *perpateh* tradition of Negri Sembilan, there are twelve tribes presided over by various chieftans. The *adat perpateh*, following matrilineal tribal forms except when electing a king, is usually interpreted by village elders and clan chieftains.[2] The pithy sayings handed down from generation to generation and known to all provided the basis for customary law. Thus the basis of rules of exogamy are contained in such sayings as, "Our boys are wed to other clans"; and, "A stranger weds into our clan. For every stranger that weds into our clan, a share is set with just consent."[3] Conciliation was a primary means of settling disputes. Thus, aside from "Kadi-justice" which would predominate, there might be some "empirical justice" but little "rational justice."

In separating justice into "Kadi," "empirical" and "rational" justice, we are primarily describing the system of administering justice,

[1] Inche Ahmad bin Mohamed Ibrahim, "Islam and Customary Law in the Malaysian Legal Context," see *infra*.

[2] Joseph Minattur, "The Nature of Malay Customary Law," see *infra*.

[3] *Ibid.*

and by implication the institutions which administer the law, rather than characterizing the substantive law itself. Thus, while we talk of "Kadi-justice" as being bound by sacred tradition or revelation, we are referring primarily to the means of settling disputes. As Weber describes "Kadi-justice": "The single case that cannot be unambiguously decided by tradition is... settled by concrete 'revelation' (oracle, prophetic dicta, or ordeal—that is, by 'charismatic' justice)...." While in part we are reflecting upon the nature of the substantive law itself, we are substantially concerned with the system of administration.

How can we characterize this substantive customary law which emanates from the varied pre-literate and peasant societies of Asia? What are its common attributes?

In the first place this traditional customary law has been subject to a multitude of influences. The great religions and cultures of Asia—in particular Islam, Buddhism and Hinduism, as well as what we may loosely characterize as Confucianism in its religious and ethical connotation—have had substantial impact upon, and have in turn been influenced by, customary law.

Buddhist ethics have had an influence upon Burmese customary law, as have Confucian ethics upon Chinese customary law. Thus, for example, the Six Rites necessary to validate a marriage according to traditional Chinese customary law were based upon the rules of propriety (*li*) of the Chou dynasty, i.e., were a part of the Confucian ethic.[1] While customary law determined the method by which these rites would be performed, and indeed there was substantial variance in methods in different parts of China, nevertheless, there was mutual influence between custom and the rites.[2]

Not only has the *adat temenggong* of Malay society received Hindu influence, but as Joseph Minattur has shown, the *adat perpateh* was also subject to Indian influence.[3] The matriliny practiced by the Nyars of Kerala and other South Indian areas probably influenced the Malay institutions of Minangkabau, and thus of Negri Sembilan.[4]

As has been noted, despite the fact that the essence of Muslim marriage is the "contract effected by *akad nikah*,.... [t]he most outstanding feature of a Malay marriage is the *bersanding* or the sitting in state of

[1] Vermier Yanatak Chiu, "Some Notes on Chinese Customary Marriage," *infra.*

[2] The Six Rites also received recognition by the law code.

[3] Joseph Minattur, "Some Notes on Indian Influence on Malay Customary Law," see *infra.*

[4] *Ibid.* Even the Mapillas, Muslims of the Sunni sect, were held to be governed by principles of matrilineal descent by the Madras High Court, indicating the strength of this customary institution.

the bride and bridegroom on the bridal throne, the 'Rajas for a day.' This ceremony, which is Hindu in origin, holds a greater significance to the ordinary Malay than the proceedings of the *akad nikah*."[1] This aspect of the marriage is so important that it "in effect reduces the Muslim marriage ceremony to the status of an engagement."[2] As a result of one of the rulers of old Malacca taking a Chinese bride sent by the Emperor of China, "[a]mong the Malays of Malacca, Johore, Negri Sembilan and Selangor it is also customary to dress the bride in ancient Chinese costumes on a night of the *berhinai* ceremonies.... Through the centuries what began as a fashion became an integral part of Malay wedding customs."[3] Similarly: "The Malay customary rules regarding the *maskahwin* represent a compromise between Muslim law and the ancient Malay custom."[4]

Traditional Hindu law was derived in part from ancient customary rules, and details of caste and customs collected in the nineteenth century have formed a source for contemporary Hindu law.[5] The influence of Hindu ethics and religion upon the law of Burma, Thailand, Cambodia and Laos is well known, as is the influence of Confucian Chinese ethics upon the customary and formal law of Korea, Vietnam, Japan and regions on the periphery of China. Muslim influence on customary law is extensive and exists throughout Asia including China, the Philippines, Indonesia, Malaya, Borneo, Thailand, etc. Buddhist influence on Chinese customary and formal law, as well as the customary law of Burma, Vietnam, Laos, Cambodia, India, Mongolia, Tibet and other regions is also quite obvious.

Thus there are major religions and ethical systems as well as cultures that have influenced customary law and formal legal developments throughout Asia,[6] in particular the Muslim,[7] Buddhist, Hindu and Confucianist schools. While in fact these religious-ethical systems and their "codes" have become intertwined with customary law, it is worthwhile differentiating these ethical legal principles from customary law. It is

[1] Inche Ahmad bin Mohamed Ibrahim, "Islam and Customary Law in the Malaysian Legal Context," see *infra*.

[2] *Ibid.*

[3] *Ibid.*

[4] *Ibid.* Unlike Muslim law which recognizes the groom's gift to the bride, *mahr*, while Malay custom demands "...a whole series of conventional presents...." Malay custom also fixes the amount of *maskahwin*.

[5] S. P. Khetarpal, "Codification of Hindu Law," see *infra*.

[6] The peculiar influence of Christianity on the formal law of the Philippines is also to be noted. Of course Christianity has also influenced legal developments in Madras and other parts of India for a very long time.

[7] Of course one of the sources of Muslim law was custom, *urf*, and usage, *adat*.

also necessary to differentiate customary law from the secular codes and binding cases of the "greater tradition" of traditional peasant society. The great ethical, religious and secular codes and binding cases of Asia tend to be in written form, and thus of a more permanent and rigid nature. Customary law is generally unwritten,[1] and thus more flexible.

Van Vollenhoven found common elements in customary law in Indonesia that are also of use in characterizing customary law; i.e., "(1) a preponderance of communal over individual interests,... (3) an all-pervasive 'magical' and religious pattern of thought, (4) a strong family-oriented atmosphere..."[2] While (3), the "all-pervasive 'magical' and religious pattern of thought" may be more significant in pre-literate and certain peasant societies than it would be in others, a modified version might more appropriately characterize traditional customary law, i.e., a pervasive (rather than "all-pervasive") magical and religious pattern of thought which was reflected in the law. The strong family law atmosphere which van Vollenhoven describes relates to both the administration of justice (in that family related institutions such as the lineages and clans helped to administer the law), as well as to the fact that the law was pervaded by family status relationships and analogies thereto. Status is generally quite important in customary law and the hierarchical nature of the family, for example, was reflected in the law as was the status of chieftains, gentry, royalty and other principal groups. Status, however, is also important in common law, as Pound has so clearly shown.[3] "The common-law lawyer... thinks of the relation of principal and agent and of powers, rights, duties and liabilities, not as willed by the parties but as incident to and involved in the relation."[4] While the "original type which provided the analogy" is the relationship of landlord-tenant at common law,[5] the father-son relationship generally provides the analogy for many customary law relationships in Asia. Thus duties and liabilities arise from the nature of the relationships in both the common law and customary law of Asia.[6]

[1] In recent years customary law in such places as Sarawak has been incorporated into written form, generally at the instance of the government in order to make the principles known to officials who are ignorant of the tradition as well as for the benefit of the younger generation, similarly ignorant.

[2] S. Takdir Alisjahbana, "Customary Law and Modernization in Indonesia," see *infra*. Number (2) and the latter half of (4) of van Vollenhoven's classifications seem less related to substantive law, and have thus been omitted.

[3] Roscoe Pound, *The Spirit of the Common Law* (Boston, 1949) (Beacon ed.) pp. 14–31, see particularly p. 21.

[4] *Ibid.*, p. 21.

[5] *Ibid.*, pp. 22, 23.

[6] It should be noted that Pound says: "In the industrial and urban society of today classes

In summary, customary law in Asia is generally unwritten; it tends to reflect group or communal rather than individual interests; it often be comes intertwined with and permeated by "magical" and/or religious patterns; family law relations are of much significance and analogies thereto are of substantial significance in the law; and the law is concerned with details as well as broad principles and has substantial local variants. The system of administering customary law is generally either "Kadijustice" which prevails particularly in pre-literate societies and in the "little tradition" of peasant societies or "empirical justice" which is prevalent in the "greater tradition" of peasant society. "Rational justice" may also be administered in the "greater tradition."

How can customary law be differentiated from custom? The answer to this turns on the age old question of how we define law. While this is not the place to undertake a re-examination of this problem, Hoebel's definition (while not without difficulties) is a useful one, i.e.: "A social norm is legal if its neglect or infraction is regularly met, in threat or in fact, by the application of physical force by an individual or group possessing the socially recognized privilege of so acting."[1] Thus customary law would be that aspect of the law which manifested the attributes described above.[2]

II. Customary Law and the Formal Legal Institutions: Interaction and Conflict

In the nineteenth century the religious, family-oriented, rural Asian culture came into contact with the secularized, rational and industrialized West. The Western powers soon assumed the role of the former rulers of Asian society.[3] The law and social institutions of traditional Asia felt the impact of contemporary technology.[4] Customary law, related religious-ethical law and the secular positive law of tra-

and groups and relations must be taken account of no less than individuals." Thus status and legal consequences arising from relations are still significant contemporarily.

[1] E. Adamson Hoebel, *The Law of Primitive Man* (Harvard University Press, 1954) p. 28. Force is defined by Hoebel, who refers to MacIver, as: "Force, unqualified, means coercion—the condition that exists whenever men act, or refrain from acting, in a manner different from that which they themselves would have chosen in a given situation, because others deliberately limit the range of their choice either directly, through present control over it, or indirectly, through the threat of consequences.... The essentials of legal coercion are general social acceptance of the application of physical power, in threat or in fact, by a privileged party, for a legitimate cause, in a legitimate way, and at a legitimate time. This distinguishes the sanction of law from that of other social rules." at p. 27.

[2] This of course is just a working and tentative definition which can only be refined after continual criticism and examination by scholars and legal practitioners.

[3] S. Takdir Alisjahbana, "Customary Law and Modernization in Indonesia," see *infra*.

[4] See for example Max Rheinstein, "The Law of Family and Succession," *Civil Law in the Modern World* (La. 1965) A. N. Yiannopoulos, editor, p. 27ff.

ditional Asian society came into contact with Western legal institutions and were often administered by Western or Western-trained personnel. The results varied, however one can discern certain patterns. The former secular codes, such as the Chinese *Ta-Ch'ing Lü-Li*, were often replaced by Western codes that had little significance for Asian society. The religious institutions were to some extent undermined by rational Western techniques. Customary law—although similarly affected, particularly by the breakdown of pre-literate and peasant institutions—remained very significant in most societies. Without the traditional codes and traditional formal machinery for dispute resolution, customary law was indeed important. While the "greater tradition" was seriously weakened and in part displaced, the "little tradition" remained—although of course not unchanged. On the other hand in some societies the positive ethical-religious codes came to be interpreted by the Western style courts as if they were Western codes and thus were regarded as fixed postulates which were used as a basis for deciding individual cases — a characteristic they often did not possess in their natural habitat.

In the family law field there are two contrasting policies that can be distinguished regarding the administration of traditional Asian family law by the Western powers or Western influenced judicial personnel. In the English colonies, customary law was generally discouraged and English law was utilized except in the family law area where room was left for the "traditional customary law" of the people of the colony. Aside from outlawing certain facets of family law which the English found abhorrent, the overt policy of the English government was to recognize the traditional, religious and customary family law of the natives in the courts. In fact as we shall see, the enforcement of this overt policy encountered many complications.

Dutch colonial policy, however, differed somewhat. Whereas the English generally imposed their laws on the native population in many areas and merely excepted family law from this imposition, the Dutch, under the influence of C. van Vollenhoven, came to exalt customary law. It was regarded as a satisfactory basis for building a national legal system. Though customary law "...was adulated for its 'wholeness' and its subtle refinement in satisfying the community's sense of justice and feeling of mutual responsibility...." attempts to put this theory into practice also met with several difficulties.

Western legal institutions are primarily rational in nature and thus are in contrast to the predominantly "Kadi" or "empirical" justice of Asian institutons. Legal institutions in the West tend to be relatively important arenas for the peaceful resolution of domestic relations disputes. Social institutions such as lineages and clans are not major institutions of social-legal control. The reverse situation existed and in fact still exists throughout much of Asia. In traditional Asian society the formal law courts were often considered a last resort, and in fact certain opprobrium and shame were attached to their use. Ideological support was often given for this attitude by the government. Such feelings continue to exist in Asia with regard to the new "Western" courts, although at times briefs are filed in the Western courts as a means of pressing people to negotiate.[1]

Conciliation was and remains a most significant aspect of legal procedure in Asia. The procedures for conciliation—which was often carried out by certain prestigious local leaders, gentry, tribal chieftains, clan or lineage heads, etc.—were and are delicate. Open conflict was to be avoided and the pride of each party to be maintained. Even the lower level formal courts in China promoted and continue to promote conciliation in what we may loosely term civil cases. Where Western courts are established, however, there is generally little room for such activity unless one can regard some of the pre-trial[2] conferences and family court proceedings, out of court settlements, etc., as a form of conciliation. The adversary proceedings of the common law courts are particularly ill-suited for conciliation procedures, in view of the pressure on each party to overstate his case and become identified with a particular point of view pending a relatively clear cut victory. Furthermore, as Maine has shown, legislation is most appropriate in the nation state which has effective central political organs; nevertheless it was used extensively by colonial legislatures which really did not have political institutions that deeply affected the customary family law of the villages of Asia. Thus various incompatibilities were inherent in the establishment of Western courts in Asia.

Nevertheless as a result primarily of colonial pressures, most Asian societies have "received" in smaller or larger part civil and common law institutions. While European law was, at least in the family law area, not generally imposed directly upon the populace, the results of various methods were often the same. Where European institutions were not directly adopted, traditional Asian institutions were interpreted by common or civil law methods, thus either rigidifying the

[1] See K. Ishwaran, "Customary Law in Village India," *infra*.

[2] But see Maurice Rosenberg, *The Pre-trial Conference and Effective Justice—A Controlled Test in Personal Injury Litigation* (New York, 1964), where pre-trial conferences (at least in personal injury litigation in New Jersey) seem neither to refine nor shorten trials nor increase settlements.

institution or turning it into some hybrid legal form more closely resembling its European parent.

Even in Indonesia where, "Although it was repeatedly stressed that for the Indonesians law was to be a natural outgrowth of their own society, it was yet inconceivable that in a dualistic society where one group dominated another, the concrete task of giving form and content to this customary law would be performed by the native people living in rural village communities."[1] As a result, "...customary law could only be applied where it did not conflict with the interests and policies of the colonial system."[2] Thus the customary law, administered only when convenient to the colonial government, without real recognition of social change, and which continued to emphasize local variations, became in fact an impediment to national unity.

In Burma, as in many of the English colonies, it was noted by the early representatives of the crown that justice in family matters would be administered according to the established laws of Burma. However, despite several English language publications on the subject, one of the earliest representatives of the crown was under the mistaken impression that Burmese courts had no law code to guide them, and that "all their decisions were arbitrary."[3] Though he lacked knowledge of the Burmese language, Mr. Maingy was reluctant to employ native officials to administer the law directly. As a compromise, after dismissing Burmese law as "very complicated," he prepared his own "Code of Regulations," but at the same time he made allowance for local custom by providing that one learned in Burmese law would be present at the judicial proceedings to advise the Commissioner. A jury was also impanelled. "The result was that [these]... judicial proceedings assumed a remarkably Anglo-Burmese character."[4] But even this was more than the British authorities in India, who directed the administration of justice in Burma, could tolerate. Thus the "codes, statutes and regulations passed by the British Governor-General of India and meant for the Indians came to be extended to Burma...."[5] However, as was the case in most British colonies, family law was exempt from the direct imposition of Indian, i.e., English, law.

The Burma Laws Act, 1898, provided in Section 13 that in family

[1] S. Takdir Alisjaabana, *infra*.

[2] *Ibid.* In Indonesia customary law was applied to larger areas of the law and not restricted to family law, as it generally was in English colonies, as noted *supra*.

[3] U Hla Aung, "The Effect of Anglo-Indian Legislation on Burmese Customary Law," see *infra*.

[4] *Ibid.*

[5] *Ibid.*

law matters the courts shall apply "the Buddhist law in cases where the parties are Buddhists...." The problems caused by this provision have been manifold.

> On the basis of their knowledge about Hindu... and Muslim law, the English took for granted, in their ignorance of Buddhism and Burmese customary law, that the relationship between law and Buddhism with regard to marriage, divorce and inheritance must be the same. In fact, *in the strict sense of the term, there is no such thing as Buddhist law; there is only the influence exercised by Buddhist ethics on changes that have taken place in customs.*[1]

Furthermore the British took the Dhammathats and applied them with the rigidity of a statute, something they never possessed in Burmese law. The result was many peculiar decisions.

Similarly in Malaya and Singapore the English judiciary generally relied upon a questionable and partial translation of the code of the Ch'ing dynasty as a basis for administering "customary" Chinese law. The importance of the cases, rites (*li*), and real customary law was generally unknown. "Expert" evidence upon which the court relied for definition of customary law was frequently inaccurate. The role of *stare decisis* in this English model judiciary, whereby the higher courts are generally bound by their own decisions, tended to rigidify customary law. At odd instances English law was applied to the Chinese. For example, the English Statutes of Distribution were applied to the primary and secondary wives of the Chinese, contrary to traditional Chinese customary law. The result in part was to put a premium upon the acquisition of the status of secondary wife, for women were in effect offered a substantial financial reward for entering such a relationship. Claims thus arose against the estates of the well-to-do on the basis of some tangential relationship. Wives of long standing could be made to share equally with these claimants.[2] Adoption ordinances modeled on English law were passed, making it time-consuming and expensive to adopt children, and causing antipathy in the Chinese community which had long practised adoption, as Maurice Freedman has shown. Anachronisms of the common law that were being whittled away by the courts of the Commonwealth and England were enacted into law as late as 1961 in Singapore, when a statutory enactment of *Hyde* v. *Hyde* was imposed upon the people of Singapore. Thus in a community long practiced in polygamy and which indeed had received sanction under the English model legal system for this practice, the jurisdiction

[1] *Ibid.* Emphasis supplied.
[2] Buxbaum, David C., "Chinese Family Law in a Common Law Setting...," see *infra*.

of the court for purposes of divorce, etc., was determined in part by an English definition of marriage that refused to acknowledge even potentially polygamous unions as having the status of marriage.[1] Finally the Privy Council, sitting in far off England—whose decisions were influenced in part by colonial policy, and which lacked any real knowledge of local social circumstances and customary law despite the ostensible assistance of experts—was and is the highest court in Malaysia and Singapore.

Under such circumstances, how could the courts (despite the weakening of the social institutions, e.g., lineages and clans) become a major arena for the peaceful settlement of disputes? How indeed could a "common law" be built?

In the Borneo states, Sabah and Sarawak, the courts, in part because of political-legal realities and in part as a result of a liberal Charter granted by the Gladstone government, had evolved a somewhat more rational method of determining Chinese customary law. The court apparently looked to the customary law of the group to which the people before the court belonged at the time of the decision. While there were dangers and difficulties in this approach, e.g., the problem of ascertaining contemporary customary law, and thus the need for careful social investigation as well as the potential danger of sanctioning social trends antithetical to national goals, nevertheless there is also substantial potential benefit to be derived from attempting to make the judiciary meaningful to the people of the region. The courts at times also seem to give judicial recognition to conciliation by social institutions, thus utilizing this important institution.

Even Thailand, although not under direct colonial tutelage, nevertheless felt various pressures to Westernize family law. "It was felt that the Western powers, still enjoying the privilege of consular jurisdiction, would be more inclined to admit the competence of the local courts if they found that the law applied by these courts was nearer to their own."[2] Thus it was felt, as it was in China due to the hope held out by the colonial powers,[3] that Westernization of the law would "...facilitate future negotiations for abolition of extraterritoriality which a number

[1] *Ibid.*

[2] Adul Wichiencharoen and Luang Chamroon Netisastra, "Some Main Features of Modernization of Ancient Family Law in Thailand." See *infra*.

[3] Although in fact, despite substantial Westernization of Chinese laws, aside from the Soviet Union and one other exception, most colonial powers retained extraterritoriality until the latter part of World War II, when they had little choice and it was to their political advantage to rid themselves of this jurisdiction.

of Western powers enjoyed in Thailand at that time."[1] Certain Thai institutions were also deemed old fashioned, and fear that they would subject the Thais to Western criticism was voiced. Thereby certain Western legal institutions were adopted, causing (as shall be discussed *infra*) certain social problems.

Thus Western legal institutions have come to affect legal developments in Asia. The formal judiciary in its Western garb was and is generally remote in thought and form from the society wherein it administers law. Usually managed by Westerners or Western trained legal personnel, any deviation from Western law is viewed by some as a threat to their special position. At times these people are unacquainted with the society and customary law of the nation in which they work, and are thus incapable of analyzing indigenous legal institutions. Furthermore, attempts to use Western courts of law which operate on the basis of Western procedural rules to administer traditional customary law does not often stimulate beneficial results. Thus while social institutions are losing their legal viability, if the courts of law are not amenable to reasonable dispute resolution, added social pressures and problems will result—something modernizing societies need not encourage.

III. Customary Law and the Family in Modernizing Society

Family law, which is closely related to "Kadi-justice" and very important in the "little tradition," differs in many societies. Even within societies such as Malay and Indian society there are many variations in this field of law, as there are in China. Religious-ethical codes are important in this field of law, which is particularly subject to religious, historical and customary influences. English family law for example, prior to the Norman conquest, was administered by the bishop of the diocese and the alderman, who sat together deciding both civil and ecclesiastical matters.[2] After the Norman conquest, the ecclesiastical courts were separated from the civil courts at the instance of the Roman court. The ecclesiastical courts asserted jurisdiction over marriage and related matters, since marriage was a sacrament of the Church. The ecclesiastical courts applied the common law of marriage which was based in part upon Jewish law, Roman law, the Scriptures, writings of the Church Fathers and periodic regulations of the Popes

[1] Adul Wichiencharoen and Luang Chamroon Netisastra, see *infra*.
[2] William Blackstone, *Commentaries on the Law of England* (Oxford, 1768) Vol. 3, p. 61.

and Council.[1] It was not until the time of Henry VIII that appeals from the English ecclesiastical courts to the Papal Curia were ended,[2] and it was only in the Matrimonial Causes Act, 1857, that the ecclesiastical courts were deprived of their jurisdiction. Thereafter ecclesiastical law and common law were gradually harmonized. English family law was also influenced by the doctrine of the Church of England. Thus for example it was not until the Marriage Act, 1836, that English law "...permitted marriages to be solemnized on the authority of a certificate in other ways than according to the rites of the Church of England, thus for the first time recognizing the validity of a purely civil marriage."[3] And even today under the most recent Marriage Act, 1949, and recent amendments[4] publishing of the banns in the parish church can be an essential part of a marriage solemnized by the Church of England[5] although marriages may now also be solemnized by other rites.

English marriage was defined by Lord Penzance in the famous case of *Hyde* v. *Hyde*[6]: "I conceive that marriage, as understood in Christendom, may for this purpose be defined as the voluntary union for life of one man and one woman, to the exclusion of all others." He further noted, "But marriage is one and the same thing substantially all the Christian world over." And we "...regard it as a wholly different thing, a different status from Turkish or other marriages among infidel nations, because we clearly should never recognize the plurality of wives.... This cannot be put on any rational ground, except our holding the infidel marriage to be something different from the Christian and our also holding the Christian marriage to be the same everywhere." Thus the court held that it could have no jurisdiction over a Mormon "marriage," which apparently was in fact monogamous but was potentially polygamous. This decision of course has been subject to much criticism and some

[1] E. L. Johnson, *Family Law* (London, 1958) at p. 1. See also F. Pollock and F. W. Maitland, *History of English Law* (Cambridge, 1952) II, pp. 364 *et seq.* The common law courts were able to affect family law and marriage indirectly; for example, by refusing dower to widows not married *in facie ecclesiae* and refusing to recognize legitimization for purposes of inheritance of children whose parents married after their birth, contrary to ecclesiastical practice.

[2] W. Blackstone, at p. 67.

[3] P. M. Bromley, *Family Law* (London, 1962) at p. 38.

[4] Marriage Act, 1949 (Amendment) Act, 1954; Marriage Acts Amendment Act, 1958; Marriage (Enabling) Act, 1960.

[5] Although the marriage could also be solemnized on authority of a common license granted by a parish church, special license granted by the Archbishop of Canterbury, or superintendent registrar's certificate in any church or chapel where the banns may be published.

[6] (1866), L.R. I P. and D. 130, at p. 133.

recent modification in England and the Commonwealth, and is only presented here to indicate particular religious influences upon the development of English family law. Similarly the civil law countries perhaps differ among themselves more in family law than in any other aspects of the law. It is not unnatural that family law will be heavily dependent upon religious, customary and historical influences. Thus the adoption of the substantive family law of the West by Asian countries where entirely different religious, customary and historical influences prevail, seems particularly inappropriate. It is for this reason that the courts in Asia have had much trouble with family law, particularly where unmodified Western legal institutions were adopted.

Polygyny, which was often sanctioned by both the traditional customary religious-ethical and secular codes and cases in Asia, has been a major source of legal friction. In Thailand for example it was felt by some that polygyny "...was old fashioned and inappropriate for the modern days...."[1] and might be the cause for Western criticism of Thai morality. For these reasons, and in the hope of eliminating extra-territoriality, polygyny was abolished and the old Thai codes, which embodied customary law and were broadly drawn to allow for change, were replaced by more detailed Western codes.

> However, the Thai experience since the promulgation of the new family law in 1935 indicates that the law has not succeeded in eradicating polygamy, which it has attempted to do. Statistics are not available, but the general impression is that, in spite of the law, the practice of polygamy seems to continue undiminished. Such a departure of law from custom has created added social problems of unmarried mothers and consequently of illegitimate children to a degree unknown under the ancient polygamous law. However, in so far as illegitimacy is concerned, a counter-acting measure is found in the provision for affiliation procedure whereby a child born out of wedlock may be legitimized upon consent or request of the father. But in practice, there are not many cases of legitimization. Regarding the unmarried mother, the law turns its back on her and her problems, and the term "unmarried mother" becomes more and more of a stigma.[2]

Similarly in Singapore where polygyny was sanctioned by traditional Chinese customary law and formal law, as well as by Confucian ethics, and also recognized and perhaps indirectly encouraged for a long time by the English courts of Singapore, it was prohibited in 1961, criminal sanctions being provided for enforcement. Singapore adopted by statute the *Hyde* v. *Hyde* definition of marriage. Thus, while obviously not putting an immediate brake upon polygyny, the practice of which may be fairly widespread[3] in Singapore, children of these secondary

[1] Adul Wichiencharoen and Luang Chamroon Netisastra, see *infra*.
[2] *Ibid.*
[3] Buxbaum, David C., see *infra*.

unions will be stigmatized as illegitimate and secondary wives will be deprived of their status.[1] The potentiality of criminal prosecution on the other hand seems somewhat remote, and in any case would indeed be harsh. There is no necessary connection between polygyny, and modernization, nor with polygyny and a harmonious family situation. "That it can be made to work smoothly is perfectly clear from the evidence of ethnography."[2] Whether polygyny conforms to contemporary notions of social justice is another question, but it would seem that gradual, realistic and less harsh methods of attempted elimination could be utilized with better results.[3] Burma for example has not prohibited polygamy, but has provided that the husband must have the consent of the first wife before taking an additional spouse. Adultery on the other hand is grounds for divorce. Parenthetically, from the point of view of children, in a society where it is acceptable polygyny may be psychologically and emotionally preferable to the successive marriage patterns of some Western societies.

Divorce (while handled more rationally than polygyny by most Asian jurisdictions) has caused conflict between Western substantive law and traditional customary Asian law in the few jurisdictions which have adopted strict nineteenth century Western law. Several Western jurisdictions are moving towards allowing divorce by mutual consent in fact, or at least a more moderate position on divorce. The Catholic Church is reexamining its position on this matter and in fact in New York State—where adultery has for a long time been the sole grounds for divorce, the Church did not stand in the way of legislative change. The old New York law interestingly enough was known to have encouraged perjury, as well as make divorce primarily available to the wealthy, who could afford to leave the jurisdiction and establish residence elsewhere.[4] Adversary divorce proceedings have been criticized in

[1] "The unfortunate, and often tragic, status of the illegitimate child in the great majority of modern Western family laws is an outcome of the Christian conception of the monogamous marriage." W. Friedmann, *Law in a Changing Society* (Penguin ed., 1964) at p. 209.

[2] G. P. Murdock, *Social Structure* (New York, 1960) at p. 30. Of the societies sampled in this book, 193 were characterized by polygyny, only 43 by monogamy and 2 by polyandry. Polygyny was defined as existing only where plural marriages are contemporaneous and where the marriages involved "residential cohabitation and economic cooperation as well as sexual association."

[3] See Buxbaum, David, *infra*.

[4] W. Friedmann, *op. cit.*, p. 182 in discussing the techniques that have permitted an expansion of divorce in the West notes: "The second, probably the most important and certainly the most ominous, technique is acceptance of the practice of faked evidence. The result, that parties sufficiently wealthy to afford the cost of litigation, and of the various agreements outside and inside the court, which are necessary for the procedure to be brought to a successful conclusion, can, in effect, obtain divorce by consent, discredits the law. It is reached by fraud, and not infrequently perjury, no less objectionable for having become

many Western jurisdictions, and special family courts, domestic relations courts, mandatory reconciliation services, conciliation services, etc., have been established in an attempt to avoid the need to become involved in mutual invective which thus exacerbates feelings and ends the possibility of reconciliation. However in a jurisdiction that long sanctioned divorce by mutual consent, an adversary proceeding for divorce was instituted for the Chinese of Singapore in 1961.[1] Thus another product of Western family law under its own particular religious influence was instituted at this late date in Singapore; whereas traditional Chinese customary law was in some respects more in keeping with contemporary Western trends.

Generally speaking, however, each Asian jurisdiction's attitude toward divorce (in contrast to attitudes towards polygyny) depends in part upon religious and customary law influences. Very often divorce by mutual consent in accordance with traditional customary law is sanctioned. For example traditional Chinese law (although having as a result of Confucian ethics incorporated seven provisions when divorce was expected and three when divorce could not be granted) nevertheless in customary law and positive law permitted divorce by mutual consent.[2] In fact one suspects that this was probably the most frequent means of divorce in Ch'ing times.[3] Contemporarily Title IV of the Civil Code permits divorce by mutual consent or judicial determination in Taiwan. In mainland China, Article 17 of the Marriage Law, 1950, permits divorce by mutual consent with the sanction of the court. There is also provision for divorce by judicial determination. These statutes directly and by inference elevate the power of the wife to initiate divorce proceedings in comparison to traditional customary law. Thailand, under Civil and Commercial Code, Book V, permits divorce by mutual consent as well as by judicial determination.

settled practice. It is hypocrisy, inertia, and the interest of some in the maintenance of the existing state of affairs, which stand in the way of a reform of the law that most serious commentators have long recommended. The façade of a semi-puritan ethics is preserved at the cost of sacrificing the integrity of the law and often creating one law for the rich, another for the poor."

[1] There has been discussion recently of changing this regulation in Singapore.

[2] See Tai Yen-hui, *Chung-kuo Shen-fen Fa-shih* (Taipei, 1959) at p. 69.

[3] It should be recognized that much of the power of divorce rested in the hands of the husband and the husband's family. However the wife and the wife's family were not always powerless. The wife's family could attempt to redeem their daughter, for example, as was done. The wife's family in the situation where the husband married into the wife's family was of course in the dominant position. The provisions of the marriage contract would also in part determine the power of the parties to instigate divorce proceedings.

Traditional Hindu law influenced by Hindu religion generally only permitted divorce via customary law among lower castes. Contemporary legislation permits divorce upon certain specific grounds, e.g., adultery, insanity, virulent leprosy, venereal disease, etc.,[1] for all castes; while retaining customary divorce for lower castes.

While at Muslim law the "...husband had unlimited power to terminate the marriage by the process called *talāq*, the wife had no means of relieving herself from a yoke that had become almost unbearable."[2] Thus the Dissolution of Marriages Act, 1939, in India, provided that the wife could obtain divorce upon such conditions as desertion (for four years), failure to maintain (for two years), failure to perform marital obligations, insanity, etc.[3]

Malay custom was more lenient with regard to divorce than Muslim law. An attempted reconciliation, *bersuarang*, was a necessary precondition for a husband contemplating divorce. He would hold a feast and invite his wife's relatives to air his grievances.[4] Nevertheless divorce could be granted and generally a wife could herself return her dower use (or another method of payment) and obtain a divorce if she were refused one by a blameless husband.[5] Now in Malaysia, where Malay customary law is mixed with Muslim law, it is common "...to require the husband to make a condition or *ta'alik* to enable the wife to obtain a divorce if the husband should abandon her, fail to maintain her for a stated period or assault her."[6] Some states in fact require this *ta'alik*. The wife also has power in Malaysia to apply to the Kathi for divorce.[7]

Thus much of the divorce legislation discussed above reflects the customary and religious practices of the communities in the light of certain contemporary trends. Principal exceptions are Singapore, where English law predominates, the Philippines and Vietnam. Law which has grown out of traditional customary and religious law as modified by certain contemporary pressures is generally more meaningful to the population. The law of divorce with some noticeable exceptions stands in contrast to the laws on polygyny which have often evolved less rationally.

[1] S. P. Khetarpal, "Codification of Hindu Law," see *infra*.

[2] Asaf A. A. Fyzee, "Recent Developments in Muhammadan Law in India, 1900–1960," *International and Comparative Law Quarterly*, Suppl. no. 8 (1964) 46 at p. 48.

[3] *Ibid.*

[4] Haji Mohamed Din bin Ali, "Malay Customary Law and the Family," see *infra*.

[5] Inche Ahmad bin Mohamed Ibrahim, see *infra*. Although according to the *Ninety-nine Laws of Perak* no divorce was permitted if the husband was blameless, nevertheless in most jurisdictions in Malaysia it was so permitted.

[6] *Ibid.*

[7] *Ibid.*

Generally customary law is more flexible than religious law and more easily subject to social change. Religious law having certain idealized written codes is less amenable to modification. It is also more easily subject to strong emotional ties and thus less likely to be a potential basis for unifying legislation in communities where there is religious diversity, as there is in most Asian societies. While undoubtedly there is an interrelationship between customary law and religious-ethical law, it would seem to be advantageous where feasible to build new legal institutions on the basis of customary law. Van Vollenhoven was not entirely wrong in seeing certain unifying elements in customary law, and as we have tried to show, there are others that can provide a basis for the development of truly national legal systems, i.e., a "common" law. Techniques that were and are meaningful in traditional customary law (e.g., the use of status and conciliation) could be used to develop contemporary institutions.

Conclusion

Customary law is important particularly in the family law field in much of the world today. In Asia, revolutionary governments such as that on mainland China have recognized the importance of customary law. Thus it has been noted that in attempting to establish their legal program: "The policies of the [Chinese] Government find obstacles in their way, to which the authorities are inclined to make concessions. By and large they show consideration for the customs of the masses...."[1] Various legal provisions such as the right of descendents to inherit property to provide for the ancestral cult have been upheld, at least until recently, as a concession to customary law.[2] In Pakistan it has been suggested that the Criminal Law Amendment Act, 1963, is really a return to the traditional Jirga system and thus in part to customary law.

It of course is not only in Asian, or even in pre-literate, tribal or peasant societies that customary law is of importance. Thus for example in France, custom is more important than in common law jurisdictions. There are numerous references to custom and usages as a source of decision regarding consensual transactions in the Civil Code. Thus under the category of *secundum legem* or those linguistic or additive

[1] M. H. van der Valk, "The Law of Succession in China," V *Law in Eastern Europe* 297 at p. 319.

[2] *Ibid.*, at p. 320. At p. 326 it is noted that the *chui-fu* situation is governed in part by customary law.

usages, primarily statutory and also contractual duties are interpreted within the statutory framework. Ambiguous language is interpreted according to usages. Custom is probably a more important linguistic guide to interpreting statutes than at common law.[1]

However there is a second category of custom, *praeter legem*, which is custom that develops into new rules of law independently but not in derogation of statutory law; for example, the series of rules governing the disposition of family heirlooms or burial places. The codes make no reference to these matters of inheritance or community property, thus the courts apply customary law indirectly.[2]

There is a third category known as customs *adversus legem*, or those that derogate from the statutory text. While there is much disagreement here and the courts are not likely to admit this usage in the *droit civil*, nevertheless recognition of such a custom may occur indirectly via interpreting the intention of the parties in a particular transaction as derogating from the *droit supplétif*. On the other hand if there is a mandatory provision in the statute, it may be interpreted in a manner not in conflict with custom.[3]

Thus in a civil law jurisdiction, which prides itself for reliance upon a code, custom plays a role in contemporary decision making. The role of customary law in contemporary common law is perhaps somewhat more restrictive, although a thorough examination of this question has yet to be made. For example, it has been suggested by Max Gluckman that the concept of a "reasonably prudent man" is really a customary law standard. Also commercial institutions and other social institutions have certain customary rules that may in fact even receive judicial recognition. We also must recognize on the other hand that customary law in contemporary Western society has certain characteristics which may differentiate it from peasant, tribal or pre-literate societies, where it often is more embracing and more powerful, and not as readily subject to change in fact by statute.

The reception of Western substantive law, particularly in the family law area has generally meant that the law of the formal judiciary is not

[1] René David and Henry P. de Vries, *The French Legal System* (New York, 1958), see section on Custom.

[2] *Ibid.* The courts have also created certain remedies via customary law. Generally the term usages rather than customs is used.

[3] *Ibid.* For example, where the civil code had a fixed rule contrary to commercial custom regarding the payment of interest on current accounts of reciprocal debits and credits, the courts held the code inapplicable to current accounts, in accordance with commercial custom.

that of the people.[1] Similarly the legal institutions have not been suitable places to administer customary law. The rules of procedure, form of trial and method of inquisition were generally hostile to the development of customary law or to the conciliatory procedures commonly associated with traditional litigation. The desirability of insisting upon adversary procedures seems limited. The role of *stare decisis* in an English model judiciary where the courts, and especially the highest court, are bound by their own decisions is peculiarly inappropriate to societies in a state of rapid social change. The tradition of codification of the civil law countries, while useful perhaps in the commercial law field, is again inappropriate for family law, where provision should be made for change more readily than by resort to legislation. The need for certainty in the family law field is less pressing than in the areas relating to modern commerce. The desirability of reflecting changing social patterns is substantial.

The result of the intrusion of Western law is that the courts are generally not arenas for the peaceful settlement of disputes and places to seek justice, but become instead arenas for attacking a hostile situation that has become so out of balance that normal methods of resolution according to recognizable norms have no chance of redressing a balance.[2] On the other hand they have become in some societies places to threaten an adversary in order to force him to come to some agreement. They become in a sense traditional governmental institutions, except their redeeming features are minimal. They do not stress conciliation of disputes, they are very expensive, and their law is neither just nor intelligible to the common people. Of course this description is perhaps the worst side of the picture, and does not fit every jurisdiction in Asia and a small minority of Western educated people might find the courts amenable. Nevertheless in the family law field this picture is appropriate for a number of Asian societies.

Solutions to this problem are not easy. They depend in large part upon local circumstances, the amenability of the courts to change, the legislative interest in reform, etc. It would seem that—as a necessary minimum—the judicial and other relevant personnel should become acquainted with the traditional methods of settling disputes and substantive law. Thereafter they should acquaint themselves with the relevance and viability of traditional forms in relation to their con-

[1] *E.g.*, see E. Adamson Hoebel, "Fundamental Cultural Postulates and Judicial Lawmaking in Pakistan," 67 *American Anthropologist, Special Publication*, No. 6, Part 2 (December, 1965) 43 at p. 45.

[2] *Ibid.*

temporary society. They should then be prepared to make the legal institutions relevant to the solution of family law problems by ridding them of those aspects of Western substantive law and institutional procedure which are inappropriate to the customary and religious law of their society. Finally, they should—armed with their constitutions or other idealized national goals—attempt to implement such changes as are efficacious to circumstances and justice.

It should be remembered that the law of England was long referred to as "the customs of the realm" or *leges et consuetudines angliae*. Even in Blackstone's time, the area of Kent retained the custom of gavelkind.[1] In fact English common law grew from the collections of tribal customs made by Alfred, Edgar, and Edward the Confessor.[2] The royal courts, once they had obtained national jurisdiction, welded these local customs into a "common law" for all the nation. This technique may be of use in Asia.

It is interesting to note that the courts in Pakistan are "ostensibly seeking to identify the basic postulates of Islam as set forth in the Quran and to relate them to contemporary needs through the Formal National Law."[3] Thus the text of the *Quran* has been the basis for reform which allows divorce to the wife in order to prevent her from going astray. Without evaluating the efficacy of this particular decision, the technique used is of substantial interest. If this can be accomplished with religious law, then certainly customary law could be a basis for similar approaches. The organic growth of law out of traditional persisting custom is generally preferable in the family law area to the wholesale importation of foreign law.

Some sanction also can be given to village leaders, as perhaps has been done in Borneo. There, headmen were made elective officials—a modern concept which undoubtedly works imperfectly, but their decisions as to conciliation or "arbitration" of family disputes were recognized by the courts. At the same time marriages were to be registered, which was proof of marriage, although one could still prove the existence of a marriage if no registration had taken place. Customary law is recognized, but it is the customary law of the parties at the time of the decision. Gradually local leaders, the traditional legal institutions, and the law are being incorporated into a modern legal framework. While there are substantial problems with this approach, and in particular

[1] Charles Sumner Labinger, "Customary Law" III *Encyclopedia of the Social Sciences* (New York, 11th printing, 1954) 662 at 664 f.
[2] *Ibid.*, at p. 665.
[3] E. Adamson Hoebel, "Fundamental Cultural Postulates..." *op. cit.*, at p. 53.

the question as to whether the courts can feasibly determine changing customary law—something which they seem to be ineffective at accomplishing most recently; nevertheless such methodology has potential.

There is a need to ascertain what local customary practice is, not merely as the Historical School might suggest to thereafter posit it in legislation, but rather to see how it may be reflected in the formal law so that the courts may become more responsive to the people's needs and at the same time to see how local customary law may be realistically modified so as to make progress towards the specific or general goals of each Asian nation. "Customary law... is both a rule of conduct and a norm for decision..."[1] and thus can be given cognizance by the courts without the need for intervening legislation. This both permits flexibility in approach and prevents the development of a large hiatus between law and society. On the other hand, legislation can on occasion be used to realistically modify customary law where it is in conflict with national goals. Such legislation will only have real effect where the courts are actually resolving the disputes of society and reflecting and affecting the custom of the realm. If the courts are ignored by the people, then the effect of legislation—especially outside the criminal sphere—becomes minimal. Of course law cannot generally be an instrument for social change without education and social understanding. While the need to establish courts which administer "rational justice" is an important part of building a modern technological society, the field of family law, even in the West, is pervaded with religious and customary law and administered in part by "Kadi" and "empirical" justice. Family law in different societies has reflected local religious, ethical and customary divergences, that it may continue to do so for some time should not seriously impede modernization.

Organic growth from traditional institutions to modern institutions as rapidly as is feasible and just is preferable to the useless establishment of meaningless or unjust institutions. From traditional institutions of conciliation, modern institutions can gradually be constructed. The flexible customary law can be incorporated into responsive legal institutions; local customary variations can be welded together on the basis of unifying elements and techniques, such as status relationships, to build a law common to an entire society. The common law case method can provide a useful technique for such unification provided that the courts retain flexibility and do not interpret the role of *stare decisis* too strictly.

[1] Eugene Ehrlich, *Fundamental Principles...*, at p. 449.

The following papers are divided into three parts for the sake of convenience, although there is much overlapping between parts. The material for the Introduction was drawn in part from these articles, though, as will be obvious, not all participants were in agreement on each and every point discussed at the Conference. There was however much general agreement. Nevertheless the Introduction naturally reflects my own conceptualization of the problems and conclusions.

DAVID C. BUXBAUM

PART I

THE NATURE OF CUSTOMARY LAW IN DIVERSE ASIAN SOCIETIES

I. CUSTOMARY LAW AND MODERNIZATION IN INDONESIA

In the innumerable, ever changing manifestations of reality, the realm of events, man has a special position as a behaving and acting being. Through the development of his mind, he is able to overcome the static harmony between vegetative and animal behaviour and to interact with the surrounding world in a continuous dynamic dialectical interplay between his behaviour and his environment. The decisive moment in this dialectical interplay occurs when man, with the capacity of his mind to evaluate continuously the things, relations and occurrences in his surroundings, arrives at decisions in terms of his human motivations and goals, i.e., values. What we call cultural behaviour is nothing else than value-oriented behaviour and the totality of culture is nothing more than the realization of a system of values at a certain place and at a certain time.

In the analysis of the evaluating capacity of the human mind, we discern the theoretical and economic values which are related to the progressive aspect of culture, the religious and aesthetic values which are related to the expressive aspect of culture; and the power and solidarity values which determine the social organization of culture. Through the theoretical evaluating process of the mind, i.e., our thought process, the sense images of the empirical world become knowledgeable. It is the economic evaluating process aiming at utility which uses this knowledge of the empirical world and transforms it into useful goods for the maintenance and comfort of life. The religious evaluating process, based on intuitive feeling and contemplation, brings the human mind into direct contact with the reality of the holy, the sacred, or the numinous through the receptivity of the senses. Viewed from this holy reality, the empirical theoretical and economic realities are only a small realization of the all-embracing holy reality, they are only "ash and dust." The aesthetic evaluating process faces the surrounding world which enters through the senses as the manifestation of an aesthetic reality, which like the religious reality speaks directly to the feeling and imagination. The aesthetic value we call beauty. In the social evaluating processes of power and solidarity man faces his fellow man. With the power evaluating process, he faces his fellow man in terms of power, i.e., the urge for self-assertion, for expanding the self. The solidarity evaluating process faces the fellow man not as the power evaluating process in terms of striving, competition, struggle, rank order of power, but as essentially independent beings, valuable because of their own possibilities for unfolding and development.

The social evaluating processes of power and solidarity, representing the relationship between man and man, form the two axes of the social organization of society. The power evaluating process represents the vertical axis and the solidarity evaluating process the horizontal axis of social organization.

It is against this background of the broad social and cultural process that we will be able to understand the conflict between modern and customary law, and eventually to formulate its solution. If we have accepted the proposition that every culture is basically the realization of the six values described and the differences between cultures are differences in the characteristics and in the pattern of these six values, then all cultural behaviour in the context of a certain culture is determined by the system of values of that culture.

If the values of every social or cultural group are a more or less integrated pattern system, it is clear that in order to achieve this system of values, the relations and behaviour of the members of the group too must form a more or less integrated system. It is through *the norms* of the social group that the members of the group participate in a certain standardized pattern of social relations and social behaviour, and that understanding, and consequently cooperation, is made possible between the members of a social group. Viewed from this standpoint the norms of a social group are standardized generalizations of expected social relations and behaviour, which not only restrain the behaviour of the group members, but also mold, organize and direct them for the achievement of the values of the group.

Thus the system of social norms, which organizes and integrates social relations and social behaviour in a social group, facilitates or even aims at the achievements of the goal, i.e., the values of the social group. In the last analysis the social norms are nothing more than the dynamic manifestation of values and it is the function of the organization of power in society to determine and maintain the norms of society.[1]

[1] For a fuller treatment of the meaning and function of values for individual, social and cultural behaviour, see my *The Place of Values in the Behavioural Sciences*, Malay Studies, University of Malaya, Kuala Lumpur, 1963; further *Values as Integrating Forces in Personality Society and Culture*, to be published by the University of Malaya Press.

From this point of view the interaction and conflicts of modern positive law and customary law, which took place in the countries of Asia during the colonial period, were in their very essence cultural conflicts par excellence. The European nations, which during the Renaissance were emancipated from the religious oriented culture of the Middle Ages during the Enlightenment and especially during the 19th century, developed more and more secularized cultures. Already in the 15th, 16th and 17th centuries, they started to develop an empirical science; a technology developed, which was parallel to a continuous expansion of economic life and which gave to the European nations a tremendous physical power over other races through the development of greater and more manageable ships, and especially through the development of more effective arms. Driven by an insatiable urge for material gain and adventure, they roamed the seas and oceans, bringing their goods to the remotest parts of the world and taking home the products of other countries. It was through this seafare and trade that they gradually acquired political power over large parts of Africa, Asia and America. In the competition among themselves in their trade with the countries of Africa, Asia and America, gradually they accumulated more and more political power over distant countries, since it was through political power that they assured themselves of trade with these countries. It was especially during the 19th century, when the European countries experienced the greatest expansion in their science and technology which paralleled the tremendous upsurge in industrialization and commerce, that these modern European cultures, in which the theoretical and the economic values are the dominant and determining values, had a direct impact on the native cultures in the political context which we call colonialism. The colonial political organization attempted everywhere to change and influence the native social and cultural order to further facilitate the aims of their traders, planters, industrialists, etc., in their goals, which were determined by their secular culture.

In order to have an idea of the impact of the colonial government on the native society and culture in South East Asia, we need a short characterization of this native society and culture at the time of the first encounter. In general it can be said that in the whole of South East Asia, the native society and culture can be discerned in two aspects: first the society and culture of the upper strata, centered around the king and the court. This society was the result of a mixture of an earlier culture of the people of South East Asia with the high cultures of India and Islam. In their political structure, they have been characterized by what we may loosely term feudalism, in which the king was an absolute monarch. The power of the king was closely related to the religious system. In the Indian system, he was a direct incarnation of God, while in the Islamic system, he was the *chalifah.* In this atmosphere of feudalism and religion, the court was the center of a refined culture, manifesting itself in refined arts and a refined system of ceremonies and etiquette. Through the power of the king the capital also was the economic center of the country with a more or less extensive industry and trade.

The second aspect of native society and culture was represented by the villages. In contrast to the feudal culture, with its bureaucratic hierarchy and its splendid arts, ceremonies and etiquette, the culture of the village was that of simple, economically more or less autarkic peasant communities, with a strong attachment to the soil and a strong bond of solidarity between its members. The religion of these village communities has been only superficially affected by the great religions and is dominated by the concepts of animism, dynamism and magic, which also form the basis of their economic thinking, their attachment to the soil and their group solidarity. In the arts, this culture was much less sophisticated than that of the court.

However great the difference was between the high culture of the courts influenced by the Indian and the Islamic cultures, and the still primitive culture of the village communities, as compared to the culture of the Europeans during the 19th century in Africa, Asia and America, both aspects of the native culture were in one very important way akin to each other. The religious value of the holy dominated both cultures; feeling and imagination played an important role in group life and the religious myth was the guiding and moving concept in the life of the people. It is clear that rational life and economic sophistication had developed further in the culture around the court, but compared with modern Western secularized culture, even this was still pre-Renaissance, pre-Enlightenment and pre-industrial.

The decisive event in the political contact between the Western colonial powers and the colonized countries was that the Western powers at an early date took the positions of the former feudal rulers, who were shunted aside or became mere Western puppets. It is interesting to see, for example, how in Indonesia the Dutch government became master of all the land through the Domeinverklaring, which was based on the assumption that monarchs are absolute owners of the land.

Through the defeat of these native potentates, the colonizing power automatically took over all their power and rights. The laws deriving from the former native kingdoms were gradually replaced by new laws made by the colonizing power. The colonial structure was formulated by these new laws, the colonial penal law kept order in the conquered areas, protecting the achievements of colonial ambitions. The civil law, the law of contracts, the law of commerce, etc., which were related to the colonial economic and trade interest, were also of importance.

It is in this new social and cultural order, administered and maintained by the colonial civil service, courts and police, and favourable to the policies of economic exploitation, that the colonial government had to decide to what extent it wished to proceed towards change of the total social and cultural order of the colonial territories. In this respect two trends were clearly discernible, one aiming at a radical change of the culture of the colonial subjects, the other restraining itself to the most necessary measures for the achievement of the colonial political and economic aims.

The first trend manifested itself with missionary zeal, aiming at the conversion of the natives to the Christian religion. Its interest was more religious than economic. This attitude was more dominant in the Spanish colonial empire, where early efforts were made to convert the natives. Thus the values and norms of the native culture were to be replaced by the values and norms of a Christian European culture.

We shall limit our concern to the second trend, since the conflict of European positive law and native customary law is primarily a conflict between a secularized, rational, individualistic and economic culture, on the one hand, and a communal and religious-oriented culture on the other. After occupying the political and administrative position of the native rulers, and promulgating the laws necessary to secure the achievement of its political and economic interest, the colonial government faced the question of how far it wanted to mix with the social and cultural life of the village masses in shaping its colonial empire. In general it can be said that there were areas where the colonial values and norms were in conflict with the native values and norms, and other areas where the two systems had very little to do with each other.

One school of thought, which consequently pursued the rational and economic logic of Western culture, attempted to resolve the conflict by contending that the whole of Western law of commerce, of contract, of land title, etc., should be imposed on the population, so that modern economic institutions and enterprises would have the greatest possibility of expansion. In this unification of law, the whole native population gradually would become a part of the new social order under the regulation of modern European laws, which as we know have been influenced by the abstract and individualistic Roman law.

It was clear, however, that the backward native village population would be greatly disadvantaged in the competition with the more sophisticated urban people. In a minimum of time their valuable land would fall into the hands of economically stronger groups, consisting mostly of foreigners. Such a radical change in the possession of land would not only make real paupers of the village population, but would also uproot them from their traditional culture, creating a host of new problems for the colonial government, which neither had the will nor the energy to elevate the colonized people to their own standard of living.

It was in this context that a variation of the above scheme presented itself as a logical solution. The colonial government imposed its laws according to its needs, and left the population to its own norms where there was no contradiction in interests with colonial governmental policies. Thus the concept of maintenance of customary law was born and acquired an official status and sanction in the legal system of the colonial government. This idea of different types of law for different classes of residents was considered the liberal attitude toward the cultural heritage of alien peoples, and received strong support from a legal theory popular in Europe in the 19th century. As expressed by F. K. von Savigny, the central concept of this "historical school" was that law is the evolutionary product of a nation's growth; it is part and parcel of a national culture and cannot be imposed from outside the culture. Seen as a general historical phenomenon, this theory of course is invariably true: it is easy to look back into history, and find the functional position of law in a culture.

The chief analyst and proponent of this theory which celebrated its highest triumph in the Dutch East Indies was C. van Vollenhoven, whose ideas have dominated both Dutch and Indonesian legal thinking on the kind of law to be put into practice for the Indonesian people over the last 50 years. By using ethnological concepts and comparing the existing customary law in the various regions of Indonesia, van Vollenhoven demonstrated with great skill that there were certain common elements in all. He found, *inter alia*, (1) a preponderance of communal over individual interests, (2) a close relationship between man and the soil, (3) an all-pervasive "magical" and religious pattern of thought, and (4) a strongly family-oriented atmosphere in which every effort was made to compose disputes through conciliation and mutual consideration. With these basic common elements, the great variegation of Indonesian customary law could be seen as expressing a fundamental unity, which had in various places through the accidents of history undergone certain changes—through the intervention of Indonesian-Indian, Indonesian-Islamic and later Dutch governmental and legal structures. By the masterly quality of his writing, van Vollenhoven was so successful in revealing the peculiar beauty of this customary law that a whole new generation of Indonesian jurists, who wanted their people to rise as rapidly as possible to the level of other progressive nations, grew up willing to accept his ideas of customary or *adat* law as essentially the most satisfactory basis for a national legal system.

In the broadest sense van Vollenhoven found in Indonesia only what he himself, as a European reacting against the individualism and formalism of European law (especially its Romanized civil law), was looking for, namely, certain primordial elements in ancient European customary law, such as had existed among the Germanic tribes before they were conquered by the Romans. In this light one can see that the exaggerations in his analysis and his picture of Indonesian customary law were the results of his own personal ideals and sentiments, which in turn were simply the manifestations of certain currents within one legal school flourishing in Europe at that time. But one can also say that in Indonesia this was the beginning of a sort of romanticism of customary law. It was adulated for its "wholeness" and its subtle refinement in satisfying the community's sense of justice and feeling of mutual responsibility.

But the attempts to put this theory into practice once again revealed the paradoxical dualistic quality of colonial society. Although it was repeatedly stressed that for the Indonesians law was to be a natural outgrowth of their own society, it was yet inconceivable that in a dualistic society where one group dominated another the concrete task of giving form and content to this customary law would be performed by the native people living in rural village communities. In the general framework of colonial relationships it was inevitable that the final word on the form and content of customary law would lie with van Vollenhoven and other jurists of similar views. This meant, essentially, that customary law could only be applied where it did not conflict with the interests and policies of the colonial system. Nevertheless, the colonial government could now congratulate itself, not only for not undermining, but even for protecting the cultural life of its colonial subjects.

In Dutch colonial history, this "customary law" school goes indeed by the name of the "ethical" group. It differed from the "reactionary, capitalistic liberal" group which sought to impose written European law on the Indonesian people in order to facilitate the smooth running of its plantations and various industrial and commercial enterprises.

The facts of modern economic life demanded a clearly articulated written law allowing the entrepreneur to make accurate calculations as to the consequences of business agreements over a long period. Giant economic organizations (often with branches in other parts of the world) were helpless in the face of an unwritten customary law, familial in character and adapted to the small-scale community, where each individual was known personally to his fellow, and where law could be adjusted to varying circumstances.

Should we, however, be surprised at the ease with which the "customary law" group, with its strong "ethical" position, succeeded in winning the hearts of the younger Indonesian jurists, thirsty for praise of the values of their society and culture, which had suffered so many humiliations in the last centuries? Their new awareness of the values of this legal system, handed down from generation to generation, so idyllically depicted by van Vollenhoven, gave them a great feeling of confidence in themselves and in their people. We should, therefore, not be surprised to find paeans of praise for this customary law, flowing (on more than one occasion) from the pen of romantics like the late Muhammad Yamin. It was full of poetry; and within its framework, man's spirit was as yet unfragmented, unlike in the modern world. Art and religion could still be united within the forms of law.

And even apart from this, the traditional customary law had created a legal structure which protected the land rights of economically unsophisticated, poverty-stricken Indonesians from the depravations of rich, world-wise foreigners who were eager to buy up their land. If we also remember that those who wanted the introduction of modern European law into Indonesian life were precisely those European entrepreneurs who are usually called "capitalists," and who represented to Indonesian eyes the worst possible aspects of colonialism, it is not hard to see why most educated Indonesians supported the champions of customary law—van Vollenhoven and his followers.

In consequence, a group of Indonesian jurists rose to prominence who were fully persuaded that customary law was the legal system most truly "in harmony" with the Indonesian idea of justice. They were the products of the teachings of van Vollenhoven at Leyden and later of

Ter Haar and Supomo at Jakarta. They never really understood that the peculiar synthesis of nationalist sentiment and ideals of Indonesian progress within the modern world, expressed by their whole concern for customary law, soon brought the development of Indonesian law and Indonesian legal thinking to a hopelessly confused and tangled impasse. All clearly defined goals were lost sight of; and any rational understanding of the problems of law, as faced by Indonesia in the 20th century, completely vanished.

This Indonesian case shows clearly to what confused legal thinking the doctrine of customary law has led. The Dutch East Indies is the place where the concept of customary law has been developed most consequentially and in the most sophisticated manner, due to the great personality and scholarship of van Vollenhoven and to the vigour of customary law among the Indonesian people. Thus in the Dutch East Indies customary law was, and is, not only validated as to the rules for marriage and inheritance, but also for landrights, and for various political and economic activities within the village community. In some cases it also has the character of administrative and penal law. Traces of this trend are of course also discernible in other ex-colonies in South East Asia, where at least the laws of marriage, of inheritance, etc., of the native population were left untouched. These and other religious problems were too complicated and subtle to be handled by a foreign government, while at the same time they were of very little relevance to the colonial political and economic interests.

In order to understand the *cul-de-sacs* to which the doctrine of *adat* law can lead, it is very instructive to analyze the Indonesian case further in the contexts of the ideals of an independent modern Indonesia.

First of all the acceptance of the doctrine of customary law tends to split Indonesia up into various customary law areas, since customary law, despite van Vollenhoven's discovery of its basic unity, is in fact nothing other than the norms of social behaviour of small, isolated communities. Customary law is thus a great handicap to the development of a unified Indonesian civil law, attuned to modern needs and conditions, since it is deeply rooted in the sacred tradition of a culture which has vanished or is in the process of vanishing. In facing the necessities of progress in modern times customary law favours an irrational, familial, unbusinesslike and conservative attitude. It tends to keep the village in its old isolation and prevents the village man from participating in modern intellectual and economic progress. In colonial times customary law was in part defended as protecting the landrights of ignorant and poverty-stricken Indonesians, but after independence it gradually but obviously became a barrier to economic development along modern lines.

Let us take for example the land-law in the Minangkabau territory. In this area with a powerful and highly articulated customary law on property rights, the entire land, including mountains and jungles, has usually long been divided up among numerous clans and families. It would probably be fair to say that there is no land there now which does not already belong to some group. Anyone not belonging to one of the Minangkabau clans or families has absolutely no chance of acquiring a plot for himself (although there may be plenty of untilled land) unless he becomes a member of one of these clans or families by a special customary law ceremony. The fact is that while it is often easy for Minangkabauers to buy land in other parts of Indonesia (in Java, for example), it is almost impossible for an outsider to do the same in the Minangkabau territory. The central government itself has run into this obstacle in its various efforts to stimulate a transmigration program. It has become quite obvious that people who come from other areas of Indonesia are going to find it very difficult to acquire and open up land in this area, whether for agriculture, cattle-breeding or industrial purposes. Thus large areas of useful and perhaps necessary land remain untilled and unusable.

Another impediment, which has long been felt, is the vast number and variety of laws governing inheritance in the customary system. As intercourse and interassociation between Indonesians have grown steadily over the years, this legal heterogeneity has caused great legal complications. Eventually inter-regional customary law either becomes hopelessly confused, or loses its use and validity for ordinary purposes.

We can thus see that, though it was not suspected at the time, the real interests of a progressive independent Indonesia demanded a style of legal thinking which differed radically from van Vollenhoven's but could have been quite in harmony with the capitalist entrepreneurs, who were seeking to establish throughout the world a clear written legal system based on the general assumptions of modern business enterprise. The development and growth of a modern Indonesian state required a clearly articulated legal system which as far as possible would reflect the unity of Indonesia, and yet also adapt itself where possible to the models of other modern nations. And for this purpose, a customary law based on small isolated village-cultures was of very little use.[1]

It is clear from this Indonesian case that a piecemeal change of the *adat* law will only result in a complicated patch-work, which will not be to the advantage of systematic modernization of the law, nor to the social and cultural integration of the country. Moreover it is the very spirit of *adat* law which is unfavourable to efforts toward modernization—now the most urgent problem in the countries of Asia. If we still sometimes hear some modern Asian intellectual praising customary law, it must be considered the expression of a confused mind in the face of the tremendous spiritual and material change which is taking place in Asia and elsewhere. If he is a man of the modern world, very often his adulation of *adat* law is the expression of the nostalgia of a tired modern man for a more peaceful archaic society. Or it can also be the reaction of a modern nationalist who, with the realization of the political and economic defeat of his culture during the last centuries, attempts to acquire some self-confidence and self-satisfaction in the thought that customary law is the manifestation of higher spiritual values than those of the individualistic, abstract and materialistic laws of modern culture. But this kind of appreciation of traditional law as a part of the traditional spiritual culture is the illusion of a negligible number of people, as is witnessed by the fact that so very little of this concern has been crystallized in the modern constitutions of the newly independent nations of Asia. Even in the modern educational system of the Asian countries we discern very little of the great religious and aesthetic values of the region, not to speak of the concepts and ideas of traditional customary law.

Indeed the cultural change which has taken place in the Asian countries is greater and more radical than we usually profess to accept. The norms of customary law are relics of a time forever past, for modern, secularized culture has penetrated even into the holiest of our holy religions. The time is already long past when we can speak of a controversy between the cultures of the Western and Eastern nations. Our constitutions and our systems of education clearly reveal that we have already accepted the modern way of thought and life, dominated by modern political, theoretical and economic values. Whereas formerly it was the colonial government which imposed the concept of modern positive law, now after independence it is the modern Asian leaders

[1] For the description of the conflicts in Indonesian *adat*-law, I have drawn heavily on the chapter "Confusion in Legal Thinking" in my work *Indonesia in the Modern World*, published by the Congress for Cultural Freedom, New Delhi, 1961.

themselves who decide to create the modern laws which are necessary for the modernization of their countries.

With the concept of the six cultural processes (which can be combined into three processes, namely: the progressive cultural processes, determined by the theoretical and economic values; the expressive processes determined by the religious and aesthetic values; and the social organization processes, determined by the power and solidarity values), not only can the tremendous complexity of any culture be reduced to its simplest common denominator, but we can analyze and understand the confusing criss-crossing of currents and countercurrents, the complicated conflicts and tensions, as well as the failures and successes in the great transformation of Asian cultural life. In the final analysis the kaleidoscopic confusion in the Asian cultural scene of today can be considered as a short recapitulation of the development of Europe after the Renaissance. European culture, which during the Middle Ages was dominated by religion and the value of the holy, gradually made way for a more secular culture in which science, technology and economics play a most important role. This process of secularization and rationalization has brought Western culture to an unprecedented vitality and activity, resulting not only in the development of science, technology and economics, but also in the conquest of a large part of the world by European nations.

In the most general sense, we can say that at the time of early contact of the Asian people with European sailors and merchants, the Asian culture, dominated by religious beliefs and tradition, was more or less in a stagnant position. It was in the unpleasant contact between the colonizer and the colonized during the last century that Asian people came to realize that in the superiority and productivity of the European secular culture in science, technology and economics lay the very basis of their defeat and humiliation by Western conquerors. And when the Western colonizers opened the possibility for a small number of Asians to learn science, technology and modern business, neither the Europeans nor the Asians expected that this decision would have the most devastating consequences for the power position of the Europeans in Asia, as well as for the continuation of the traditional, religious oriented culture of Asia.

We now know that these few Western-educated Asians opened the struggle against Western colonialism in the form of nationalism, resulting in so many new free nations in the Asia of our day. On the other hand, it was also this Western-educated minority which struggled against the stagnation, apathy and backwardness of the old society and culture. With all its power and knowledge, it attempted to change its own society and culture in the direction of the culture of post-Renaissance Europe. From a cultural point of view, Western-educated Asians became allies of the European in the creation of what we call modern culture, i.e., secular, progressive culture, dominated by science, technology and economics.

It is clear that in this great modernization process in Asia static customary law acquires another coloration. Primary interest is now in the change of society and culture, not in the conservation of the old. A progressive secularized culture is replacing the static, expressive, religious-oriented culture. And it is logical that in this cultural attitude, law has a more dynamic function than that formulated in the theory of von Savigny's historical school. Law is not just the outgrowth of a developing society, but it has a more important role in stimulating and guiding a society's growth. In this sense law is the twin of education, each helping the other to shape the new society and its culture. And it is in this sense that we can fully understand the building of great legal structures such as the modern constitutions of the new nations of Asia, out of which emerged a host of other laws regulating the growth of the new order in economic life, in education, in land reform, social relations, etc.

Does all this mean that religion and other higher spiritual values are vanishing in the new nations of Asia? Undoubtedly not, since it is clear that science, technology and economics will not be able to solve all human problems. For a full understanding of this complex cultural change, it is necessary to refer also to the crisis which has taken place during the last century within the modern culture of Europe and America, as described by writers like Spengler, Toynbee, Sorokin, Schweitzer and others. The complaints in modern countries about the demoralization of the youth, the increasing emptiness of life, the debasing of moral and aesthetic standards in mass culture, the various kinds of fear, anxiety, frustration, neurosis and psychosis resulting from a loss of the ethical integrating force in the personality, urge many Asians to consider their own eagerness for modernization in the light of a broader concept of their culture, in which the progressive and expressive aspects should come to a fuller synthesis.

It is out of this consciousness of the crisis of modern culture with its successes as well as its failures and aberrations that personalities like Tagore, Iqbal, Buber and many others arise who attempt to provide the modern Asian with a deeper anchorage in his awareness of the religious foundations of life, and a deeper enjoyment through the unfolding of aesthetic creativity. It is interesting to see how through their broadened concept of the modernization of their cultures these Asian cultural thinkers come to an early alliance with the great cultural thinkers of the Western world, men like Schweitzer, Teilhard de Chardin and others. From this point of view, the struggle between the progressive and the expressive aspects of the cultures of Europe and America and the conflicts in Asian cultures are gradually coming to resemble each other.

II. THE NATURE OF MALAY CUSTOMARY LAW

Introduction

Malay customary law is called *adat*, a word borrowed from the Arabic. *Adat*, in general, means right conduct; and in common usage, it stands for a variety of things all connected with proper social behaviour.[1] Thus it will connote rules of etiquette and the ceremonies prescribed for a particular occasion, such as marriage, as well as those customs which have "legal consequences."[2] It is in this last sense that the word is generally used in this paper.

It has been said:

> A social norm is a customary mode of behaviour—it is what people in a given society are expected by their fellow members to do, not only because such behaviour is usual but also because it is deemed good. The man who upholds the norms will be rewarded by his fellows—with approbation, honours and the like; these are positive sanctions. The man who does not uphold the norms will be punished by negative sanctions. These may take many different forms ranging from minor social sanctions, such as ridicule and refusal to interact with him, to the most extreme—that of ostracism by the community. Economic sanctions such as refusal to cooperate in economic activity and political sanctions such as the depriving of an elected person of one's support and vote may be applied. Legal sanctions are those in which force may be used by a recognized authority.[3]

Attempts have been made to redefine law so that the definition may cover customs which have legal consequences. "A social norm," writes Hoebel, "is legal if its neglect or infraction is regularly met, in threat or in fact, by the application of physical force by an individual or group possessing the socially recognized privilege of so acting."[4] S. Roy would define law as "a body of rules of human conduct, either prescribed by long established usages and customs or laid down by a paramount political power."[5] Sir Arthur Goodhart defined it as "any rule of human conduct which is recognized as being obligatory."[6] Dr. T. O. Elias attempted to improve upon the definition by suggesting that "the law

[1] Dictionaries give the following meanings, among others, for *adat*: custom, customary law, customary behaviour, proper behaviour, courtesy.

[2] C. Snouck Hurgronje, *De Atjeher* (The Achinese) Vol. I, p. 357. To connote the *adat* that has legal consequences, he used the Dutch expression "adatrecht" i.e. "adat law."

[3] P. C. Lloyd, *Yoruba Land Law*, 1962, p. 14.

[4] E. A. Hoebel, *The Law of Primitive Man*, p. 28.

[5] S. Roy, *Customs and Customary Law in British India*, p. 4.

[6] Quoted in T. O. Elias, *The Nature of African Customary Law*, p. 53.

of a given community is the body of rules which are recognized as obligatory by its members."[1]

Writing of Sumatra more than 150 years ago, William Marsden stated:

> There is no word in the language of the island which properly and strictly signifies law; nor is there any person or class of persons among the *Rejangs* regularly invested with legislative power. They are governed in their various disputes by a set of long-established customs (*adat*) handed down to them from their ancestors, the authority of which is founded on usage and general consent. The Chiefs, in pronouncing their decisions, are not heard to say, "so the law directs," but "such is the custom."[2]

It may be that *adat* will weld the society as sweetly and well by any other name, such as *sadachara*[3] or "native law and custom."[4]

Adat Melayu (Malay Custom)

The Malay community may be classified into two different groups: one following *adat temenggong* and the other, *adat perpateh*. *Adat perpateh* is adhered to by the Malays inhabiting Negri Sembilan and certain parts of Malacca, especially Naning. Malays in other parts of Malaysia are supposed to follow *adat temenggong*. Though both the *adat* originated from tribal organizations in the past, it is in *adat perpateh* that the remnants of tribal structure are clearly evident at present. To cite one instance, marriage between two persons belonging to the same clan is regarded as incestuous and is strictly prohibited. Another characteristic of *adat perpateh* is that it adheres to matriliny while *adat temenggong* favours patriliny.

The two *adat* are believed to have been called after two legendary law-givers, Parapatih nan Sa-batang and Kei Tamanggungan. According to the *terombo* (song of origin) familiar to the present day followers of *adat perpateh*, these law-givers held sway over different parts of Minangkabau in Sumatra, Parapatih ruling over the hilly inland region and Tamanggungan governing the coastal region. According to legend, they were half-brothers. Why Parapatih insisted upon matriliny and exogamy for his followers, while his half-brother was inclined to patrilineal descent and endogamy is not known. A legend narrated by Willinck[5] may explain the prevalence of exogamy in *adat perpateh* society, but it does not indicate why it is not followed in *adat temenggong*

[1] *Id.*, p. 55.
[2] William Marsden, *The History of Sumatra*, 3rd Edition, 1811, p. 217.
[3] A Sanskrit word used by text writers to mean approved usage.
[4] A term used by British colonial administrators. No distinction was made between law and custom, and as P. C. Lloyd (*op. cit.*, p. 15) remarks, "it was perhaps not intended to be made."
[5] G. D. Willinck, *Het rechtsleven bij de Minangkabausche Maleiers*, p. 121.

society. According to the legend, Parapatih, when young, went on a long journey. On his return he married Putri Zamilau, without knowing that she was his half-sister. Later when it was discovered that they were blood relations, Parapatih and Tamanggungan, horrified by the incestuous connection, decided to divide the Minangkabaus into two groups, Koto-Piliang and Bodi-Chaniago, and ruled that no one should marry within his own group.

In general, it is the *adat perpateh* group which seems to follow its *adat* strictly, and therefore it is not unlikely that when the *adat temenggong* group gradually gave up exogamy, the other group adhered to it. The adherence to matriliny seen in the *adat perpateh* society may also be due to its general tendency to adhere strictly to the *adat*. Assuming that matriliny was indigenous to Minangkabau, it is not improbable that the system gained strength from the South Indian settlers who followed a similar rule of descent. But the possibility of its having been introduced into Minangkabau[1] by South Indians cannot be absolutely ruled out. It could be that the South Indians in Minangkabau were those who followed matriliny in their own native land and they either introduced the system into the country of their adoption or incorporated it with the indigenous system.

As it is the *adat perpateh* society that follows its *adat* scrupulously, when one speaks of Malay *adat*, one is more inclined to think of *adat perpateh* than of *adat temenggong*. Wilkinson wrote in 1908: "The difference between the *adat perpateh* and the *adat temenggong* is visible in these days of British administration. Whenever a miscarriage of justice occurs in Perak, Pahang and Selangor, the Malays take it very calmly; but in the Negri Sembilan the whole population is excited by any non-recognition of the local *adat*."[2]

[1] Despite all legends concerning the origin of the name Minangkabau, it is probable that it originally meant the portion (or division) of land allotted to *Mennoki* (Malayalam, literally, a Superintendent). *Menoki* was also a baronial title in North Kerala. *Menokibhagam* (the chief's or superintendent's portion) could easily have been corrupted to *Minangkabau*. See also the *bau* or *bu* endings in place names like Rembau, Jelebu which may once have been *Rem* (Rama?) *bhaga*, *Jelabhaga*. *Lembaga* originally seems to have meant a territorial division. *Bahagian* in Malay vocabulary indicates that the Sanskrit *bhaga* was not unknown to the Malay world.

If this etymological interpretation be correct, it is possible that the baron and his kinsmen who occupied the fenced area (Pagar Ruyong) and its surroundings followed matriliny, while their local tenants or dependents followed the (indigenous) system of patriliny. It could as well be that while the baron and his kinsmen followed matriliny, those who adhered to patriliny were those of the chief's followers who, though they also came from South India, were given to following the rules of patrilineal descent in their own country. It was only certain sections of the Kerala community (for example, the Nayars, and certain groups of Tiyas and Mapillas) which followed matriliny.

[2] Wilkinson, "Law: Introductory Sketch," pp. 19–20 (in *Papers on Malay Subjects*).

This paper concerns itself more with *adat perpateh* as representing Malay customary law than with *adat temenggong*. The digests dealing with *adat temenggong* are "mixed with relics of Hindu law and overlaid with Muslim law."[1] Thus the Malacca Laws (Undang Undang Melaka) though entitled Risalat Hukum Kanum (A Tract on Customary Law) is a digest "grafting the Islamic Law of the new Sultanate [of Malacca] on to the earlier law of a Hindu court."[2] One is, therefore, on surer ground in dealing with Malay customary law when such rules of *adat perpateh* as could be gleaned from traditional sayings are selected for discussion.

Basic Laws

It is arguable that even the Austinian definition of law would cover the fundamental rules of the Malay customary law, as they were laid down by the two law-givers, Parapatih and Tamanggungan; they were rules, (if one gives credence to their legendary origin), "set by political superiors to political inferiors."[3] But it may be conceded that the Malays follow their *adat* not merely because it is believed to have been laid down by the law-givers, but also because it is expressive of an instinctive sense of right, of the common consciousness of the people (*Rechtsüberzeugung*).

What the law-givers proclaimed for the observance of their followers may be regarded as the basic rules of the *adat*. Tamanggungan laid down:

Who casts the net shall jump to drag it in;
Who commits an offence shall compensate;
Who owes shall pay; who slays shall be slain.[4]

Parapatih declared:

A debt adheres to the tribe [clan] of the debtor;

[1] Winstedt, *Malays, A Cultural History*, 4th Edition, p. 91.

[2] *Id.*, p. 99. See also Haji Mohd. Din bin Ali, "Two Forces in Malay Society," *Intisari*, Vol. I, No. 3; p. 15, where he says in regard to the inheritance of Malay holdings in the "Islamic-cum-Temenggong States": "Take away the Hukum Shara and the residual adat and that which is Temenggong would be beyond recognition," (p. 19). He also says: "At present the amalgamation of Islam and the Adat Temenggong is so complete that it is well nigh impossible to separate one from the other." (p. 20)

[3] Austin's *Jurisprudence*, (1911 Edition) p. 87.

[4] Siapa menjala, siapa terjun, / Siapa salah, siapa bertimbang, / Siapa berutang, siapa membayar; / Siapa bunoh, siapa kena bunoh.

The translation quoted is that of A. Caldecott, "Jelebu Customary Songs and Sayings," *J.S.B.R.A.S.* Vol. 78, p. 3, at p. 17.

Most of the translations of *perbilangan* in this paper are those of A. Caldecott, J. L. Humphreys, Parr and Mackray, Wilkinson and Winstedt.

A mortgage becomes a lien on the tribal land;
Who wounds shall pay smart-money, who kills shall give restitution.[1]

These by no means seem to have constituted all the rules of conduct followed by the Malay society and generally contained in *kata pesaka* (traditional sayings) or *perbilangan* (customary sayings). According to tradition, these were the laws first formulated. The rest of the customary laws may be regarded as springing from them.

The history of the development of his customary law is not a secret to the Malay. For as the *perbilangan adat* (customary saying) puts it

The old men know tradition,
The young men hear report.[2]

And the law of the tradition is:

The pattern becomes the mould;
The example becomes the type;
Precept passing into usage,
Practice passing into custom,
The custom handed down by our forefathers from generation to generation:
Transplanted it withers,
Uprooted, dies.[3]

Here in a few words is summarized the development of traditional or customary law (*kala tua*) which may be distinguished from the custom of the country (*resam negri*) expressed in such sayings as:

Duty gives and receives again,
Courtesy repays kindness.[4]

Adat Law and Custom

From the sayings it is not always easy to distinguish between the

[1] Hutang nan berturut, chagar bergadai; / Chinchang pampas, bunoh beri balas.
This again is from Caldecott's "Jelebu Customary Songs and Sayings." Some versions of the *terombo* (for instance, the one familiar to the people of Naning) contain many more rules. See J. L. Humphreys, "A Naning Recital," *J.S.B.R.A.S.*, Vol. 83, p. 1. See also Haji Mohd. Din bin Ali, "Two Forces in Malay Society," *op. cit.*, p. 15. I prefer the Jelebu version as laying down the basic law. The various rules given in the Naning version appear to be either elaborations of the basic principles or mere matters of procedure. See below, section on administration of the *adat*.

[2] Pebilangan pada nang tua-tua, / Perkhabaran pada nang kechil-kechil.

[3] Berlukis berlambaga, / Berturas berteladan; / Nang di-ucha di-pakai, / Nang di-pesar di-biasakan, / Turun-menurun dari-pada nenek moyang: / Di-anjak layu, / Di-chabut mati.

[4] Shariat palu-memalu, / Berbudi orang berbahasa kita.

customs that have legal consequences and those that do not have such consequences. Here again what ascribes legal consequences to a custom is the law of tradition: if, according to tradition, the pattern has become the mould which the clansmen will be interested in maintaining intact with whatever coercive powers they may possess for the purpose, one may assume that that pattern has passed from custom into customary law. It is obvious that when it is said:

Clansmen of a clan, tribesmen of a tribe,
With kin both far and near;
To those afar we hearken,
Those near we mark and obey.[1]

the hearkening (*di-dengar-dengarkan*) cannot be enforced.

But the rule of exogamy contained in "Our boys we wed to other clans"[2] should not be broken, for a breach would bring in its train dire consequences on the offender. Again, the saying

A stranger weds into our clan.
For every stranger that weds into our clan
A share is set with just consent[3]

contains a rule of law which will be enforced by the community.

The sayings handed down from generation to generation are known to every one so that in fact ignorance of law can be no honest or valid excuse. According to a derisive saw, dull-witted may be the people of Minangkabau, who have no footing on the sea, but they and their kinsmen in Malaysia are smart enough to know and remember their *adat*.

The sayings are simple and can be easily memorized. This memorable quality does not always make for easy comprehension. Thus the pithy saying

Pound rice in a mortar,
Cook rice in a pot.[4]

is explained to mean that complaints should be made to the proper court.[5] It is also supposed to imply that punishment must fit the crime.[6]

[1] Bersuku berwaris, / Jauh pun ada, dekat pun ada / Jika jauh di-dengar-dengarkan, / Jika dekat di-pandang-pandangkan.

[2] Yang jantan di-semendakan ka-orang.

[3] Menerima pula orang semenda. / Tiap-tiap menerima orang semenda itu, / Di-tentukan pula dengan benar dengan muafakat:

[4] Menumbok di-lesong / Menanak di-periok.

[5] See J. L. Humphreys, "A Collection of Malay Proverbs," *J.S.B.R.A.S.*, Vol. 67, p. 108; also Winstedt's "Notes to Caldecott's Jelebu Customary Songs and Sayings," *J.S.B.R.A.S.*, Vol. 78, p. 29.

[6] Winstedt's "Notes," *op. cit.*, p. 29.

A third explanation given is to the effect that a person should attend to his business in the proper manner.[1]

There is probably no harm if a saying signifies many things, provided all of them are in conformity with the accepted social norms.

In spite of a variety of meanings attributable to some of them, the interpretation of these saws appears to be less difficult than the interpretation of a statute in a common law court; for the interpretation of the saying along with the significance of the metaphor or other figure of speech contained in it is handed down from generation to generation. This recourse to what one might regard as the preparatory work to the enunciation of the rule makes the saying not unduly difficult of understanding.[2]

Constitutional Structure

Adat perpateh appears to envisage a hereditary constitutional monarchy. The ruler of Negri Sembilan, Yang di-Pertuan Besar (one who is acknowledged as the great lord) is, in theory, elected by the *Undangs* of Sungei Ujong, Jelebu, Johol and Rembau. But as Wilkinson observes: "Nowadays the choice of a Yamtuan[3] is a foregone conclusion; his election is a mere form."[4] In 1934 when Muhammad Shah died, his son Abdul Rahman succeeded him. All that the *Undang* of Sungei Ujong declared in this connection on behalf of the four electors at the installation ceremony was that "...This day we have installed Tuanku Abdul Rahman, son of the late Yang di-pertuan Besar Muhammad Shah, on the Lion Throne of the Kingdom of Negri Sembilan."[5] Neither the matrilineal principle nor the rule of primogeniture is accepted in relation to the succession to the throne. It is up to the electors to choose a younger son of the late Yang di-Pertuan Besar in preference to the eldest, if the latter is found unsuitable for the position; but no Yang di-Pertuan Besar is elected from outside the royal family.[6] The democratic principle, however, appears to be maintained in the tradition that the Yamtuan should marry a woman who is one of his subjects and not of royal descent.[7] The opinion is sometimes expressed that the royal con-

[1] Wilkinson, "Law: Introductory Sketch," *op. cit.*, p. 17.

[2] Differences in interpretation as well as differences in the text do occur in different areas; this may be because there are variations in the custom between one area and another.

[3] A colloquial term for Yang di-Pertuan.

[4] Wilkinson, "Sri Menanti," p. 39 (in *Papers on Malay Subjects*).

[5] J. J. Sheehan, "Installation of Tuanku Abdul Rahman," *J.M.B.R.A.S.*, 1936, p. 237.

[6] See the Laws of the Constitution of Negri Sembilan, Article VII (3) which reads "No person shall be elected Yang di-Pertuan Besar of the State unless He ... is a lawfully begotten descendant in the male line of Raja Radin ibni Raja Lenggang."

[7] P. E. de Josselin de Jong, *Minangkabau and Negri Sembilan*, p. 151.

sort should be a member of the Ayer Kaki family of the Batu Hamper clan, the family to which Raja Melewar's wife belonged.[1] But no such rule is considered obligatory at present.[2]

The principle of election is recognized in the choice of the *undang*, the *lembaga* and the *buapa*. The *buapa* is to be elected by the members of his *perut* and approved by the *lembaga* who can dismiss him at will.[3] In the election of the *lembaga*, the principle of *giliran* or *pesaka bergelar*[4] is followed, that is, every *perut* in turn has the right to supply the *suku* chief. The principle thus postulates, as de Moubray puts it, "that each *perut* should have its equality in this matter ensured by being placed as it were on a roster."[5] In Rembau and Naning, the *lembagas* elect the *undangs* by unanimous vote from different *perut*, offshoots of the original Malacca house.[6] In Jelebu, Johol and Sungei Ujong, there are electoral colleges for the election of the *undangs*. Though the principle of election, direct or indirect, is recognized, one finds that the choice for the electors is strictly circumscribed, and, in some instances, as, for example, in the case of the election of the *Undang* of Sungei Ujong, the electors themselves generally have to be members of certain specified families. No election or dismissal of a *lembaga* is valid until confirmed by the *undang*.[7] A *buapa* may be dismissed at will by the *lembaga*.[8] In spite of the democratic elements evident in the *adat perpateh* society,[9] one cannot be oblivious to the hierarchical pattern, based on blueness of blood and ancient lineage, in the general social structure.

A king has his royal annals,
A chief his geneological tree,
A tribal headman [*lembaga*] his song of origin.[10]

[1] Wilkinson, "Sri Menanti," p. 22 (*Papers on Malay Subjects*).
[2] *Ibid.*
[3] Winstedt, *The Malays, A Cultural History*, p. 82.
[4] The Minangkabaus call it *adat sansako*.
[5] G. A. de C. de Moubray, *Matriarchy in the Malay Peninsula*, p. 106.
[6] Winstedt, *op. cit.*, p. 85.
[7] *Id.*, p. 84.
[8] *Id.*, p. 82.
[9] According to customary sayings in Jelebu, "If a chief dies, election by the common voice is required. A family by common consent can elect or dismiss its elder; elders by their common consent and with the support of the enfranchised members of the clan can elect or dismiss the headman of a clan. The headmen of clans by common consent can elect or dismiss an undang. The chiefs by common consent and with the support of the lembagas can elect or dismiss the King."

Ganti mati barkebulatan / Kebulatan anak buah membuat atau memechat buapa / Buapa bulat, waris-nya rapat, membuat atau memechat tua; / Kebulatan tua, boleh membuat atau memechat undang; / Undang bulat, lembaga rapat, waris sedia, membuat atau memechant raja.

Caldecott, "Jelebu Customary Songs and Sayings," *op. cit.*, pp. 34–35.

[10] Raja bersejarah, / Penghulu bersalasilah, / Lembaga berteromba.

This need not be a matter of surprise when one considers that the *adat* originated in a tribal organization, with its paramount chief, subordinate chiefs, headmen and elders.

This hierarchical set-up is evidenced by the saying:

The king rules his world;
The chief rules his province;
The lembaga rules his clan;
The elder rules his own people;
The peasant rules his house.[1]

Another saying describes the dignity attributed to the king and the chief:

The king has Majesty, the chief Honour;
The king decrees, the chief orders;
The king rules the world, the chief rules the clan.[2]

The nature of the jurisdiction of the various dignitaries is expressed in the *perbilangan*:

The Raja is the fount of equity;
The Chief carries out the law;
The cord for arrest is the tribal headman's,
The execution creese is the territorial chief's,
The headman's sword is the Raja's –
He can stab without asking leave of any suzerain.
He can behead without reporting it to any suzerain.[3]

In spite of his being able to wield the headman's sword (or the sword of execution), he had only limited powers as may be seen from the fact that:

The King does not own the soil nor can he levy taxes;
he is the fountain of justice and may levy definite fees for his maintenance.[4]

As a Jelebu saying puts it, "The highroads with their stepping stones

[1] Raja menobat di-dalam alam; / Penghulu menobat di-dalam luak; / Lembaga menobat di-dalam lingkongan-nya; / Ibu bapa menobat pada anak buah-nya; / Orang banyak menobat di-dalam teratak-nya.

[2] Raja berdaulat, penghulu berandika; / Raja bertitah, penghulu bersabda; Raja berkhalifah, penghulu bersuku.

[3] Raja sa-keadilan; / Penghulu sa-undang; / Tali pengikat daripada lembaga; / Keris penyalang daripada undang; / Pedang memanchong daripada keadilan, / Tikam, ta' bertanya, / Panchong, ta' berkhabar.

[4] Ada-pun Raja itu tiada mempunyai negeri dan tiada boleh menchukai kharajat, melainkan berkeadilan sahaja serta permakanan-nya.

belong to the prince and the bulbuls."[1] Any attempt on his part to levy taxes would cause him to be expelled, or in the picturesque language of the traditional saying, he would be cast out upon "a waveless sea and a grassless field."[2]

Under the *keadilan* (the fountain of justice) the jurisdiction of the various chiefs and headmen was well defined and carefully graded.

Wilkinson wrote:

> In itself the gradation of official powers is no protection of the liberty of the subject. Its effectiveness in Negri Sembilan lay in the fact that the higher authorities were like our own appellate or assize courts: they could not initiate an attack on an individual. If the peasant committed a petty offence, he was judged by his own people: the chief could not interfere. If he was charged with a graver crime, he was heard by his own people and if a *prima facie* case was made out against him, he was handed over to the higher authorities for trial.... The (territorial) chief could not proceed against any one except the tribal headman [Lembaga], nor was he strong enough to attack any single Lembaga unjustly in face of the opposition that such a proceeding would arouse among the rest.[3]

The other members of the hierarchical order also had their allotted position and sphere of influence:

> Disputes among their families
> Are the province of the elders.
> When a husband disputes about the property
> acquired by his own and his wife's joint labour
> It is the province of his family.
> Within the four threshold beams of his house
> Is a husband's province.[4]

Land Tenure

The importance of landed property to an immigrant people like the Minangkabau settlers in the Malay Peninsula cannot be exaggerated, especially when they were given to the felling of trees and the tilling of land rather than to commercial business. In spite of all the acquisitiveness one might expect of them, the Minangkabau settlers seem to have been guided by a remarkable sense of justice in the acquisition and apportionment of land. According to the customary saying current in Jelebu,

[1] Winstedt, *op. cit.*, p. 88.

[2] *Ibid.*

[3] Quoted in Winstedt, *op. cit.*, p. 89.

[4] Anak buah yang berchalun / Ibu bapa yang punya / Orang semenda yang gadoh bersuarang, / Anak buah yang punya. / Lingkongan bendul yang empat, / Orang semenda yang punya.

When the first clod was upturned
And the first creeper severed,
And the first tree felled –
Our custom and system of entail were not yet established.[1]

When holding was dovetailed into holding,
When our stretches of rice-field were made,
When the shoots of our plants swayed in the breeze,
When our betel palms grew up in rows
Then were established our custom and system of entail.[2]

In determining rights to property, the social position of a person and his lineage are of significance. It is recognized that

The highroad with its stepping stones
Belongs to the king.[3]

and

Stretches of rice-field
Old betel-nut palms
Ancestral coconuts
Belong to the tribal headmen [lembaga]
The path over the knolls in the swamps
Belongs to the tribal headmen [lembaga]
The Sakai path with its tree-trunk bridges
Belongs to the clan that owns the soil.[4]

While the land cleared and cultivated by the immigrants was regarded as belonging to them, the aborigines and their heirs whose lands the immigrants had taken possession of also had rights recognized under the *adat.*

Ravines and valleys
Hills and hill-bases
Belong to the territorial tribe and their chief.[5]

The *adat* attempted to be fair to the birds and fishes too.

[1] Sa-bingkah tanah terbalek, / Sa-helai akar yang putus, / Se-batang kayu rebah – / Adat dengan pesaka belum di-adakan.

[2] Tetekala / Kampong sudah bersudut, / Sawah sudah berjingang / Puchok sudah meliok, / Pinang sudah berjijir / Adat dengan pesaka di-adakan, ia-itu.

[3] Jalan raya titian batu / Raja yang empunya.

[4] Sawah yang berjinjang / Pinang yang gayu / Nyiur yang saka / Lembaga yang punya. / Jalan paya titian permatang / Lembaga yang empunya. / Jalan Sakai titian batang / Waris yang empunya.

[5] Gaung guntong, / Bukit bukan, / Waris dan penghulu yang punya.

The high way with its stepping stones,
Hills and hill-bases,
Lonely forest,
Deep ravines,
Broad plains,
Sloping water-courses,
Belong to the birds.
Deep pools
To the fishes.[1]

While the king shared with the birds the highroad with its stepping stones, the *waris* and their chief shared with them the hills and the hill-bases.

As Wilkinson observes, ownership of land was based on real working tenure.

The *adat*

did not allow a landlord to lock up valuable land at his own discretion or to exact a heavy tax from would-be workers. To use a homely metaphor, it allowed the dog-in-the-manger to levy toll on the cows to the extent of the value of the manger to the dog, while English law allows toll to be levied to the extent of the value of the manger to the cows.[2]

The *adat* expected its adherents to take good care of their property, for

Rice-crops unfenced become waste grass,
Buffalos unpent become wild cattle.[3]

The conditions of entail are also laid down. When the land bears clear evidence of occupation, it is considered heritable.

Idle fallow, land with stubble,
Land with tree-stumps left by the feller,
land that has been levelled –
These can be inherited.[4]

And the inheritance under *adat perpateh* is in the female line.

Our heritage comes from our women,
Men wear the insignia of hereditary office,

[1] Jalan raya titian batu, / Bukit bukau, / Rimba yang sunyi / Gaung yang dalam / Lepan yang lebar / Bandar yang sundai, / Si-barau barau yang punya. / Lubok dalam si-kitang kitang yang punya.

[2] Wilkinson, "Law: Introductory Sketch," *op. cit.*, pp. 28–29.

[3] Padi ta' berpagar lalang / Kerbau ta' berkandang seladang.

[4] Pesaka / Yang bersesapan, yang berjirami, / Bertunggul, berpemarasan.

The inheritance belongs to the women
The man cherishes it.[1]

As a measure of social security envisaged to prevent a member of the clan ending up landless and homeless, certain restrictions on the alienation of ancestral property were contemplated under the *adat*.

The woman's nearest of kin can approve or prevent;
The full members of the woman's clan elect to find the money;
If there are full members of her clan, they can subscribe to save the tail;
If there are next of kin, they can bar the sale;
If the property in question has an owner already, the sale cannot proceed;
The tribal headman can quash the sale.[2]

Husband's Position

Contrary to popular belief, this system of inheritance does not mean that the husband is under a petticoat government in the *adat perpateh* society. His high position in the family is guaranteed to him under the *adat*.

Within the four threshold beams of his house
Is a husband's province.[3]

His importance in the home is again acknowledged in the saying

Slaves can offend against the masters,
Pupils against their teachers,
Children against parents,
Wives against husbands.[4]

This clearly indicates that wives are expected to be obedient and faithful to their husbands. It is also said

Warder of the wife is the husband
Warder of the husband his wife's family.[5]

[1] Terbit pesaka ka-pada saka, / Si-laki-laki menyandang pesaka; / Si-perempuan yang punya pesaka, / Orang semenda yang membela.

[2] Sah batal ka-pada sa-kadim; / Kata berchari ka-pada waris-nya; / Tinggal waris menongkat; / Tinggal sa-kadim melintang; / Tinggal harta bertuan ta' jadi; / Tinggal tua batal.

[3] See p. 26, note 4.

[4] Salah hamba ka-pada tuan / Salah murid ka-pada guru / Salah anak ka-pada bapa / Salah bini ka-pada laki.

[5] Kunchi bini laki / Kunchi semenda tempat semenda.

Because the wife's family happens to be his warder, a husband may occasionally find himself in certain unenviable situations:

When a man marries and goes to his wife's family,
If clever, he will be a friend in council;
If a fool, he will be ordered here and there.
A tall man, he will be as a sheltering buttress,
Prosperous, he will be as a laden branch that gives shade.
The married man must go or stay as he is bid.[1]

It is also said,

A bridegroom among his wife's relations
Is like a soft cucumber among spiny *durian*;
If he rolls against them, he is hurt,
And he's hurt, if they roll against him.[2]

If he follows the customs of his wife's family and makes himself useful, he may find his life among his wife's relations not too unhappy, though,

If a fool, he will be ordered about
To invite guests distant and collect guests near.[3]

but,

If he is strong, he shall be our champion.[4]

A fool's position may hardly be better elsewhere.

The husband among his wife's relations is naturally expected to observe the customs of her family:

When you enter a byre, low;
When you enter a goat's pen, bleat;
Follow the customs of your wife's family.
When you tread the soil of a country and live beneath its sky,
Follow the customs of that country.[5]

It would not be fanciful if one assumed that the position of the man

[1] Orang semenda bertempat semenda. / Jikalau cherdek, temen berunding; / Jikalau bodoh, di-suroh di-arah. / Tinggi, banir tempat berlindong; / Rimbun, dahan tempat bernaung; / Orang semenda pergi karna suroh, / Berhanti karna tegah.

[2] Orang semenda dengan orang tempat semenda / Bagai mentimun dengan durian, / Menggolek pun luka, kena golek pun luka.

[3] Jikalau bingong di-suroh arah, / Menyeput nan jauh, mengampongkan nan dekat.

[4] Jikalau kuat di-bubohkan di-pangkal kayu.

[5] Masok kandang kerbau, menguak; / Masok kandang kambing, membebek; / Bagai-mana 'adat tempat semenda, di-pakai / Bila bumi di-pijak, langit di-junjong, / Bagai-mana adat negeri itu di-pakai.

in a matrilineal society should be more than enviable. Though matrilocal residence of the wife and the customary requirement that the husband should live in the wife's home may bring in certain problems of human relations, especially in his association with the in-laws, one cannot overlook the fact that he has his "province," his sphere of influence and power within the four threshold beams of his house, and that he also has a cherished place in his own family and clan. In his capacity as uncle or brother, he may be the manager of the family and it is not unlikely that he is or he becomes an elder or chief in his clan.

Even when he suspects a shade of unfairness, he should be philosophic enough to console himself with the thought that

> The hap of this life goes by turns,
> Awhile to him, anon to me.[1]

This is specially relevant if his wife's male relations forget that "courtesy repays kindness" (*Berbudi orang berbahasa kita*), the relatives of their own wives may be equally forgetful of the adage.

If the wife's relations exercise some control over him, it seems to be justified for two reasons. The well-being of the family is mainly their concern, and it is their responsibility to see that the husband of their sister or niece contributes to that well-being. Further, they have taken upon themselves a good deal of responsibility for him. For the *adat* stipulates

> To unravel disputes,
> To pick up the fallen and search for the lost,
> To pay debts and receive dues
> Is the business of a man's wife's family.[2]

For this extreme solicitude envisaged in the requirement about picking up the fallen and searching for the lost, the price he pays in the inconvenience of his being ordered about, if he be a fool, is small in comparison with the value of the benefits he receives. *Noblesse oblige.* All that the *adat* seems to enjoin on him in return, apart from attending to his duties in his new surroundings, is that he should pay due regard to the customary law of marriage which stipulates:

> Two familiar spirits in one household,
> Two ladders to one sugar-palm,[3]

[1] Dunia berganti-ganti, / Sa-kali di-orang sa-kali di-kita.

[2] Kusut menyeleosaikan, / Chichir memungut, hilang menchari / Utang membayar, pintang menerimakan / Oleh tempat semenda.

[3] These two lines signify a man's union with another woman of the same clan as his wife during the wife's life.

Sprouts without seed[1]
Are offences against morals.
Custom looks for signs of guilt;
When custom declares the offence proved,
It is not a peccadillo to be mildly corrected.
Nor can recourse be had to religious law –
For this crime of taking two brides when a man has been given one.[2]

Whatever discomforts he may consider himself to be put to by his wife's relations, the *adat* prescribed a fair distribution of property between the husband and the wife, if a divorce is decided upon.

What a man has got by his wife remains with her clan,
What the husband brought goes back to him;
Property in partnership is split up,
The common property acquired by a man and wife's joint labour is equally divided;
Any loss or profit on the wife's estate is a matter for her clan;
The man's person is restored to his own clan.[3]

The husband's absence of independence among his wife's relations does not seem to deprive him of his rights to a fair share in the division of property. After all,

What is the custom of the land?
Duty gives and receives again.[4]

Administration of the Adat

The Malay, in general, is not a litigious person. When he happens to be a litigant, he appears to be unhappy about it. It is said,

Victory – a defeated foe,
defeat – a bowed head,
agreement – a joining of hands.[5]

[1] A euphemism for bastards.

[2] Pelesit dua sa-kampong / Enan sa-batang dua sigai / Mata tumboh tiada berbeneh / Sumbang ka-pada tabiat. / Adat menuju ka-pada tanda / Bila 'Sah' kata adat tiang / Tanggal ta' boleh di-patoh lagi, / Salah ta' boleh di-hukum / Ia-itu suatu di-beri, dua di-ambil.

[3] Dapatan tinggal, / Pembawa kembali / Kutu di-belah / Suarang di-ageh / Rugi laba pulang ka-tempat semanda / Nyawa darah pulang kapada waris.

[4] Nama mana resam negeri? / Shariat palu-memalu.

[5] Menang berkechudang / Alah berketundokan / Sa-rayu berjabat tangan.

What he likes to do when conflicts arise is expressed in the saying

> The injured is made whole,
> The tangled is made straight.[1]

The injured is made whole by applying the customary remedy, which in most cases, especially in *adat perpateh* society, consists in awarding compensation.

In a tribal society such as the one envisaged by the *adat*, "arbitration" plays a very important role. Petty disputes were referred for "arbitration" to the village elder. Only when "arbitration" failed or when the dispute was serious enough to require stronger measures were the services of the *lembaga* sought. He could make an arrest and, if he found it necessary or expedient, hand the offender over to the *undang* who could command the use of the execution creese.

> Small matters are the place for "arbitration,"
> great for the application of custom,
> the most weighty for ancient ancestral right.[2]

Though no doctrine of judicial precedent, as applied in common law jurisdictions, is recognized under the *adat*, the phrase *menchari adat* (search for the custom) is significant in that a search for a precedent remedy is usually made. The saw is

> A day of loss is a day of search,
> The hurt is healed, the wound is stanched.[3]

The judges are usually the village elders or the chiefs of the clans who uphold the norms of their society. As they are not bound by precedent, though a precedent may have great persuasive value, it is not difficult for them to reinterpret the *adat* in the light of modern needs. The sayings in which the *adat* rules are couched may be reinterpreted in such manner as to suit present day conditions. As interpretation of *perbilangan* has not been developed into an esoteric science, there will be no serious objection to re-interpretation which is intended to keep pace with the times. One could therefore argue that customary law needs no modification. Whatever modification is necessary is being made in the application of the *adat* by those who are interested in upholding the norms of their community. Until the *adat* rules are written down, and

[1] Burok di-baiki / Kusut di-selesaikan.
[2] Dudok dengan aturan kechil nama mepakat; / besar nama Adat: gedang, bernama pesaka sembah.
[3] Sa-hari hilang sa-hari di-chari / Sakit di-ubat, luka di-tasak.

the meanings of words and phrases are quibbled over by lawyers conversant with the interpretation of modern statutes, there will be no need for the modification of these rules, as they are easily adaptable to the demands of rapid social changes.[1]

Though a search is made for a precedent, there may be a few cases for which no precedent can be found. In such a situation, the procedure followed by the Rejangs in Sumatra is described by Marsden.

> It is true, that, if any case arises, for which there is no precedent on record (of memory), they deliberate and agree on some mode that shall serve as a rule in future similar circumstances. If the affair be trifling, that is seldom objected to; but when it is a matter of consequence, the *pangeran* or *kalippah* (in places where such are present) consults the *proattins* or lower order of chiefs who frequently desire time to consider it, and consult with the inhabitants of their *dusun*. When the point is thus determined, the people voluntarily submit to observe it as an established custom....[2]

This procedure in its essentials seems to have been adopted in Malaysia too, though no case is known where the inhabitants of a *mukim* were consulted before laying down a principle for its decision; but it may be assumed that the elders or chiefs who act as judges are aware of the common consciousness of the people. When once the law is "discovered," it is applied in the same way as

> When a coat is ready, it is put on,
> When a mould is there the metal is poured in.[3]

A good judge is he who is skilled in the art of the wriggling lizard,[4] and not one who will automatically apply a precedent remedy without taking trouble to make a cautious and thorough inquiry. Like the wriggling lizard which climbs slowly from the foot to the top of a tree, the judge should proceed carefully and cautiously, not unwilling to retrace his steps when his line of inquiry has been found wrong.

> Astray at the end of the track –
> Back to the start of the track,
> Astray at the end of the talk
> Back to the start of the talk.[5]

A method of inquiry that is discountenanced by the *adat* is that of in-

[1] See the observations of P. C. Lloyd, *Yoruba Land Law*, p. 17.
[2] William Marsden, *The History of Sumatra*, 3rd Edition, 1811, p. 217.
[3] Baju sudah di-sarongkan / Lembaga ada di-tuangi.
[4] Malim biawak bengkong.
[5] Sesat ka-hujong jalan – / Balek ka-pangkal jalan; / Sesat ka-hujong kata – / Balek ka-pangkal kata.
In some versions of the *terombo* these lines are included among the laws declared by Parapatih nan Sa-batang.

sufficient discrimination and is described as the judgment of the thrusting fish trap (*hukum serkap*), for a cone-shaped trap when thrust down in shallow water may enclose indiscriminately a myriad catch of fish.[1]

Under *adat perpateh*, circumstantial evidence is preferred to oral evidence tendered by witnesses.

> Change a sarong behind the house,
> Change a word behind the tongue.[2]

It is easier to commit perjury than to change clothes; no built-up privacy is required for the feat.

> Customary law requires signs of guilt,
> Religious law calls for witnesses.
> When religious law meets circumstances obscure,
> It throws wide its net to catch the offender...
> There is a clear case says custom,
> When there is evidence of guilt and information laid,
> When a man is chased from the scene of the crime and is found panting.
> When there are hacks and cuts;
> If evidence be at hand, it requires to be shown it,
> If it be not at hand, it requires it to be related.[3]

When there is no such clear case, circumstancial evidence is relied upon and becomes more significant. In relation to the laws of theft, twelve circumstances are forbidden. They range from being found with booty snatched or stolen by force to being found with a fluttering heart. In this reliance placed on circumstantial evidence, it is probable that mere coincidence will be mistaken for cause and effect.

> The branch breaks as the hornbill passes.[4]

The purpose of the *adat* in accepting circumstantial evidence may have been that men should be encouraged to walk warily, avoiding

[1] J. L. Humphreys writes: "I regret to say that this proverb is commonly used, not without a certain aptness, to describe some phases of English justice, especially the summary trial and conviction of batches of prisoners, such as gang-robbers, hawkers or gamblers." (J. L. Humphreys, "A Collection of Malay Proverbs," *J.S.B.R.A.S.*), Vol. 67, p. 111.

[2] Beraleh kain ka-balik rumah, / Beraleh chakap ka-balik lidah.

[3] Adat bertanda, hukum bersaksi; / Adat yang tiba ka-gelap menjala. / Sah, kata adat. / Apa-bila tertanda, terbeti; / Terkejar, terlelah; / Terpakok, terpauk; / Dekat, tertunjokkan; / Jauh, terkatakan.

[4] Enggang lalu, ranting patah.

suspicious proximities.[1] After all, *adat* is approved behaviour, apart from its being customary law.

What is contemplated under the *adat* is perfect, even-handed justice.

The quart measure that is full,
The gallon measure that is true,
The weight that is just,
The scales that are even.[2]

The compensation to be paid for a wound would vary according to the intensity of the provocation and also according to the place where it was inflicted—in the language of the *adat*, whether it "grows on the hill, on the slope or in the valley," (*tumboh di-bukit, di-lereng, di-lembah*) that is, on the head, on the body or on the leg.[3]

The saying

It is forbidden by custom
To conceal and abet.
It is approved by custom
To bring to light and compare facts.[4]

indicates the high sense of civic duty the Minangkabau settlers possessed. To conceal and abet would be socially dangerous acts and the *adat* forbids them in the interests of social justice and general well-being.

Restitution rather than retribution was the keynote of the humane administration of criminal justice under the *adat*.[5] But this statement should not be taken to imply that all offences were compoundable. Incest was punishable by death and was usually punished with outlawry and confiscation of property.[6]

[1] Tergesek kena miang, / Tergegan kena embun.
(Rub against the stem of a bamboo and you itch, / Shake it and you are sprayed with moisture.)

[2] Chupak yang pepat, / Gantang yang piawi, / Bongkal yang betul / Teraju yang baik.
Caldecott has the marginal note "We seek for perfect justice" for these lines; but he adds in a footnote that Malay casuists distinguish four points in these four lines: (i) if the bench of judges be full (ii) if the judges have full authority (iii) if the weight of evidence is sufficient (iv) if the judges are just. (A. Caldecott, "Jelebu Customary Songs and Sayings," *op. cit.*, pp. 28–29.

[3] See J. L. Humphreys, "A Collection of Malay Proverbs," *J.S.B.R.A.S.*, Vol 67, pp. 107–108.

[4] Kepantangan adat, / Di-lindong di-endapkan. / Kepejatian adat, / Di-terang di-bandingkan.

[5] For wounding smart-money is the penalty, / For slaying substitution of a person to the dead person's clan. / The children of the murderer are invited to the feast of atonement, / And one of his kin given to the clan of the murdered man.
Chinchang pampas; bunoh beri balas, / Anak di-panggil makan, / Anak buah di-sorong 'kan balas.

[6] Parr and Mackray, "Rembau,"*J.S.B.R.A.S.*, Vol. 56, p. 78.

The requirement in the *adat* that there should be absolute unanimity for every decision and every election may have been induced by the concept of *laras*, (harmonious, belonging together).

> The greatness of men lies in taking counsel together;...
> As a bamboo conduit makes a round jet of water,
> So taking counsel together rounds men to one mind.[1]

The imposition of a decision of the majority might leave the minorities discontent, while a unanimous decision would make every one feel a sense of harmony, a feeling of belonging together. This requirement of unanimity was probably desirable and certainly effective during the days of close-knit clan organizations.

Conclusion

One of the versions of the *terombo* has the line:

> Adat sentosa di-dalam negeri.[2]
> (Custom brought peace on the land.)

This appears to have been the purpose of the *adat*—to bring peace and harmony induced by a sense of justice. And this purpose was achieved by letting covenants develop into customs.

> What in the beginning are covenants
> Grow up into customs;
> Custom is lord over covenants.
> Water proceeds along water-ways,
> Sanction proceeds from covenant;
> A country grows up with its customs.[3]

This growth is accelerated by the scrupulous observance of the traditional injunction:

> Each shall get his share and portion;
> Take ye not the goods of others;
> Squander not the children's birth right.[4]

[1] Kelebehan umat dengan muafakat, / Bulat ayer karna pematong, / Bulat manusia karna muafakat.

[2] See Caldecott, "Jelebu Customary Songs and Sayings," *op. cit.*, p. 17.

[3] Tetekala kechil bernama muafakat / Tetekala besar bernama adat: / Si-raja adat kapada musfakat / Ayer melurut dengan bandar-nya, / Benar melurut dengan pakat-nya, / Negeri bertumboh dengan adat-nya.

[4] Berumpok masing-masing / Berharta masing-masing, / Harta orang jangan di-tarek / Untok anak jangan di-berikan.

In its pursuit of justice and fair play, the *adat* considers itself to be in harmony with religious law. It declares:

> Customary law hinges on religious law,
> Religious law on the word of God.
> If custom is strong, religion is not upset;
> If religion is strong, custom is not upset.[1]

If there is any difference between the two, it is only a difference in emphasis:

> Our customary law bids us
> Remove what is evil
> And give prominence to what is good;
> The word of our religious law
> Bids us do good
> And forbids our doing evil.[2]

If the difference, according to the followers of the *adat*, is so negligible, can there be any serious conflict, in their view, between religion which is ideal law and custom which is real law?[3] If there is no major conflict, why should they be persuaded to forsake their *adat* and adopt a tantalizing hybrid, *adat ketemenggongan*? The Mapillas of North Kerala, a Sunni Muslim group, are not regarded any the less Islamic in their life because of their adherence to matriliny. They are predominantly matrilocal too.[4]

In the same way as covenants grow up into customs, covenants can destroy custom.[5] An enactment, passed by a majority of votes, can effectuate the destruction more easily still. But it will be harder to retrace one's steps and resurrect the *adat*.

It may be suggested that customary law should be regarded as the common law of the people in those spheres of their lives where it is applicable. To equate "native law and custom" with local customs in England and to treat them as facts to be proved in court as is done in Malaysia does not seem fair, because they deserve to be regarded as common law rather than as local customs. That this is not such a fantastic suggestion as might appear to some may be shown from a

[1] Adat bersendi hukum / Hukum bersendi kitabullah. / Kuat adat, ta' gadoh hukum, / Kuat hukum, ta' gadoh adat.

[2] Pada adat menghilangkan yang burok, / Menimbulkan yang baik; / Pada shara menyuroh berbuat baik, / Meninggalkan berbuat jahat.

[3] Adat yang kawi, / Shara yang lazim.

[4] See Schneider and Gough (Ed.), *Matrilineal Kinship*, pp. 415 *et seq.*

[5] Hilang adat karna muafakat.

decree issued in 1708 by Johan van Hoorn, Governor-General of the Dutch East Indies. He ordered that all civil and criminal matters in the Preanger districts should be decided in the courts of the regents who would render justice according to the local laws. The Dutch officials had only the duty to see that the local laws and customs were faithfully applied and justice impartially administered.[1] Commenting on the decree, a Dutch historian said, "In the Preanger there were continuous conflicts between the Batavian and the regency courts but the principle had been stated that native law would not be superseded by western law."[2]

When the Westerner looks at the customary law of the East, he may see it blurred; the *kathi*, trained in the ways of religion and immersed in Arabic culture, may find it far too worldly for his sympathetic understanding; and one does not learn the rules of Naning games in London's Lincoln's Inn Fields. The only persons who can be expected to have a clear understanding and a proper appraisal of customary law are the traditional leaders of the community. They are interested in maintaining the norms of their community and to them should be entrusted the administration of customary law. They will know how to reinterpret it to keep pace with social changes—changes which their own community has accepted as being relevant to it. Speaking of Yoruba customary law P. C. Lloyd says:

> Customary law is constantly being reinterpreted to satisfy the needs of a commercial economy; one would use the word *reinterpreted* and not *changed*. Many modern transactions, such as sale, were not illegal a century ago and legal today—a century ago they were inconceivable to most Yoruba... each generation sees its own problems, though the law may remain basically unchanged.[3]

Adat is

> Uncracked by the sun,
> Unworn by the rain.[4]

[1] B. H. M. Vlekke, *Nusantara*, pp. 222–23.
[2] B. H. M. Vlekke, *op. cit.*, p. 223.
[3] P. C. Lloyd, *Yoruba Land Law*, pp. 11–12.
[4] Tak lekang dek panas / Tak lapok dek hujan.
See Tunku Hussain bin Tunku Yahya's article "Uncracked by the sun," *Intisari*, Vol. I, No. 3, p. 45, from which the translation of these two lines is taken.

III. SOME IBAN (SEA-DAYAK) CUSTOMARY LAW IN SARAWAK

Sarawak is inhabited by a plural group comprised of the Iban, Kayan, Kenyah, Kelabit, Murut, Kejaman, Skapan, Melanau, Bidayuh (Land Dayak), Malay and Chinese. Of all these races, only the Malays and some Melanaus are Muslims, while most of the others are animists—believing in God and various other deities.

The Sea-Dayaks, the largest of the animist group, believe in Sengalang Burong (Brahmany Kite), Simpulang (Sangyang) Gana, Ini-Inda, Anda Mara, Selampeta and Sera Gindit. They believe that these deities are messengers between God (*Petara*) and man. To pray to them, the Dayaks hold several kinds of festivals in which they are able to make offerings.

Legends say that these deities gave the Sea-Dayaks' ancestors natural law which has now turned into customary law. It is on the basis of this customary law that all Dayak cases are settled by their chiefs and headmen of the long-houses and districts.

All the Sea-Dayaks live in long-houses. Each long-house has its own headman and its own Farm-chief, Tuai-Umai. In the old days these were hereditary, but since 1900 these men have been elected by the community. The headman is responsible for looking after the well-being of his people, while the Farm-chief only deals with the annual farm labours.

As the Sea-Dayaks are *padi* planters, it follows that any offence committed during the farming season would be settled by the Farm-chief according to the customary law. The worst offence is to steal anything from someone's farm. If this is not settled by fine and sacrifice of birds and pigs, it is believed that such sin would provoke God to anger and cause him to punish the human race with floods and hunger.

It is the duty of the long-house headman to settle all kinds of disputes of the people under his jurisdiction. Anybody who offends another must be fined according to customary law. If the offender is not satisfied with the finding of the headman, he is free to appeal within fifteen days to the court of the District Chief, the *Penghulu*.

In modern times, since some Ibans have been converted to various Christian denominations and other faiths, it has become difficult for the native chiefs and headmen to settle disputes between the Pagan and Christian Dayaks of the same long-house.

Customs Regarding Engagement, Marriage, and Widowhood

Nanya Bini (*Engagement*)

If a man wishes to marry, the first thing he should do is to tell his parents of his desire. The age for a man to marry is after he reaches his twentieth year and a girl can marry after her seventeenth birthday. If the family's close relatives have a daughter, she may be the one the man's parents will ask for. If such a request is agreeable to both families, the bridegroom's parents fix a day when they will come again with their relative to ask for the girl in a formal manner known as "*Nanya Bini.*"

During the ceremony, the bride's parents will demand from the bridegroom's family a certain amount as "dowry," known as "*Berian*" and "*Bunga Pinang.*" If this is agreeable to the bridegroom's family, the "dowry" ranging from twenty-five to one hundred dollars must be paid by them to the bride. The *Bunga Pinang* fee will be from one to five dollars.

Melah Pinang (*Marriage feast*)

About a fortnight after the *Nanya Bini* ceremony, the marriage feast will be held in the bride's house. Many guests and village headmen will be invited to attend. During the feast, the "dowry" and *Bunga Pinang* fee are paid according to the agreement made during the *Nanya Bini* ceremony. This payment is witnessed by many village headmen and principal guests. If the union is incestuous, then it must be propiated with the blood of birds or pigs in accordance with the customary law. If this is not done the union will become illegal.

Having done this, the chiefs who witness the marriage are asked to tell all present that if the bridegroom divorces his wife, except for cases such as adultery, jealousy or madness, he will lose the "dowry." In the case of the bride, if she divorces her husband she must refund the "dowry" as well as paying half of it again with her own money.

Sarak Belega (*Temporary Divorce*)

Within a week after the marriage feast, if either the husband or his spouse see or hear forbidden birds, snakes or animals or have a dream which foretells bad luck in his or her marriage, the custom allows them to *sarak belega* (divorce temporarily) for one month. During this time the husband is free to court other girls and the wife is also permitted to be courted by the bachelors.

After a month of *sarak belega* is ended, the husband and wife must reunite as demanded by customary law. If one of them refuses to do so, he or she will be fined for divorce in accordance with the customary law.

Sarak Rama (*Ordinary Divorce*)

If the husband and wife divorce one another due to a quarrel or other similar matter, the one who does not wish to continue the marriage must pay the usual fine for divorces.

Sarak Manis (*Mutual Divorce*)

If the husband and his wife both agree to divorce one another, they are allowed to do so by exchanging rings in the presence of the headman (or headmen if one of them is from another long-house).

Bedua Reta (*Division of Property*)

When a man divorces his wife after a week of marriage, the one who followed the other to live in his or her parents' house shall have to gather possessions within that period. But if they have been married for a number of years, they must divide their property equally according to the number of persons in the family. This division is known as "*Bedua Lauk.*" The property to be divided at divorce is everything which the parties possess, including the rubber plantations they have planted together.

Bedua Anak (*Division of Children*)

When divorcing one another, a man and his wife must divide their children equally. If they only have one child, it will automatically stay with the guiltless parent. If they cannot settle this between themselves, the dispute must be brought to the court of the chief for settlement.

Balu (*Widowhood*)

If the husband dies, the wife will undergo either one of the two kinds of widowhood, *Balu Mata* (unripe widowhood) or *Balu Mansau* (ripe widowhood).

If the widow is undergoing an unripe widowhood, she must not wear red clothes, nor powder her face nor use perfumes to attract a man.

If she does this, she will be accused by her in-laws of being disrespectful to them. She is also forbidden to know any man or marry before she is released by her in-laws from her three months' widowhood.

If a widow is undergoing a ripe widowhood, she must not marry until her deceased husband has been honored by her in a "*Gawai Antu*" (festival held for the soul of the dead). This festival takes place once in every ten or more years.

Berangkat Tulang (*Uprooting the deceased's bones*)

If a widow marries within a week after her husband's death, this is a very serious offence known as *Berangkat Tulang*, and must be heavily fined according to customary law.

Ngemulu Antu (*Disrespect of the deceased husband*)

If a widow is caught committing sexual intercourse with a bachelor during her widowhood, she will be accused in the District Chief's Court by her in-laws as committing *Ngemulu Antu*, and the offenders will be heavily fined.

Butang Antu (*Disrespect of the dead by adultery*)

If a widow commits adultery with a widower, she is accused as "*Butang Antu*," which causes both herself and her partner to be heavily fined according to customary law. But if they marry one another, the offence will become worse and is known as "*Berangkat Antu*" (went off with dead woman's husband, while he was still undergoing his widowerhood). Their marriage is only allowed after they have paid their fine.

Bebini Maioh (*Polygamy*)

No Dayak is allowed to marry more than one wife at a time. If the husband wishes to marry another woman, before doing so, he *must* divorce his wife first. In the old days the offence of polygamy (though very rare) was considered as most grievous, which caused the offenders to be sentenced to death by being pierced with bamboo spikes. Today, in place of this, if any such offence occurs, the offenders will be imprisoned.

Codification of Customary Law

During the Brooke rule in Sarawak, the Sea-Dayak customary law was preserved. In case of petty disputes, the government always disapproved of bringing such cases before the civil court, but ruled that they were to be settled amicably by the native headmen and *Penghulus* (chiefs) in their respective courts.

In 1907, the Resident of the Second Division at Simanggang, Mr. A. B. Ward, recorded some of the Sea-Dayak *adats*. These customary laws were used by the native district courts in the Second Divison to settle the Dayaks' major disputes. Mr. Ward's original code has been published in full in the *Sarawak Museum Journal*.

In the Third Division the first conference to record the Sea-Dayak customary law in print was held in 1932. Another conference took place in Sibu in 1952 to revise these *adats* for the Sea-Dayaks, and was published in a book entitled "*Tusun Tunggu*" (Iban code of fine).

The last conference to record the customary law was held in Simanggang in 1962 and was attended by many senior *Penghulus* and *Lemambangs* (bards) of the Second Division. The results obtained in the conference were written and published in a book entitled "*Adat Dayak*" (Dayak Law).

In the state of Sarawak, the codification of customary law seems necessary in order that all native customs which come from similar roots can be made uniform throughout the country. Unless there is codification, the future generations, particularly those living in the towns, will be ignorant of customary law. If customary law is fully codified, it will benefit the long-house headmen, and the magistrates of native district courts, who settle disputes in their respective jurisdictions.

IV. SOME NOTES ON CHINESE CUSTOMARY MARRIAGE

Customary marriage, or old-fashioned marriage as it is sometimes called, is marriage according to the traditional customs that have accumulated in China from time immemorial and are transmitted from generation to generation. These customs are, to a large extent, constructed on the foundation of the rules of propriety, especially the rules of propriety of the Duke of Chou of the Chou Dynasty (1122–255 B.C.). Therefore, in order to have a better understanding of Chinese customary marriage, a study of its socio-historical background is necessary.

(*A*) *The Six Rites*

In this perspective, a matter of the utmost importance are the so-called Six Rites which are as follows:

1. "*Na tsai*" or offering of presents to the girl-elect in an attempt to find out whether or not she is marriageable.
2. "*Wen ming*" or asking for the full name and date of birth (year, month, day and time) of the girl-elect.
3. "*Na chi*" or the procedure of finding out (by horoscope, divination *etc.*) whether or not the match will be suitable and felicitous.
4. "*Na cheng*" or payment of money in settlement of the marriage. This is the final step in the betrothal.
5. "*Ch'ing ch'i*" or asking for the fixing of the day of the wedding.
6. "*Ch'in ying*" or the procedure of the bride being welcomed by the bridegroom at his home.

(*B*) *The Master of Matrimony and the Go-between*

"*Chu hun*" or the master of matrimony is a person (usually the paterfamilias) who controls the marriage from beginning to end—from the selection of the bride, the employment of the go-between and the procuring of the full name and date of birth of the girl-elect in "*na tsai*" and "*wen ming*", the decision on the suitability of the match, the payment of money in settlement of the marriage and the fixing of the day of the wedding in "*na chi,*" "*na cheng*" and "*ch'ing ch'i,*" to the performance of the last of the Six Rites in "*ch'in ying*" on the wedding day. Thus in all customary marriages it is the master of matrimony, and not the parties to the marriage themselves, who have no say in the matter, with whom every decision concerning the marriage lies. His presence is still utilized in the modern wedding, though a master of matrimony has practically none of his former power, and only a remnant of his authority survives to this day.

All customary marriages are brought about by the "command of the parents and the unctuous words of the go-betweens." Go-betweens are middlemen (or rather middlewomen) who usually are matchmakers by profession. They know every eligible bachelor and every marriageable damsel in the neighbourhood and are always ready and willing to render their services at a price to those who want them. Their names invariably appear in the marriage document even in modern marriages; not, however, under the name of go-between, but with the more dignified title of "introducer."

Thus a customary marriage is deemed invalid (1) if it is not brought about by the parents or grandparents or by a senior member of the family who invariably becomes master of matrimony; (2) if it is not negotiated by a go-between who verbally settles the marriage contract between the two families; (3) if it is not preceded by a betrothal which is a condition precedent to all customary marriages; (4) if the betrothal is incomplete by not being evidenced by payment of money and/or by a formal contract of betrothal; (5) if it is not celebrated publicly by bringing home the bride with a bridal sedan and music; and (6) if the bride and bridegroom fail to kowtow to the bridegroom's ancestral tablets and to his parents and senior members of his family.

(*C*) *Position of Women in Old China*

In the days of yore a woman's position in China was quite pitiable. At home she was under the control of her father; after she was married, she was under the restraint of her husband; after the death of her husband, she submitted herself to the direction of her eldest son. Politically, she was incapable of holding office in the government or of succession to any title of nobility; and socially, she was deemed inferior to men. A familiar Chinese proverb says metaphorically: "Married to a chicken, a woman becomes a chicken; married to a dog, a woman becomes a dog."

In the Sung Dynasty (A.D. 960–1279) the doctrine of the "Three Obediences and Four Virtues of Women" was supplemented by extending the doctrine of chastity to include the remarriage of widows. Thus, despite the fact that no law had ever prohibited a woman from remarrying after the death of her husband, she was nevertheless considered unchaste if she contracted a second marriage.

(D) Concubinage—Secondary Wives

The origin of concubinage may be traced to the time when feudalism flourished in China. Under the feudal system a king was entitled to marry one wife and eight concubines, a feudal lord was given the right to wed one wife and six concubines, a "*tai fu*" (an official from the first to the fifth rank) could take one wife and two concubines, a "*shih*" (an official from the sixth to the ninth or lowest rank) could have one wife and one concubine, and a commoner could marry only one wife. Originally, therefore, the taking of concubines was a privilege belonging exclusively to the ruling class. But after feudalism had disintegrated, gradually it became quite a common occurrence for the rich to take as many concubines as they could afford, until in the course of time a man's wealth and social prestige were measured by the number of concubines and slaves he possessed.

Concubines may be classified into three categories, as follows:

1. Concubinage resulting from "*pen*" or failure to observe the Six Rites. The Book of Rites says: "*P'in* maketh marriage; *pen* maketh concubinage." "*P'in*" means the taking of a woman in marriage by observing the Six Rites and "*pen*" means the taking of a woman into the household by running away from the Six Rites, *i.e.*, without observing the Six Rites.

2. Concubinage by "*mai*" or purchase, which was by far the most common way of taking concubines in China.

3. Concubinage by "*ying*." "*Ying*" refers to a woman who accompanies the bride to the wedding. This type of concubinage has long fallen into disuse but it has some historical value nevertheless. As already stated above, a monarch could marry nine women and a feudal lord was entitled to take seven women in wedlock. But bigamy was a crime from time immemorial, so only one of these women, *i.e.*, the bride, performed the marriage rites while the others deliberately refrained from observing them. The one who had performed the marriage rites became "*hou*" or queen, while the others who had accompanied the bride to the wedding but who had not observed the marriage rites became "*fei*" or royal concubines. These royal concubines were women who made up the entourage of the bride whom they had accompanied. As a matter of fact they were more or less the queen's bridesmaids, except that they were expected to become royal concubines after the wedding.

(*E*) "*Ju Kung*"

The taking of concubines must be in accordance with certain formalities called "*ju kung*" (enter the household), or ceremonies of initiating the concubine into the family. In these ceremonies the prospective concubine is made to pay obeisance to the wife by kowtowing to her and serving her tea. In the province of Kwangtung where concubinage was most prevalent, the wife would in addition give a new name to the concubine. A banquet is usually given on such an occasion at which time the affair is publicly announced and the concubine presented to the participants.

(*F*) "*Fu Cheng*"

After the death of the wife, the husband may either marry another woman according to the Six Rites, or he may promote one of his concubines to the position formerly occupied by his deceased wife. In either case the second wife is called "*t'ien fang*" (filling up the room), meaning a woman who is taken into the family to fill the place left vacant by the death of the first wife.

If the husband, instead of marrying another woman after the death of his wife, promotes one of his concubines to be his wife, he must observe certain formalities called "*fu cheng*" before the second union can become a valid marriage. Now, "*fu*" means to lift and "*cheng*" means principal. The two words combined together would mean an act of lifting or promoting the concubine to the position of a principal wife. Since the concubine is already an acknowledged member of the family, the ceremonies to be performed for "*fu cheng*" are thereby simplified. All that is required for such an occasion is for the concubine in question to perform, openly and in the presence of relatives and friends, the ceremonies of kowtowing to heaven and earth and to the husband's ancestral tablets and to kowtow and serve tea to the husband's parents. The husband is required by custom to give a banquet at which he publicly announces to the participants that he has lifted or promoted the concubine in question to the position of a principal wife.

(*G*) "*Chien T'iao*"

"*Chien t'iao*" is a system of domestic relations whereby a man may have more than one wife at the same time. Now, "*chien*" means concurrent and "*t'iao*" means ancestral shrine, connoting the idea of a man who is responsible for the worship of two or more ancestral shrines, as well as for the propagation of the future generations of two or more branches of the family. In order to fulfill this dual responsibility, he is obliged to marry two or more wives, depending on the number of branches of the family he represents—one for each branch of the family.

In order to become a "*chien t'iao*" son, the following three conditions must be fulfilled:

First, a "*chien t'iao*" son must be an only son and the one and only male descendant of all the branches of the family.

Secondly, a "*chien t'iao*" son must be an adopted son of his paternal uncle or uncles by blood.

Thirdly, there must be a formal adoption or adoptions.

(*H*) "*T'ung Yang Hsi*"

Another curious custom which has prevailed in China and which has a much wider application, especially in the villages, than "*chien t'iao,*" is the practice of "*t'ung yang hsi*" (foster daughter-in-law) or the practice of fostering the future daughter-in-law from childhood.

To call "*t'ung yang hsi*" "child betrothal" is just as incorrect as to describe it as "child bride"; for, while to some extent it partakes of the characteristics of both, it differs in substance and purpose from each. The system is primarily economic and thrives best under conditions where tillers of the soil are hard-pressed for helpers in general chores in the home, or in the field. A "*t'ung yang hsi*" is neither a bride nor a betrothed for the simple reason that there is neither a betrothal nor a wedding when she is taken into the household. She is a member of the family (a future daughter-in-law fostered from childhood) and becomes a bride only when marriage ceremonies are performed after the boy of the family (her future husband) has reached the marriageable age.

(*I*) *Some Customary Restrictions on Marriages*

Restrictions on marriages in old China may be classified into the following categories: 1) Restrictions on grounds of consanguinity and affinity, whereby near relatives are forbidden to marry. 2) Restrictions on grounds of seniority. Persons of a senior generation cannot marry those belonging to the junior generation. 3) Restrictions based on the clan system. Persons of the same surname cannot marry. 4) Restrictions based on differences in social status. A slave cannot marry a free person.

V. SOME NOTES ON INDIAN INFLUENCE ON MALAY CUSTOMARY LAW

The purpose of this paper is a modest one. It is intended to indicate that some rethinking in regard to the early period of Malaysian legal history is necessary. With all due respect to R. J. Wilkinson, who has done excellent work on Malay language, it is proposed that *adat perpateh*[1] was influenced by Indian customs as much or more than *adat temenggong*.[2] It is generally assumed that *adat temenggong* was gleaned from Indian fields. I would suggest that Malay *adat* in general, irrespective of whether it is *adat perpateh* or *adat temenggong*, owed a great deal, probably its very soul, to Indian influences.

In a paper published in 1944, Sir Richard Winstedt stated:

> With little exaggeration it has been said of Europe that it owes its theology, its literature, its science and its art to Greece; with no greater exaggeration it may be said of the Malayan races that till the nineteenth century they owed everything to India; religion, a political system, medieval astrology and medicine, literature, arts and crafts.[3]

After elaborating this thesis he concluded:

> Though he is unconscious of it, from the cradle to the grave the Malay is surrounded by survivals of Indian culture. Even his nursery tales are many of them derived from Bidpai's Fables, the Jataka tales and Somadeva's *Ocean of Story*. India found the Malay a peasant of the late stone age, a "frog under a coconut shell," and it left him a citizen of the world. It taught him the weaving of silk and embroidery and metal work, and it gave him its clothes and material comforts. It taught him to tame the elephant and improved his methods of fishing. The customary law of the tribe it broadened into the law of the State. It introduced the Malay to Hindu and Persian classics and induced into an illiterate people a passion for knowledge. It gave him the science of the middle ages, and converted to Islam, it gave him the ideal of democracy. But now that steamships have brought the Malay world into close relations with Arabia and Egypt, England and Holland, all these things are to its inhabitants no more than a tale that is told by Indian and European scholars.[4]

If he were to write now, he would probably make special mention of the Constitution of Malaysia which is derived, in a large measure, from

[1] The custom (*adat*) followed mainly by the Malays of Negri Sembilan and Naning. It is characterized by exogamy and matriliny.

[2] The custom followed by Malay communities in other parts of Malaysia.

[3] Winstedt, "Indian Influence in the Malay World," *Journal of the Royal Asiatic Society*, 1944, p. 186.

[4] *Id.*, p. 195.

the Constitution of India as adapted in part by Pakistan in its Constitution of 1956.

De Josselin de Jong thinks the view that Malayan races owed everything — religion, political system, etc., — to India is "to put it mildly, greatly exaggerated. "[1] Though one cannot vouch for this "everything" in Sir Richard's allegedly exaggerated statement, one need have no hesitation in protesting that when he said "the customary law of the tribe it broadened into the law of the State" he was probably indulging in an understatement. For India not only broadened the customary law of the tribe, but also strengthened that law by adding to it sizable chunks of India's own customary law with the result that in a few spheres at least, the Malay customary law has been able to withstand the onslaughts of Islamic law and English law. I may cite, for instance, the survival of the formalities of the installation ceremony observed in Negri Sembilan and elsewhere which were undoubtedly borrowed from Indian practices. Whether the Yang di-Pertuan Besar,[2] if elected and installed without these ceremonies[3] would be entitled to exercise the powers granted to him under the Constitution may be a nice point for discussion in constitutional law, but one may venture the suggestion that the Malay society in Negri Sembilan will have to pass through many more vicissitudes before it is likely to have a Yamtuan accepted as its ruler without these ceremonies.

The instance from Negri Sembilan has been cited with a view to pointing out that Indian influence in *adat perpateh* society was no less potent than in *adat temenggong* society. One would probably find much clearer indication of indebtedness to India on the part of the former than the latter; for most of the institutions of the latter are found all over the world, while those of the former are not so widespread and when one looks at the details, similarities are so striking as not to be easily dismissed as accidental.

Ever since Wilkinson wrote his "Law: Introductory Sketch" published in the series *Papers on Malay Subjects* it has been an article of faith among students of Malaysian legal history that *adat perpateh* is the indigenous customary law of the Malays, or to use Wilkinson's own words, "the pure Malay law of Minangkabau."[4] Following Wilkinson, they believe that *adat temenggong* represents the old Minangkabau

[1] P. E. de Josselin de Jong: *Minangkabau and Negri Sembilan*, (Leyden, 1951), p. 29.
[2] The Head of State in Negri Sembilan.
[3] Under the Constitution of Negri Sembilan, he is to be elected in accordance with the custom of the State. Article VII (2).
[4] *Papers on Malay Subjects:* "Law: Introductory Sketch," by Wilkinson, p. 2.

jurisprudence in a state of disintegration after many centuries of exposure to the influence of Hindu despotism and Muslim law,[1] and that the Minangkabau immigrants who brought with them *adat temenggong* to the Malay Peninsula came by way of Palembang. The "ancient Malay kingdom of Palembang had come under the influence of the old Hindu civilization of Java and had entirely abandoned its Minangkabau customs."[2]

With respect, it is submitted that both these views appear to be erroneous. Apart from the many undisputed facts of history with which we are familiar, there is ample evidence to be derived from social anthropology and etymology which would induce, if not compel, acceptance of contrary views.

The view that *adat temenggong* is *adat perpateh* in decay under Hindu and Muslim influences may be easily disposed of. As both *adat perpateh* and *adat temenggong* existed (and still exist) in Minangkabau, there is no good reason to assume that certain groups of Minangkabau people who temporarily settled in Palembang permitted a state of disintegration in their own *adat* and when they later on migrated to the peninsula brought along with them what was left of this *adat* which had by now assumed substance as *adat temenggong*. The *kampongs* in Minangkabau are traditionally grouped into four *suku* (= quarters), i.e., *Bodi*, *Chaniago*, *Koto* and *Piliang*. They are further grouped into two, *Bodi-Chaniago* and *Koto-Piliang*, and these two groups are considered to have their own *adat*. Each *nagari* in *Minangkabau* considers itself as belonging to one of these two groups, either to *Bodi-Chaniago* group with its *adat perpateh* or *Koto-Piliang* group with its *adat temenggong*. This division into two groups does not mean that there are no *kampongs* belonging to *adat temenggong* in the *Bodi-Chaniago* area or vice versa; it only indicates that *kampongs* belonging to the *adat temenggong* traditionally occupy a prominent position in a *nagari* of the *Koto-Piliang* group and those of *adat perpateh* occupy a similar position in the *Bodi-Chaniago nagaris*, which may have among them *kampongs* following *adat temenggong*. After all, the two groups are described as forming *lareh*,[3] which means harmonious or belonging together.[4] According to legend,[5] the two law-givers, *Kei Tamanggungan*[4] and *Parapatih nan-Sabatang*, after whom the *adat* are called, were half-

[1] *Id.*, p. 36.

[2] *Id.*, p. 2.

[3] *Lareh* is Minangkabau for Malay *laras*. Note the saying: adopun mandirikan pajueng Koto-Piliang hanjo Bodi-Tjaniago (Bodi-Chaniago sets up the umbrella of Koto-Piliang).

[4] For details, see de Josselin de Jong, *Minangkabau and Negri Sembilan*, *op. cit.*, p. 12.

[5] The legend is narrated by G. D. Willinck, *Het rechtsleven bij de Minangkabausche Maleiers*, p. 121.

brothers.[1] It is true that according to the version of the *terombo* (the song of origin) of the *adat* familiar to the people of Naning and the neighborhood, the two law-givers chose two separate spheres of influence: Tamanggungan chose the coastal area

Where the water comes in rolling billows,
Where the waves break white in foam,
Where the beaches glare in the sun,
Where the sand-banks stretch seaward,
Where the long islands lie on the tide,
Where the merchandise goes out and in
Where the traders sell and buy.[2]

Parapatih chose for himself the inland region

Where squirrels race and frisk on the trees,
Where monkeys leap from branch to branch,
Where long-armed apes dangle and swing,
Where mouse-deer nightly come to bathe,
.... A place of snakes sleeping and coiled,
A place of wild cats sleeping curled......
A place of high hills and open glades.[3]

Though the *terombo* speaks of two different spheres of influence for the two law-givers,[4] we know as a matter of fact that in Minangkabau from

[1] William Marsden gives the name as Kei Tamanggungan (*History of Sumatra*, 3rd edition, (1811) p. 332). According to de Josselin de Jong, the full name is (presumably in Dutch spelling) Kjai Katumanggungan. As in the case of Parapatih, this name also appears to be a title, which may mean the Chief of the (King's) Companions, if it is not a corruption of Sanskrit *dharmanatha* (lawful protector) with *agung* added to it. The final *an* in the name probably serves the purpose of indicating masculine gender. Considering the duties traditionally attributed to a *temenggong*, one would incline to think that this title or official designation had something to do with *dharma* (justice, law). It is not improbable that the title has been adapted from Sanskrit *dharmagna*, *dharmanatha*, *dharmavid* or *dharmadhikarin*.

[2] See Haji Mohd. Din bin Ali, "Two Forces in Malay Society," *Intisari*, Vol. I, No. 3, p. 16. As a Minangkabau saying has it, Dato Katumanggungan possesses the kingship, Dato Parapatih possesses the (royal) umbrella (the symbol of sovereignty). (Datue Katumanggungan punjo karadjoan, Datue Parapatih punjo pajueng.) Quoted in de Josselin de Jong, *op. cit.*, p. 73.

[3] These lines are quoted from J. L. Humprey's translation of the *terombo*: *J.S.B.R.A.S.* No. 83, p. 13. It may be recollected that the *terembo* was composed in the Peninsula as may be seen from the following lines:

Our sires, our origins, / Forget not our origins! / Minangkabau our overlord, / Johor our Raja, / Siak our ally, / Malacca our landing place, / Naning our mother, / The land of Jelebu our offshoot!

[4] See the *terombo* lines:

Di-situ lah pembahagian Dato Temenggong dengan Dato Perpateh nan Sa-batang / Menghilir ka-Kampar Kiri dan menghulu ka Kampar Kanan.

There was the place of division / Of Dato' Temenggong and Dato' Perpateh – / Downstream to Kampar Kiri, / Upstream to Kampar Kanan.

olden times to this day, *nagaris* following *adat perpateh* and those following *adat temenggong* exist together and in harmony, in conformity with the concept of *lareh*. *Adat temenggong* could therefore have been brought by certain sections of the Minangkabau people to the Malay Peninsula direct from the country of its origin. It was certainly unnecessary for them to have gone and sojourned in Palembang to adopt *adat temenggong* and then to import it to the Peninsula.

The other Wilkinsonian myth that *adat perpateh*,[1] an institution utterly indigenous to the Malays, flourished in its pristine purity in Minangkabau, uncontaminated by Indian influences, probably requires more detailed discussion. It is known from inscriptions found in Kedah, Province Wellesley and East Borneo that there were Indian settlements in Malaysia as early as the 4th century A.D., if not earlier.[2] Coedès has proved beyond reasonable doubt that most of the settlements were of South Indians.[3] He says that the Indian adventurers on their arrival found a people who were fairly advanced in civilization. According to him one of the characteristics of their civilization—the Austroasiatic civilization—was the recognition of descent by the female line.[4] It is found among the Khasis of Assam in N.E. India, an Austroasiatic community. The Garos of Assam as well as the Jaintias who are closely related to the Khasis also follow matriliny. Considering that matriliny was not unknown to the Austroasiatics, it is not suggested that this social system was introduced into Minangkabau from South India, where it was prevalent in the area now comprised in the State of Kerala; but the probabilities of such introduction cannot be ruled out when one recollects that in various parts of Sumatra, Malayalis settled down along with other South Indian immigrants. This may be seen from the old clan names in Sumatra. Thus one comes across in the sub-division of Marga Simbiring of the Karo Batak names like Coliga, Pandija, Melijala, Pelavi and Tekang.[5] In this company, it is not difficult to

[1] *Adat perpateh* is believed to be named after Dato Parapatih nan Sa-batang. The Dato's name appears to be variously given; thus, Wilkinson would have Perpateh pinang Sa-Batang while Hyde has it as Merpateh pisang Sa-batang. (*J.M.B.R.A.S.*, vi, iv. p. 51) *Parapati* is a Sanskrit compound meaning "overlord" and "nan" appears to be a corruption of the Sanskrit suffix "nam." Wilkinson's innovation to "pinang" and Hyde's alteration to "pisang" may be due to the presence of the word Sa-batang which means a single stem. Probably Sa-batang was used, in contrast to *suku* (quarter) or *saka* (branch), as connoting the whole tribe and hence the title indicated the headship of a tribe.

[2] See B. H. M. Vlekke, *Nusantara*, p. 21; P. Wheatley, *The Golden Khersonese*, p. 273. Winstedt, *A History of Malaya*, (1962) p. 31.

[3] George Coedès, *Les Etats hindouises d'Indochine et d'Indonésie*, p. 25 *et seq.*

[4] *Id.*, p. 21. See also P. Wheatley, *The Golden Khersonese*, *op. cit.*, p. 193.

[5] N. J. Krom, *Hindu-Javaansche Geschiedenis*, translated by H. B. Sarkar, *Journal of Greater*

recognize Melijala for Malayalam,[1] corresponding to the present day Kerala, Pelavi for Pallava and Tekang for Dekhan.

From 500 A.D. there were Indianized states in Sumatra; the oldest of them was probably Melayu with its capital at Jambi, near Minangkabau. It would appear that the Srivijaya empire brought this state under its power and influence.[2] When the empire declined the ancient kingdom of Melayu seemed to have come to life again[3] under the name of Dharmasraya. In 1275 King Kirtanagara, the ruler of a Javanese kingdom called Singasari, entered into relations with Melayu. As may be gathered from an inscription of 1286, these relations led to a successful expedition against Melayu. Tribhuvanaraja Maulivarmadeva, the King of Dharmasraya, became an ally of the King of Singasari.[4] These historical facts deserve notice because of the geographical proximity of Melayu and Minangkabau, and because of the significant circumstance that the kingdom in Melayu had an Indian name, and the king had an Indian name as well as an Indian title.

In the next century a prince who was educated in the Indianized kingdom of Java set up a kingdom for himself in Minangkabau and ruled over it for about thirty-five years, from 1340 to 1375. He was called by an Indian name, Adityavarman.[5] It may therefore be safely assumed that Minangkabau during those days was not without some impact of Indian culture. According to the tradition current in Negri Sembilan, it was in 1388,[6]—that is, thirteen years after the reign of Adityavarman—that some sections of the Minangkabau people migrated to Negri Sembilan. A Minangkabau prince who was elected Yang di-Pertuan in Negri Sembilan in 1773 is referred to as Raja Melewar, which appears to be a title rather than a name, for Melewar (or Melavar) in Tamil and Malayalam would mean a superior or overlord.

The first Minangkabau king mentioned in *Sejarah Melayu* also appeared to have had an Indian name, Sang Sapurba,[7] which Winstedt

India Society, Vol. XVI, p. 26. Dr. Krom's Dutch spelling for these names is retained here. See also H. Kern, *Verspreide Geschriften* (Collected Writings), Vol. III, pp. 67–72.

[1] Malayalam usually denotes the language of Kerala, but with the addition of *nadu*, and the resultant dropping of the final *m* in the first word (i.e. Malayalanadu, but more often Malanadu, land of hills) it may stand for the State of Kerala.

[2] B. H. M. Vlekke, *Nusantara*, *op. cit.*, p. 28.

[3] *Id.*, p. 64.

[4] See de Josselin de Jong, *op. cit.*, pp. 895–96.

[5] See B. H. M. Vlekke, *Nusantara*, *op. cit.*, p. 70.

[6] Parr and Mackray, "Rembau," *J.S.B.R.A.S.*, Vol. 56, (1928) p. 2.

[7] His full title was Sang Sapurba Trimurti Tribhuvana; the last two words are undoubtedly Sanskrit. His original name Nila Pahlawan also consists of Indian words.

reconstructs as Prabhu.[1] His queen's name[2] was undoubtedly Indian, Wan Sundari,[3] which means "sylvan beauty." It may be that the Indian settlers gave their beautiful queen from the wilderness a complimentary appellation. According to the Minangkabau legends, the first ruler had the name Maharajadhiraja, which is actually an Indian title and may be translated as "supreme ruler."

In Negri Sembilan, *di-Pertuan* in the designation Yang di-Pertuan Besar appears to be Malay transliteration for the Sanskrit compound *atipradhan.* The hereditary titles of the four *Undangs* of Negri Sembilan have in them a number of Indian words: Putera Indera Pallawa (Sungei Ujong), Lela Perkasa Setiawan (Johol); Maharaja Lela Sedia Raja (Rembau) and Mendika Mentri Paduka (Jelebu). The hill above the old Istana in Negri Sembilan is called Bukit Sri Indera, after a Hindu deity. One of the *orang empat istana* (four men of the place) has the title Raja diwangsa, that is Rajadhivamsa in Sanskrit, meaning ruler of the chief tribe. The Yamtuan's throne is referred to as *singahsana* which is the Sanskrit word for throne. The tiered bathing-pavilion meant for the ceremonial lustration of the Yang di-Pertuan Besar and his consort has a Sanskrit compound word for its name, *pancha persade.* The musical competition held on the occasion is referred to as *sepat rega* which probably stands for the Sanskrit *sapta raga,* seven tune-types.

To refer to a number of institutions connected with their matrilineal system, Minangkabaus and Negri Sembilan people use Indian words, some of which are the very words used by the people of Kerala to denote their own institutions. For instance, Minangkabau *bako* denoting patrilineal relationship, is heard in Negri Sembilan as *baka* and in Kerala as *vaka. Harto pussako* of Minangkabau and *harta pesaka*[4] of Negri Sembilan have in them two Sanskrit loan words: *arta* meaning wealth and *saka* meaning branch, used in relation to the branch of a matrilineal family group in all three areas. The same *saka* appears in Minangkabau in the phrase *Kata saka* or *kata pesaka* in the sense of *perbilangan,* sayings. *Kata* also is a Sanskrit word. What one observes occasionally in the vocabulary of Minangkabau and Negri Sembilan is that some names denoting certain institutions and territorial units are exact translations either into Malay or into Sanskrit of Dravidian

[1] Winstedt, *History of Malaya, op. cit.,* p. 41. If *prabhu* was the title of the Minangkabau ruler, *Melewar* may be regarded as an exact translation of this title into Tamil or Malayalam.

[2] See Shellabear's edition of *Sejarah Melayu,* cheritera II.

[3] The use of *wan* for grandmother in Negri Sembilan can probably be traced to this royal ancestress.

[4] These words denote ancestral property in matrilineal society.

names used in Kerala. For instance one comes across the strange word *ebu bapa* which means father-mother (not mother-father, as is sometimes seen translated) and which appears to be a translation of Malayalam *ammaman*, meaning "he-mother." Negri[1] is given a specialized meaning in Negri Sembilan and Minangkabau and stands for Malayalam "*nadu*."[2] In Kerala one becomes familiar with such phrases as *nadum nagariym*, literally country and town, but used indiscriminately in the sense of territorial units. *Taluk*, an Arabic loan-word, denoting a territorial unit in Kerala, seems to be evident in the Minangkabau *Luhak* and Negri Sembilan *luak*. *Kotta* (fortress) a Dravidian word, appears in both Minangkabau and Negri Sembilan, though in the specialized sense of village in Minangkabau and that of a small town Negri Sembilan. As used in these areas, it probably meant, in the beginning, a fortified area.

Peru is another interesting word. It means name in Kerala, and may include the name of the family by which a person is identified, in the same way that a surname in the West helps to identify a family member. *Parui* (womb) in Minangkabau and *perut*[3] in Negri Sembilan, stand for the matrilineal clan to which one belongs.

Again, the Negri Sembilan expression *orang semenda* may be a derivative from Malayalam *sambandhakaran*,[4] the expression used to denote a man who has entered into a marriage relationship in the Kerala matrilineal society. *Harta dapatan* or *harta pendapatan* would appear to be derived from *dattam*[5] (given) in Sanskrit. These Sanskrit words were

[1] *Nagara* in Sanskrit means a city. In Malay *negri* would usually connote a country or settlement. Negri Sembilan seems to denote nine settlements.

[2] Usually used in the sense of principality or province, but sometimes used to specify a district; also used to connote the country as opposed to town.

[3] *Per* in Malayalam would mean giving birth. See p. 58 note 3 below.

[4] *Sambandham* is from Sanskrit and means bond or tie and hence marriage. *Karan* is a Dravidian suffix indicating a person who belongs to or possesses what is connoted by the preceding part of the word. Hence *sambandhakaran* is one who is bound or wedded. Applying the usual rules of Malay syntax, one whould have *karan sambandha* or *aran sambandhak*. It is not unlikely that instead of accepting *karan sambandha*, the Malay adopted a semi-articulated "k" at the end of *sambandha* and assumed that "aran" was the substantive. He may have been right in this assumption as probably "k" in "sambandhakaran" was employed solely for euphony. Later "k" may have been dropped and *aran* altered into *orang*. It may be observed that "g" in *orang* is seldom distinctly heard. In a phrase like *orang di-tarek* (the adopted person) the "k" seems to be retained, if the expression is derived from Malayalam *tarakaran*, one who has, or is given, a foundation on which a house is to be built, that is, one who is accepted into the lineage group. It is interesting to note that Wilkinson commenting on the word "*orang*" in his Dictionary writes: "It is also used in national, descriptive or tribal names like 'man' in Englishman." (*A Malay-English Dictionary*, p. 821). *Karan* in Malayalam serves the same purpose.

[5] See Manu (ix, 194) where he speaks of *dattam pritikarmani* (what was given in token of love) as forming part of the property of a woman.

commonly used by the higher classes in Kerala.[1] Pramanikal[2] who, in medieval Kerala, assisted the chief of a *desa* (district) in police and judicial matters and decided disputes in his court, seems to correspond to *penghulu* in Malaya.

Perhaps the most important institution in a matrilineal society is woman. This may be true in other societies as well, but it is assumed this is especially so in matrilineal societies. The commonest word used in Malaysia as well as Indonesia to denote a woman is *perempuan*, a Dravidian derivative, from the Dravidian *penpirannavar*.[3] If one applied the usual rules of Malayan syntax to the Dravidian compound and also dropped the last two syllables in the compound, it would not be hard to come by the Malay word, *perempuan.*

Almost all the Sanskrit words one comes across in Malay are those which an educated Melayali would have used and which are still current in modern Malayalam. There are a large number of Dravidian loan words and derivatives in Malay, a few of which can be easily traced to the exclusive vocabulary of the speech current among Mapillas and Tiyas in North Kerala. To cite one instance, the word *peteras* which Wilkinson explains as arrogance and says is an Indian word, without giving any further indication about its etymology, is heard only in North Kerala.

In Kerala matriliny was practised by Nayars from time immemorial. In North Kerala, Tiyas and Mapillas also had the same system of social organization. In *Kunhi Pathuamma and others* v. *Sundara Aiyar and another*,[4] Chief Justice Leach of the Madras High Court held that a Mapilla family is "governed by *Marumakkattayam law* (that is, matrilineal descent) in all matters relating to property unless there happens to be private property undisposed of by will."[5] Mapillas are Muslims belonging to the Sunni sect. Most of them were originally converts from

[1] Dr. Gundert in his *Dictionary* (1872) quotes *artam dattam ceitu* (gave wealth) from *Hora Vyakhyanam* to illustrate the meaning of *dattam.*

[2] *Pramanikal* is plural, and *pramani* singular; but the plural form is generally used as an honorific and may denote one person.

[3] One who is born a woman as different from *anpirannavan*, one born as a man. Compare the colloquial *orang jantan* which may mean a person born as *tan. Tan,* in the sense of "you" was a polite form of speech, used as late as the twenties of the present century in Kerala, while addressing a respectable male person. It is still used, but not often. One wonders whether the Malay "*tuan*" has been derived from Malayalam "*tan*". *Tan* is sometimes used as a titular honorific in Malay, as in *tan dewa sakti* in Perak. *Puan,* in the same way, may have been adapted from *pen,* (*pon* in Tulu, another Dravidian language) a Dravidian word meaning woman or maiden, on the analogy of *tuan,* though the vowel sounds in the original words are different.

[4] A.I.R. 1941 Madras 32.

[5] *Id.*, p. 33.

Hinduism, and, in spite of embracing a new faith which prescribed a different rule of inheritance, they cherished their own matrilineal system, until inroads were made into it by legislation.[1]

Assuming that matriliny was indigenous to Minangkabau, it is not unlikely that this local institution was influenced by South Indian settlers who were familar with a similar system and who, when they were in Minangkabau and took wives from there and adopted certain local customs, were interested in creating a synthesis of the local institution with their own. Even if no conscious attempt at synthesis was made either by the settlers or by the local community, the Minangkabau and the Kerala institutions had many points of similarity which may not be due to coincidence. The fact that the same words or related words are used in both the countries to connote some of the characteristics of this social structure points to a relationship that cannot be dismissed as purely accidental. In Negri Sembilan, Sanskrit names are heard in relation to a greater number of such characteristics, covering a wider field. It is not likely that old indigenous institutions would fall for foreign names at first sight. To adopt foreign names for an institution, the institution must have been introduced or been thoroughly subject to the impact of the foreigners, or at least so often mentioned by the local people while speaking to the foreigners that the former found it easy to refer to it by its foreign name. When one knows from one's understanding of South East Asian history that South Indians settled in Sumatra and the Malay Peninsula, and that some groups of the South Indians followed matriliny and some of the matrilineal institutions in Minangkabau in Sumatra and Negri Sembilan in the Malay Peninsula are called by Indian names, it is difficult to rule out South Indian influence on such institutions, just as one may not feel convinced if one is told that the name Raffles Institution was coined by a Malay poet at the court of the Sang Aji of Tumasek for its euphony, when one knows that Raffles was the founder of Singapore, that the English ruled over Singapore when the institution was founded and the word "institution" is an English word, as we know it, though of Latin origin and borrowed from Old French.

One may in passing refer to an observation made by M. Zaborowski who said:

> I have seen in India, on the Malabar Coast,[2] and especially at Beypur, Calicut, and the surrounding country, various natives of *Malaisoid* type, whose features struck

[1] See the (Madras) Mapilla Marumakkattayam Act, 1939.
[2] In the State of Kerala.

me owing to their close resemblance to those of the Nias.[1] Among the Tiyans... this resemblance is great...; but those in whom the resemblance struck me most, were a... Kurumba man and woman, mendicants met in the vicinity of Calicut. It was on my return from Nias, and the impression they produced was a lively one... I do not wish to affirm that the Nias are descended from the Tiyans, or from the Kurumbas; but from the description of their physical characters, their customs and their legends, results the possibility of a common origin between Nias and Kurumbas.[2]

We shall now consider a few institutional similarities between *adat perpateh* and the law of the *Dharmasastra.* Wilkinson seems to think that *adat perpateh* awards compensation for offences while Indian law of the olden days inflicted severe punishment on offenders,[3] as was done under *adat temenggong*. While not disputing that the *Dharmasastra*[4] made provision for severe punishment for heinous crimes which were called *sahasa,* it may be mentioned that atonement for murder and slaughter by way of payment of blood money was not uncommon in India. Jolly, in *Hindu Law and Custom* writes,

Roth... has proved that in the Vedic age a blood money of 100 cows was paid to the relations of a murdered person. Baudhayana (1,19,1) prescribes fines of 1,000, 100, and 10 cows and a bull to be paid to the king for the murder of a Kshatriya, a Vaisya and a Sudra respectively.... As Buhler ingeniously suggests, probably the king did not keep these fines for himself, but gave them to the family of the murdered person. The blood money of 100 cows reminds us of the 100 cows which have to be given as price of an adoptive son or as the price of a bride.[5]

Jolly proceeds to say that even in modern days payment of blood money consisting of pieces of land or village was in vogue in Rajputana and cites Sir Alfred Lyall who has made mention of a case of robbery in the first quarter of this century by a frontier tribe in Rajputana. It

[1] The Nias occupy the island of Nias, off the west coast of Sumatra, and not far from Jambi and Minangkabau.

[2] Zaborowski, Malgaches – Nias-Dravidians, *Bull. Soc. d'Anthropol.*, Fasc. 2, 1897, quoted by Edgar Thurston, Malagasy-Nias – Dravidians, *Madras Museum Bulletin*, Vol. II, No. 2, 119.

After referring to the resemblance between the clothing of the Irulas of Malabar and the Malagasy of Madagascar, M. Zaborowski proceeded to observe: "In studying the customs of our Indo-Chinese wild tribes, I have naturally been struck with the similarity of their taste for interminable rolls of copper which they wear on the fore-arm, the profusion of bracelets, and especially with the habit of dilating the lobes of the ears, and suspending therein rings of copper, with the tastes and practices of the Dayaks of Borneo. Now I find the same tastes, and almost the same practices among the Dravidian tribes of Southern India. Irulas, Paniyans and doubtless the Kurumbas cover themselves with bracelets and rings of copper and insert in the lobes of the ears light discs, rolls of cajan, doubtless to suspend therein ear-rings, and even strings of copper, which stretch them. This last custom is very widespread at Nias, and it is met with in Madagascar. *Its point of departure, its origin, is then not in Borneo, but in Southern India*". (*Id.* p. 120, emphasis added).

[3] See Wilkinson, "Law: Introductory Sketch," *op. cit.*, p. 33. He however mentions eight offences as "potentially capital crimes." *Id.*, p. 34.

[4] Code of laws.

[5] Julius Jolly, *Hindu Law and Custom*, 1928, p. 284.

ended with the tribe agreeing to pay "the usual bloodmoney" for a Brahman shot down in the fight.[1]

Writing early in the 5th century A.D., Fahsien, the Chinese traveller, observed that the administration of criminal law in India in his time was mild, that most crimes were punished by fines only and that capital punishment was practically unknown.[2]

It may further be mentioned that under *adat perpateh* compensation was not invariably the method of punishment to which an offender was subjected. There was provision for death and exile. Parr and Mackray state that in Rembau incest of near relations was nominally a capital offence, but actually punished with outlawry and confiscation of property, a penalty which the *Undang* had no power to commute.[3] They also add that in Naning the death penalty was exacted and refer to a legend current in Pulau Sebang, Naning, according to which a man and a woman found guilty of incest were placed in baskets and drowned in a stream.[4]

The saying

Keris menyalang daripada Undang
Pedang pemanchong daripada raja.
(The execution-keris is the Chief's;
The sword of execution is the King's.)

also indicates that execution as a mode of punishment was not unknown to *adat perpateh*. It may not be seriously contended that the Raja and the *Undang* were invested with these powers for their own personal entertainment.

The principle of substitution in *adat perpateh* may be an adaptation of a similar principle, namely, *pratinidhi*, in Hindu law. The concept of *pratinidhi* was evolved to meet cases in which the original could not be produced. A familiar substitute was a fixed monetary payment in place of penances prescribed for expiation.

The rules of evidence in *adat perpateh* may also have been taken from Hindu law. The *adat*, it is said, relied too much on circumstantial evidence.[5] The most conclusive sign of guilt, as Wilkinson observes, is expressed in the saying,

[1] *Id.*, p. 285.
[2] Cited by R. K. Choudhury, *Studies in Indian Law and Justice*, p. 33.
[3] Parr and Mackray, "Rembau," *op. cit.*, p. 78.
[4] *Ibid.*, footnote (2).
[5] P. P. Buss-Tien, "Malay Law," *American Journal of Comparative Law*, Vol. 7, No. 2, p. 261.

Enggang lalu, ranting patah.
(The twig breaks as the hornbill flies past it.)[1]

It is said that

When customary law meets circumstances obscure
It throws wide its net...
Crime leaves its trail like a water-beetle;
Like a snail, it leaves its slime;
Like a horse-mango, it leaves its reek;
A stream that knows not its source or its mouth,
Like that is a man who cannot account for his doings;
Where a dog barks is where the iguana climbs.[2]

In connection with the undue reliance placed on circumstantial evidence, one hears:

Pass through flames and you are scorched,
Rub against a bamboo stem and you itch,
Shake it and you will be sprayed with moisture.[3]

With these may be compared what Narada says about the criminal cases in which a person may be convicted merely on suspicion even where there is no witness to prove the guilt. "He who is seen with a firebrand will be known as an incendiary; he who is seen with a weapon, as a murderer; he who is seen with the wife of another, as the adulterer; he who is seen with an axe in his hand will be known as the destroyer of forests."[4]

It is not proposed to deal in detail with *adat temenggong*, for it is generally accepted that there was considerable Indian influence upon this *adat*. But this conclusion has been reached partly on the basis of doubtful reasoning. It is assumed that because it was autocratic and cruel, it must have been influenced by the Indian concept of autocratic arbitrary rule and severe punishments.[5] The Hindu rulers of India were subject to the *Dharmasastra*. The sanction behind the *Dharmasastra* may be only a continuing cycle of births and deaths; but there were certain other practical considerations which kept the Indian kings within the limits set by public opinion as voiced in the king's council of

[1] Wilkinson, "Law: An Introductory Sketch," *op. cit.*, p. 33.
[2] R. Winstedt, *The Malays, A Cultural History*, 4th Edition, p. 93.
[3] A. Caldecott, "Jelebu Customary Songs and Sayings," *J.S.B.R.A.S.* Vol. 78, p. 29.
[4] Cited by J. Jolly, *Hindu Law and Custom, op. cit.*, p. 299.
[5] See Wilkinson, *op. cit.*, pp. 39–40, 45.

advisors. The classical instance of a king yielding to public opinion, even against the dictates of his own conscience, may be seen in the *Ramayana* where Lord Rama abandons his faithful queen in the forest because the public gossipped about her life as a captive in the palace of King Ravana. It is again doubtful whether *adat temenggong* as observed in Malaya was as autocratic as it is made out. Wilkinson, who speaks of the autocratic nature of *adat temenggong*, has the following anecdote to give from Malacca, a region governed by this *adat*. In the old city of Malacca, he writes,

> a certain chief asked the sultan to surrender an offender. The sultan demurred. When the matter was pressed, the sultan procrastinated in order to allow time for the chief's wrath to pass away, but at last handed over the criminal with a request that the chief might be merciful to his captive. The chief replied by taking up his elephant-goad and splitting open the prisoner's skull in the sultan's very presence.[1]

One wonders whether the sultan or the law he administered was autocratic. Wilkinson does not say anything at all about what happened to the chief; he merely remarks: "A criminal was a prize to be fought for; he was not a man to be tried."[2]

One may in passing refer to etiquette in relation to the royalty in Malaysia which is called *adat istiadat* and which in the main is derived from India. For instance the language traditionally used for persons of royal blood and chiefs consists largely of Sanskrit words or derivatives. When a chief speaks, he makes *sabda*,[3] a Sanskrit word which means sound, while a commoner makes *chakap*, probably an onomatopoeic Malay word. When a member of the royal family is angry, he is said to be *murka*, again a Sanskrit word, while a commoner is content with being *marah*. The royalty gives *anugerah*, from Sanskrit *anugraha*, when making a gift, while a commoner only *beri* or *bagi*. These instances are given only to suggest the influence of Indian ways and manners on the etiquette accepted in Malaysia.

In our study of Malaysian law and its history, what we usually notice is an Anglo-centric approach. In this approach the early part of Malaysian legal history is treated as if it were a prelude to the history of the introduction of English common law into Malaysia. It may be alleged that the present paper is Indo-centric. It is true that as the subject of the paper is Indian influence, much is said about India; but

[1] Wilkinson, "Law: Introductory Sketch," *op. cit.*, p. 43.
[2] *Ibid.*
[3] *Sabda* is used in relation to a *penghulu andeka* in Minangkabau and an *undang* in Negri Sembilan. The saying is Rajah berdaulat / penghulu berandeka / Rajah bertitah / penghulu bersabda.

the attempt has been to view the Malaysian institutions in their historical, and to that extent, their proper, perspective. It is not an attempt to point out, because it would not be true to history, that there was a legal chaos in Malaysia, and that the only salvation lay in adopting Indian laws which the Indian settlers were willing and ready to help the indigenous people to adopt. Neither the Indian rulers nor the Indian settlers seem to have endeavoured to change the local customs by imposing their own; but, in their own sphere of activities they tended to follow practices familiar to them in India and some of these were adopted by the local people. In some spheres, as in the case of royal ceremonies, and the details of matrilineal descent and matrilocal residence, the influence seems to have been great.

Finally, it may be mentioned that the study of Malaysian legal history should be Malaysia-oriented and not Anglo-centric, as it has so far been. Now that Malaysia is regarded as having been weaned from England it is time she revised her laws retaining only as much of the English law as is considered essential and reviving as many of the old local laws as are found suitable to the genius and circumstances of the people who are to be governed by them.

PART II

CUSTOMARY LAW AND THE FORMAL LEGAL INSTITUTIONS: INTERACTION AND CONFLICT

VI. THE EFFECT OF ANGLO-INDIAN LEGISLATION ON BURMESE CUSTOMARY LAW

I. *Introduction*

The Coming of British Rule

Burma lost her sovereignty to the British in 1885 and regained her independence in 1948. Thus, British rule over the whole of Burma lasted sixty-three years, although, if we take into consideration three years of Japanese occupation during the Second World War, the period of effective British rule in Burma was only sixty years. It must, however, be mentioned that the establishment of British authority in Burma did not take place all at once and the coming was not as peaceful and honourable as the going; for the British government, which by the beginning of the 19th century was already firmly established in India, had to fight three costly wars with the Burmese before being able to take over the entire country. These wars stretched over a period of more than sixty years. The first Anglo-Burmese War was fought in 1824, in which native Indian troops were used for the first time by the British to invade and subjugate a foreign country. The British, by virtue of their superiority in naval power and modern artillery, won the war as a result of which the Treaty of Yandabo was concluded in 1826. Under this treaty the Burmese King had to cede to the British government the two coastal provinces of Arakan and Tenasserim.

Having thus gained a firm foot-hold in Burma, the absorption of the whole country into the British Empire was just a matter of time. And although Article 1 of the Treaty of Yandabo[1] stipulates that "there shall be perpetual peace and friendship between the Honourable (East India) Company on the one part and His Majesty the King of Ava on the other" the British government did not find much difficulty in picking another quarrel with the Burmese King and consequently the second Anglo-Burmese War was fought in 1852 and the sizable territory of southern Burma consisting of Pegu, Rangoon, Bassein and Prome, was annexed to the British Empire. Finally, in 1885, the third Anglo-Burmese War ended in the banishment to India of the last of the Burmese Kings and the remaining territory of Burma was officially annexed to the British Empire early in 1886.

[1] For the full text of the Treaty, see 13 *British and Foreign State Papers*, 1825–1826, at p. 362. See also Alleyne Ireland, *The Province of Burma* (1907), Vol. I at 345; Maung Maung, *Burma in the Family of Nations* (1957) at 157.

Introduction of English Law

The first attempt at introducing the English legal system into British-acquired territories in Burma was made in 1825 when one Mr. Maingy was sent to Tenasserim under the supervision of the Governor of Penang, then a Presidency of India. In the "proclamation" which he issued on arrival at Mergui in September 1825, Mr. Maingy declared *inter alia* that "proper measures shall be immediately adopted for administering justice to you according to your own established laws so far as they do not militate against the principles of humanity and natural equity."[1]

When, however, Mr. Maingy set about implementing the declaration, he found that administering justice "according to your own established laws" was easier said than done. The reasons appear to be quite simple. In the first place, Mr. Maingy was not acquainted with Burmese law and custom and the Burmese system of administering justice and he was for some time under the mistaken impression that "the Burmese Courts of Justice had no code of laws for their guidance" and that "all their decisions were arbitrary."[2] This ignorance on the part of a British Commissioner is quite surprising in view of the fact that by the time Mr. Maingy arrived in Tenasserim Major Symes had already published the account of his first mission to the Burmese Court,[3] in which he observed that "the Birman system of jurisprudence is replete with sound morality, and is distinguished above any other Hindoo commentary for perspicuity and good sense" and that "it provides for almost every species of crime that can be committed, and adds a copious chapter of precedents, and decisions to guide the inexperienced in cases where there is doubt and difficulty." He added that laws were "in general conscientiously administered."[4]

In the second place, although there were numerous native officials of the late Burmese government who were experienced in the administration of justice, Mr. Maingy did not want to employ them, because "they possessed such unbounded influence over the natives that to reinstate them would greatly diminish the estimation we are now held in."[5] Thirdly, the Burmese law and judicial procedure contained in the Burmese lawbooks were all in the native language which Mr. Maingy

[1] See J. S. Furnivall, "The Fashioning of Leviathan" XXIX *J.B.R.A.S.* (Reprint) (1939) at 6.

[2] *Id.* at 21.

[3] See Major Michael Symes, *An Account of an Embassy to the Kingdom of Ava* (London, 1800).

[4] *Id.* at 304. See also *Mill's History of British India* (4th ed. by H. H. Wilson, 1840) Vol. II at 225.

[5] See Furnivall, *op. cit.* at 20.

did not understand and he dismissed the whole system as "very complicated." He therefore followed the easiest course by preparing his own "Code of Regulations"; but to make allowance for local law and custom, he provided that "there shall always be a person in attendance, skilled in Burman law and usages and well acquainted with the decisions that would have been given by the late judges."[1] The Commissioner, his Deputy, or Assistant, was to sit as the sole judge. Thus, Mr. Maingy attempted to strike a happy medium between the principle of English law and the Burmese ideas of justice and a Jury was empanelled whenever the Commissioner sat as a Sessions Judge. The result was that his judicial proceedings assumed a remarkably Anglo-Burmese character.

When these proceedings came to the notice of the British judges in Bengal, they were "scandalised and perplexed."[2]

> In one case both complainant and accused were sentenced to be tom-tomed round the town. They were husband and wife who had repeatedly troubled the court with frivolous complaints until neither the judge nor the jury wanted to see any more of them. In another case the complainant had been punished instead of the accused—a woman who had brought a charge of rape was convicted of seducing the accused to commit adultery with her. An absconding husband was sentenced to be forcibly employed on Government work and part of his wages made over to his wife. Similarly a thief was set to work until he should have made good money that he had stolen. Another accused was sentenced to "exposure," that is, to stand up in the public bazaar with a placard showing his offence.[3]

These decisions may be bad in law, that is, English law, but they are sound in commonsense and certainly a more effective means of preventing and discouraging crime than the punishment provisions of the Penal Code.[4] But all this was more than the Honourable Judges could stand, and consequently, the administration of justice in Tenasserim and Arakan was placed under the direct supervision of the High Court in Bengal. This put an end to Mr. Maingy's way of administering justice "according to your own established laws."

The Court System Under British Rule

The organization of British courts in Burma had proceeded in a haphazard fashion and was based more on expediency than on any systematic plan. Up to 1862 the territories of Tenasserim, Arakan and the delta area, which were taken over by the British after the first and

[1] *Id.* at 22.

[2] See J. S. Furnivall, *Colonial Policy and Practice* (1956) at 32.

[3] *Ibid.*

[4] See Robert E. Knowlton, "The Punishment Provisions of the Penal Code" 2 *Burma Law Institute Journal* (1960), at 13.

second Wars, were separately administered by Commissioners, who were entirely independent of each other and subject to no common local administrative head. But in January of that year, the Foreign Department of the Government of India took steps to reorganize the administrative structure. The three areas mentioned above were united into a single unit known as "British Burma" and placed under one Chief Civil Officer called the Chief Commissioner. This official was invested with the powers of a Judicial Commissioner with jurisdiction to hear appeals from the Divisional Commissioners. Two separate courts were also established at Rangoon and Moulmein "with full powers of Civil and Criminal jurisdiction analogous to those exercized by the Recorder of Prince of Wales Island and Singapore with the exception of the power to try cases in which European British subjects are charged with capital offence."[1] In 1872 the Court of Judicial Commissioner of Lower Burma was established at Rangoon and the Chief Commissioner was relieved of his judicial duties. This marked the separation of the judiciary from the executive although at lower levels the Commissioners and Deputy Commissioners continued to exercise both executive and judicial powers. In 1900 the Court of the Judicial Commissioner was transformed into the Chief Court of Lower Burma as the highest civil and appellate court.

Imposition of "Direct Rule"

When Upper Burma was occupied by the British and Indian forces in the Third Anglo-Burmese War, the problem before Lord Dufferin, the Governor-General, was how to administer the country. In his Minute dated the 17th February 1886 submitted to the Secretary of State for India, he said he had considered two alternatives: The first alternative was to transform Burma into a "buffer" state.

> Under this arrangement, the Native Alompra dynasty would have remained upon the throne; the ruling Prince, like the Amir of Afghanistan, would have been perfectly independent in matters of internal administration, and all that we should have required would have been the right to supervise his external relations.[2]

The other alternative was to make Burma "a fully protected State, with a native dynasty and native officials, but under a British Resident, who should exercise a certain control over the internal administration as well as over its relations with foreign Powers." He had even considered the possibility of

[1] See Ireland, *op. cit.* at 92.
[2] See *Burmah No.* 3 (1886)*: Further Correspondence Relating to Burma.* Command 4887.

permanently placing the civil administration of the country in the hands of British officers, at the same time that the position occupied by its former kings was assumed by a Llama or some similar ecclesiastical dignitary such as is found in other Buddhist States. By this means it might be possible, I imagined, to give a certain amount of satisfaction to that national sentiment with which the Burmese, in common with all other people, must be credited, to console them for the disappearance of their own Royal House....[1]

However, on his visit to Burma in the same year Lord Dufferin found the Burmese too patriotic and the possibility of the French extending their influence to Burma so strong, that he finally recommended "annexation pure and simple, and the direct administration of the Province by British Officers" as offering "the best prospect of securing the peace and prosperity of Upper Burmah and our own Imperial and commercial interests."[2] This recommendation was of course accepted by the "Home Government."

Thus, by historical accident, Burma became an integral part of what was then known as "British India." The authority of the Chief Commissioner of Lower Burma was extended to Upper Burma. In 1897 both Lower Burma and Upper Burma were "promoted" to the status of a Province of India and the Chief Commissionership was raised to a Lieutenant-Governorship with a "Legislative Council." A year before, the Court of the judicial Commissioner for Upper Burma had been established. In 1922 the High Court of Judicature at Rangoon was established by Letters Patent consolidating the powers and jurisdictions of both the Chief Court of Lower Burma and the Court of the Judicial Commissioner of Upper Burma. When Burma was formally separated from India in 1937, a new High Court replacing the High Court of Judicature was established under the Government of Burma Act, 1935 with headquarters at Rangoon. This High Court continued to function when Burma became an independent Republic in 1948 but with a new set of Judges. A Supreme Court was also established as the final Court of Appeal with powers previously exercised by the Judicial Committee of the Privy Council.

II. Codes versus Custom

Indian Codes for the Burmese

The logical result of direct rule as an Indian Province was that the codes, statutes and regulations passed by the British Governor-

[1] *Id.* at 24.
[2] *Ibid.*

General of India and meant for the Indians came to be extended to Burma as a matter of course. By that time the British-Indian government had produced a large amount of legislation for India. According to Mr. Justice Baden-Powell, in the days of the "Regulations" (1793–1834) no less than 596 regulations of the Bengal Code were passed. The number of Acts passed from 1834 to 1862 was 793 and those from 1862 to the close of 1883 amounted to 546.[1] Among the codes and statutes extended to Burma were: the Indian Penal Code, the Criminal Procedure Code, the Code of Civil Procedure, the Indian Contract Act, the Transfer of Property Act, the Indian Evidence Act, the Specific Relief Act and the Indian Trusts Act, to mention just a select few.

> This massive monument of law has been built up in little more than a quarter of a century by a "legislature" whose very existence is unknown to many well-educated persons and the men, who planned and drafted these Codes, who discussed and amended and passed them, are almost unknown in England even by name.[2]

All these codes and statutes with the exception of those dealing with family and ecclesiastical matters were based on English law. This was "as unjust and impolitic as it would be to establish the Muhammedan or Hindoo law in England."[3] But if the law introduced was modern English law to be found in the latest statutes and rulings, the situation would have been better. However, Mr. Justice Baden-Powell has told us that the English law incorporated into these codes and statutes was "that of a period when the law itself was the most technical, the least systematic and the least founded on general, equitable and coherent principles that the world has ever seen."[4] Sir Joshua Child, Chairman of the Court of Directors of the East India Co., had described the laws of England as "a heap of nonsense, compiled by a few ignorant country gentlemen, who hardly knew how to make laws for the good of their own private families, much less for the regulating of companies and foreign commerce."[5] In England public opinion has prevented the evil effects of the law from being felt, but "where English law has been introduced into countries where this public opinion or a free press did not exist, the evil effects have been lamentable."[6]

The most common criticism made against English legislation in India is that they are not prepared

[1] See B. H. Baden-Powell, "English Legislation in India" II *The Asiatic Quarterly Review* (1886) at 365. The numbers given also include those repealed or amended.

[2] See John D. Mayne, "The Anglo-Indian Codes" IV *The A.Q.R.* (1887) at 351.

[3] See F. J. Shore, *Notes on Indian Affairs* (1837) (Vol. I) at 302.

[4] See Baden-Powell, *op. cit.* at 372.

[5] Quoted by F. J. Shore, *op. cit.* at 117.

[6] *Ibid.*

in such a way as to meet the real wants and sympathetically appreciated conditions of Indian provincial life, and with a view to their being really assimilated by native magistracy on whom ultimately the administration of law to the masses depends; [but that] the great objects aimed at are legal acumen, accuracy and technical smoothness in the lines of English law.[1]

The system of English law is so incompatible with the habits, sentiments and circumstances of the people, that if attempted to be forced upon even that part of the field of government which belonged to the administration of law, it would suffice to throw the country into the utmost disorder, would subvert almost every existing right, would fill the nation with terror and misery and would leave the country in a state hardly different from that in which it would have been under a total absence of law.[2]

These criticisms might sound a bit harsh, but they were made by well-meaning British officials who had lived in India for many years and who had had personal experience in the administration of those laws among the Indian population. If such was the position in India, one can imagine what the situation would be with the Burmese whose language, religion, manners and customs were vastly different from those of the people of India. In the case of India where a large population of Hindus and Muslims with their own ancient laws and customs were living together, there might have been some justification for the adoption of English law instead of either Hindu law or Muslim law. But in the case of Burma where ninety per cent of the population are Buddhists, it would have been possible to adopt Burmese law and custom as the basis of modern legislation. In any case, the Anglo-Indian statutes should have been revised to suit the manners and conditions of the Burmese people. On the contrary they were imported wholesale into Burma with no modification whatever.

This policy of engrafting English law in a foreign culture has been attributed to a disposition on the part of the English "to estimate themselves, their customs and institutions above those of all others."[3] This characteristic is said to manifest itself more strongly in the English lawyers who have been "brought up to believe that the English law is the perfection of human wisdom" and "being convinced of the immense superiority of the English law over all others, they conceived that they were conferring a benefit upon the people by introducing it into India."[4] However, if one remembers that the English came to India and Burma not merely as traders in search of wealth but as conquerors in search of an empire, such an attitude on the part of the ruling group is not at all

[1] See Baden-Powell, *op. cit.* at 374.
[2] See Shore, *op. cit.* at 302.
[3] *Id.* at 274.
[4] *Id.* at 301.

surprising. In fact, "flag follows trade" has always been their policy.

It is a matter of common knowledge that in almost all the British colonial territories the only area that has been exempted from the "benefit" of English law is that of family relations and religion. The reason generally given for this is that indigenous and English ideas in the fields of contract, tort and criminal law show many similarities and that English law was adopted simply because it was convenient to do so.[1] In 1845 Sir Lawrence Peel, the Chief Justice of Bengal gave the assurance that "the English law as to contracts, the most fruitful source of litigation, is so much in harmony with the Mahomedan and Hindoo laws as to contracts" that no technicality, complication or uncertainty would result from the introduction of English law.[2] It has also been observed that "actions of assumpsit between Hindus constitute the great proportion of the business of the courts" and that "allowing for a few peculiarities their law of contract does not vary materially from our own. Any good English lawyer with the 8th and 9th chapters of Manu in his hand would solve with facility and correctness at once many a dispute between Hindus upon the more ordinary subjects of litigation among them."[3] It would appear that the authorities just cited have exploded the myth, created by the protagonists of English law, that before the coming of British rule, neither India nor Burma had *lex loci* "apart from their personal laws." "When they have no personal law, they have no law, except what we choose to invent for them."[4] It is submitted that the myth was little more than an excuse for the adoption of English common law to the exclusion of all others.

Some of the principles of Burmese law governing contract, tort and crimes have also been found to be very similar to those of the English common law since Burmese customary law can be traced to the ancient Hindu Code of Manu as modified through the course of many centuries by Burmese custom and the Buddhist religion.[5] And yet when one examines the provisions of some of the Anglo-Indian codes and

[1] See T. O. Elias, *British Colonial Law*, London (1962) at 128.

[2] See Sir George Rankin, *Background to Indian Law*, Cambridge (1946) at 90.

[3] See Strange, *Notes of Cases in the Court of the Recorder and in the Supreme Court*, 1798–1816, Madras (1816), Preface, p. 6 cited in Rankin, *op. cit.* at 90.

[4] See Mayne, *op. cit.* at 335.

[5] See Hla Aung, "Buddhism and Domestic Law" II *Burma Law Institute Journal* (1960) at 62. For a more detailed examination of the origin, nature and development of Burmese Customary Law, see Maung Htin Aung, *Burmese Law Tales: The Legal Element in Burmese Folk-lore*, (London 1962) 4–39; Maung Maung, *Law and Custom in Burma and the Burmese Family*, (The Hague 1963); E. Maung, *The Expansion of Burmese Law*, (Rangoon 1951); S. C. Lahiri, *Principles of Modern Burmese Buddhist Law* (6th ed., 1957, Calcutta).

statutes, one can find many rules which are at variance with the established principle of native customary law such as Hindu law, Muslim law and, more particularly, Burmese law.

Criminal Law and Procedure

Let us, therefore, examine briefly some of the fundamental differences between English law and Burmese law. One of these could be found in the attitudes of the two legal systems towards law itself. The Burmese derived their idea of law from the Dhamma, the moral law. To the Buddhist this is not divine law or law of God; it lacks the element of "command" which Austin, one of the foremost English jurists, took to be an essential element in law. The Burmese regard law rather as a statement of cause and effect, like the laws of nature. Every act or omission entails certain consequences in this world or the next.[1] Thus, in Burmese law, reasonableness is more important than legality. Decisions were arrived at not by application of arithmetical rules as under the English legal system but by contracts and compromises obtained by argument, expostulation among themselves, all parties appealing more or less to what is right or just.[2] Under the English system of "rule of law" judges are more concerned with what is legal or what they consider to be legal as distinguished from what the Burmese regard as reasonable or just. For most of the British judges, to be legal is to be just. How often do we hear English judges quoting the oft-repeated maxim—"justice must not only be done but it must be seen to be done!" But how can the poor litigant, who in most cases is just the common man, be expected to be convinced that justice has been done to him if the decision, though perhaps strictly legal, does not seem to him to be reasonable? This is the trouble with most of the Anglo-Indian codes and statutes.

Take, for instance, the world-famous Indian Penal Code, which is supposed to be the best and the most successful of the codes that the British had promulgated for India. It has been described as far in advance of the original law which is administered at any assizes or quarter sessions in England "free from the refinements, subtleties and artificial constructions which disfigure so much of our law."[3] If the Penal Code is successful, perhaps it is not only because it embodies the best of English law but because some attention has been paid to India's

[1] See Furnivall, *op. cit.* at 131, 132.

[2] See Sir John Jardine, J. C. in *Selected Judgments of the Judicial Commissioner of Lower Burma* (1870–92) at 197.

[3] See Mayne, *op. cit.* at 339.

special problems "which arise not merely out of the religion and usages of the people, but out of the distances, the contours, the climate of the country and the racial distinctions among those who in different ages have poured into it from the north."[1]

One finds, however, that attention had been paid in the wrong way. Take, for example, the classification of offences. Theft, no matter how trivial, is an offence against the State, is not compoundable and is cognizable by the police; whereas an assault, no matter how serious, unless it causes grievous hurt, is purely a private affair with which the police have nothing to do. If the person assaulted wants to prosecute he must do so himself, pay his own expenses and engage his own lawyer. If he cannot afford these, he must go without a redress. To most people, however, whether they be Indian or Burmese, a petty theft is seldom a serious matter. They place more value on their body and on their personal dignity and self-respect than on a trifling piece of property. To them, therefore, the classification is artificial and unreasonable.

Again, giving attention to India's special problems does not mean that Burma's special problems have also been taken into consideration. Take the question of adultery for an illustration. Section 497 of the Penal Code makes adultery a crime punishable with five years in jail and fine. There is of course nothing wrong with this. What is wrong is the rule embodied in the section that only the man is punishable and the "poor innocent" woman is permitted to go scot-free even though she may have been primarily instrumental in the commission of the offence. The reason given for this exemption is that

> ...the condition of the woman in this country is unhappily very different from that of the women of England and France; they are married while still children; they are often neglected for other wives while still young [and that] they share the attention of their husband with several rivals. To make laws for punishing the inconstancy of the wife, while the law admits the privilege of the husband to fill his senana with women is a course which we are most reluctant to adopt and throw into a scale already too much depressed, the additional weight of the penal law.[2]

If these considerations were applicable to India of the mid-nineteenth century, they certainly were not applicable to Burma where child marriages were practically unknown and where the age of majority for women had been fixed by custom at twenty. Even with regard to India it would appear that the Law Commissioners had exaggerated the situation somewhat and the commentators of the Code have expressed

[1] See Rankin, *op. cit.* at 209.
[2] See Ratanlal, *Law of Crimes* (19th ed.) at 1242.

the view that the reasons given for not punishing a wife as an abettor are "neither convincing nor satisfactory" and that "it would be more consonant with Indian ideas if the woman were also punished for adultery."[1] We have already seen that under Burmese custom the woman would also be punished for seducing the man to commit adultery with her.[2]

If this is the position of the Penal Code, which Sir James Fitzjames Stephen described as "triumphantly successful,"[3] that of its companion —the Code of Criminal Procedure—is no better. Of these two codes, a British civil servant, who had served in Burma and India for more than a quarter of a century, had this to say:

> ...The perspective of the Indian Penal Code is wrong. It is taken from English law, which is also wrong, that is, opposed to common sense.... But that is nothing to the wrongheadedness of the Criminal Procedure Code. For, whereas the Penal Code only partly offends the people, the Court procedure is wrong from top to bottom. Its very foundation principle is wrong.
>
> What is its principle of a trial? Is it a means of finding out the truth? Is it an impartial inquiry into what has happened? Not in the least. A trial is a duel. It is the lineal descendant of the duels of the Middle Ages. The place is changed, it is a Court and not a field; weapons are witnesses and tongues, not swords nor spears; the parties fight by champions, not in person, and the umpire is called a judge, but the principle is the same. Take any criminal trial. On one side is the Crown prosecutor, on the other the Advocate of the accused. They fight. All through the case they fight. The prosecutor calls his witnesses, asks them only the questions the answers to which will help his case. The other champion cross-examines, bullies, confuses them, tries to make them contradict themselves, drops in irrelevant matter, and tries to destroy what the other side has built. When the defence is on, the state of affairs is reversed. Neither wants the truth. Each plays to win and that alone. If either knows evidence which would help the other side, he suppresses it. The judge is almost helpless. He has to take what is given. He sees *Lacunes* in the evidence, he cannot fill them. He can't get down from off the bench and go out into the country finding evidence for himself....
>
> A clever barrister or advocate will secure an acquittal where a cheaper man would fail. That is notorious everywhere.... The poor man loses and the rich man wins. The poor man goes to gaol, the rich is acquitted or gets a light sentence. The exact truth of a case is never known....[4]

These, then, are the practical effects of the Criminal Procedure Code which Sir John Strachy has described as "complete, efficient and successful."[5]

[1] *Ibid.*

[2] See p. 69, *supra.*

[3] See Sir James Fitzjames Stephen, *A History of the Criminal Law of England*, (1883) (3 vols.) Vol. III.

[4] See H. Fielding-Hall, *The Passing of Empire*, London (1913) at 83–86.

[5] See Sir John Strachy, *India: Its Administration and Progress*, cited in Ireland, *op. cit.*, note 1, at 175.

Civil Law and Procedure

There is much Anglo-Indian legislation dealing with such matters as contract, property, partnership and business transactions. All these statutes are based on English law and their effect on native life and custom has been far-reaching. Take, for instance, the question of land tenure which affects millions of Burmese peasants and the rural population. Before the introduction of English law, land tenure in Burma was governed by local custom and usage. The man who reclaimed for himself a piece of land out of the jungle became by his industry proprietor of the clearing without reference to anyone else. He thus acquired an alienable right to his tenure with no dues to pay whatever except the annual revenue which the village headman might levy—usually ten per cent of the annual produce. The landed proprietor could dispose of the land in any way he liked; otherwise it descended to his heirs and assigns in order of succession; but the estate left by the original occupier was seldom broken up. The heirs tilled part of it or gathered the whole crop in successive years so that the land did not need to be split up into infinitesimal parts. It was open to anyone at any time to carve a holding of his own out of the forest so that there was no temptation to sell or break up the original family lands. In the words of Sir George Scott:

> The fondness with which the people cling to their ancestral lands has something of almost religious fervour in its tenacity. In Upper Burma, land is never sold as the term would be understood in Europe. The transaction which goes by the name of sale is, in reality, a kind of mortgaging, or more exactly pawning, if such a term can be used with regard to land. The estate passes from one occupant to another for a certain sum of money, and it is clearly understood that if at any time the owner is in a position to reclaim his property, he may do so whether the purchaser likes it or not. Farther than this even the buyer cannot sell the land to a third party without first obtaining the consent of its former owner.[1]

All this changed with the coming of British rule and introduction of English law. The courts defined and restricted family rights and made land subject to the Western law of property. Under Burmese customary law there was no such thing as an outright sale; if a proprietor "sold" his land, the understanding was that he or any member of the family might redeem it at any time, but the British courts came to treat such conditional sales as final. Again under Burmese custom the interest on a debt could not accumulate beyond the sum originally borrowed, but the British courts, applying English law, recognized no limit. Nor did

[1] See Shwe Yoe (Sir George Scott), *The Burman: His Life and Notions* (3rd. ed., 1927) at 532.

they recognize the claim made by Burmese peasants that all who had taken part in cultivation were entitled to a first claim upon the produce. Indian money-lenders, who had come to settle in Burma in large numbers, thanks to the liberal immigration policy of the British, would not grant loans, which the peasants were badly in need of, if they could not recover more than the original loan as interest or if they could not sell mortgaged lands to realize their claims. Those "out-moded" customs were burdensome; economic progress must take precedence over social welfare. Consequently, Western ideas of sanctity of contract and individual property in land were substituted for the Burmese custom of family possessions. Transactions which the Burmese peasants regarded as mortgages were construed as sales; debts were allowed to accumulate and labourers lost their security of payment for their labour.[1] Ownership of land passed gradually into the hands of non-agricultural Indian landowners. Thus, rural indebtedness and absentee landlordism became the principal characteristic of the Burmese economy under British rule.[2] The result was that under the "rule of law" of the British

> all social relations were dominated by the economic motive, the desire for material gain, continually pitting the individual against society, and that consequently the social order disintegrated and Burma had been transformed from a human society into a business concern.[3]

So much for the substantive aspects of the civil law. As regards its procedural aspects, the incredible expense, delay, complexity and corruption that attend the civil proceedings in courts today are a matter of notoriety. The situation has been candidly described by Dato Sir James Thomson, Lord President of the Federal Court of Malaysia, in the following terms:

> ...The actual machinery of the administration of English law today is archaic, cumbrous, slow, expensive and complicated beyond belief. For proof of this I need only refer to the practice and procedure of the Supreme Court, the so-called "White Book" which lies on all our desks. The cover of the book may be virginal white; the contents, however, are darkness and obscurity. It contains some 4000 pages and some 2,000,000 words in which it sets out the actual procedural mechanism of the courts and even so, as we all know to our cost, we sometimes look in it in vain for the answer to a problem. No wonder the ordinary man thinks at times that there is something wrong with the working of the law. It is for us lawyers, who are in a position to realize the real difficulties of the problem to apply our minds to finding a solution to try to evolve some sort of order out of what can almost truly be described as chaos.[4]

[1] See Furnivall, *op. cit.* at 134.

[2] See J. L. Christian, *Burma and the Japanese Invader* (Bombay, 1945) at 118.

[3] See J. S. Furnivall, *An Introduction to the Political Economy of Burma* (3rd. ed., 1957) Preface at p. 1.

[4] Dato Sir James Thomson, speaking at the occasion of the opening of the Federal Court of Malaysia see *The Straits Times* (October 2, 1963), at p. 7.

Speaking of English law Dato Thomson continued:

A great American judge has said that the law is the government of the living by the dead. That is perhaps peculiarly true of the law of England which for the reasons I have indicated has become the modern law of Malaysia. But we all know for historical reasons the law of England has for centuries been divorced from the mainstream of law in the continent of Europe which comes from the Roman law and as embodied in logical codes by the great continental jurists of the eighteenth century. In the law of England, however, there are no codes. There is much that is good. There are, however, anomalies, anachronisms and peculiarities dating back to long forgotten pages in the history of England and which have now become a burden and an obstacle to justice in modern England itself and far more so in countries like this, with far more different historical background and social organization. We hear much of the principle that justice should not only be done but that it should be seen to be done. It will not be seen to be done by the people of this country so long as the windows of our courts are covered with the dust of outmoded legal rubbish.[1]

This gloomy picture of the law in Malaysia depicted by the Lord President is of course equally applicable to the situation in Burma where, under British rule, the judicial system became more and more the apparatus of a foreign government. Those who administer the law are now in most cases Burmese judges, but on the bench they were living in a world different from that in which they lived at home. Undoubtedly, most of them knew the law or at least some of it and applied it as conscientiously as they could, but as the law had no roots in the community, they applied it literally and mechanically. Thus, there was a wide gap between law and life and to the common man the "rule of law" came to be almost synonymous with caprice.[2]

III. Judicial Legislation: Courts versus Custom

Saving of Personal Laws

As has been mentioned above, the only area in which the British government had allowed the Burmese people to continue to be governed by their own law and custom is that of family relations such as marriage, divorce, inheritance, succession, adoption and religious usages. The relevant provision is section 13 of the Burma Laws Act, 1898, which, shorn of irrelevant parts, reads as follows:

(1) Where in any suit or other proceeding in Burma it is necessary for the Court to decide any questions regarding succession, inheritance, marriage or caste or any religious usage or institution, [the Court shall apply]
  (a) the Buddhist law in cases where the parties are Buddhists,
  (b) the Mohammedan law in cases where the parties are Mohammedans,

[1] *Ibid.*
[2] See Furnivall, *op. cit.* at 135.

(c) the Hindu law where the parties are Hindus shall form the rule of decision, except in so far as such law has by enactment been altered or abolished, or is opposed to custom having the force of law.

(3) In cases not provided for by sub-section (1), or by any other enactment for the time being in force, the decision shall be according to justice, equity and good conscience.[1]

To a casual observer, this delightfully brief provision might seem simple and clear enough and eliminate any difficulty in applying it to concrete situations. On the contrary, this apparently simple provision has been interpreted and applied by the British courts in such a way that it has given rise to many conflicting and sometimes even self-contradictory decisions. The number of reported cases bearing upon this provision alone has exceeded one thousand. It will, therefore, not be possible to discuss all these cases in this brief paper; nor is it our purpose here to state in detail the Burmese customary law as it is applied by the courts at present. Discussion in the remaining part of the paper will, therefore, be confined to cases in which the courts have, by means of what may be termed judicial legislation, overridden some of the express provisions of Burmese customary family and ecclesiastical law. This has been mainly due to three important factors: (1) the ignorance on the part of the British authorities concerning the nature of Burmese law; (2) the tendency of the British judges to uphold private interest at the expense of social welfare; and (3) the ambiguity of the term "justice, equity and good conscience" appearing in section 13(3) of the Burma Laws Act.

Ignorance Concerning the Nature of Burmese Law

As its name implies, the Burma Laws Act is a local Act being applicable to the term "Province" of Burma only. Prior thereto the only rule laid down for judges both in India and Burma in civil matters was that they were to administer to Hindus, Muslims and Buddhists their own personal laws in matters of succession, inheritance, marriage, caste and religious usages and institutions and that in all other matters not provided for by specific legislation, they were to act according to justice, equity and good conscience. It is therefore clear that the purpose of the Burma Laws Act was to render into statutory form the general rule that the courts had already been administering for some years. And although ninety percent of the population of Burma were (and still are) Buddhists, we find that Hindus and Muslims are also mentioned in the Act perhaps because at the time of the enactment of

[1] See I *Burma Code* (1955) at p. 9.

this law a sizable number of Hindus and Muslims were already living in the country.[1]

The main source of the trouble is the term "Buddhist law" used in section 3(1)(a) of the Act. Professor Rhys Davids has attributed this to the ignorance of the English concerning the relationship between law and Buddhist religion.[2] On the basis of their knowledge about Hindu law and Muslim law, the English took for granted, in their ignorance of Buddhism and Burmese customary law, that the relationship between law and Buddhism with regard to marriage, divorce and inheritance must be the same. In fact, in the strict sense of the term, there is no such thing as Buddhist law; there is only the influence exercised by Buddhist ethics on changes that have taken place in customs. To quote Professor Rhys Davids,

> no Buddhist authority, whether local or central, whether lay or clerical, has ever enacted or promulgated any law. Such law as has been administered in countries ruled over by monarchs nominally Buddhist has been custom rather than law; and the custom has been in the main pre-Buddhistic, fixed and established before the people became Buddhist. There have been changes in custom. But the changes have not been the result of any enactment from above. They have been brought about by change of opinion among the people themselves....[3]

It is, therefore, clear that the term "Buddhist law" as used in the Act is nothing but the customary law of the Burmese Buddhists. This customary law is mainly unwritten and can be gathered partly from the *Dhammathats* and *Phyat-htones* and partly from the prevailing customs and usages of the people. Of the three sources, the *Dhammathats* have always been considered to be of higher authority than the other two and cited by the British courts almost to the exclusion of the *Phyat-htones* (judgments or rulings). This is not the place to go into the history of these Burmese law-books,[4] suffice it to say, however, that the *Dhammathats* are "a body of authority consisting of many texts, sometimes contradictory but yet in their entirety forming what may be called the institutional Buddhist law."[5] A perhaps more accurate definition can also be found in section 2 of Kinwun Mingyi's Digest in

[1] According to the census of 1901, the distribution of Burma's population by religion was as follows: Buddhists – 9,184,121; Muslims – 339,446; Hindus – 285,484; Christians – 147,525. The total population then was 10,363, 613. See Ireland, *op. cit.* at 71. The present population of the Union of Burma has been estimated at approximately 23,000,000.

[2] See T. W. Rhys Davids, "Buddhist Law" in VII *Encyclopedia of Religion and Ethics* (2nd ed., 1932) (Edinburgh) at 827.

[3] *Id.* at 827.

[4] For a detailed study of the history and development of Burmese Law, see Forchammer, *The Jardine Prize: An Essay on the Sources and Development of Burmese Law* (Rangoon, 1885). See also Sir John Jardine, *Notes on Buddhist Law*, Parts I–IV. (1882–1883)

[5] The Privy Council in *U Pe* v. *Maung Maung Kha* (1932) 10 *I.L.R.* (Rangoon Series), 261.

which a *Dhammathat* is described as "a collection of rules which are in accordance with custom and usage and are referred to in the settlements of disputes relating to person and property."[1] There are altogether thirty-six *Dhammathats* of which eleven are in verse, twelve in prose and thirteen in Pali. The date of the oldest *Dhammathat* is 727 A.D. Some of them, like the *Manugye*, were compiled by order of the King himself and some later received royal sanction.

The British judges, including the distinguished members of the Judicial Committee of the Privy Council, were at first unable to appreciate the nature of the *Dhammathats* and tended to give these law-books an authority and rigidity which they had never possessed under Burmese rule, and tried to interpret and apply them strictly like statutory law. It was mainly because of this that polygamy came to be legally recognized in Burma although it was rarely practised among Burmese Buddhists. The real culprits were the Burmese kings and their officials who were mainly responsible for the practice of this institution. Sir George Scott has expressed the view that "polygamy is recognized and permitted, but practically does not exist now."[2] Similarly, the rule that the Orasa or the first-born child of age is entitled to a larger share in the estate of the deceased parent is also contrary to the prevailing custom in Burmese society where all the children share the estate equally among themselves. Unfortunately, however, this obsolete rule is still applied by the courts.

Dhammathats not being statutes, the principle of equitable construction, which is discountenanced in interpreting legislative enactments, cannot be excluded when seeking the meaning of the texts in them. Thus, where a provision of a *Dhammathat* is opposed to the general custom, it is safer to give more weight to the latter, for a rule contained in a *Dhammathat* is in course of time apt to change by the development of customs inconsistent with such law. Custom is, therefore, often a better guide than religious law-books.[3]

Also, in one of the leading cases[4] the Privy Council laid down that where the *Manugye* was not unambiguous, one need not even refer to other *Dhammathats*. Thus, a *Dhammathat* was raised to the status of a

[1] Kinwun Mingyi U Gaung: *A Digest of the Burmese Buddhist Law* (2 Vols.) (Rangoon, 1908–1909). U Gaung was one of the five Ministers of the last Burmese King whose services were retained by the British Government after the annexation of Upper Burma. He was later made a member of the Lieutenant-Governor's Legislative Council and a Companion of the Order of the Indian Empire (C.I.E.).

[2] See Shwe Yoe, *op. cit.*

[3] See *Thein Pe* v. *U Pet*, 3 *L.B.R.* 175 (F.B.).

[4] *Ma Hnin Bwint* v. *U Shwe Gon* (1914) *A.I.R.* 97 (P.C.).

statute making its application more rigid and the utilization of customary law more difficult than before.

The first High Court Judge to "rebel" against the august authority of the Privy Council was Sir Arthur Page, the Chief Justice of the Rangoon High Court, who, in a case decided in 1936, declared:

> ...The time has come when some Judge should be courageous enough to point out, albeit with diffidence and the utmost respect, that while great value is attached in Burma to the rulings in the *Manugye*, Burmese jurists do not regard this *Dhammathat* as sacrosanct and that from time to time some embarrassment has been created as the result of following the *Manugye* in the teeth of what has been laid down in the *Dhammathats*. One not insignificant reason why this *Dhammathat* is so frequently cited is because the *Manugye* was the first, if it is not the only *Dhammathat*, to be wholly translated into English and thus it is the authority to which those unversed in the Burmese tongue most readily, if not inevitably, turn.
>
> Where, therefore, a certain rule of Burmese law is to be found in the *Dhammathats* and also in decided cases and in the modern practice and views of Burmans, the Court is not only at liberty but is bound to decide the case in accordance with Burmese Customary Law as it obtains today, rather than to perpetuate the outworn shibboleths of bygone ages, notwithstanding that some sanction for their continuance may be found in extracts from the *Manugye Dhammathat*. Burmans are not to be doomed to live for ever under the rulings and customs by which they were governed in the days of King Alompra.[1]

This shining example of Page C.J. was followed fifteen years later, when Burma was already independent of British rule, by Justice U E Maung of the Supreme Court in a case decided in 1951 in which he declared that "the *Manugye Dhammathat* was not the paramount authority in the body of Dhammathats as enunciated by the Privy Council."[2]

Private Interest and Social Welfare

We have seen earlier that the general trend of judicial interpretation in Burma under the rule of English law had been to favour private interest over social welfare. This, as pointed out by Dr. Furnivall, "was a heritage from a legal system which had been transplanted in Burma by judges and lawyers, either British or called to the English Bar."[3] This trend could be seen in many of the cases involving interpretation of the Burma Laws Act. This writer has pointed out elsewhere[4] how judicial misapplication of this very important law had resulted in grave injustice to the Burmese Buddhist women who married the Muslims,

[1] *Ma Hnin Zan* v. *Ma Myaing*, *A.I.R.* (1936) Rangoon 31 at 34.

[2] See *Dr. Tha Mya* v. *Daw Khin Pu*, (1951) *B.L.R.* (S.C.) 108.

[3] See his foreword to Maung Maung, *Burma's Constitution* (2nd ed., 1961) at xi.

[4] See Hla Aung, "Sino-Burmese Marriages and Conflict of Laws" I *Burma Law Institute Journal* (1958) 25.

Hindus and the Chinese, whereby they were deprived of all their legitimate rights and benefits which they would have enjoyed under Burmese customary law and how the legislature had to step in and pass a statute for their protection.

In their anxiety to uphold private property rights at the expense of social welfare, the courts had encroached upon a purely religious area where the Burmese Buddhist monks were governed not by the *Dhammathats* but by the rules of their Order called the *Vinaya*. Now a Buddhist monk is prohibited by the rules of the *Vinaya* from possessing property other than that given as a religious gift, either to him or another monk.[1] Thus, in a case decided in 1915 involving the question of whether a Buddhist monk is capable of entering into a valid contract for selling or mortgaging land, it was held that he was prohibited by his personal law from doing so.[2] This was the ruling made by the Judicial Commissioner of Upper Burma. This ruling was later confirmed by the High Court in *U Teza* v. *Ma E Gywe*[3] where it was held that an agreement to purchase a house by a Buddhist monk was void, the transaction being opposed to his personal law, *Vinaya*, and hence immoral within the meaning of section 23 of the Indian Contract Act.[4] It is submitted that both these decisions are correct in the sense that they are in accordance with the sentiments of all the Buddhists in Burma.

When, however, in 1929 the same question came up before the High Court again, Mr. Justice Carr, doubting the correctness of the said two decisions, the latter decision being that of a single Judge of the High Court (Maung Ba, J.), referred the question to a Full Bench for an authoritative pronouncement of the law governing the matter. The question was: "Is the sale of immovable property to a Burman Buddhist monk void on the ground that a monk is prohibited by the rule of the *Vinaya* from entering into such pecuniary transactions." This Reference was heard by a Full Bench of four High Court Judges, but the opinion was equally divided between them with two Judges, namely, Rutledge C. J. and Maung Ba, J. answering the question in the affirmative and the other two in the negative.

[1] See *Kinwun Mingyi's Digest, op. cit.* Vol I, section 409.

[2] See *U Tilawka* v. *Shwe Kan*, 29 *I.C.* (1915) 613.

[3] *A.I.R.* (1928) Rangoon 3.

[4] Section 23 of the Indian Contract Act provides: "The consideration or object of an agreement is lawful, unless—it is forbidden by law or is of such a nature, that if permitted, it would defeat the provisions of any law; or is fraudulent or involves or implies injury to the person or property of another or the Court regards it as immoral, or opposed to public policy.

"In each of those cases, the consideration or object of an agreement is said to be unlawful. Every agreement of which the object or consideration is unlawful is void."

The case had, therefore, to be referred again to another Full Bench of five Judges none of whom participated in the previous Reference. This time the opinion was unanimous, all the five Judges answering the question in the negative, namely, that the sale of immovable property to a Burmese Buddhist monk was not void on the ground that a monk was prohibited by the rules of the *Vinaya* from entering into such pecuniary transactions and that a Buddhist monk was not disqualified from contracting under section 11 of the Contract Act.[1] The *ratio decidendi* of the decision is:

> The definition of the word "laws" in its juridical sense is that "laws" are rules of civil conduct enforced by the State. From this it follows that the rules of conduct as laid in Vinaya for the guidance of Buddhist monks cannot be deemed to be "laws" unless they are enforced by the State. According to section 13(1), Burma Laws Act, they are not enforced by the State except in cases in which questions regarding any religious usage or institution arise. A sale being a pure matter of contract is not "a question regarding any religious usage or institution." A Buddhist monk therefore is not disqualified from contracting by law within the meaning of s. 11, Contract Act.[2]

Thus, by adhering strictly to the letter of the law and ignoring its spirit, the British Judges had, by judical legislation, struck down in one stroke the time-honoured rule, originally laid down by Lord Buddha and observed by millons of His disciples throughout the centuries, that "a rahan(monk) who does buying and selling is guilty of *Nissagi pacittayam.*"[3] No good Buddhist would appreciate the reasoning of the Full Bench. The only explanation one could think of is that to British Judges the "legal" always precedes the "reasonable" and private interest must come before social welfare.

"Justice, Equity and Good Conscience"

This phrase is very familiar, particularly to those who have lived under the influence of English law. Its meaning is obscure and is as variable as the colour of a chameleon. It is the convenient phrase put into a statute to fill gaps in the law. Thus, if, in deciding cases, the courts can obtain no help or guidance from legislative enactments or religious law-books or other authorities, the Judges are expected to act in accordance with "justice, equity and good conscience." This usually means what each judge thinks best to do in the particular case. But

[1] See *U Pyinnya* v. *Maung Law, A.I.R.* (1929) Rangoon 354. Section 11 of the Contract Act says: "Every person is competent to contract who is of the age of majority according to the law to which he is subject, and who is of sound mind, and is not disqualified from contracting by any law to which he is subject."

[2] *Id.* at 362.

[3] See the opinion of Maung Ba, J. *Ibid.*

for judges, who are either British or British-trained, the phrase generally means principles of "English law if applicable to the society and circumstances of Burma."[1]

However, in the field of personal law such as marriage, divorce, inheritance and succession, principles of English law are hardly applicable. Thus, in a case dealing with the question of validity of a marriage between a Burmese Buddhist woman and a Chinese Confucian, section 13(1) of the Burma Laws Act did not apply because one of the parties was not a Buddhist. So section 13(3) came into play and the question had to be decided according to justice, equity and good conscience. But to apply the principles of English law to such a case would be ridiculous. Chinese customary law would not be applicable either, because it was foreign law and to apply it would not be in accordance with justice, equity and good conscience. The court, therefore, arrived at the same result by applying Burmese customary law as *lex loci contractus* and the marriage was held valid.[2] This case was decided in 1937 by which time the practice of applying Chinese customary law to Burmese-Chinese marriages had already stopped thanks to the ruling of a Full Bench in the case of *Ma Yin Mya* v. *Tan Yauk Pu* where Rutledge, C.J. held that (1) the Burmese Buddhist law regarding marriage was *prima facie* applicable to Chinese Buddhists as the *lex loci contractus* and (2) that to escape from the application of Burmese Buddhist law a Chinese must prove that he is subject to a custom having the force of law in Burma and (3) that the application of such custom would not work injustice to the Burmese woman.[3]

IV. Conclusion

It has been said that "the impact of English law has not affected appreciably the ancient Hindu, Mohammedan and Buddhist Laws...."[4] However, the foregoing analysis would seem to have shown us that the introduction of English law into India and the wholesale and un-

[1] See *Dr. Tha Mya* v. *Ma Khin Pu*, *A.I.R.* (1941) Rangoon 81. For a historical examination of the phrase, see J. Duncan M. Derret, "Justice, Equity and Good Conscience" in J. N. D. Anderson, (ed.) *Changing Law in Developing Countries*. (London, 1963).

[2] See *Ma Kyin Mya* v. *Maung Sit Han*, (1937) R.L.R. 103.

[3] See Hla Aung, *op. cit.* at 32–33.

[4] See Dr. Ba Han, *A Legal History of India and Burma*, (Rangoon, 1952) at 107. But another Burmese scholar has observed that "the impact of the English legal system introduced into the country after the annexation of 1886 shook Burmese customary law to its very foundation, just as Burmese society itself rocked with the shock of the impact." See Maung Htin Aung, "Customary Law in Burma" in Philip W. Thayer (Ed.) *Southeast Asia in the Coming World* (Baltimore, 1955) at 203.

thoughtful importation of Indian codes and statutes into Burma had shattered the whole fabric of Burmese law and had unfortunate social consequences. It is true that both India and Burma have inherited from the British the concepts of democracy, individual freedom and the idea of a Judiciary independent of the Executive. But recent events in Burma seem to have shown that Western institutions, however excellent they may be, do not take root in an Oriental country where the common people have been subjected to a legal system which did not take into account their customs and traditions and which did not promote their social and cultural welfare. And if the British system of law and government has lasted longer in India than it has in Burma, it is probably because India has lived much longer under British rule than Burma, and therefore has been able to build up a sort of tradition. Even then it is still premature to be too optimistic about the future of Western institutions in the East in general, and in India and Malaysia in particular, which shared the same fate under British rule as Burma.

As for the innumerable codes, statutes and other laws which have remained as a legacy of British rule, it is neither desirable nor possible to get rid of all of them within a short time. And although most of these laws are outmoded and anachronistic, some of them are undoubtedly useful, and indispensable for economic and industrial development, and for the promotion of international trade and commerce. The only thing that is necessary with regard to these laws is to make a systematic study of them with a view to introducing suitable reforms.

It is, therefore, perhaps fitting to conclude this paper with another quotation from Dato Sir James Thomson, who declared:

> ...We must now consider whether the time has not come to make changes in the actual law itself, and that is a problem which has so far attracted very inadequate attention in the context of all the new emerging nationhood of Asia. The time has now come for each of the new nations, each new master in its own house, to consider how much of its legal heritage is altogether suitable to the changed circumstances of today, how much of it should be retained and how much of it should be discarded. Here again it is the lawyers that must take the lead. Law reform, if it is to achieve lasting results, must be carried out by people with knowledge; otherwise the end may be worse than the beginning....[1]

[1] See *The Straits Times*, (October 2, 1963) at p. 7.

VII. SOME MAIN FEATURES OF MODERNIZATION OF ANCIENT FAMILY LAW IN THAILAND

Thailand is a country of statutory law. Even before the work on modern codes was first undertaken towards the end of the last century, the entire field of ordinary civil and criminal justice was covered by written law. Although much legislation enacted at various times embodied new or modified legal rules, most other legislation was simply the expression of long established custom, and ancient Thai family law was customary in this sense.

The family law now in force is contained in the Civil and Commercial Code. The present family law lays down many new rules which depart from ancient customs, the fundamental change being the substitution of monogamy for polygamy. This reflects the triumph of modernity over tradition; in fact, it symbolizes the Westernization of the country. To the supporters of monogamy, the new law prohibiting polygamy was an important advance in Thai morality; but to its opponents who pleaded for realism, arguing that morality was relative, the new law was without foundation and was destined to become inoperative, thus causing more harm than good. The debate lasted for more than two decades and finally, in 1935, three years after a constitutional form of government was established, the present family law providing for monogamy was promulgated as Book V of the Civil and Commercial Code.

The Ancient Law

The ancient law on matrimony, known as *Kodmai Laksana Pua Mia*, consisted of a number of laws enacted by different kings of the Ayuthya period—a period in Thai history covering four hundred and seventeen years. These laws were the embodiment of ancient customs of the Thai people. Together with other private and public laws they were compiled into a general code of laws in 1804, during the reign of King Rama I of the present Chakri dynasty.

It may be of interest to note that the work on codification both of private and public laws was ordered by the King as a result of the final appeal on a divorce case brought before him. In the days of absolute monarchy the kings were the law givers and supreme judges. In that historic case, the husband appealed to the King, claiming it was contrary to justice that his wife who committed adultery should have had the right to seek and be granted a divorce by the jury, while he himself had done nothing wrong.

The King, having heard all the facts, declared that the judgment was contrary to justice. He examined the written law and discovered that the judgment was in accordance with the legal provisions. Believing that the written provisions were an erroneous representation of the customary rules of law and that such an error might have crept into other laws, the King set up a commission of eleven jurisconsults to work on codification. He himself made final revisions where he thought they were required by justice. The result was a general code of laws[1] which lasted until recently.

There is no indication when customary family law was first reduced to written form. This may have occurred soon after King Ram Kamhang invented the Thai script in A.D. 1283. But since there is evidence that a number of statutes enacted during the Ayuthya period were also written in Khmer script, early statutes compiled from customary law might have preceded the invention of Thai script. However the first known statute was the one enacted in A.D. 1361.

This statute dealt with a number of questions including polygamy, adultery, rights and duties of married persons, matrimonial property, dissolution of marriage and its effects on property. Following this statute, it is not certain how many more were enacted during the whole Ayuthya period of over four centuries, because the statutes eliminated by the codification of 1804 were not listed.[2]

Two main features characteristic of the ancient Thai law, in contrast to the modern law, are polygamy and the conjugal power of the husband.

[1] Prince Damrong, an eminent authority on Thai history, believed that this code was not the first one that Thailand had. According to him, codification was a technique resorted to at different times during the Ayuthya period. Prince Damrong, *Tamnan Kodmai Muang Thai* (History of Thai Laws).

It is most unfortunate for Thai scholars that almost all of the early written records of the Kingdom were burnt when the ancient capital of Ayuthya was destroyed after its capture by the Burmese in the war of A.D. 1767. Much of what was written later, on the ancient history of the Kingdom was the result of many decades of arduous work of collecting and piecing together the scattered fragments of material; much may have been lost forever. At any rate, little is known of the historical development of Thai laws.

[2] There was at any rate an additional statute enacted in 1362, one year after the main statute was promulgated, which concerned an unprecedented and complicated case of dispute over the distribution of matrimonial property upon the dissolution of marriage.

Polygamy

Under the ancient law, polygamy was legal. The family law classified wives into three categories, namely, the major wife, the minor wife, and the slave wife.

The major wife, or *mia klang muang* (commonly known as *mia luang*) was married with the consent of her parents, and with the understanding that she would be the major wife. Since no provision of law prescribed the contrary, it had been interpreted that it was possible for a man to have more than one major wife.

The minor wife or *mia klang nok* (commonly known as *mia noi*) was married with the understanding given by her husband that she would be a minor wife.

If a man took as his wife a woman slave belonging to him or to his close relatives, she had the status of a slave wife, or *mia klang thasi* (commonly known as *thasa phalays*). By law she became a minor wife when her bondage was lifted by the master or when she bore a child. Irrespective of whether bondage was lifted or whether she bore a child, a slave wife became free upon the death of her husband.

The legal distinction between the different classes of wives had two functions. First, it served the purpose of determining the amount of compensation which the adulterer was made to pay to the husband. The higher the class of wife, the greater the amount of compensation the adulterer had to pay. Secondly, wives of higher classes were entitled to larger shares of the husband's estate after he died.

In addition to these three classes of wives, the law recognized another special class of wife, commonly referred to as *mia prarajathan*, of a higher status than the *mia klang muang*. The *mia prarajathan* was the one given by the King to a nobleman as a reward for meritorious service to the country.

Conjugal Power of the Husband

Under ancient law, a woman was at all times under someone's protection. If single, no matter how old, she was under the care and protection of her parents; when married, she was under her husband's protection. Parental power was converted into conjugal power and transferred to her husband.

It is not easy to define what the conjugal power consisted of. It is doubtful as to whether originally conjugal power involved the right to give one's wife away with or without her consent. However, it was clear that the law recognised the husband's right to administer bodily punishment to his spouse when she was guilty of misconduct, provided that the degree of punishment was in proportion to the misdeed. If the punishment was out of proportion, she was entitled to bring action against him, and disproportional punishment also constituted a ground for divorce.

Argument for Modernization

It should be mentioned that in the debate on modernization of family law there was no dispute regarding amending the strong conjugal power of the husband in favour of a higher conjugal status for women, for in fact existing conditions had raised the status of the wife at that time. In spite of the law, women had always played an important role in Thai society and actually managed family finance.

The question as to whether the new law should substitute monogamy for polygamy was highly controversial. The debate started during the reign of King Vajiravudh. The King himself wrote a memorandum, dated June 1, 1913, stating his view on the subject in reply to Prince Svasti, who advocated monogamy as the basis for drafting the new marriage law. The King's memorandum is most interesting to read and indicative of the many aspects and extensiveness of the considerations given to the subject by the lawdrafters. It is here quoted in part:

> When I instructed Prince Charoon about drafting the Marriage Law, I did not rely upon my personal opinion alone. I submitted the question in the Cabinet Council, which on that particular occasion was meeting at Sanam Chandra Park. When a decision had been arrived at, which, if I understand rightly, was to the effect that the number of wives should not be restricted to one, I instructed Prince Charoon in the presence of my Ministers that registration should be adopted as the legal evidence of marriage or cohabitation of husband and wife.
>
> For myself, I shall neither gain nor lose by the adoption of either the system of monogamy or polygamy, so that I feel that I am competent to state a disinterested opinion on the subject.
>
> The opinion which I have stated to Prince Charoon, together with certain other added ones, is as follows.
>
> 1. The making of Law to deceive the world, i.e., the appearance of a Law that is not true in reality, appears to me to be a downright cynical lie. Therefore, if we are going to have a lot of wives, I do not think it right that we should state that we are adopting the monogamous system as a principle of our Marriage Law; because if we adopted such a principle and could not generally practice it, it would amount to a want of respect for the Majesty of the Law. And if the Executive does not enforce strict obedience to the Law, it amounts to deceiving the world at large by enacting a Law merely to be evaded, a thing that does not appear to me to enhance the dignity of either the King or the Nation.
>
> 2. When it had been resolved in council, that the principle of Polygamy should be allowed to continue, I suggested the system of registration, in order to regulate promiscuity of irregular unions, since I have noted that in our country people so easily become "Man and Wife" that it is sometimes difficult to get evidence of such a

union. In general, women who become minor wives ("Mia Noi") or secret wives ("Mia Lab") are very unhappy. The reasons for a woman becoming a minor wife are either through love of the man who she expects would treat her as a wife, or else by purchase from her parents. Such a girl does not necessarily have any love for the man, but she consents to the union either through fear of the parents or trough pity for their poverty. Such a girl has all my pity for she is a most unfortunate creature, and her unhappiness is not the direct result of her own concupiscence, but rather that of her love and pity for the parents, and desiring the parents' happiness above all else. Such an unfortunate one is in a worse plight when the man who bought her forsakes her, for it is most difficult for her to find another husband; and if she has had some children, then it becomes still worse. But even women, who have consented of their own free-will to cohabit with men who have deceived them by specious promises, are also to be pitied; and those women, when forsaken by the men, have many of them turned to prostitution out of necessity. That is why I believe that, if it could be clearly laid down that only those who have been registered are legally "Man and Wife" ("Phu Mia Kan"), it would serve in a small measure to protect girls from being deceived, for at least a girl would always have the means of proving the seriousness of a man's intentions towards herself, whether he really meant to give her the status of a wife or not.

3. As to the statement that even in Europe, where the Law is founded on the monogamous system, men of wealth also have a number of concubines, I admit it to be a fact. But, in my opinion, European women who become mistresses or concubines and Siamese women who become minor wives are different. European women know very well the consequences of such acts, they know very well they are acting immorally and do so with their eyes wide open, so that when they are forsaken, they have no one else to blame but themselves. The principle of monogamy has been established in Europe so long, that people have got accustomed to it for ages past. But not so in Siam. We have for a long time had polygamy, and the system is deep-rooted in the understanding of our people; therefore, even though it may be set down in Law that only the major wife is to enjoy the status of wife in the eyes of the Law, yet neither women nor parents understand things as they are understood in Europe. The minor wives would still continue to consider themselves "wives," unless it were expressly enacted that "*A man who has already contracted marriage with one woman, and thereafter has connection with another woman, shall be condemned to have committed adultery, and his legal wife shall be entitled to a divorce.*" Unless such a provision has been enacted, I do not believe our women will understand that to become a minor wife does not carry with it the status of a wife. They would still stick to the old way, and even though they may have ceased to entertain any affection for the men, they would still not dare to run away, since they still consider themselves bound. Also, should the minor wife of one man have connection with another man, she would still be deemed an adulteress. Besides, the Buddhist Church would still condemn as guilty of adultery both the man who has connection with another man's minor wife and the woman herself, because no Law could overcome Canonical Law and the commandments of Our Lord. It should be remembered, that Laws are made not only to be understood by judges and lawyers, but they must also be understood by laymen. Therefore, unless people could be made to appreciate the fact clearly, that a minor wife is *not* wife, and that when she no longer desires to cohabit with the man who has been keeping her she may leave him *without suffering any ill-consequences whatsoever*, the problems I have already stated would not have arrived at a satisfactory solution, and men would still be able to take unscrupulous advantage of women's credulity. The reason why I suggested a system of registration was really to give women a chance of suffering a little less from the deceit of men.

4. It is stated that if it were set down in our Law that if we allowed man to have

more than one wife, it would amount to a confession that we were on a lower moral plane than that of the Western Nations. I can not agree with this statement, because the monogamous system of the Europeans is the result of their religion, which ordains that a man may have only one wife and a woman only one husband, and that married people who have connection with others than their own spouses are said to commit adultery.

Our own religion, however, does not limit the number of wives that man may have. I once asked the Holy Prince Vajirayana to explain the meaning of the word "*Sandosh*" (uncovetousness), and he explained that it meant "being satisfied with that which one has, and not desiring that which belongs to others." I further asked whether a man who possesses many wives should be considered a man who is "Sandosh" (uncovetous), and he replied that "the number of wives does not signify, the only thing that matters being the desire for someone else's wife, which would then be called sinful covetousness; so long as a man does not desire or plot to take away another's wife, he would be "Sandosh," no matter how many he may himself keep." This clearly shows that our religion does not forbid polygamy, and does not condemn it as immoral. Only if a man should seek connection with another's wife, or a woman who is already a wife (no matter whether a major wife or minor wife) should seek connection with a man other than her husband, such a man or woman would be said to have committed adultery. According to our religion, the major wife and the minor wife are equally "prohibited women," which is not the case in Europe, where a concubine or mistress could not be "prohibited" from forming connection with anyone, because the religion of Europe does not recognise the minor wife as bound in any way to a man. This being so, it cannot be said that the Siamese who has several wives is on a lower moral plane than the European with only one wife, because to admit such a proposition would mean that we shall have also to admit that the Buddhist Religion itself is also on a lower moral plane than the Christian Religion, which naturally I for one *cannot* admit.

5. If, however, it be considered good policy for us to admit that we have hitherto been on a lower moral plane than the Europeans, and that it is therefore necessary to raise ourselves to their moral level, then many questions would have to be considered. For example, should we or should we not limit the relationship of those who may marry one another because the Christian Religion does so most distinctly....

I have brought this matter up in order to demonstrate that our moral plane and that of the Europeans could not very well be compared with fairness, because they are so different, and it is most difficult to judge who is on the higher plane and who on the lower. Therefore to drag the subject of Moral Planes into the drafting of Marriage Law appears to me to be rather inapt. Besides, if we set down that we are on one moral plane, and in reality remain on another, it does not mitigate my scruples about telling lies.

6. The most important thing in my opinion, and one about which Phya Kalyan Maitri agrees with me, is that when we have *no illegitimate children in our Laws, it is not desirable to provide for their coming into being*. It is true that at present there are already many cases of children who are not acknowledged by their fathers, but there are no laws to strengthen the position of such unnatural fathers. Should, however, the monogamous system be adopted as the principle of our Marriage Law, a father who does not wish to acknowledge the children of a minor wife would simply take refuge behind the Law. But if provision is to be made to compel a man to acknowledge his children, no matter by whom borne, then my anxiety is in a measure lessened. But I do not agree with Prince Svasti in his citing the Japanese and Chinese systems of acknowledging children, (and I might also beg to differ from the opinion expressed in his memo, that the Marriage and Concubinage Systems of Japan and China are the same as ours. I believe I am right in saying that our system came directly out of

the Code of Manu. Whereas the Chinese system was evolved in China itself, although the Code of Manu might also to a certain extent have contributed to its evolution). The Chinese and Japanese are people who most ardently desire children because both Shintoism and Confucianism require that a man should have sons to perform the rites of ancestral worship; and therefore, even when a man has no sons of his own he needs must have recourse to adopting someone else's child as his own, the adopted son becoming his heir. We Siamese, however, have no such belief, so that it cannot be hoped that the natural son would be so easily acknowledged as in Japan or China. Some sort of provision will have to be made to compel a man in Siam to acknowledge his natural children; otherwise, such children would be unfortunate, fatherless children, unable to look anybody in the face.

7. Even though there were to be a law compelling a man to acknowledge all his children, whether born in wedlock or bastards, I still feel that the children of the minor wife would be unfortunate beings, because although the Law compels them to have fathers, yet that same Law will not allow them to have mothers. Are they to become born in lotusses, like Brahma who sprang from the navel of Vishnu in Hindu Mythology? Besides, I still recollect the words of my Father, who propounded a curious question, for he asked: "If you consider the minor wife only as a mere vessel, should you not also consider the children of the minor wife as children born from a mere vessel?" I remember this saying very vividly, because I thought then how just it was, and I am firmly convinced that to treat the minor wife as a vessel would bring most undesirable consequences. In the first place, the child of the minor wife who would please his father would have looked down upon his own mother; in the second place, if the child is really fond of his mother, he would have a grievance against his father for not treating his mother as a woman, but as a mere vessel. For a child to be in the one state is as bad as to be in the other, and may lead to grave consequences. Even looking at it from a wordly standpoint, it appears certain that the child must necessarily be on bad terms with either its father or its mother. From the standpoint of religion, the position would be no better, for the child must inevitably lose respect for either its father or its mother, whereas our religion expressly teaches one to consider one's father and mother as one's Brahma (i.e., creator). If a child must be taught that it *must* consider its father's major wife as its mother (and to take *no* notice of the woman who really gave it birth), it would mean that the child is taught to lie from the day of its birth to the day of its death. I maintain that no one could possibly reconcile himself to such untruthfulness, for it is most difficult to love one's step-mother or foster-mother as one's own. It would only be mere outward show, and one would be forever enacting a lie. It practically amounts to training the child from birth to recognise that neither Honesty nor Truth are as important as Expediency. When such an immoral precept becomes firmly imbedded in the child's mind, he will, when grown up, still continue to put Expediency above Honesty and Truth in all things and under all circumstances.

Besides, if we are to hold that all children acknowledged by a man become legally the children of his wedded wife, will the Europeans believe that we are really monogamists? Supposing a man had 20 or 30 children, could anyone be made to believe that they are all born from the same mother? No, certainly not. They would know very well that the man had more than one wife. And therefore to pretend that he is a monogamist would not only be quite useless; he would still be called a polygamist just the same.

8. The statement (by Prince Svasti), that Europeans also have more than one "Mia" and that the fact of keeping one or many women simply depends upon the wealth of the man might be true of Europe, but it does not have quite the same meaning here. I have already explained in paragraph 3 the difference in the position of the women themselves, but I would like here to add something else. It may be true

that wealthy Europeans also practically have minor wives, but such women do not have children as a rule, as is evidenced by the fact that in France, where people are fond of keeping mistresses, the result is seen in the falling of the birth-rate, until the French Governments have had to resort to the policy of encouraging childbirth. In our country, however, the minor wives bear children just the same as the major wife, so that the problem can hardly be said to be quite the same here as in Europe. I maintain that we must look at the question from a different point of view.

9. As to Prince Svasti's statement, that polygamy in our country is only confined to the upper classes and is not common among the lower classes, and that the Law should be made for the benefit of the majority rather than the minority, I beg to offer the following replies:

(a) As to the Law being made for the benefit of the majority, and taking the majority as the criterion, I have nothing to say in opposition to that, since it is the fundamental basis of Law.

(b) As to the statement that polygamy is confined to persons of the upper classes, I must ask a question in return, namely, where is the line to be drawn between the upper and the lower classes? For example, are the servants (Mahadlek) of Princes to be considered of the upper or the lower class? I know a good many such men who are by no means monogamists; that is why I ask the question.

(c) In our country, there is a proverb to the effect that "the behaviour seen to be proper amongst the gentry is imitated by the slaves" (meaning thereby that the slaves will ever ape their superiors), which I observe is still very true even in these days. Therefore, in legislation one has to take the upper classes as the criterion. Any law that is able to command the obedience of the upper classes would not be found oppressive by the lower. Those who make outcries and create disturbances are not of the Mass, but belong rather to the gentry (at least that is so in Siam).

Summing up his discussions, the King posed these questions for decision:

(1) Shall we adopt the principle of monogamy as the basis of our Marriage Law?

(2) If it is so decided, shall we adopt strict monogamy or otherwise what difference would there be between it and downright polygamy?

(3) What status will the minor wife enjoy? Is she to be considered as a human being or a human chattel? Shall she be allowed to participate in any benefit derived from the husband's property after his death?

(4) Shall any distinction be made between the children of the minor wife and those of the major wife? If the Japanese system is to be adopted, the children would (apparently) receive equal treatment. Shall that be the case?

(5) If a man does not acknowledge his child, will the child have any means of compelling the father to do so? If so, what will be the means?

To those questions, the King offered his personal opinion as follows:

(1) The principle adopted should be that which is the most expedient for the majority.

(2) If plastic monogamy is to be adopted, I consider it to be better to adopt polygamy outright, because then there would be no compulsion, and each man could choose to have only one wife or several wives, according to his own inclination and convenience.

(3) In my opinion, the minor wife should be treated as a human being, and not as chattel; therefore, so long as she still cohabits with her husband, she should enjoy the status and the protection proper to a wife, and she should have a share in her hus-

band's property after his death. But it is only natural that her share should be less than that of the major wife who brought her dowry. At least, the minor wife ought to receive some recognition for her services and for being the mother of the man's children.

(4) In my opinion, all the children should receive equal treatment; that is to say, the father should expressly state in his will who is to be his heir to carry on the honours of his family, and the rest should receive such portions as he names in his will. But should the father die intestate, the eldest son of the principal wife (i.e., the one who brought a dowry) should become the heir, all the rest of the children receiving such portions as may be willingly given them by the said heir (who in this case would stand *in loco parentis* to his brothers and sisters.) In this way, with the exception of the said heir, all the children of the deceased would receive equal treatment, no matter whether they be the children of the major wife or the minor wife.

(5) The child who is not acknowledged by his father should be provided with easy means of seeking acknowledgment.

It is interesting to note that the foreign legal experts employed by the Thai government took caution in dealing with this controversial subject, leaving the issue to the Thai to discuss and decide among themselves. Mr. Padoux, the Legislative Advisor at that time, stated in his memorandum of May 9, 1913, that,

...I took from the very beginning the view that all Europeans could do in a matter intimately connected with Siamese life and customs was to collect the existing law to the best of their ability, to put it in the shape of articles of Code, to make only such modifications as were necessary for the adjustment of the various provisions, and to suggest no more alterations than those which were clearly required by the recent changes introduced in the administration and social organisation of Siam. I was—and I am still—strongly of opinion that the initiative of fundamental reforms in questions of marriage, divorce, parentage, inheritance, must lie only with the Siamese Statesman and legal men. Europeans, however long they may have lived in this country never know sufficiently the Siamese customs and the Siamese life to be in a position to make authoritative suggestions on the matter. The Siamese Government alone can know what Siam may require and how far the old rules of the Siamese Family Law may be altered.... I say that not because we are afraid to take responsibilities, but because this is a matter on which I feel we are not qualified to submit proposals to the Government.... We would have been of course quite prepared to substitute monogamy for polygamy in the draft, if instructed by the Government to do so. But it would have been mere presumption on our part even to simply raise the point. It seems very difficult for a man who has been born and brought up in one of the systems to form an independent opinion as to whether monogamy is superior to polygamy or not.

The proponents of monogamy, especially Prince Svasti who later in 1916 became Chief Judge of the Supreme Court, judged polygamy by Western moral standards: polygamy was old-fashioned and inappropriate for the modern days and thus, as Prince Svasti stated in his memorandum,

should not appear in the Civil Code; as it would lead to no good result, and may be the means... [where by] foreigners... criticise our morality by saying that our law is not of the same standard as the Western laws, thereby bringing disgrace on our country.

It should be noted that, setting aside the moral attitude underlying the proposal to substitute monogamy for polygamy in the new family law, there was also a feeling that the substitution of monogamy for polygamy would help to facilitate future negotiations for abolition of exterritoriality which a number of Western powers enjoyed in Thailand at that time. It was felt that the Western powers, still enjoying the privilege of consular jurisdiction, would be more inclined to admit the competence of the local courts if they found that the law applied by these courts was nearer to their own.

The debate on whether it was advisable to substitute monogamy for polygamy in the new family law, starting in 1912, went on unabated for some time. Later it was felt that it was better to let the matter take its own course. Time decided in favour of monogamy. In January, 1934, the draft family law providing for a form of monogamy came before parliament for discussion and decision. In March, 1935, the vote was taken, passing the law as Book V of the Civil and Commercial Code.

The Modern Law

The substance of the rules in the new family law generally conforms to the international standard as expressed in most legal systems of Western nations. In addition to the substitution of monogamy for polygamy, the Civil and Commercial Code Book V, while retaining all former rules which are still appropriate, has introduced many new provisions. Some main features which are characteristic of the modern law will be discussed.

Marriage

Since the promulgation of the Civil and Commercial Code Book V, the only mode of making a legal marriage is by registration of the union at the local District Office. Previous to the promulgation of Book V, a legal marriage could be proved by the couple living together openly as husband and wife. But from 1935 onwards, the law recognizes no union unless that union has been duly registered. Apart from the registration of marriage, there are no other formal ceremonies required by law. But customarily a Thai marriage generally consists of a semi-religious ceremony wherein the couple to be married receives the blessing of their elders, followed by a marriage feast, however this ceremony can easily be dispensed with. As long as the couple has registered the union, the law considers them husband and wife.

The law lays down certain conditions which must be fulfilled by the person who wishes to marry. Section 1445 of the Civil and Commercial Code provides that a marriage can take place only if:

(1) the man has completed his seventeenth year of age and the woman her fifteenth year;

(2) the man and the woman are not blood relations in the direct ascendant or descendant line, or brother or sister of full or half blood;

(3) the man or woman is not already the spouse of another person; (to increase the force of this restriction, another requirement is made that a person who has registered his marriage once must prove to the satisfaction of the Registrar that his or her previous marriage has been legally dissolved;)

(4) the man and the woman agree to take each other as husband and wife;

(5) neither the man nor the woman is a person of unsound mind.

If the woman is a widow or a divorcee, the marriage can only take place if not less than three hundred and ten days have elapsed since the dissolution of the marriage; but this rule shall not apply if:

(a) a child has been born during such period, or

(b) the divorced couple remarry, or

(c) there is an order of the court allowing the woman to marry.

Apart from the above conditions listed in Section 1445, the law prohibited the marriage between adopter and the adopted. Another condition is added in the case of a marriage of a minor. He or she cannot marry without the consent of his or her parents or guardian; and such consent must be given in one of the following ways:

(a) the person entitled to give consent may affix his signature in the register at the time of registration of marriage; or

(b) he may give consent by a document in writing stating the names of the parties to the marriage and signed by him; or

(c) in case of necessity, he may declare his assent verbally before at least two witnesses.

Such consent, once given, cannot be revoked.

Concerning the giving of consent, a question arises whether the consent of both parents is required. On this matter, the principle underlying this rule requiring consent seems to be that the minor must receive the consent of the person or persons with whom he lives who have the parental power over him. Thus when his father and mother are alive and living together, he needs the consent of both of them. But when the parents live apart, only the consent of the one with whom he is living is required. When the court has appointed a guardian, however, the consent of the guardian alone seems to be sufficient even though the parents are still alive.

Normally, the Registrar will refuse to register a marriage of a minor when the required consent has not been obtained. However, once there has been a registration of such marriage, the marriage is deemed valid. But the law gives the person whose consent is required the right to bring an action for the cancellation of such marriage. The power of cancellation must be asserted within six months of knowledge of the marriage, and when the minor has ceased to be a minor, or when the woman has become pregnant, the action for cancellation cannot be brought at all.

Apart from the conditions and restrictions described above, Thai family law has no other marriage restrictions in connection with class distinction, special profession, or differences of races. There is, however, one exception: according to the Buddhist Hinnayana rules of orders, the priests of this sect are not allowed to marry.

As has already been stated, normally the Registrar will refuse to register any marriage contrary to the condition of marriage. However, if such marriage has taken place, the law prescribes different effects to it according to the condition which has not been fulfilled.

Firstly, in case of a union in which one or both spouses are below marriageable age, such a marriage is valid but subject to cancellation by the court on application of any interested person other than those who have consented. But such cancellation cannot be made if both husband and wife have reached the required age before the court has made the cancellation, or if the wife has become pregnant by that time.

Secondly, in the case where the marriage is made contrary to any of the conditions listed in Section 1445 (2–5), it is deemed void. These provisions cover such instances as the spouses being within the prohibited degree of kinship, or either of them already married to another person, or either being of unsound mind. This group includes the case where there has been a lack of mutual agreement by the parties to take each other as husband and wife. But in this latter case, if the agreement is defective on account of mistake as to the identity of the other spouse or on account of duress, the marriage is not void but merely voidable. The court may, on application of the person under such mistake or duress, cancel such marriage.

Thirdly, the marriage of a widow or divorcee within the period prohibited by law does not give rise to an action for cancellation of the marriage. The only apparent result of such breach of condition is that the Registrar will refuse to register the marriage. Where the registration of such marriage has been made, the marriage is valid. A child born to the wife during that forbidden period, however, is deemed to be a legitimate child of her previous husband.

Fourthly, in the case where the adopter marries the adopted, such marriage cannot be cancelled. It is therefore generally presumed that the marriage is valid and the relationship created by the adoption ceases upon their marriage.

Although these marriages are void or voidable as the case may be, for all practical purposes they are as effective as valid marriages until the court has pronounced them otherwise. This is due to the provision of Section 1488 which lays down that no person may allege that a marriage is void or voidable unless it has been so decided by judgment of the court. Further, rights acquired by *bona fide* third party before the cancellation of the marriage, and those acquired through such marriage by the person who has married in good faith are protected, as Sections 1494 and 1495 provide that the cancellation of marriage shall not prejudice such rights. Moreover, the party who has married in good faith may bring action claiming compensation from the other party, and if the *bona fide* party be the woman, she may also claim maintenance.

Apart from these, in matters concerning their property, their offspring, and the effect of the cancellation judgment in general, Section 1496 provides that after cancellation of marriage, the provision concerning dissolution of marriage in case of divorce by judgment of the court shall apply *mutatis mutandis*.

Status of the Spouses and Matrimonial Property

Prior to the promulgation of the Civil and Commercial Code Book V, a married woman might be one of the wives of a man but now a woman married under the present Code is *the* wife of her husband, legally at least. Having been so recognized by law, a married woman thus acquires greater protection with respect to her marital rights and property. Her status has now been raised to the position of her husband's equal partner.

However, since someone has to be the head of a family, the law gives that position to the husband. As the head of the conjugal union, he has the right to choose the place of residence and directs what is to be done for maintenance and support of the family. The wife is nevertheless entitled to manage household affairs and to provide for the necessaries of the family suitable to its station in life.

Thai law follows the maxim that husband and wife are one and the same, subject to the rule that he is the head of the conjugal union. Hence, as a consequence of marriage, the wife's property is automatically merged with that of the husband and becomes the common property, with the husband as the manager. In such a case, she cannot dispose of it by legal act without the consent of her husband, except for such expenses as the management of household affairs and for the provision of the necessaries of the family suitable to its station in life.

There are, of course, two exceptions to the general rule that the husband is the manager of the common property. One is when the husband and wife, prior to their marriage, have made an ante-nuptial agreement arranging the management of their common property otherwise. The other is where the court has made an order authorizing the wife to be the manager of the common property.

There is also an exception to the rule that the spouses' properties are merged automatically upon marriage, and that is, each spouse's property which is separate property (*sin suan tua*) does not merge into the common property. Therefore, the wife's separate property continues to belong exclusively to her and she has the sole right to dispose of it. The separate property consists of the following:

(1) property belonging to either spouse before marriage, which has been set aside as separate property by the ante-nuptial agreement;

(2) property for personal use according to station in life, or tools necessary for carrying on the profession of either spouse;

(3) property acquired by either spouse during marriage through a will or gift if it is declared by such will or document of gift to be separate property;

(4) fruits of the separate property;

(5) "Khongman," the property given by the man to the woman on betrothal as security for the marriage.

Since the husband is entitled to manage the common property, he is also entitled by law to bring actions concerning the common property. But in the case where the ante-nuptial agreement has made her the manager of the common property, the wife has the right of action.

In addition to what has been described above, a married woman can, without her husband's consent, do any act binding on their common property and bring actions in connection with it under the following conditions:

(1) in case it is uncertain whether the husband is living or dead;

(2) if the husband has been adjudged incompetent or quasi-incompetent;

(3) if the husband has deserted her;

(4) if the husband, because of unsoundness of mind, is placed in a hospital to be taken care of, and

(5) if the husband has been sentenced to an imprisonment for one year or more, and is undergoing such penalty.

Divorce

The Civil and Commercial Code Book V lays down that divorce may be effected only by mutual consent or by judgment of the court.

The recognition of divorce by mutual consent greatly differentiates Thai family law from that of Western countries. To the people of Christian faith, it was generally believed and accepted that dissolution of marriage should be justified only by death of the spouse. Hence, although divorce is now generally recognized among Christians, a legal device to control divorce is provided through court procedure. Divorce is therefore generally granted only after the court has made inquiries into the causes of dissatisfaction between the spouses. This practice is due to the fact that the family law of such countries is more strongly bound by religion and the belief that whom God has united, no man can separate. In Thailand, on the other hand, where marriage is not strictly bound by religion, the concept of marriage and divorce have generally accorded with popular opinion. Even before the promulgation of the Civil and Commercial Code, divorce by mutual consent was legally permitted. Marriage came from willingness and consent, and thus should be capable of dissolution in the same way.

Divorce effectuated by mutual consent must be made in writing and certified by at least two witnesses. Moreover, where the marriage has been registered as provided by the Code, the registration of divorce must be effected by both husband and wife to make it valid. There is no law prohibiting the divorced couple from remarrying. The remarriage of such a couple would automatically revoke and annul their divorce.

In a case where the consent of the other spouse cannot be obtained, the spouse who desires a divorce can institute a divorce proceeding, alleging that the other spouse has done whatever is provided as the cause for such action by law. If it is proved that the allegation is true, the judgment is given and the marriage is dissolved.

In regard to legal grounds for divorce, Section 1500 of the Code provides as follows:

(1) If the wife has committed adultery, the husband may enter a claim for divorce. The action, however, cannot be brought if he has consented to or connived with the wife's adultery.

(2) If one spouse is guilty of gross misconduct or has caused bodily harm to the other or to his or her ascendents, the latter may enter a claim for divorce.

(3) If one spouse has deserted the other for more than one year or failed to give proper maintenance and support, or committed acts seriously adverse to the relationship of husband and wife to such an extent that the other cannot continue cohabitation as husband and wife, the latter may enter a claim for divorce.

(4) If one spouse has been sentenced by a final judgment to imprisonment for theft, snatching, robbery, gang robbery, piracy, or false money, or has been sentenced by a final judgment for any other offense to imprisonment for more than three years, the other may enter a claim for divorce. Such a claim may not be entered, however, if the spouse desiring to divorce has consented to or connived with committing of any of the above offences.

(5) If one spouse has been adjudged to have disappeared, so long as such adjudication has not been revoked, the other may enter a claim for divorce.

(6) If one spouse has been adjudged incompetent on account of unsoundness of mind which has lasted continuously for more than three years since the date of the adjudication and such unsoundness of mind is still incurable so that the continuance of marriage cannot be expected, the other may enter a claim for divorce.

(7) If one spouse has broken a bond of good behaviour executed by him, or her, the other may enter a claim for divorce.

(8) If one spouse is suffering from a communicable and dangerous disease which is incurable or may cause injury to the other spouse, the latter may enter a claim for divorce.

(9) If one spouse has defective genital organs so as to be permanently unable to cohabit as husband and wife, the other may enter a claim for divorce.

Concerning the institution of divorce proceedings, it is laid down by Section 1509 that rights of action based upon the grounds in 1, 2, 3, 4 and 7 above are extinguished after 3 months from the time when the fact which can be alleged by the claimant has been known or ought to have been known to him or her. In any case no action can be brought after two years have elapsed since the ground of action arose. However, grounds upon which a claim for divorce can no longer be based may still be proved in support of another claim for divorce based upon other grounds.

Muslim law

In passing, it should be mentioned that since a great number of persons in the far south of Thailand near the Malayan border adhere to the Islamic religion, Thai law takes cognizance of this fact and lays down that the provisions of the Thai law on family and succession shall not apply to the Muslims. Thus in the disputes concerning family and inheritance where the parties involved are Muslims, the court applies the Muslim law.

Conclusion

The modern codified family law has introduced many new legal rules, which repudiate long established customs of the country. This was undertaken because it was felt that the ancient customs were out of harmony with modern times and should, therefore, be abolished. The legislators replaced those ancient customs with a new way of life, which, to them, is rational, modernistic, and desirable, but alien to the Thai. The law-makers thought that through the legal provisions they enacted, those undesirable ancient customs would cease to exist and the new rational social relations, which they sought to establish, would take root.

Such is an attempt to use *law as an instrument of social change*. As such, law has assumed its new dimension. Traditionally, law is a social phenomenon emanating from a definite social relationship and a given legal pattern reflecting certain conditions of a particular society. Law, as such, was *a specialized form of social control*. But law in its new dimension, exemplified by the modern Thai family law, assumes another function. The attempt now in many developing countries is to use law as an instrument of social change.

However, the Thai experience since the promulgation of the new family law in 1935 indicates that the law has not succeeded in eradicating polygamy, which it has attempted to do. Statistics are not available, but the general impression is that, in spite of the law, the practice of polygamy seems to continue undiminished. Such a departure of law from custom has created added social problems of unmarried mothers and consequently of illegitimate children to a degree unknown under the ancient polygamous law. However, in so far as illigitimacy is concerned, a counteracting measure is found in the provision for affiliation procedure whereby a child born out of wedlock may be legitimized upon consent or request of the father. But in practice, there are not many cases of legitimization. Regarding the unmarried mother, the law turns its back on her and her problems, and the term "unmarried mother" becomes more and more of a stigma.

We turn now from the substance of the law to its form. As has been said, the ancient Thai family law in written form was compiled from long established customs. This ancient legislation was meant to be written evidence of customary rules of law, thus providing greater accessibility. The same was also true of the family code contained in Rama I Code of 1804. Those laws were written in broad terms, making it possible for the judicial power to render interpretations to meet new or changing situations.

The modern family code, characteristic of modern standards of codification, was so drawn as to render it complete in coverage, logically arranged, and precise and clear in phraseology. But, unfortunately, codifiers, however experienced they may be, cannot foresee the myriad questions which may arise under the provisions they frame. Thus, soon after the family code came into force, many people felt that the law was far from adequate. There are gaps to be filled, and uncertainty and confusion exist. It is worthy of note that the recently established commission of jurists for revision of the Civil and Commercial Code gave first priority to family law revision, because of the urgency and the degree of its inadequacy. However, it seems that there will be no great change in the substance and policy of the law. The revision will mostly concern filling in gaps and altering and modifying wording for greater clarity and precision.

VIII. ISLAM AND CUSTOMARY LAW IN THE MALAYSIAN LEGAL CONTEXT

I. Historical Introduction

The Malays in Malaya did not become Muslims until comparatively recent times and it is generally accepted that the Malays were not Muslims at the time when they migrated from Sumatra. When they came to Malaya they brought with them and preserved much of their ancient customary law. Muslim law has been superimposed on this. Although the Malays are generally strict Muslims they have never adopted the whole of the Muslim law, and the Muslim law which is applied in Malaya is Muslim law varied by Malay custom.

The Malays in Malaya are said to have originally come from the Minangkabau highlands of Sumatra. Some are said to have come directly and brought with them the pure Malay law of Minangkabau, the matriarchal *adat perpateh* and the tribal organization. Others are reputed to have arrived by way of Palembang, where during the centuries of Hindu and monarchical influence the tribal organization has broken down, and they are believed to have brought with them the patriarchal *adat temenggong*.

In Malaya, the greater part of Negri Sembilan and the Naning district of Malacca follow the *adat perpateh*.[1] The immigrants brought with them the *adat perpateh*, which still exists to this day. In purely *perpateh* tradition, sovereignty in the state resides in the subjects of the state. Power and authority are vested in their elected representatives. Society consists of the individual, the family, then the tribes, who constitute the components of the state. In the *perpateh* set-up of Negri Sembilan there are twelve tribes in all. Each tribe is presided over by a *lembaga* or headman and the twelve tribes in turn come under the authority of four *undangs*, each of whose jurisdiction extends in his *luak* or district. Finally, the state is governed by the ruler who is the Supreme Head of the state. "Constitutionally" it is laid down by custom that:

> The individuals elect the elder
> The elders elect the Lembaga

[1] The early immigrants from the *perpateh* hinterland of Sumatra settled on the upper reaches of the Muar River to establish the territory of Ulu Muar and Jempol; on the Linggi and Rembau Rivers to found the States of Sungei Ujong and Rembau; on the course of the Malacca River to found the States of Naning, Johol and Inas; and on the Triang River to found the State of Jelebu.

The Lembaga elect the Undang
The Undang enthrone the Ruler.[1]

Power is vested in these various chieftains after they are elected and the exercise of such powers is defined and determined. Thus:

The Ruler rules the State
The Undang rules the *luak* (district)
The Lembaga rules the tribe
The elder rules his followers.[2]

Before the integration of the various territories of Negri Sembilan each of the constituent members was ruled by an *Undang*. At this period before the Confederation of the State of Negri Sembilan in 1773, each *luak* was a state owing a remote allegiance to the *temenggong* or Sultan of Johore. It was in 1773 that Raja Melewar, a member of the Royal House of Minangkabau, was invited to be the first ruler of Negri Sembilan. This brought Negri Sembilan in line with the other states in Malaya in having rulers of royal lineage and this constitutes the *adat temenggong* element in the constitution of Negri Sembilan.[3]

In the other states of Malaya, the *adat temenggong* became identified with the Muslim system and absorbed the institution of the Sultanate. The customary *temenggong* states became Muslim Sultanate states. In time the teachings of Islam were absorbed into the *adat temenggong* and the two became parts of one system, though traces of the *adat temenggong* are still to be found, especially in the inheritance of Malay holdings.[4]

II. Federal Constitution

The Federal Constitution provides in effect that in every state, which has a ruler, the position of the ruler as the Head of the Muslim religion in his state in the manner and to the extent acknowledged and declared by the Constitution of that state and subject to the Federal Constitution all rights, privileges and powers enjoyed by him as Head of the Muslim Religion, shall remain unaffected and unimpaired. Thus

[1] Bulat anak buah menjadi buapak / Bulat buapak menjadi Lembaga / Bulat Lembaga menjadi Undang / Bulat Undang menjadi Raja.

[2] Raja memerentah alam / Undang memerentah luak / Lembaga memerentah Suku / Buapak memerentah anak buah-nya.

[3] Haji Mohamed Din bin Ali, "Two Forces in Malay Society," *Intisari*, (Singapore, 1962) Vol. 1, No. 3, p. 15f.

[4] *Ibid.*

we find it provided in the Constitutions of the States of Johore, Kelantan, Pahang, Perak, Selangor and Trengganu that the ruler shall be the Head of the Muslim religion in the state. In Negri Sembilan the ruler is the Head of the Muslim religion, but in exercising his functions, he is required to obtain the concurrence of the *Undangs*. In Malacca, Penang and Singapore it is provided that the Yang di-Pertuan Agong shall be the head of the Muslim religion in the state.[1]

The Federal Constitution provides that the Muslim personal and family law and Malay custom are matters within the legislative and executive competence and jurisdiction of the states.[2] No law with respect to any matters of Muslim law or the custom of the Malays may be made by the Federal Parliament even for the purpose of implementing a treaty, agreement or convention between the Federation or any other country or any decision of an international organization of which the Federation is a member until the government of any state concerned has been consulted.[3]

In some of the states of Malaya there is provision for the constitution of a *Majlis Ugama Islam dan Adat Istiadat Melayu* to aid and advise the ruler on all matters relating to the religion of the state and Malay custom. In Selangor, Kelantan and Pahang it is provided that the *Majlis* shall be the chief authority in these matters in the state and that the *Majlis* shall take notice of and act upon all written laws in force in the state, the provisions of *Hukom Shara* (Muslim law) and the ancient custom of the state of Malay customary law. A legal committee consisting of the *Mufti*,[4] not more than two other members of the *Majlis* and not less than two other fit and proper persons (who may be members of the *Majlis* or not) is constituted. Power is given to the legal committee and *Majlis* to make and issue rulings (*fetua*) on any point of Muslim law or doctrine or Malay customary law. It is provided that in making and issuing any such ruling the *Majlis* and the legal committee shall ordinarily follow the orthodox tenets of the *Shafii* school of law. If it is considered however that the following of such orthodox tenets will be opposed to the public interest, the *Majlis* may, unless the

[1] Federal Constitution, Article 3; Constitution of the State of Johore, Articles LVII and LVIIA; Constitution of the State of Kelantan, Articles V and VI; Constitution of the State of Pahang, Article 24; Constitution of the State of Perak, Article VI; Constitution of the State of Selangor, Article XLVIII; Constitution of the State of Trengganu, Article IV; Constitution of the State of Negri Sembilan. Articles V and VI.

[2] Federal Constitution, Ninth Schedule List II.

[3] Federal Constitution, Article 76(2).

[4] The *mufti* or jurisconsult is a specialist on law who can give authoritative opinions on points of doctrine.

ruler shall otherwise direct, follow the less orthodox tenets of the *Shafii* school. Further if it is considered that the following of either the orthodox or the less orthodox tenets of the *Shafii* school will be opposed to the public interest the *Majlis* may, with the special sanction of the ruler, follow the tenets of any of the *Hanafi*, *Maliki* or *Hanbali* schools, as may be considered appropriate. In making and issuing any such ruling the *Majlis* shall have regard to the *adat istiadat Melayu* or the Malay customary law applicable in the state.[1]

In Trengganu it is provided that the *Majlis Ugama Islam dan Adat Melayu* shall aid and advise the ruler in all matters relating to the religion of the state and Malay custom. The *Majlis* shall take notice of and act upon all written laws in force in the state, the provisions of the *Hukom Shara* (Muslim law) and the ancient custom of the state or Malay customary law. Power is given to the *Mufti* to make and issue any rulings (*fetua*) on any point of Muslim law or doctrine and to the *Majlis* to make and issue any rulings on Malay customary law.[2]

In Perlis it is provided that the *Majlis Ugama Islam dan Adat Istiadat Melayu* shall advise the ruler on all matters relating to the Muslim religion and Malay custom and such advice shall be given in accordance with Muslim law (*Hukom Shara*) and such other Malay customary laws as may be applicable in the state. The *Majlis* shall, when requested by any person or any court to do so, issue a *fetua* or ruling on questions relating to the Muslim religion or Malay custom. A *Shara'aih* committee consisting of the *Mufti*, two members of the *Majlis* and two persons, not being members of the *Majlis*, who profess the orthodox Muslim religion (*Ahli Sunnah waljamaah*) is established for the purpose of advising the *Majlis* on any matter relating to a *fetua* to be issued by it. The *Majlis* when issuing such a ruling shall follow the *Quran* and the *Sunnah* of the Prophet, but where the following of such teachings would be opposed to the public interest, the *Majlis* shall refer such ruling to the Ruler for his decision. In issuing such rulings the *Majlis* shall have

[1] Selangor Administration of Muslim Law Enactment, 1952, Ss. 5, 37, 38, 41 and 42; Kelantan Council of Religion and Malay Custom and Kathis Courts Enactment, 1953, Ss. 5, 38, 39, 42 and 43; Pahang Administration of the Law of the Religion of Islam Enactment, 1956, Ss. 5, 30, 31, 33 and 34.

[2] Trengganu Administration of Islamic Law Enactment, 1955, Ss. 9, 18 and 20.

In making and issuing any ruling upon any point of Muslim law or doctrine the *Mufti* is required ordinarily to follow the orthodox tenets of the *Shafii* school, but if the *Mufti* considers it to be in the interest and welfare of the Muslim community he may issue a *fetua* within the tenets of any of the four schools. In making and issuing any ruling upon a point of Malay customary law the *Majlis* shall have regard to the *Adat Istiadat Melayu* or Malay customary law applicable in the state; and if the point concerns in any manner the Muslim law, the *Majlis* shall refer the matter to the *Mufti* for his advice.

due regard to the *adat istiadat Melayu* or Malay customary law applicable in the state.[1]

In Perak it is provided that the *Majlis Ugama Islam dan Adat Melayu* shall advise the ruler in all matters relating to the Muslim religion and the Malay custom. No specific provision is made for the issuing of *fetuas* but it is provided that no member of the *Majlis* who is not a subject of the ruler and who is not a Malay shall take part in any discussion relating to matters of purely Malay custom. "*Adat Melayu*" is defined as that portion of the *adat* or custom having the force of law which has been acted on, or is in force in the state, and which is commonly known as "*Harta Sapencharian*" but shall not include that portion of the "*adat*" known as "*adat resam*" except as authorized from time to time by the State Executive Council.[2]

In Negri Sembilan, Penang, Malacca and Kedah the *Majlis* is the *Majlis Ugama Islam* and no provision is made for advice or rulings on the Malay customary law. The *Majlis Ugama Islam* is constituted to aid and advise the ruler (or in the case of Penang and Malacca, the Yang di-Pertuan Agong) in matters relating to Muslim religion in the state. A legal committee (in Kedah called the *Fetua* Committee) is constituted consisting of the *Mufti*, two members of the *Majlis* and not less than two or more than six other fit and proper Muslims who are not members of the *Majlis*. Power is given to the *Majlis* and the legal committee of the *Majlis* to issue *fetuas* on any point of Muslim law, and in issuing any such ruling the *Majlis* and the legal committee are ordinarily required to follow the orthodox tenets of the *Shafii* school.[3]

In Johore too the *Majlis* is the *Majlis Ugama Islam*, whose duty is to aid and advise the ruler in all matters relating to the religion of Islam.[4]

In Sarawak the *Majlis Islam* is given the English title of "Council of Religion and Malay Custom." It is provided that the *Majlis* shall aid and advise the governor on all matters relating to the Muslim religion and Malay customary law of the state and shall in all such matters be the chief authority in the state. Power is given to the *Majlis* to issue *fetuas* on any point of Muslim law or doctrine or Malay customary law

[1] Perlis Administration of Muslim Law Enactment, 1963, Ss. 4, 5, 7 and 8.

[2] Perak Majlis Ugama Islam dan Adat Melayu Enactment, 1951, Ss. 3–5.

[3] Negri Sembilan Administration of Muslim Law Enactment, 1960, Ss. 4, 37 and 38; Penang Administration of Muslim Law Enactment, 1959, Ss. 4, 36 and 37; Malacca Administration of Muslim Law Enactment, 1959, Ss. 4, 36 and 37; Kedah Administration of Muslim Law Enactment, 1962, Ss. 4, 37 and 38.

But where the following of such tenets would be opposed to the public interest the *Majlis* may follow the less orthodox tenets of the *Shafii* school, or, with the special permission of the Ruler or the Yang di-Pertuan Agong, the tenets of the *Hanafi*, *Maliki* or *Hanbali* schools.

[4] Johore Council of Religion Enactment, 1949, Ss. 2 and 3.

of the state. In making and issuing any such ruling the *Majlis* is ordinarily required to follow the orthodox tenets of the *Shafii* school.[1]

III. Malay Custom and Muslim Law in the Malaysian Legal Context

Malay custom has modified the Muslim law in its application to the Malays in Malaysia, and it is proposed to examine the modifications in relation to (a) the law of marriage and divorce, (b) the law relating to guardianship and adoption, and (c) the law relating to property and inheritance.

A. Marriage

Under the Malay custom a marriage is regarded not merely as a personal, but as a family and tribal tie as well, and there are elaborate ceremonies for the betrothal. Even outside the *adat perpateh* areas a Muslim marriage in Malaysia is often preceded by a betrothal. The first move is made by the man's family which ascertains from the girl's family whether a proposal would be favorably received. When an understanding has been reached, the parties proceed to set the date of the marriage and the precise amounts of the payments for *maskahwin* and presents. There may be a formal ceremony of betrothal at the girl's home, which finalizes the contract between the two families.[2]

In Negri Sembilan the ceremonies are more elaborate. First there is the *menghantar chinchin* or "sending the ring" ceremony. This is done by depositing a ring with the parents of the prospective bride. This signifies a request for the bride's hand on the part of an interested groom. A feast is held to which the bride's relatives are invited, the ring is shown and at the same time opinion and approval are sought. If the relatives do not approve the marriage the ring is returned to the suitor.

[1] Sarawak Majlis Islam (Incorporation) Ordinance (Cap. 105 of the Laws of Sarawak, 1958), S. 4, 33, 37 and 38.

But where the following of such tenets would be opposed to the public interest, the *Majlis* may follow the less orthodox tenets of the *Shafii* school or, with the special sanction of the Governor, the tenets of the *Hanafi, Maliki* or *Hanbali* schools. In making and issuing any such ruling the *Majlis* shall have due regard to the Malay customary law applicable in the state. Further if it is considered that the following of either the orthodox or the less orthodox tenets of the *Shafii* school will be opposed to the public interest, the *Majlis* may, with the special sanction of the governor, follow the tenets of any of the *Hanafi, Maliki* or *Hanbali* schools, which may be considered appropriate. In making and issuing any such ruling the *Majlis* shall have regard for the *Adat Istiadat Melayu* or the Malay customary law applicable in the state.

[2] See M. Siraj, "Muslim Marriages in Singapore," *World Muslim League Magazine* (January. 1964), p. 41f; Ahmad bin Mohamed Ibrahim, "Status of Muslim Women in Family Law in Malaysia," *Malaya Law Review* (December 1963), p. 314 f.

If the proposal is accepted, another ceremony is held, to which the relatives of both parties are invited. Here the *chinchin tanya* or seeking ring is circulated to be viewed and examined by the relatives present, symbolizing the discussion of the merits and demerits of the bridegroom to be. The appearance of the double ring signifies that the match is agreed upon and the agreement is sealed under the custom expressed thus:

> One ring to sound the parents
> Two rings unanimous agreement
> Approval entails the customary covenants
> Repudiation by the man he forfeits the token
> Breach by the bride she repays twofold
> Blemish of either the pact is annulled
> Insanity and lunacy are outside the pact.[1]

In Sarawak Malay custom regarding betrothal is briefly: first the boy's parents will approach those of the girl to talk about the possibility of marriage. If the boy is acceptable and agreement is reached generally the second stage is to take a *tekol*[2] to the girl's parents. This *tekol* in practice must take place within seven days of the agreement's being reached. If the boy breaks the agreement and does not take the *tekol* to the girl's parents he will be liable for the offence called *balak pengamang* and liable for a fine; but if the girl breaks the agreement before the *tekol* is received, she is not guilty of any offence. The third stage is *pertunangan* or betrothal which must take place within one month of the giving of the *tekol*, failing which the *tekol* will lapse. If the betrothal does not take place due to the default of either party, he or she will be liable to a fine; and if it is the girl who defaults, she will have to return the *tekol*. After the betrothal comes the last stage, marriage, which should be solemnized within one year of the betrothal. Failure to do so on the part of the boy will entitle the girl to sue him for *mungkir* or breach of promise to marry. If either party breaks the betrothal agreement, he or she will be liable to a fine and if it is the girl who breaks the agreement, she will have to return the betrothal gifts or their value.[3]

[1] Chinchin sabentok menanya ibu bapa nya / Chinchin dua bentok oso sekata / Oso sekata janji di-ikat, / Elah si-laki lonchor tanda, / Elah si-perempuan ganda tanda / Chachat chida berkembalian / Sawan gila luar janji.

See Haji Mohamed Din bin Ali, "Two Forces in Malay Society," *op. cit.*, p. 25.

[2] The word *tekol* is used in colloquial Malay in Sarawak to mean an object, usually a weight, placed on a lighter object to prevent the latter from being shifted or blown away. *Tekol* usually takes the form of money, precious metal or stone, such as gold or diamond rings.

[3] *Sarawak Undang-Undang Makhamah Melayu*, Sarawak, Ss. 1–20; Ahmad bin Mohamed Ibrahim, "Status of Muslim Women in Family Law in Malaysia," *op. cit.*, p. 317.

In the states of Malaya provision is made in law for breaches of the betrothal agreement. In Selangor, Negri Sembilan, Penang, Malacca and Kedah it is provided that where a party to a contract of betrothal breaks such contract without lawful reason and the other party is willing to carry out the contract, the party in default is liable to pay to the other party the sum which was agreed in the contract. If the defaulting party is the groom-to-be he has also to pay as damages the amount of the *maskahwin*, and in Negri Sembilan, Malacca and Kedah also the *hantaran*, which would have been payable together with other moneys expended in good faith in preparation for the marriage.[1] If the woman defaults she has to return the betrothal gifts, if any, or the value thereof in addition to paying the agreed damages.[2] In Kelantan, Trengganu and Pahang, if a person who has entered into a contract of betrothal refuses to marry the other party and the other party is willing to fulfill the contract, the defaulter (if male) is liable to be adjudged to pay the value of the *maskahwin* which would have been paid had the marriage taken place, together with other moneys expended in good faith in preparation for the marriage. If the woman defaults, she has to return the betrothal gifts, if any, or the value thereof, in addition to paying the agreed damages or the amount expended in preparation for the marriage.[3] In Perlis it is provided that where a party to a contract of betrothal breaks such contract, such party shall be liable to pay to the other the sum agreed in the contract and, if male, to pay the amount of the *maskahwin* payable under the contract and such other sums as may have been expended by the other party in good faith in preparation for effecting the terms of the contract; and where the party so liable is female, the return of the betrothal gifts or the value thereof, and such other sums expended by the other party in good faith in prepa-

If the engagement or betrothal is broken because of the interference of a third person, such person is liable to a fine and restrictions are imposed on the marriage of the party who broke the engagement or betrothal to the person who caused it to be broken.

[1] *Maskahwin* is the obligatory marriage payment due under Muslim law by the husband to the wife at the time the marriage is solemnised. *Hantaran* is the obligatory cash payment due to be paid under local custom by the bridegroom to the bride at the time the marriage is solemnised.

[2] Selangor Administration of Muslim Law Enactment, 1952, S. 124; Negri Sembilan Administration of Muslim Law Enactment, 1960, S. 119; Penang Administration of Muslim Law Enactment, 1959, S. 119; Malacca Administration of Muslim Law Enactment, 1959, S. 118; Kedah Administration of Muslim Law Enactment, S. 119.

[3] Kelantan Council of Religion and Malay Custom and Kathis Courts Enactment, 1953, S. 137; Trengganu Administration of Islamic Law Enactment, 1955, S. 95; Pahang Administration of the Law of the Religion of Islam Enactment, 1956, S. 117. In Pahang the female party has to pay as damages the amount agreed in the contract, by which the marriage was arranged, to be paid by her on breach of the contract.

ration for effecting the terms of the contract.[1] In the other states where no express provision is made for breach of the contract of betrothal, the consequences of the breach will be expressly provided for by the parties. In Singapore, for example, it is usual to stipulate that if the breach is on the man's side he will forfeit the presents or payments given by him; if the breach is on the girl's side the man will be entitled to payment of double the value of the presents or expenses given or incurred by him.

Although the Muslim marriage is in essence a contract effected by the *akad nikah*, that is the declaration of offer on the part of the one party and the acceptance by the other in the presence of at least two witnesses, custom imposes a number of ceremonies. The most outstanding feature of a Malay marriage is the *bersanding* or the sitting in state of the bride and bridegroom on the bridal throne, the "Rajas for a day." This ceremony, which is Hindu in origin, holds a greater significance to the ordinary Malay than the proceedings of the *akad nikah*. Indeed so important is the *bersanding* ceremony that in a form of marriage known as the *nikah gantong*, literally suspended marriage, the couple, although wedded in the eyes of religion, may not live together or even see each other in private until the *bersanding* is held months or even years later. This in effect reduces the Muslim marriage ceremony to the status of an engagement. The *berhinai* or *henna* ceremony is another evidence of the importance of custom in Malay marriage. This again is Hindu in origin although the significance of the ritual has been forgotten by most Malays. The *berhinai* ceremony is held before the *akad nikah* and the *bersanding* and the essential part of the ceremony is the staining of the finger tips (originally the anointing of the bride's forehead) and the obeisance to the guests by touching the forehead with the tips of the fingers held together. Among the Malays of Malacca, Johore, Negri Sembilan and Selangor it is also customary to dress the bride in ancient Chinese costumes on a night of the *berhinai* ceremonies. The fashion started after one of the rulers of old Malacca took as his bride a Chinese woman sent by the Emperor of China. Through the centuries what began as a fashion became an integral part of Malay wedding customs. While the *bersanding* has been made to appear as a Muslim ceremony by the recitation of Muslim benedictions or *doa* before the *pelamin*, no such attempt has been made with the *berhinai* ceremony. There are other customary practices usually followed in Malay marriages. It is usual to have ornamental trays of flowers and

[1] Perlis Administration of Muslim Law Enactment, 1963, S. 88.

betel leaves and rose water sprinklers for the engagement ceremony and for the wedding ceremony. On the day of the *bersanding*, the bridegroom is invited to the home of the bride by the sending of *sireh latlat* (bouquet of betel leaves). When the bridegroom arrives at the home of the bride it is usual for the entry of the bridegroom and his friend to be barred at one or more places before reaching the bridal throne and some token payment will be made to open the way. At the throne another payment will have to be made to the *Mak Andam* (or mistress of ceremonies) as it is customary for her to hold a fan in front of the bride so that she cannot be seen. If the payment to her is satisfactory, the *Mak Andam* will remove the fan and lead the bridegroom to the throne. After the *bersanding* it is customary to have a ceremonial bathing of the bride and bridegroom. There are also elaborate ceremonies for the *bertandang* or visit of the couple to the bridegroom's house to be introduced to his family.[1]

The Malay customary rules regarding the *maskahwin* represent a compromise between Muslim law and the ancient Malay custom. The Muslim law recognizes the payment of the *mahr*, the gift given by the groom to the bride. Malay custom on the other hand insists on a whole series of conventional presents, beginning with the betrothal and sometimes continuing till the birth of the first child or even later. A sort of compromise has been arrived at by identifying one of these many presents, the *maskahwin*, with the Muslim *mahr*. *Maskahwin* originally meant money paid by the bridegroom to the bride's parents but is now like the Muslim *mahr* paid (or more usually promised and left as an outstanding debt to be paid on divorce) to the bride herself.

While the Muslim law fixes no specific amount for the *maskahwin*, under the Malay custom the *maskahwin* is fixed and normally depends on the rank of the father of the bride. In Negri Sembilan for example the amount of the *maskahwin* must be the traditionally accepted amount as fixed by custom in the particular area. The customary *maskahwin* among the peasantry in Negri Sembilan is twenty-four dollars. A bridegroom may be asked to pay varying amounts to the bride's parents depending upon the status, education and eligibility of the bride. But whatever sum is asked for, the legal customary *maskahwin* must be the amount fixed by custom, that is twenty-four dollars. The rest is regarded as being for the personal and ceremonial expenses of the oc-

[1] M. Siraj, "Muslim Marriages in Singapore," *op. cit.* p. 43f; Dr. Mahathir bin Mohamed, "Interaction and Integration," *Intisari*, (Singapore), Vol. 1, No. 3, p. 39f; Tengku Pekirma Wira, "Custom in Trengganu," *Intisari*, (Singapore), Vol. 1, No. 4, p. 38f.

casion. Such customary expenses are called *belanja hangus* or incidental expenditures and are quite apart from the *maskahwin*. In Pahang it is provided that the amount of the *maskahwin* may be fixed from time to time by the ruler in council. In Perak according to the *Ninety-Nine Laws of Perak*, the fixed amount of *maskahwin* for all ordinary persons was a *tahil* and a *paha* of gold at the most; in the case of Hashimites (that is Arabs descended from the family of the Prophet) five *tahils* of gold. It is stated that rank has to be considered in such cases. At present the amount of the *maskahwin* in Perak varies with the status of the father of the bride ranging from fifty dollars for the daughter of a commoner to one thousand dollars for the daughter of the ruler. In the districts of Naning and Alor Gajah in Malacca which follow the Malay custom the amount of *maskahwin* is fixed at sixty dollars for an unmarried woman and forty dollars for a previously married woman.[1]

The term used for the *maskahwin* in Sarawak and Sabah is *berian*. In Sabah the minimum amount payable as *berian* in the various districts is prescribed by rules and varies from fifty dollars to two-hundred dollars in the case of an unmarried girl, and forty dollars to sixty dollars in the case of a woman who has been previously married. Among the Ilanun and Bajau races in the Kota Belud district of Sabah, the *berian* was originally paid in weight of brass cannon but this custom has been replaced by fixed cash payments, the basis of which is however still the weight of brass cannon and is so referred to locally. The amount varies according to the class to which the father of the bride belongs.[2]

An addition to the *maskahwin* provision is made in the states of Malaya for the payment of *hantaran*, the obligatory cash payment due under local custom from the bridegroom to the bride at the time the marriage is solemnized; the *pemberian*, the optional marriage settlement, in cash or in kind, made by the husband to the wife at the time of the marriage; and the *belanja* or optional expense agreed upon by both parties at the time of the betrothal. The *belanja*, *pemberian* and *hantaran* are customary, but details of them are mentioned during the religious ceremony of *akad nikah* and they are included in the marriage register.[3]

[1] Haji Mohamed Din bin Ali, "Two Forces in Malay Society," *op. cit.* at p. 27; Pahang Administration of the Law of the Religion of Islam Enactment, 1956, S. 2; Mahmud Ahmad, *Kebudayan Sa-pintas Lalu*, Singapore, 1960, pp. 144–145; *The Ninety-Nine Laws of Perak* (edited and translated by J. Rigby, Kuala Lumpur) 1908, p. 23.

[2] *Undang-Undang Makhamah Melayu*, Sarawak (Appendix); North Borneo Muslims Berian and Fees Rules Laws of North Borneo, 1953, Vol. 5, p. 353; D. Headly, "Some Ilanun and Bajau Marriage Customs in the Kota Belud District, North Borneo," 1950, *Journal of the Malayan Branch of the Royal Asiatic Society*. (Part 3), p. 159.

[3] Ahmad bin Mohamed Ibrahim, "The Status of Muslim Women in the Family Law in Malaysia," *op. cit.*, p. 329f.

The preference of custom for payments to be fixed is also seen in the rules relating to the payment of maintenance for the support of the wife in the *adat perpateh* areas. In Rembau for example where a husband fails to support his wife she can apply for maintenance in the *kathi's* court; the rate is fixed by custom at $6/– a month irrespective of the means of the parties or the number of children of the marriage. Similarly on divorce by the husband, the wife is entitled to maintenance during the *eddah* at the conventional rate of $6/– a month.[1]

The marriage feast, although encouraged by Islam, is elaborated under the Malay custom. In Negri Sembilan for a spinster, especially if hers is the first marriage in the family, the slaughter of a buffalo, or cattle, is considered the usual practice. To this marriage ceremony both the *lembaga* and the headmen of the two tribes are invited, their presence being regarded as tacit approval of the marriage. In the other states of Malaysia, the marriage feast is usually held after the *akad nikah* to give publicity to the marriage.[2]

While Muslim law forbids marriage within the relationship of agnates, the *adat perpateh* goes further and bars marriage between cognates. Thus marriage between maternal cousins is not allowed in the *adat perpateh* areas of Negri Sembilan although it is allowed and common in the other states. Marriage or liaison during a wife's lifetime with another woman of her tribe was punishable by death under the custom in Negri Sembilan, but marriage with a deceased wife's sister is a common practice, as it provides for the welfare of the children of the wife's tribe. The children of a brother and sister can intermarry, as belonging to different maternal tribes; but illogically the marriage of children of brothers, although their mothers may belong to different tribes, is forbidden.[3]

Muslim law also forbids intermarriage between persons related by fosterage but fosterage is not frequent in Malaysia. According to the *Ninety-Nine Laws of Perak*, when foster children marry according to the law of this world they may do so but their respective mothers must meet and forgive them so that they may obtain pardon. A man may even marry a woman who has been suckled by his own wife, but alms must be distributed in the mosque.[4]

Polygamy though permitted in Islam is in practice rare among the

[1] E. N. Taylor, "Customary Law of Rembau in 1929," *Journal of the Malayan Branch of the Royal Asiatic Society*, Part I, p. 17.
[2] Haji Mohamed Din bin Ali, "Two Forces in Malay Society," *op. cit.*, p. 25.
[3] *Ibid.*, p. 23; R. O. Winstedt, *The Malay* (London, 1961) p. 59.
[4] *The Ninety-Nine Laws of Perak*, *op. cit.*, p. 49.

kampong or rural Malays while common among the urban Malays. Under the custom it is an offence to take another wife within the same tribe. It is an offence, says custom, to take two when one is given. The Hindu law allowed three wives for a Brahman, two for a Kshatriya and one for the Vaisya. Similarly polygamy was a symbol of rank in old Malay society. In Negri Sembilan custom prescribed that only the ruler could have four wives, only an *Undang* or territorial chief three, only a *Lembaga* or tribal chief two, and the ordinary folk one. Monogamy is preferred under the custom as being the surest guarantee that a tribeswoman and her children will be supported. A second marriage destroys half the man's value as a tribal asset. Custom thus reduces the incidence of polygamy and encourages monogamy. In Rembau a man may not marry a second wife without obtaining the special sanction of the ruler, while in the other states which follow the *adat* the first wife's consent is expected before a second wife is taken. In Sarawak it is provided that a person is permitted to marry more than one wife, as for example where he has money or houses or estates, or is in receipt of an ample salary. The proper maintenance payable for each wife is fixed at from twenty dollars to fifty dollars a month.[1]

The usual custom in the *adat perpateh* areas in Malaya is that the husband stays with the wife or her family, and even outside the *adat perpateh* areas it is customary for the husband to live in the house of his bride for some period after the marriage ceremony. In Sarawak it is provided that if the husband, contrary to the usual custom, asks the wife to leave her family and stay with him or his family, she will not be asked to do so unless the husband can provide a separate house for her in her village, or if there is no place available in her village, at some other place. If however the husband has to stay at a particular place because of his work, then the wife must accompany him.[2]

B. Divorce

Custom lays down certain rules and rituals to be followed in the case of divorce. Just as marriage entails the co-relationship of a host of tribal relatives, if not of tribes themselves, so too divorce entails a break-up of such relationships and might produce considerable social embarrassment if not open quarrels. Custom requires that before a divorce takes

[1] R. O. Winstedt, *op. cit.*, p. 59; R. J. Wilkinson, *Malay Law*, (Kuala Lumpur, 1908), p. 54; Haji Mohamed Din bin Ali, "Two Forces in Malay Society," *op. cit.*, p. 25; Sarawak *Undang-Undang Makhamah Melayu*, s. 37.

[2] R. J. Wilkinson, *Malay Law*, *op. cit.*, p. 30; *Undang-Undang Makhamah Melayu*, Sarawak' s. 43.

place there should be due deliberation on the reasons for the intended dissolution. The husband who contemplates divorce from his wife must go through conciliation or arbitration called *bersuarang* or settlement. A small feast is held by the husband to which he invites both his wife's relatives and his own. The husband will then state his grievances, so that they may be considered by the persons present. In many cases the presence of the elders proves beneficial in patching up the differences between the parties and helps to mend a hasty decision or an irrelevant quarrel. But if the husband still insists on divorce, despite the counsel and advice given to the parties, separation will be allowed after a settlement of the conjugal property.[1]

The division of the conjugal property plays an important part in the divorce under custom and follows the principle:

Joint earnings are shared
Wife's property remains
Husband's property returned
The union is dissolved
Settlement permits a gift.[2]

Marriage property falls into three classes. That which is acquired during the marriage is called *harta charian* which is shared. That which the husband brought at the time of the marriage, called *harta pembawa*, reverts to the husband. That which belonged to the wife at the time of the marriage, *harta dapatan*, remains in the wife's possession. When this settlement is agreed upon, then the marriage is dissolved. The husband may leave a portion of his share of the property to the children of the marriage because under the *adat perpateh* the children belong to the mother and her tribe. Thereafter the responsibility of the father for the children ceases altogether under the custom, and the mother has custody of the children.[3] It has been held under the positive law of Malaysia in *Alus* v. *Mohamed*[4] that a husband is liable to pay for past maintenance of his children only if an order of the *kathi* has been made directing the husband to pay such maintenance or authorizing the wife to recover the expenses of maintenance of the children. In *Jemiah binte Awang* v. *Abdul Rashid bin Haji Ibrahim*[5] it was held that the rule

[1] Haji Mohamed Din bin Ali, "Two Forces in Malay Society," *op. cit.*, p. 26.
[2] Chari bahagi / Dapatan tinggal / Pembawa Kembali / Sekutu Belah / Suarang berageh.
[3] Haji Mohamed Din bin Ali, "Two Forces in Malay Society," *op. cit.*, p. 27.
[4] E. N. Taylor, "Malay Family Law," in 1937 *Journal of the Malayan Branch of the Royal Asiatic Society*, Part I, p. 67.
[5] (1941) *M.L.J.* 16.

under the *adat* whereby a husband after divorce is not liable for the support of his children does not apply where he is lawfully practising polygamy. Horne J. said "As he cannot do so lawfully under the *adat* I think it right to regard him as a person whose civil rights and duties in respect of wives and children fall to be dealt with under the rules of the Muhammadan law as varied by local custom."

In the other states of Malaya it has been held that a divorced wife is entitled to a share of all property acquired during the marriage. Where she has in fact assisted in cultivating the land she is entitled to one half of the jointly-acquired land and in other cases to one-third of the jointly acquired property (*harta sapencharian*).[1] According to the Malay custom the guardians at a lawful marriage should inquire as to the separate property of the man and the woman so that on divorce it may be returned to the owner, while property acquired during marriage is divided equally. If separate property has vanished during the marriage and the joint property acquired during the marriage is large, then the separate property is made good and the residue is the joint property; losses too are divided. If the husband wants to divorce his wife for no fault, then the joint property is divided into three, the man taking one share and the woman two.[2]

According to the *Ninety-nine Laws of Perak*, if a divorce was at the instance of the husband and there was no blame attached to the woman he must provide her with maintenance for three months and the personal property would be divided. Weapons and instruments of iron went to the husband, vessels of brass and household utensils went to the wife. To the wife also belonged the house or plantation, to the husband debts and dues. If a divorce was sought owing to the misbehaviour of the woman—that is on account of her adultery, or neglect of service at bed and board or refusal to do works of charity and to pray—she forfeited her settlements only and the law was that the husband must pay a *paha* of gold. Where a woman sought divorce, if she thrice made out a case of misconduct on the husband's part, she could obtain a divorce; but she must redeem herself by returning the settlements and the movable property went to the husband. If property had been brought from the parents' home, being acquired before the marriage, each party

[1] *Rasinah* v. *Said* reported in E. N. Taylor, "Malay Family Law", *op. cit.*, p. 29. In *Habsah* v. *Abdullah* (1950) *M.L.J.* 60 it was held that on divorce a woman is entitled by customary law to half of any property acquired during the marriage and such a claim is not barred or extinguished by her re-marriage.

[2] J. E. Kempe and R. O. Winstedt, "A Malay Legal Miscellany," (1952) *Journal of the Royal Asiatic Society, Malayan Branch*, Part I, p. 6.

would keep possession of it. Such property was known as separate property and was not thrown into the property to be divided on divorce, but if the parties had lived together for three years and had children, it would be included in the property to be divided.[1]

The Perak State Council has declared that the custom of the Malays in Perak in the matter of dividing up property after divorce when such property has been acquired by the parties, or one of them, during marriage, is to adopt the proportion of two shares to the man and one share to the woman. It has been held that the divorced wife's share may be increased to one-half depending upon the nature of the work actually done by her on the jointly acquired property.[2] In Pahang it has been declared that a woman can claim *harta sapencharian* on divorce. There is no fixed rule as to the share of the divorced wife but either equal or unequal shares may be awarded pursuant to an agreement between the parties or in confirming a gift or by judgment of the *kathi*.[3] In some of the states of Malaya, power is given to the court of the *kathi* to hear and determine actions and proceedings relating to the division or claims to *sapencharian*[4] property. In Sarawak it is provided that if both parties to the marriage have joined in acquiring the matrimonial property, for example—the farm or ricefield—then on divorce the wife is entitled to one-half of the matrimonial property. If on the other hand, the husband is the only earner, then on divorce the wife is entitled to one-third of the matrimonial property.[5]

The general rule of the Malay custom is that the whole matter of property should be settled and done with at the time of the divorce. The husband takes his half share of the *charian laki-bini* and goes back to his tribe; the wife takes her half and remains with her tribe. Claims to partition of *charian laki-bini* must therefore be made at the time of divorce.[6] The division of the property with respect to divorce can be enforced afterwards provided that it was claimed at the time of the divorce.[7] In *Jasin*

[1] *The Ninety-Nine Laws of Perak*, *op. cit.*, pp. 31 and 39.

[2] E. N. Taylor, "Malay Family Law," *op. cit.*, p. 41.

[3] E. N. Taylor, "Malay Family Law," *op. cit.*, p. 73.

[4] Selangor Administration of Muslim Law Enactment, 1952, S. 45(3); Kelantan Council of Religion and Malay Custom and Kathis Courts Enactment, 1953, S. 48(1); Trengganu Administration of Islamic Law Enactment, 1955, S. 25(1); Pahang Administration of the Law of the Religion of Islam Enactment, 1956, S. 37(3); Penang Administration of Muslim Law Enactment, 1959, S. 40(3); Malacca Administration of Muslim Law Enactment, 1959, S. 40(3); Negri Sembilan Administration of Muslim Law Enactment, 1960, S. 41(3); Perlis Administration of Muslim Law Enactment, 1963, Ss. 11 and 94.

[5] *Undang-Undang Makhamah Melayu*, Sarawak, S. 41.

[6] *Rahim* v. *Sintan*, E. N. Taylor, "Customary Law of Rembau," in 1929 *Journal of the Malayan Branch of the Royal Asiatic Society*, Part I, p. 114.

[7] *Si-Alang* v. *Samat*, E. N. Taylor, "Customary Law of Rembau," *op. cit.*, p. 115.

v. *Tiawan*[1] the respondent nine years after her divorce from the appellant brought a claim for half of his land according to the custom because the land was their *charian laki-bini*. It was held that claims to *charian laki-bini* must be brought at the time of the divorce and that therefore in the absence of agreement or misrepresentation at the time the wife could not succeed in her claim to the land after the divorce. In *Hasmah* v. *Abdul Jalil*[2] however it was held that proceedings to recover land which was *charian laki-bini* can be commenced within a reasonable period after divorce. In this case the wife was divorced on 2nd November, 1955, and commenced the proceedings on 30th August, 1956. It was assumed that the *adat* in Kuala Pilah is different from that of Rembau, which was followed in *Jasin* v. *Tiawan*. Evidence was given that on divorce the wife's relatives should decide what should happen to the property and that if the relatives refused or were not asked to do so, a *lembaga* must decide. In the absence of mutual agreement therefore the matter can be referred to the *lembaga* for arbitration or as in this case referred to the court within a reasonable period.

In Sarawak, too, provision is made for the division of the *pencharian* property at divorce. Moreover it is provided that if the married couple has debts and the *pencharian* property is insufficient to pay the debts, the divorce will not be allowed unless the husband undertakes to pay the debts. If the husband has deserted the wife and failed to maintain his wife and children for any period, he will be ordered to pay the arrears of maintenance, the amount being fixed at between $20/– to $50/– a month for the wife and between $10/– to $25/– a month for each child. If the husband is in financial difficulties and cannot pay the arrears, the amount payable will be at the discretion of the court.[3]

In Malaysia it is common at the time of the marriage to require the husband to make a condition or *ta'alik* to enable the wife to obtain a divorce if the husband should abandon her, fail to maintain her for a stated period or assault her. In some states, like Kelantan, Trengganu and Pahang the *ta'alik* is made mandatory[4]; in the other states it is encouraged. In such cases the divorce is suspended to take effect on the breach of the condition and if the husband breaks the condition, the wife can apply to the *kathi* for a divorce by *cherai ta'alik*.[5]

1 *Jasin* v. *Tiawan* (1941) *M.L.J.* 247.
2 *Hasmah* v. *Abdul Jalil* (1958) *M.L.J.* 10.
3 Sarawak *Undang-Undang Makhamah Melayu*, Section 41.
4 Kelantan Council of Religion and Malay Custom and Kathis Courts Enactment, 1953, S. 144(5); Trengganu Administration of Islamic Law Enactment, 1955, S. 102(5); Pahang Administration of the Law of the Religion of Islam Enactment, 1956, S. 124(5).
5 Selangor Administration of Muslim Law Enactment, 1952, S. 128; Kelantan Council

The wife is also given a right to apply to the *kathi* for divorce. In such cases the husband is summoned to the court and asked whether he agrees to divorce the wife or to a divorce by redemption (*kholo'*). If the husband does not agree, the *kathi* may appoint arbitrators to deal with the matter, with power for them to pronounce a divorce on behalf of the husband or to accept a divorce by redemption (*kholo'*).[1] According to the Malay custom if a husband guiltless of offence towards his wife under religious and customary law refused her divorce, she could leave him in the clothes she wore, returning her dower or otherwise paying for the divorce. If she wanted a divorce because she could not endure her husband's behaviour but not because of any offence towards her under religious law, then she could get a divorce in accordance with custom returning half her dower and all property acquired during the marriage which went to the man, each party taking his or her own personal property.[2] According to the *Ninety-Nine Laws of Perak* however, a woman wishing to be divorced from her husband may establish a complaint at the court on three occasions, and can have a divorce but must redeem herself by returning an amount equivalent to her dowry. But if there is no fault on the part of her husband she may not have a divorce.[3] In Sarawak, a wife who insists on leaving her husband, who is not shown to be at fault, will be given a period of fifteen days in which to reconsider. If she still insists on the divorce, thereafter, she will be required to pay a fine and to return the amount of the *berian* to the husband as *tebus talak*. When the *berian* is outstanding it will be regarded as compensation for the *tebus talak*. If the wife is unable to pay the *berian* she will be asked to return to her husband. When a wife has committed adultery, she will be fined and asked to repay the *berian* as *tebus talak*. If the *berian* has not been paid in full by the husband, the balance of the *berian* will be regarded as the compensation for the *tebus talak*. If the

of Religion and Malay Custom and Kathis Courts Enactment, 1953, S. 147; Trengganu Administration of Islamic Law Enactment, 1955, S. 105; Pahang Administration of the Law of Religion of Islam Enactment, 1956, S. 128; Penang Administration of Muslim Law Enactment, 1959, S. 123; Malacca Administration of Muslim Law Enactment, 1959, S. 123; Negri Sembilan Administration of Muslim Law Enactment, 1960, S. 123; Kedah Administration of Muslim Law Enactment, 1962, S. 123; Singapore Muslims Ordinance, 1957, Ss. 32 and 34.

[1] Kelantan Council of Religion and Malay Custom and Kathis Courts Enactment, 1953, S. 146; Trengganu Administration of Islamic Law Enactment, 1955, S. 104; Pahang Administration of the Law of the Religion of Islam Enactment, 1956, S. 127.

[2] J. E. Kempe and R. O. Winstedt, "A Malay Legal Miscellany," *op. cit.*, p. 6.

[3] *The Ninety-Nine Laws of Perak*, *op. cit.*, p. 22 and 34. The ancient customary form of divorce called *beli laki* is obsolete; it was only applicable where a man contracted a polygamous marriage and both wives lived in Rembau – see E.N. Taylor, "Customary Law of Rembau" *Journal of the Malayan Branch of the Royal Asiatic Society*, 1929 (Part I) p. 19.

wife is unable to repay the *berian*, she is liable to be sent to gaol.[1]

Under the Muslim law the period of *eddah* or compulsory waiting after a divorce, generally consists of three periods of purity after menstruation but it would appear that according to the Malay custom the period of *eddah* on divorce is three months and ten days.[2]

Under the custom of the old Malay communities, fornication was the accepted road to marriage. While the Muslim law prescribed death as the punishment for *Zinah* (fornication), the old Malacca digest prescribed a fine as the penalty for fornication by the unmarried, the Pahang digest or the other hand, prescribed a hundred strokes and banishment for a year. In the Minangkabau Legal Digest from Perak it was provided that where there was circumstantial evidence of fornication between a free man and woman, the judge should order them to marry; if either the man or the woman refused to marry, he or she was to be fined. According to the *Ninety-Nine Laws of Perak* the seducer of a betrothed girl was merely fined and married off on payment of double the dower, half of which was for the jilted suitor. If the seducer could not pay the fine and the dower, he was to be beaten and banished. It was also provided that a couple guilty of illicit intercourse could marry or settle the matter between themselves. Where a man was charged with illicit intercourse the judge would make an order for the parties to get married.[3] These Malay customary rules have been enacted in the *Undang-Undang Makhamah Melayu* in Sarawak. It is provided that if a man has illicit intercourse or has committed an act which is considered as wrong (*salah*) in Malay custom with a woman whom he can marry, the parties will be asked to marry and the *berian* or *maskahwin* in such case shall not exceed $50/–. If the man refuses to marry the woman he is liable to pay a fine and to pay the *berian* of $50/– to the woman, and if the woman is pregnant he is liable to pay the expenses of her maintenance of the child until the age of two years. But if the woman refuses to marry the man cannot force her. If a man has illicit intercourse with a woman who is in her *eddah*, he is liable to a fine but the parties can marry after the completion of the *eddah*.[4]

Under the Muslim law a husband who has repudiated his wife in a revocable manner has a right to take her back as long as she is still in

[1] *Undang-Undang Makhamah Melayu*, Sarawak, S. 41 and Addenda.

[2] J. E. Kempe and R. O. Winstedt, "A Malay Legal Miscellany," *op. cit.*, p. 4.

[3] Sir Richard Winstedt, "An old Minangkabau Legal Digest from Perak," 1953, *Journal of the Malayan Branch of the Royal Asiatic Society*, Part I, p. 2 and 6; *The Ninety-Nine Laws of Perak*, *op. cit.*, pp. 5–6; 33–34; 37–38; 44–45.

[4] *Undang-Undang Makhamah Melayu*, Sarawak, Ss. 14, 15, 17, 20, 48, 50 and 57.

her period of *eddah*, provided the marriage has not in the meantime become illicit for any other reason. Malay custom however, to some extent helps to protect the woman who is forced to return to her husband against her will. According to the *Ninety-Nine Laws of Perak* the law applicable in the case of a woman who was divorced and whose husband wanted her back within three months and ten days was that if she was unwilling she might be forced to return to her husband, but the husband must give her settlements in cash. If he was forcibly rejected the woman must pay the amount of the marriage settlement.[1] In Selangor, Negri Sembilan, Penang, Malacca, Kedah and Perlis it is provided that in every case in which revocation takes place after the expiration of one month from the divorce, the *kathi* shall make inquiry from both the husband and the wife to satisfy himself that the divorce has been lawfully revoked.[2] In Kelantan and Trengganu it is provided that if after a revocable divorce the husband has pronounced a revocation of the divorce, then if (a) the wife has consented to the revocation, she may, on the application of the husband, be ordered to resume conjugal relations unless she shows good cause in accordance with Muslim law to the contrary, in which case the *kathi* appoints arbitrators to deal with the dispute; (b) if the wife has not consented to the revocation for reasons allowed by Muslim law, she must not be asked by the *kathi* to resume conjugal relations but on her application the *kathi* may require her husband to divorce her and on refusal should appoint arbitrators to deal with the dispute.[3] In Pahang it is provided that where after a revocable divorce the husband pronounces a revocation of the divorce, whether the wife has consented to the revocation or not, she may on the application of the husband be ordered by the *kathi* to resume conjugal relations unless she shows good cause in accordance with the Muslim law to the contrary, provided that the *kathi* shall impose such conditions in accordance with Muslim law as he thinks appropriate.[4]

Under the Muslim law where a woman has been divorced by three *talaks* or for the third time, she is not allowed to remarry her previous husband, unless prior to such marriage she is lawfully married to some

[1] *The Ninety-Nine Laws of Perak*, *op. cit.*, p. 48.

[2] Selangor Administration of Muslim Law Enactment, 1952, S. 127; Negri Sembilan Administration of Muslim Law Enactment, 1960, S. 122; Penang Administration of Muslim Law Enactment, 1959, S. 122; Malacca Administration of Muslim Law Enactment, 1959, S. 121; Kedah Administration of Muslim Law Enactment, 1962, S. 122; Perlis Administration of Muslim Law Enactment, 1963, S. 93.

[3] Kelantan Council of Religion and Malay Custom and Kathis Courts Enactment, 1953, S. 151; Trengganu Administration of Islamic Law Enactment, 1955, S. 109.

[4] Pahang Administration of the Law of the Religion of Islam Enactment, 1945, S. 126.

other person and such marriage is consummated and later lawfully dissolved. The device has been adopted in such cases of employing a person to marry the woman on the promise to divorce her after consummation of the marriage, so as to enable her to remarry her former husband. Such a person is called "*muhallil*" in Arabic and the derisive "*China-buta*" (or blind Chinese) in Malay. The device has been given legislative sanction in Sarawak where it is provided that where the divorce is by three *talaks* or for the third time, the parties cannot remarry again except by the device of *China-buta*.[1]

C. Adoption

Adoption is not recognized as a mode of establishing parental rights and obligations in Muslim law but in the parts of Negri Sembilan and Malacca which follow the *adat perpateh* adoption was recognized under the *adat* as creating family relationship. Full adoption (*kadim adat dan pesaka*) gives a woman (and her children whether born before or after the adoption) all the rights of inheritance and all the responsibilities belonging to the natural daughters and grand-daughters of her adopter. A man if fully adopted becomes eligible for office in his adopting tribe. Limited adoption (*kadim adat pada lembaga*) of a girl of one's own tribe or sub-tribe gives her a right only to property expressly declared and bestowed during the life of the adopting mother. The practice of adoption by *kadim* rites is disapproved by Islam and was abolished in Rembau in 1940.[2]

The basic principles of *kadim* or adoption as practised in the various *luaks* or tribal districts were the same though there might have been some minor differences as regards details and procedure. In Johol and Inas the adopted daughters, if of non-Malay origin, were precluded from inheriting the customary estates of their adopted mothers, but the transmission of those estates was made directly to the children of the adopted daughters. According to one authority an adopted child of non-Malay parentage could not inherit her adopted mother's customary lands but might be given lands purchased from the *harta charian* of her parents. Most *adat* experts however agree with the principle and practice as carried out in Temabau whereby a fully adopted child had all the rights and liabilities of a natural child, both direct and collateral, and became entitled to inherit all property of whatever kind, to which

[1] *Undang-Undang Makhamah Melayu*, Sarawak, S. 58.

[2] E. N. Taylor, "Customary Law of Rembau," *op. cit.*, p. 39f; Inche Lokman bin Yusof, "Custom as seen in Land Inheritance," *Intisari*, (Singapore) Vol. 1, No. 4, p. 17f.

a natural child would succeed. The approval of the *wariths* and the consent of the *lembaga* were necessary before adoption or *kadim* could take place. A feast was held for which a buffalo or a goat was slaughtered. The feast was attended by the *lembaga*, the *buapaks*, the *besars* and the *warith kadims*. A *berchechah darah* ceremony would be performed, at which a member of the adopting family and the person to be adopted dipped their fingers in a bowl containing the blood of the slaughtered buffalo or goat followed by the sprinkling of the *tepong tawar* (pounded rice mixed with water). The child was then proclaimed as having been adopted into the tribe. The *kadim* or adoption ceremony was usually held when the adopted child reached the age of between 8 and 10, but some parents preferred to wait until the child was *pulang rumah tangga*, i.e. given away in marriage. The *adat* did not prescribe when the ceremony should be held. If the foster-mother died before the ceremony was performed, then the responsibility for holding the *kadim* passed on to the *wariths*. A problem might arise if the *wariths* subsequently refused to admit the adopted child into the tribe. The adopted child could not be admitted otherwise than with the full consent of the *wariths*. It would, therefore, be in the interest of all concerned that the *kadim* ceremony should be held with as little delay as possible.[1]

Adoption within the family circle or *perut* was called *tarek*, and the *adat* enjoined—

Poultry which is tied is given food
A person who is adopted is given property.[2]

Adoption of this kind must also be proclaimed and publicized. A family feast would be held; the *lembaga* need not be present himself, but it would be preferable for the *buapak* or the *besar* to be present in case of a possible dispute later regarding the validity of the ceremony.[3]

A person properly *di-tarek* or adopted succeeded to the customary estate of the "foster-mother"; but it was doubtful if she could also receive a share from the estate of her natural mother. E. N. Taylor stated that she was not precluded and was entitled to receive such but opinions and practice have not been unanimous. The validity or propriety of adoption was often disputed at the time of the disposal of customary estates of the foster-mothers, and it sometimes became necessary for the

[1] *Ibid.*
[2] Ayam di-tambat di-beri makan, / Orang di-tarek di-beri harta.
[3] Inche Lokman bin Yusof, "Custom as seen in Land Inheritance," *op. cit.*, p. 18–19.

Collector to hold a separate enquiry to determine the validity of the previous adoption.[1]

Kadim rites were a survival of pagan practice and would appear to be objectionable to Islam. The practice of dipping one's fingers into a bowl containing blood as a means of forging a blood relationship is most objectionable from the Islamic point of view for blood is an unclean thing. Its continued practice was deplored by certain sections of the people and from time to time there had appeared articles in the Malay press calling for its immediate cessation. In Rembau, adoption was abolished in 1940. Its abolition was sanctioned by the *kebulatan* of all the *lembagas* and the four *Orang Besar Undang*. The motive for its abolition was however not so much because of religious conviction as a desire to exclude outsiders from inheriting and enjoying the rights and privileges which would normally be conferred upon adoption. The change was dictated by economic motives rather than religious orthodoxy. The tribes no longer want their limited *tanah pusaka* to be given to others by way of admission or adoption into the tribes.[2]

Adoption is recognised by Malay custom in Sarawak and if registered in accordance with the laws of Sarawak, the effect of such adoption is that the adopted child stands in the same relation to the adopting parent or parents as would a child born in lawful wedlock, though this is not in accordance with the Muslim law.[3] In Sabah, it has been held that although under the Muslim law adopted children take nothing in intestacy, the Muslim law must be applied subject to section 7 of the North Borneo Civil Law Ordinance (No. 2 of 1938) which provided that adopted children were to be treated as children[4]; the Civil Law Ordinance has now been repealed but the provisions of the Adoption Ordinance, 1960,[5] would appear to apply to Muslims, so that in effect adopted children are placed in the same position in relation to the

[1] *Ibid.*

[2] *Ibid.* Some have questioned the wisdom or even the validity of the order prohibiting *kadim.* They argued that the practice of *kadim* was an essential and integral part of the *adat*, and to do away with *kadim* was an act *ultra vires* the *adat.* A test case was brought in 1944 during the Japanese occupation. A certain member of the Suku Biduanda Dangang tribe was admitted into the Sedia Raja Warith which is one of the two Warith Dua Charak in Rembau. As the result of this the Buapak, the Besar and the Dato' Mangkubumi – (the last named was one of the Orang Besar Undang drawing a political allowance of $200/– per month) were dismissed from their tribal posts. The *Undang* found them guilty of transgressing the *adat*; they had permitted a *kadim* ceremony to be held contrary to the *kebulatan* made in 1940 which abolished the institution of *kadim* once and for all insofar as the Luak of Rembau was concerned. The tribal officers concerned lodged an appeal againstt heir dismissal in 1946. The British Military Administration Authority however upheld the *Undang's* decision.

[3] *Sheripah Unei* v. *Mas Poeti* (1949) *Sarawak Law Reports*, p. 5.

[4] *Matusin bin Simbi* v. *Kwang* (1953) *Sarawak Law Reports*, p. 106.

[5] No. 23 of 1960.

adopting parents as would children born in lawful wedlock. Similarly in Singapore, a Muslim adopted under the provisions of the Adoption of Children Ordinance[1] is placed in the same position as a child born in lawful wedlock; and in Sarawak in an adoption registered under the Adoption Ordinance the adopted child stands in the same relation to the adopting parent or parents as would a child born in lawful wedlock with regard to the obligations and estate of the adopting parents.[2] In the states of Malaya however, it is specially provided that the Adoption Ordinance, 1952, shall not apply to any person who professes the religion of Islam either so as to permit the adoption of a child by such person or so as to permit the adoption by any person of a child who is a Muslim.[3]

D. Property and Inheritance

In its origin the law of the Malays relating to property was based on the *adat* or tribal custom and the *adat* continued to govern the ownership and devolution of property in the period before the Malay states came under British influence. The Malay rulers were Muslims but in matters of property followed the old Malay *adat*. Sir William Maxwell recorded that in the state of Perak the lands and houses of the deceased descended to his daughters equally while the sons divided the personal property. The latter were supposed to create landed estates for themselves by clearing and planting land which they may select or at all events to obtain the use of land by marrying women who may have inherited it. The early minutes of the Perak State Council note that it was customary among Malays of rank or position for a husband to appropriate a particular house to the use of his wife at the time of the marriage. She was entitled to live there during coverture and if she was divorced by the husband the house was regarded as hers and was assigned to her for her use during her life. According to the Minangkabau Legal Digest from Perak property jointly acquired by husband and wife, being rice-fields, garden and landed property in general, was divided equally between them; if the property was perishable two-thirds went to the husband and one-third to the wife, and if there was a child, one-third is taken from the father's share and given to the child. If there were two children, male and female, ancestral property was divided into three, one portion for the male and two for the female. The girl got the homestead with its trees and apparel and jewellery.

[1] Chapter 21 of the Revised Edition.
[2] Adoption Ordinance (Cap. 91), Sections 2 and 6.
[3] Adoption Ordinance, 1952 (No. 41 of 1952) Secton 31.

Livestock was divided equally between them.[1] About 1886 the Perak State Council ordered the land of a major chief, Tengku Long Jaffar, to be transmitted in the female line. Since then however, Muslim law has been more extensively adopted and the customary laws in the Malay states (other than Negri Sembilan and Malacca) have only survived in relation to the rights of widows and divorcees. Among the country people, many estates are still divided according to *adat kampong*, but this can only take place by consent. In case of disputes the courts and the collectors of land revenue have tended to apply the Muslim law. Thus the law of inheritance in the Malay states, other than Negri Sembilan and Malacca, is now the Muslim law, except for the special right of the spouses. Questions of property and inheritance are seldom litigated between a woman and her children but are often settled by agreement, and the tendency has been that in such agreements the widow receives more than her share under Muslim law. In the vast majority of Malay families, one-eighth of the estate, which is the share of the widow under Muslim law, will not provide her with subsistence. The matter was therefore regulated by Malay custom rather than by Muslim law. The fact that Muslim law allows distribution of the estate of a deceased person to be settled by consent of the heirs has enabled many arrangements which are in reality applications of the *adat kampong* to pass as distributions according to the Muslim law.[2]

An illustration of the application of the *adat kampong* or *adat temenggong* is given in the case of *Shafi* v. *Lijah*.[3] In that case the question

[1] Sir William Maxwell, "Law and Customs of the Malays with reference to tenure of land" in *Journal of the Straits Branch of the Royal Asiatic Society*, No. 13 (1884), pp. 75–220; R. J. Wilkinson, *Malay Law, op. cit.*, p. 36–37. Sir Richard Winstedt, "An old Minangkabau Legal Digest, from Perak," *op. cit.*, p. 2 and 12.

[2] E. N. Taylor, "Malay Family Law," *op. cit.*, p. 7f.

[3] *Malayan Law Journal* 1948–49, Supplement p. 49. Callow J. in this case said:

I am satisfied that in the absence of strong evidence to the contrary, which was not forthcoming, the lack of endorsement on the titles of customary land precludes the *adat perpateh*. It is always open to a land owner to request the endorsement of title as customary, and it could be inferred from the omission in this case that the late Abdul Majid did not desire the land to be subject to the *adat perpateh*, although I do not believe inheritance or succession in accordance with the law of the *Shafii* sect of the *Sunni* school of Islam was ever contemplated. But although the more defined tenets of the *adat perpateh* may not in this case be adhered to, there remains the still older and perhaps more fundamental *adat temenggong*, which one might perhaps almost term the common law behind the more statutorised *adat perpateh*, though whereas in England statutory law evolved from the common law, in this country one might almost conclude the reverse – that the *temenggong* is from the law or codes of by-gone generations. I suggest this notwithstanding Wilkinson's observations at page 40 of his work "The true *adat temenggong* of Malaya was an unwritten law"; it was and is unwritten, deriving its origin from the lawgivers of ancient times. Another simile is that *adat temenggong* was as the royal prerogative, and exercised in suitable cases where strict adherence to the *adat perpateh* would cause hardship. The holder of the Ministerial Office of *temenggong* exercised on behalf for decision was whether the inheritance of certain real property should be in accordance with the *adat* or the Muslim law. The land was acquired during wedlock but the titles of the land were not endorsed "Customary Land." It was held that the lack of endorsement on the titles of customary land precluded, in the absence of strong evidence to the contrary, the *adat perpateh*. It was held further on the evidence that it was clear that the deceased intended some form of local customary law to apply and that therefore the *adat temenggong* should be applied in this case and the estate distributed equitably between the claimants.

Where the Muslim rules of inheritance on intestacy are applied they are subject to the following modifications:

(a) on the death of a peasant his widow is entitled to a special share in is estate as her share in *harta sapencharian* unless provision has been made for her *inter vivos* by registering land in her name. If the deceased has no children and the estate is small, she may take the whole estate; in other cases she takes a half or less according to circumstances;

(b) the residue of the estate is distributed according to Muslim law but inasmuch as the widow's special share is discretionary, her one-eighth share or one-quarter share can and should be taken into consideration in assessing the special share.[1] In Sarawak where both the spouses work together on the land the *pencharian* property is divided equally between them (and this is the custom followed under Melanau custom). Where the husband is the sole wage-earner the *pencharian* property is divided into three parts, the husband taking two parts and the wife one part.[2]

of the ruler the prerogative which could not be challenged, it was an autocratic decree and should in proper circumstances the *adat perpateh* conflict or differ from the code of conscience the *adat temenggong* could be invoked and so over-rule the former. It seems to me clear, and I accept the evidence of Lijah accordingly, that the deceased Abdul Majid acquired this property for the benefit of his widow and adopted daughters. He did not contemplate the administration of his estate in accordance with the inheritance scales contained in the *Shafii* school of Muhammedan law. He intended some form of local customary law to apply, although he was probably quite vague as to detail or principle. Therefore, although the *adat temenggong* is depreciated by Wilkinson (at page 45), and although Taylor regards it as essentially the same as the *adat perpateh* (*Royal Asiatic Society Journal* May 1937, page 3) I distinguish the two *adats* and rule that the *adat temenggong* should apply. This means that the estate should be distributed equitably between the claimants, such division being decided by the circumstances of the particular case before the court. It is not a division necessarily to be followed in every such case.

[1] E. N. Taylor, "Inheritance in Negri Sembilan," in 1948 *Journal of the Malayan Branch of the Royal Asiatic Society*, Part 2, p. 47f.

[2] Sarawak *Undang-Undang Makhamah Melayu*, s. 41; *Serujie* v. *Hanipah* (1953), Sarawak Law Reports, p. 40.

In the parts of Negri Sembilan and Malacca which follow the *adat perpateh* the fundamental principle that is followed is that property is tribal rather than personal. The social unit is not the family but the tribe and therefore all rules affecting persons tend to maintain the integrity of the tribe and all rules affecting property are designed to conserve the property in and for the tribe. The tribe is the unit and it is matriarchal and exogamous. The main object of the *adat* is to provide for the continuance of the tribe through its female members and to prevent alienation of property so that it may always be sufficient to provide maintenance for the woman through whom alone the tribe can be continued. The cardinal principles of distribution are fourfold:

(a) all property vests in the tribe, not in the individual;
(b) acquired property, once inherited, becomes ancestral;
(c) all ancestral property vests in the female members of the tribe; and
(d) all ancestral property is strictly entailed on tail female.

From the basic principle that property is tribal rather than personal and that the man passes into his wife's tribe upon marriage, it follows that all property owned by a married pair is joint property and that it belongs to the tribe of the wife so long as the marriage subsists.[1]

The *adat* lays down certain fundamental rules regarding the distribution of movable and immovable property in the event of death or divorce. Ancestral property devolves upon the daughters of the deceased in equal shares, the share of the deceased daughter, if she predeceases her mother, devolves on her female descendants. In the absence of direct female descendants, ancestral property devolves on the female descendants of the nearest common ancestress in equal shares, *per stirpes*, but subject to the rights, if any, of the sons and brothers of the deceased to statutory life-occupancy. The various degrees of *kadimship* or relationship among the heirs in the family are termed *sanak ibu* if the mothers were sisters, or *sanak dato'* if the grandmothers were sisters, or *sanak moyang* if the great-grandmothers were sisters. These *kadims* or *wariths* became the indirect heirs to a deceased's customary estate in the event of failure of direct heirs, subject to the rule that the nearer in degree excludes the more distant. In default of both direct and indirect heirs the land will be auctioned, and it will be a condition of the sale that members of the same tribes should have priority to bid at the auction before it is thrown open to members of other tribes. The

[1] E. N. Taylor, "Customary Law of Rembau," *op. cit.*, p. 8f.

proceeds of the sale will go to the deceased's son or sons or her maternal brothers or uncles as the case may be.[1]

Life-occupancy is granted to the deceased's male issues or to her maternal brothers in default of direct customary heirs; the rights of the sons prevail over those of their maternal uncles. Life-occupancy permits the occupants to enjoy the produce of the land during their lifetime. Generally the life-occupants are seldom found living on the land or cultivating the *sawah* land or rice-field. Nonetheless the bestowal of life-occupancy is normally insisted upon to serve as an assurance and a safeguard against failure on the part of the female *wariths* to maintain or cherish a destitute or a divorced relative.[2]

The fundamental principle of division of property among the members of the tribes are:

Husband's property is returned
Wife's property remains
Joint earnings are shared
On death of husband, they go to wife
On death of wife, they go to husband.[3]

That is to say, what is brought by the man to the woman's house at the time of marriage goes back with him on divorce, or to his *wariths* on his death; that which is found in the possession of the wife at the time of the marriage remains with her on divorce or it goes to her customary heirs on her death; that which is acquired during the period of wedlock is to be equally divided between them on divorce and on the death of the husband it goes to the wife, and vice-versa, provided there are no children from the marriage.[4]

Harta charian bujang or property acquired by a man while he is still single devolves on the nearest female relatives of the deceased. Property given to a son by his parents ranks as *charian bujang*, and become *harta pembawa* on his marriage and this reverts to his *wariths* on his death. Similarly a gift to a married man by his family also ranks as *pembawa* and not a *charian* of the marriage. Both *harta pembawa* and *harta dapatan* must be declared before the elders at the time of the marriage, and in the event of death, claims for the return of *harta pembawa* must be made on the 100th day funeral feast.[5]

[1] Inche Lokman bin Yusof, "Custom as seen in Land Inheritance," *op. cit.*, p. 17.
[2] *Ibid.*
[3] Pembawa, Kembali; / Dapatan, Tinggal; / Charian, bagi; / Mati laki, tinggal ka-bini; / Mati bine, tinggal ka-laki.
[4] Inche Lokman bin Yusof, "Custom as seen in Land Inheritance," *op. cit.*, p. 17.
[5] *Ibid.*

Difficulties often arise with regard to the separate estates of the spouses, that is the *harta pembawa* of the husband and the *harta depatan* of the wife. These are inherited by the nearest *wariths* or *kadims* of the respective spouse in his or her tribe. Complications may occur if the deceased has been married twice or more and acquired some property during one marriage and some during another. Property acquired in the first marriage may be *harta pembawa* or *harta dapatan* of the second marriage. If *harta pembawa* increases in value during marriage, the increase or *untong* ranks as *charian laki-bini*. Similarly, if *harta dapatan*, say a buffalo, has a natural increase during the married period, the increase also ranks as *charian laki-bini*. Many complicated and vexing problems will arise regarding devolution and distribution of property following death or divorce, but however difficult or insoluble the problems may appear the basic principles for dealing with them remain unchanged, namely, *Pembawa, Kembali*; *Charian, bagi*; *Dapatan, Tinggal*.[1]

The basic principle of the custom is that all the ancestral property of the family is to be divided equally *per stirpes*. The property is therefore distributed equally to direct female descendants *per stirpes*, but due regard is made for any partial distribution which may already have been made. The rule applies only to the proper share of the proprietor, so that if the deceased was registered as the holder of all land derived from her mother and left one sister, the sister would be entitled to half, and the daughters of the deceased the other half in equal shares. Acquired property is divided into two classes according to its origin—*charian bujang* which plainly belongs to one tribe and that acquired by the joint efforts of a married pair, *charian laki-bini*, in which the tribes are interested. *Harta pembawa* means the personal estate of a married man, the property brought by him to his wife into which he passes on marriage; it may include property of three kinds, viz., his own earnings as a bachelor (*charian bujang*), his share of the earnings of any former marriage, and any ancestral property of his own family in which he has an interest. *Harta dapatan* means the separate estate of a married woman and also includes three kinds of property, viz., her own acquisitions as a spinster, divorcee or widow (*charian bujang* or *janda*), her share of the earnings of a former marriage and her ancestral property. *Charian bujang* thus becomes *harta pembawa* or *dapatan* of a subsequent marriage.[2]

The rules for the distribution on death of acquired property are as follows:

[1] *Ibid.* See also p. 134 note 3.
[2] E. N. Taylor, "Customary Law of Rembau," *op. cit.*, p. 14f.

(1) The *harta dapatan* or *pembawa* reverts on death to the *waris* of the deceased, that is the nearest female relative in the tribe of the deceased, (in the case of a man his sister, in the case of a woman her daughter).
(2) The *charian laki-bini* is apportioned
    (a) on the death of either spouse without issue of the marriage the whole remains to the survivor;
    (b) on the death of the husband leaving issue—the whole remains with the widow and issue;
    (c) on the death of the wife leaving issue, it is divided between the widower and the issue, but not necessarily equally; the principle of the division, by agreement or otherwise, is to make provision for the issue.[1]

In the non-tribal parts of Negri Sembilan (Seremban and Port Dickson) the tribal organization had ceased to be effective by 1874, and it would appear that the practice adopted was the *adat temenggong*. In general the distribution follows a family settlement or *pakat* but where there is dispute the distribution tends to follow the rules laid down by the *adat temenggong* (which is not as definite as, but tends to follow, the *adat perpateh*), though there also appears to be a tendency to follow the rules of Muslim law.[2]

The basic principle of *adat perpateh* relating to the tenure of *harta pesaka* is that property vests in the female members of the tribe, in tail female. The individual holder of the property at any time holds it on behalf of the tribe; the right is transmissible but not alienable. Under strict customary law a male cannot acquire any proprietary interest in *harta pesaka* except the interest of beneficial life occupancy in the event of failure of direct customary heirs, but the reversionary interests remain in the nearest female relatives.

The introduction of the Torrens system of land registration introduced a revolutionary change in the concept and practice of customary land tenure. The occupant of tribal land has now become the registered proprietor of land held under entries in the *Mukim* registers; the area is surveyed by the Survey Department; she possesses a document of title; dealings have to be executed in statutory forms, duly attested, and the instruments have to be presented and registered under the provisions of the Land Code. She is responsible for the payment of the quit rent and for the observances of the conditions in the title either ex-

[1] *Ibid.*
[2] E. N. Taylor, "Inheritance in Negri Sembilan," *op. cit.*, p. 80.

pressed or implied. The result is that registered proprietors are asserting their individual rights of possession to the exclusion of other members of the tribe. This is a departure from the old concept that the land is the property of the tribal community, and that the right of the individual extends only to its use. There is no doubt that land registration gives the registered proprietor a greater sense of security regarding land tenure and a greater incentive to practice good husbandry; but at the same time it tends to weaken the very basis on which the *adat* rests, and may in the end lead to the disintegration of the *adat*.[1]

Until the passing of the Customary Tenure Enactment, 1909, there was no restriction in law to stop dealings in tribal or ancestral lands, although strictly under the *adat* dealings outside the tribe were forbidden. The Customary Tenure Enactment, 1909, was enacted with the express object of preventing dealings in tribal lands with those outside the tribes. The Enactment empowered the Collector to inscribe the words "Customary Land" on titles held subject to the custom. Unfortunately, this provision of the law has not been systematically complied with and there are still many titles in the *mukim* registers which are undoubtedly ancestral lands but which have not been inscribed. All titles which are derived from the old Malay Grants are *prima facie* ancestral lands, but if the titles are not endorsed "Customary Land" under the provisions of the Customary Land Tenure Enactment, there would appear to be nothing to stop the registered proprietors from disposing of the lands under the provisions of the Land Code even though this practice is contrary to the *adat*.[2]

The Customary Tenure Enactment, 1909, was repealed and replaced by the Customary Tenure Enactment, 1926. The object of the latter Enactment was to consolidate and amend the law relating to customary tenure. "Customary Land" is defined to mean land held by an entry in the *Mukim* register which has been endorsed under the provisions of that Enactment or under those of the previous Enactment. In spite of this definition, the expression "Customary Land" is ambiguous, and this ambiguity gave rise to misunderstanding and confusion of interpretation and decision. Where the titles are endorsed, no difficulty arises on the question as to whether or not the land is held subject to the custom. The endorsement on the title is in itself conclusive evidence that the land is held subject to the custom, and all dealings and transmission connected with the land are dealt with under the Customary

[1] Inche Lokman bin Yusof, "Custom as seen in Land Inheritance," *op. cit.*, p. 14.
[2] *Ibid.*

Tenure Enactment. Where the titles are not so endorsed, the procedure regarding the distribution of a deceased's estate was governed by section 184(iii) of the Probate and Administration Enactment, now repealed and replaced by section 12(7) of the Small Estates (Distribution) Ordinance, 1955,[1] which requires the Collector to ascertain, in such manner as may be most appropriate, the law applicable to the devolution of the estate of the deceased, and to decide who in accordance with such law are the heirs and beneficiaries and the proportions of their respective shares and interests.[2]

In trying to find out the law or the custom having the force of law applicable to the deceased, the Collectors are often confronted with two vexing problems; firstly, how are they to find out whether or not a particular piece of land is held subject to the custom; and secondly whether the custom (*adat perpateh*) is the law applicable to the deceased. It is difficult to get two *lembagas* or *buapaks* or *besars* (who are supposed to be experts on *adat*) to be unanimous on their interpretation on any point raised concerning the *adat*; nor are members of the tribes unanimous in their preference as to whether any particular estate should be distributed according to *adat* or the Muslim law of inheritance. Their choice would naturally depend on the form of distribution which would benefit them.[3]

In the case of *Re Kulop Kidal*,[4] Acton J. enunciated the principle that the *adat* follows a person like his own shadow. He held that a will made by a person subject to the *adat Rembau* is inoperative as the custom governs the devolution of estates subject to the *adat* to the exclusion of wills. This principle was followed in *Re Haji Pais*[5] in which Burton J. held that the *adat* is a personal custom and affects the land by virtue of its ownership by persons subject to custom. Burton J. in that case said, "If then the custom is personal and attaches to the person, it follows that there is no place for inheritance according to Mohammedan law. It is not possible with a personal custom that certain property descend according to the custom and some according to the Mohammedan Law."

As a result of the decision in *Re Haji Pais*, the Customary Tenure Enactment, 1926, was amended in 1930, to provide as follows:

4.(i) In the case of any land particulars of which have been or may hereafter be

[1] No. 34 of 1955.
[2] Inche Lokman bin Yusof, "Custom as seen in Land Inheritance," *op. cit.*, p. 14.
[3] *Idem.*
[4] E. N. Taylor, "Customary Law of Rembau," *op. cit.*, p. 92.
[5] E. N. Taylor, "Inheritance in Negri Sembilan," *op. cit.*, p. 61.

entered in any of the mukim registers of the districts of Kuala Pilah, Jelebu and Tampin in accordance with the provisions of the Land Code, 1926, or of any previous Land Enactment it shall be lawful for the Collector, at the instance of himself or of any interested party, to enquire whether or not such land is occupied subject to the custom. If he be satisfied that such land is occupied subject to the custom and that it is registered in the name of a female member of one of the tribes included in schedule B the Collector shall add to the entry in the mukim register the words "Customary Land" and authenticate them by his signature; and the addition of such words so authenticated to any entry in the mukim register shall, subject to the result of any appeal to the Resident under section 15, be conclusive proof that the land to which such entry relates is occupied subject to the custom.

If the Collector is not satisfied that such land is occupied subject to the custom he shall record his decision to that effect and such decision shall, subject to the result of any appeal to the Resident under section 15, be conclusive proof that the land to which the entry relates is not occupied subject to the custom.

It was also provided that nothing in the Enactment shall affect the distribution of the estate, not being customary estate, of any deceased person.

The effect of this Enactment was for a time misunderstood. In *Kutai* v. *Taensah*,[1] Mudie J. held the view that under the Customary Tenure Enactment, 1926, as amended in 1930, land in the customary districts must be either customary or non-customary, and that the only land which can descend according to the custom is "Customary Land," namely, that which is endorsed. If it is not endorsed, then its devolution has to be according to the Mohammedan law. This decision was followed by Pedlow J. in *Re Imah deceased*[2] and by Raja Musa J. in *Re Teriah deceased*.[3]

The position was so confusing that in the case of *Re Haji Mansor bin Duseh*[4] the Collector referred a case for the opinion of a High Court Judge and for a ruling as to what were the rules of distribution of an estate, other than ancestral land, or lands which have their titles endorsed, or deceased proprietors in the customary districts. In a lengthy judgment, Cussen J. ruled that the Customary Tenure Enactment, 1926, is not exhaustive of the *adat*. If a title has been inscribed "Customary Land" the *adat* governs succession but the converse is not true. The absence of the words "Customary Land" does not prove that the land is not occupied subject to the custom. The only conclusive proof that the land is not so occupied is a recorded finding by the Collector to that

[1] (1933–34) *F.M.S. Law Report* p. 304; E. N. Taylor, "Inheritance in Negri Sembilan," *op. cit.*, p. 83.
[2] E. N. Taylor, "Inheritance in Negri Sembilan," *op. cit.*, p. 86.
[3] *Ibid.*, p. 90.
[4] (1940) *M.L.J.* 110.

effect under section 4 of the Customary Tenure Enactment. As regards land occupied subject to the custom in respect of which the titles are not so inscribed, the customary law of succession applied. In coming to this decision, the learned Judge endorsed the earlier judgment by Burton J. in *Re Haji Pais*, and he dissented from the judgment of Mudie J. in *Kutai* v. *Taensah*.

The decision of Cussen J. in *Re Haji Mansor bin Dusch* was followed by Horne J. in *Sali* v. *Achik*[1] and *Haji Hussin* v. *Maheran.*[2] In the earlier case he held that the absence of the words "customary land" (which means ancestral land) does not prevent devolution according to the *adat*. The Collector has to consider what rules are applicable for the distribution of the estate of the deceased person, and these are stated in the Distribution Enactment to be the rules of Mohammedan law as varied by local custom. In the latter case he considered the effect of section 4 of the Customary Tenure Enactment and said: "A decision under section 4 that the land is not 'occupied subject to custom' means that the land is not at the time the decision is given 'ancestral property.'" Such a decision is therefore "conclusive proof" that the land is "acquired property." It is open to the Collector in proceedings under the Probate and Administration Enactment to transmit the acquired property of the deceased in accordance with the personal law of the deceased. The law is the Mohammedan law as varied by local custom. Under the Probate and Administration Enactment the Collector is concerned with the law applicable to a person. Under the Customary Tenure Enactment, section 4, he is concerned with the character of a certain kind of property, viz. land. But under the custom it must be remembered that there is no difference between land and other property. All is property and is either acquired property, *harta charian*, or ancestral property, *harta pesaka*. There is therefore no conflict between the decision under section 4 and the decision under section 129 of the Probate and Administration Enactment. These decisions were followed in *Anyam* v. *Intan*[3] in which Taylor J. held that under the Probate and Administration Enactment, the Collector has to distribute the estate of the deceased according to the law or custom having the force of law applicable to the deceased. Where a deceased was a member of a tribe, that law is almost always the *adat*. The absence of the words "Customary Land" in the land register does not by itself prove that the land

[1] (1941) *M.L.J.* 14.
[2] (1946) *M.L.J.* 116.
[3] (1949) *M.L.J.* 72.

was not occupied "subject to custom" or that it was not ancestral. Where the *adat* is relied on it is necessary to prove it.

In a recent case dealing with *harta pembawa*, *Tano* v. *Ujang*,[1] Callow J. in his judgment said:

> It seems right to require proof of *adat* before the Shariah can be set aside. Indeed, it is strange to me to find a desire to set aside the Shariah which is the law of God to every Muslim; and in this case it appears a perverted custom to deprive a widow and the children of the father's property.

The claim was dismissed in that case as there was no proof that the land in question had been declared to be *harta pembawa* before or at the time of the marriage and that a claim had been lodged before or at the hundredth day ceremony of the deceased.

In *Derai* v. *Ipah*,[2] where the land had been alienated to a male, it was held that it had not been proven that the land was "Customary Land." Pretheroe J. said "If the land is not customary land it will devolve according to the rules of Mohammedan law as [the] deceased was a Moslem." He therefore directed that the land should devolve to the widow and the two daughters in accordance with the rules of Mohammedan law. This case seems to go against the authority of the cases of *Re Haji Mansor bin Duseh* (*supra*), *Sali* v. *Achik* (*supra*) and *Haji Hussin* v. *Maheran* (*supra*).

In *Minah* v. *Haji Sail and two others*[3] the appellant, *Minah*, appealed against the Collector's decision in ordering the distribution of her deceased husband's estate according to *Hukom Shara*. The appellant claimed that the land was *harta charian laki-bini* and this fact was not disputed, but the Collector held that the land was not held subject to the custom because the title was not endorsed "Customary Land." He further held that, since the deceased was a Muslim, his estate must devolve according to Muslim law of inheritance. On appeal it was held that the *adat* must prevail over Muslim law, and the appeal was allowed. Bellamy J. said "The words 'Customary Land' which have been said 'merely to operate as a caveat to protect the rights of the tribe to their control of entailed land' do not in any way affect the classification of the land under the *adat* or its devolution." After referring to the cases of *Romit* v. *Hassan* and *Re Kulop Kidal* (*supra*) he continued, "The land in question having been acquired by the deceased during his marriage to the appellant was clearly *charian laki-bini* and

[1] Seremban Civil Appeal No. 5 of 1948.
[2] Seremban Civil Appeal No. 6 of 1949.
[3] N.S. Civil Appeal No. 4 of 1953.

should have devolved to the widow, the appellant. The *adat* must prevail over the Muslim law."

In *Teriah* v. *Baiyah and three others*[1] the appellant, Teriah, claimed transmission of her deceased son's land to her on the ground that it was *harta pembawa*. The Collector held that the land was not held subject to the custom because the title was not endorsed, and accordingly granted Letters of Administration to the deceased's widow, Baiyah. Teriah appealed against the Collector's decision, but the appeal was dismissed by Abbott J.

In the case of *Maani* v. *Mohamed*,[2] Ismail Khan J. said "In the case of non-customary lands the legal position is in my view correctly set out by Cussen J. in *Re Haji Mansor bin Duseh* and followed by Horne J. in *Sali binte Haji Salleh* v. *Achik*. The general effect of these two judgments is that the distribution of such lands is governed by the personal law of the deceased, and if it is proved in a particular case or if it is generally accepted in the district that the Muslim law of descent is varied by local custom (*adat*) effect should be given to such custom (*adat*) as the personal law of the deceased. In the case of *Sali binte Haji Salleh* v. *Achik*, it was held that the fact that the title of the land is not endorsed "Customary Land" does not preclude the Collector from considering the personal law of the deceased which may be the Muslim law varied by local custom (*adat*). In a latter case *Haji Hussin* v. *Maheran* it was held that notwithstanding a finding by the Collector under section 4 of the Customary Tenure Enactment that the land was not customary, it was still open to him to distribute the land in accordance with the custom (*adat*)."

Under the Muslim law a person cannot validly dispose of more than one-third of his property by will. The rule of the *adat* is stricter than that of the Muslim law, a person cannot under the custom dispose of his property by will at all (*Re Kulop Kidal deceased*)[3]; and an agreement made during life to vary the succession is void (*Romit* v. *Hussan*).[4]

E. Death

There are no special rites regarding funerals in Islam but the Muslims are enjoined to bury and participate in the funeral upon knowing of the death. Islam does not require heavy expenditure on funerals nor does it encourage the holding of *tahlils* or feasts in commemoration of

[1] N.S. Civil Appeal No. 9 of 1954.
[2] (1961) *M.L.J.* 88.
[3] E. N. Taylor, "Customary Law of Rembau," *op. cit.*, p. 92.
[4] *Ibid.* p. 63.

the dead. During the days of the Prophet it often happened that some relatives of the dead or others who were well off paid *sadaka* or charity by giving money or coming to the aid of the family, as for example by cooking for them as they were busy in their misfortune. In Malay custom however, funeral expenses are a matter of great importance. They include not only the actual burial charges but also the expenses of the last illness and the cost of the customary feasts which are held on the third, seventh, fourteenth, fortieth and hundredth day, and are called respectively, *meniga hari, manujoh hari, dua kali menujoh, ampat puloh hari* and *saratus hari*. Some of these may be omitted; the most important one is the last, especially in the case of a married person because on that day the two families meet together with their respective tribal authorities (not always the *lembagas*) to settle the questions of property which necessarily arise on the disruption of the link between the two tribes.

Funeral expenses are chargeable:

(a) in the case of a child or unmarried girl—on the joint property of the parents;

(b) in the case of an unmarried man—on his personal acquired property or, if he had none, on his mother's or sister's ancestral property;

(c) in the case of a married person of either sex—on the joint property of the marriage, primarily on movable property, and failing that, on land;

(d) in the case of divorced or widowed persons—on the shares of property acquired before, or during, or after, marriage and failing that, on the ancestral property of the mother's family.[1]

It is a rule that where any individual leaves acquired property the funeral expenses must, if practicable, be limited to that amount, (*Re Badoh deceased*)[2]; only in the last resort may recourse be had to the ancestral property. An aged woman, however, may distribute her property among her daughters or nieces, reserving only a portion by way of *kepan* or funeral expenses; in such a case her funeral expenses are chargeable on the property so allocated and the relative who pays them is entitled to the *kepan* in addition to her ordinary share.[3]

The funeral expenses are by the custom an actual encumbrance on the appropriate property[4] If it appears that the wrong party has paid

[1] E. N. Taylor, "Customary Law of Rembau," *op. cit.*, p. 10–11.
[2] *Ibid.*, p. 150.
[3] *Re Miut deceased, Ibid*, p. 219.
[4] *Re Dahil deceased, Ibid*, 113; *Re Sitam deceased, Ibid*, p. 222.

them (as he often does where there is a dispute in the family) an order for transmission may be made conditional on the repayment of those expenses[1] and the Collector has power to order a portion of the estate to be auctioned if necessary.

IV. Conclusion

The integration of the *adat* and Islam in Malayan law is an established fact and although there are points of conflict between them, these have normally been glossed over by alleging that both systems are in fact directed to the same end:

> Our customary law bids us
> Remove what is evil
> And give prominence to what is good;
> The word of our religious law
> Bids us do good
> And forbids our doing evil.[2]

The one system depends upon and supplements the other:

> The custom is based on the religious law.
> Religious law is based on the Quran.[3]

Conflicts between them should be avoided and one system should not infringe on the other:

> Custom infringing on Muslim law excludes the latter.
> Muslim law infringing on Custom excludes the latter.[4]

Custom has historically played an important part in the development of Muslim law. Recent research has shown that the details of the Muslim law were developed during the Umayyad Caliphate in the second century of the Hegira (670–720 A.D.) on the basis of the Umayyad administrative practices and regulations and the ideas and custom of the peoples including those of the conquered territories. Muslim law grew out of customary and administrative practices which were impregnated with religious and ethical ideas based on the teachings of the Holy *Quran* and the Prophet.[2] The Muslim legal system recognizes the

[1] *Niah* v. *Alias*, *Ibid*, p. 81.

[2] Pada adat, / Menghilangkan yang burok / Menibulkan yang baik / Kata Shara / Menyurohkan berbuat baik / Menegahkan berbuat jahat.

[3] Adat bersendikan hukom / Hukom bersendiran Kitabullah.

[4] Adat ka-hukom mati hukom / Hukom ka-adat mati adat.

[5] J. Schacht, *Origins of Muhammadan Jurisprudence*, (Oxford 1959); J. Schacht, "Pre-Islamic Background and Early Development of Jurisprudence and the Schools of Law and Later Development of Jurisprudence," *Law in the Middle East*, (Washington, 1955); Fazlur Rahman, *Islamic Studies*, (Karachi, 1962 and 1963).

force and validity of custom in establishing rules of law. The validity of such laws rests on principles somewhat similar to those of *ijma* or consensus, which is one of the accepted sources of Muslim law. The customs and practices which prevailed in Arabia in the time of the Prophet are accepted where they have not been abrogated by the Holy *Quran* or the practice of the Prophet. As to customs which have appeared since that time, their validity is justified on the authority of the tradition, which lays down that whatever the people generally consider to be good for themselves is good in the eyes of God. Custom has come to be an important source of law in some Muslim countries, especially in Morocco, where the principle of *amal* or judicial practice has been developed by the jurists. In Malaysia too, the *adat* has played an important part in the development of Muslim law and there would appear to be no reason why it should not continue to do so, especially in those spheres where it helps to maintain the status and position of women in society. A synthesis between the *adat* and Muslim law is possible if on the one hand the principles of the Muslim law as contained in the *Quran* and the *Sunnah* are subjected as they were in the early days of Islam to the free activity of interpretation through *ijtihad* – *ijma*[1] to meet the ever-changing social and economic conditions, and if on the other hand the *adat* itself is subject to modification to meet the needs of such social and economic conditions:

> If chipped, you mend,
> If broken, you rivet
> If bushy, you prune
> If old, you renew.[2]

[1] The Muslim law developed through the deductive reasoning (*ijtihad*) of individual jurists which was later accepted by the other jurists and the Muslims generally (*ijma*).

[2] Sumbing-sumbing di-titek, / Patah-patah di kimpal / Rimbun-rimbun di-tutoh / Burok-burok di baharui.

IX. CHINESE FAMILY LAW IN A COMMON LAW SETTING

A Note on the Institutional Environment and the Substantive Family Law of the Chinese in Singapore and Malaysia*

INTRODUCTION

The development of Chinese family law in Malaysia and Singapore provides an interesting case study of an attempt to fuse elements of two disparate legal systems in a foreign social climate. The present court system of Malaysia and Singapore and the adjective law are based in large part upon principles of English common law, while the substantive family law applied to the Chinese people is in part a reflection of "traditional"[1] Chinese law. These diverse legal orders function in a social setting which, although substantially influenced by Chinese tradition, is nevertheless a distinct environment, and which on the other hand certainly bears little resemblance to the native habitat of the common law.

Thus ancient principles of the common law, such as *stare decisis* and the rules of evidence, are applied to cases dealing with the status of secondary wives or the prerequisites for a valid ceremony of marriage according to venerable Chinese judicial precepts. Traditional Chinese family law, which was heavily dependent upon local customary variation,[2] is treated as a great unity by the common law courts of Singapore and the states of Malaysia, other than Sabah and Sarawak. Expensive statutory procedures having English law antecedents are enforced in order to legally effectuate important customary family law procedures such as adoption. The courts of Malaysia and Singapore, largely bound

* I am in substantial debt to Maurice Freedman, James Clarkson, Wen Chung-chi and G. William Skinner, as well as to Jack Dull and Richard and Leigh Kagan, for their very important suggestions regarding this manuscript, published with the permission of *The Journal of Asian Studies,* wherein it first appeared (Vol. xxv, no. 4, August, 1966).

[1] The courts of Malaysia have generally regarded the law of the Ch'ing dynasty (1644–1911) as the prototype of traditional Chinese law. In that many Chinese emigrated to Malaysia during that period, and in that the legal innovations promulgated by Yüan Shih-k'ai and the Nationalist Government (1912–1949) etc., perhaps helped to undermine the ancient social and legal structure but presumably did not have a substantial impact upon prevailing legal attitudes in China particularly in the family law field, such a designation is not unreasonable. (The ineffectiveness of the courts especially in the rural areas, the importance of custom in family law matters, the Japanese invasion and the weakness of the central government were some of the many factors that muted the effectiveness of these legal innovations.) In this paper we shall mean Ch'ing China when referring to traditional China.

[2] See for example *Chung-kuo Hsien-tai Shih-liao Tzu-shu* No. 6 (Taiwan, 1962) pp. 121f.

by their own decisions in this English model judiciary, are unable adequately to reflect change in a dynamic social environment. Furthermore common law precedents which have become anachronisms in England and the Commonwealth were enacted into law as a step towards "modernization" in Singapore in 1961. Finally a judiciary largely trained in England is expected to deal with Chinese law principles with which it is often almost totally unacquainted[1] and indeed about which the available literature in Malaysia and Singapore is limited.

The results therefore of this strange union of common law and Chinese law are, not surprisingly, often awkward compromises which at times cause serious injustices, thereby reinforcing the role of social institutions and undermining the position of the courts as an arena for the settling of family disputes. The social institutions, however, have been deprived of much of their "legal" power and therefore are at times unable to manage their traditional functions of mediation and dispute resolution adequately, thus engendering social chaos.

Some of the errors of judgment in the development of the Malaysian judiciary may be attributed to the myopia of the colonial period, where the institutions of common law were regarded as implements for the civilizing of foreign peoples. A description of the pitfalls encompassed in an attempt to incorporate elements of two diverse legal institutions in order to form a single body of family law, without careful scrutiny of social development, is nevertheless of contemporary relevance. Several Asian countries no longer under the aegis of colonial rule are now determined to reconstruct portions of their legal institutions.[2] They are drawn by nationalistic pride to the traditional customary family law as a basis for this renovation, and yet are attracted to the Western "rational and impersonal" legal system in their desire to appear and to become "modern." Often, particularly in communities with large immigrant populations, neither system is fully relevant to the social circumstances of the people.

The process of integrating legal institutions into a changing society to make them more effective organs for the peaceful resolution of disputes is one of great intricacy and difficulty. Utilization of law as a tool for

[1] Thus far only the University of London offers a course in Chinese law among the major institutions of the United Kingdom, and a Chinese law course was only instituted at the Law Faculty of the University of Singapore—the only law school in Malaysia and Singapore—in 1963.

[2] The conference (wherein this article was first presented) under the sponsorship of the Association of Southeast Asian Institutions of Higher Learning brought together representatives from eleven Asian countries to discuss the role of customary family law and colonial law in the present and future development of their legal systems.

social change (e.g., institutionalizing a system of monogamy in a community long practiced in polygamy) without a thorough understanding of the society involved, as both colonial and contemporary legislatures have attempted in Singapore, is of questionable effectiveness. This note concerning the development of the Chinese family law institutions of Singapore and Malaysia from initial recognition of "customary"[1] substantive Chinese family law to the efforts to impose the English common law of domestic relations in 1961 upon the Chinese of Singapore, will hopefully illustrate some of the problems involved in transplanting substantive law into an alien judicial and social environment.

This paper is divided into two basic sections. Section I describes the institutional environment in which the law is administered in Singapore and Malaysia. Section II undertakes to examine certain problems of the substantive law itself. Each section is preceded by a brief historical introduction designed to contrast some of the traditional judicial patterns of China with those of Malaysia and Singapore. Within these two divisions a rough historical chronology is used to develop the legal patterns. The conclusion includes not only an evaluation of previous developments, but certain implicit and explicit suggestions as to future action.

I. THE INSTITUTIONAL ENVIRONMENT

1. *Relevant Legal Institutions in Traditional China*

A. Judiciary. The judicial system of traditional China provided a hierarchy of courts of which the lowest formal administrative units, the approximately 1250–1300 *hsien-yamen*, were of most direct relevance to the population. The *hsien-yamen* had jurisdiction among other things over civil matters as well as adultery and other criminal offenses relating to domestic relations.[2] This formal judiciary, because of its

[1] While the Women's Charter 1961 (discussed *infra*) seriously modifies the applicability of substantive Chinese law to the domestic relations disputes of the Chinese in Singapore, the Malaysian states continue to apply "customary" Chinese law to these matters. What was originally deemed "customary" Chinese law by the Malaysian judiciary and legislature is in reality a fusion of both the positive law and customary law of traditional China.

[2] See *Ch'in-Ting Ta-Ch'ing Hui-Tien* (25th year Kuan Hsü, 1899 ed.) Chüan 6 (13–16) (reprinted Taiwan) pp. 0081–0082; hereafter referred to as *Ch'ing Hui-Tien*. See Chü Tung-tsu, *Local Government in China under the Ch'ing* (Cambridge, 1962) at p. 2.

See also *Ta-Ch'ing Lü-Li Tseng-Hsiu T'ung-tsuan Chi-ch'eng* (*T'ung-chih* 2nd year ed. 1863) Chüan 30 (including appended *Hsing-an Hui-lan*); hereafter referred to as *Ta-Ch'ing Lü-Li*.

The effectiveness of control seems quite remarkable in that: "With a total of roughly 1,500 magistrates in all types of *chou* and *hsien*, there was on the average one magistrate for 100,000 inhabitants (calculated on the basis of the 1749 official figures) or 250,000 (1819 limited size, was often remote. Furthermore, the potential expense, delay and shame arising from involvement in its proceedings, as well as its reputed penal character bespeaking punishment for the wrongdoer, made it in part a symbol of stern authority rather than the major active instrument of social ordering or the principal arena for the peaceful resolution of disputes.

While in fact in the *hsien* and other lower level courts the magistrate himself often effectuated a civil conciliation agreement, this was not the socially preferred method of settling disputes in part because the magistrate could use the threat of punishment to obtain this conciliation. While the harsh stipulations of the code were often mitigated in actual local level practice, there was nevertheless a potential danger in petitioning the courts for redress. Thus when a conciliation agreement was effectuated under judicial auspices, the parties, in form at least, often petitioned the magistrate to withdraw the case from the docket and to drop any potential criminal penalties. The magistrate himself on the other hand often refused pleas for civil redress, suggesting that the matter was too trifling for the courts and that the parties might best settle the matter themselves by conciliation. The population was thus encouraged to avail itself of the informal organs of control and conciliation to resolve social conflict.

B. Lineages and clans (*or surname associations*). The lineage, *tsu*, for example—which has been regarded by some as the focal point of Chinese social institutions exalted above the individual and the state[1]—was of particular importance in the provinces of Kwangtung and Fukien, from which most Malaysians of Chinese descent emigrated, and where "...lineage [*tsu*] and the village tend markedly to coincide, so that many villages consisted of single lineages."[2] Large lineages were in-

official figures)." Hsiao Kung-chuan, *Rural China, Imperial Control in the Nineteenth Century* (Seattle, 1960) at p. 5.

[1] Chen Ku-yuan, *Chung-kuo Fa-chih Shih* (1934) at p. 63.

[2] Maurice Freedman, *Lineage Organization in Southeastern China* (London, 1958) at p. 1. The lineage has been defined "...as an exogamous patrilineal group of males descended from a founding ancestor, plus their wives and unmarried daughters." S. van der Sprenkel, *Legal Institutions of Manchu China* (London, 1962) p. 80. This does not imply a biological connection. See also *Hsing-an Hui-lan*, appended to *Ta-Ch'ing Lü-Li*, Chüan 8. Here it was held in an 1828 case that, where there were no eligible relatives, a child of the same surname could be adopted and was entitled to the prerogatives of the heir although he was not of the same *tsung*—a somewhat wider grouping than the lineage. He was therefore permitted the *liu-yang*, i.e., the claim of exemption from criminal punishment in order to care for his adoptive parents. This decision could be justified on the theory that all those of the same surname were originally of the same family—a myth held in traditional China. (This myth was fortified by the law prohibiting marriage between persons of the same surname, although there were probably less than 470 surnames in China.) See also G. Jamieson, *Chinese Family and Commercial Law* (Shanghai, 1921) at pp. 131, 132.

volved in maintenance of order. Confucian virtues such as filial piety were stressed. Sometimes ancestral regulations, *tsung-kuei*, were formulated, warning against crime, violence, adultery and unfilial behavior. Expulsion from the lineage and other forms of punishment were prescribed by these regulations.[1] These rules were moral codes based upon prevailing ideology, law and custom, flexibly enforced with "...major emphasis...upon moral persuasion rather than actual punishment."[2] Generally the rules were more lenient than the law code, but they placed ultimate reliance upon state authority. These lineage rules could be registered with the government and acquire a formal and quasi-legal status and thereby develop an interrelationship with the legal organs and the law code which was one of mutual support and supplementary assistance.[3] In the cities the surname organizations (or clans), *t'ung-hsing-hui*, performed similar functions. It was generally these urban surname associations that were the prototypes of institutions reconstituted in Singapore and Malaysia which fulfilled the functions of the lineage and surname associations of traditional China. Undoubtedly the lineage and surname organizations played an important role in dealing with certain aspects of domestic relations and other social matters often dealt with by law courts in other societies. The government, recognizing the role of these institutions as one of value, promoted them by exhortations and political intervention.[4]

C. Associations, etc. Besides the lineages and clans, the guilds, *pao-chia* and *li-chia*, the gentry, and of course the secret societies played important roles in the administration of traditional Chinese law. An imposing network of institutions, designed to maintain the political, social and familial hierarchy in China, existed during the Manchu dynasty.

[1] Serious offenses such as murder, treason, etc., were dealt with by the government through the court system, etc. The lineage heads and leading officers had powers of punishment including oral censure, *yü*; demand for formal ritualistic apology; corporal punishment, *chang-tse*; expulsion from the lineage (a very serious punishment in the traditional Chinese society so that there was a provision in most regulations for re-admission upon good behavior); and finally punishment by invoking the power of the courts. Liu, Hui-chen Wang, *The Traditional Chinese Clan Rules* (New York, 1959) pp. 36–45. In a few cases, clan rules envisioned capital punishment or orders to commit suicide. At times the provisions from the penal codes were incorporated into the lineage regulations.

Hsiao, at p. 67 note 109, citing *hsien* records of the *Nan-hai* district, notes that a young man who beat his mother when reprimanded for gambling "...was put to death by order of a gentry clansman."

[2] Liu, pp. 22–24.

[3] *Ibid.* E.g., unfilial behavior was punished under many lineage rules by forty strokes; the Ch'ing code however provided a minimum of one hundred strokes of the bamboo for this offense.

[4] Hsiao, at p. 348.

In the immigrant community, on the other hand, many of the traditional organs of control and the machinery for the settling of disputes did not exist. The very symbol and the ultimate source of authority—the central government and its law code and court system—was absent. The scholar gentry, virtually the only Chinese group experienced in central government administration, did not form any significant portion of the Chinese immigrants to Malaysia. The *pao-chia* and *li-chia* were relegated to the past. The colonial government, interested in attracting Chinese immigrants, did not intrude itself into Chinese affairs during the earlier historical period. Therefore the Chinese, deprived of a role in the colonial government and lacking their own formal institutions, had to rely heavily upon the remaining instruments of authority—the transplanted and somewhat altered informal organs of traditional China as well as some institutions which were new manifestations of traditional organizations—as their initial basis for self-government.

2. *Institutions of Legal Significance in the Early Colonial Period in Malaysia and Singapore*

A. Capitan China. "The object of the British in the first place was to attract the Chinese to the new settlement of Penang so that it might profit by their industry, and to interfere with them as little as possible." In that the Chinese wished to be "...tried and governed under their own laws..." Captain Light "...committed the administration of each community to a headman or 'Captain'...,"[1] who was generally a secret society leader. The "Capitan China," an important institution throughout Southeast Asia, thus became the "broker" between the Chinese community and the English officialdom in Malaya, Singapore and Borneo.[2] The Capitan China "normally had full competence in matters of custom, religion and the family."[3] In Malaysia and Singapore, the Capitan China, although obviously in many respects very different, in

[1] Victor Purcell, *The Chinese in Malaya* (London, 1948) pp. 143ff. See also Joyce Ee, "Chinese Migration to Singapore, 1896–1941," 2 *Journal of Southeast Asian History*, (1961) pp. 33–35.

[2] On Malaya, see J. M. Gullick, *Indigenous Political Systems of Western Malaya* (London, 1958) pp. 23–25. On Borneo see T'ien Ju-k'ang, *The Chinese of Sarawak: A Study of Social Culture* (London, 1953) at p. 69.

[3] G. William Skinner, "Overseas Chinese Leadership: Paradigm for a Paradox," U.N.E.S.C.O. Symposium at p. 1. While Skinner talks particularly of Manila, Semarang and Phnom Penh, he notes this system was in existence throughout Southeast Asia. The term Capitan or Kapitan is from "the Portuguese cognate of 'captain.'" In the larger communities, the Capitan had various colleagues of rank and the system of selection was institutionalized involving both the Chinese community and the colonial governments.

effect performed a role similar in some respects to that of the Chinese gentry. Having neither the training nor the experience of the scholar gentry of traditional China, they nevertheless assumed positions of leadership in local communities on the basis of their economic position, affiliation with the secret societies, and their own individual talents. The Capitan China and the scholar gentry both provided local welfare services, engaged in arbitration, and supplied a link with the officialdom. In helping to finance Chinese education, the latter-day Capitan China in some sense became the guardian of tradition. However, lacking both the traditional intellectual training and the institutional assistance and support that existed in China, the Capitan China had to rely upon the existing political power within the Chinese community—i.e., the secret societies—for institutional support.

B. Secret Societies. These societies had their own system of law which was in part embodied in written regulations[1] of the society and dealt not only with the internal regulation of the members' behavior towards one another—including prohibitions against litigation between members, misbehavior with sons or daughters of members, etc.; but which also contained provisions promoting traditional virtues including filial piety, punishing unfilial conduct with severe penalties. Traditional Confucian familial concepts, reinterpreted in the light of the new social situation, found their way into the disciplinary code of the society. While these regulations were not framed by sophisticated members of the gentry, and were often crude and harsh, they nevertheless represent the carrying of some of the tradition by the immigrants to the shores of the new society.

C. Clans and lineage, etc. After the new immigrant community began to settle and bring its womenfolk to Malaysia and Singapore, various other organizations were founded. There were numerous associations, *hui*, which became important in family matters. Speech groups formed associations, as did surname, *hsing*, organizations, which largely displaced the lineage organizations of traditional rural China. Religious associations and commercial associations, *hong*, were among the more important groupings. Family and religious associations however, unless linked with secret society organizations, lacked the support of the courts and officials and the institutional encouragement they had received in China. Nevertheless, their roles in Malaysian Chinese society were

[1] "Rules and Secret Signs of the Toh Peh Kong Society," Leon Comber, *Chinese Secret Societies in Malaya: A Survey of the Triad Society from* 1800–1900 (New York, 1959) pp. 279–284. See also Leon Comber, *The Traditional Mysteries of Chinese Secret Societies in Malaya* (Singapore, 1961) at pp. 56–59).

important once the society had gathered sufficient stability to permit the growth of family institutions.

Thus while some of the tradition was perpetuated, the social and institutional framework of Singapore-Malaysian society was different from that of mainland China. The above institutions however are not only of historical value. Even after the establishment of the formal court system and the proscription of the secret societies (both of which were designed to usurp the prerogatives of the informal Chinese institutions and to establish the formal judiciary as the primary arena for settling disputes) these informal Chinese institutions retained vitality. In Sabah and Sarawak, the Capitan China has become an elected official, and in the Malay states and Singapore he still plays an informal role. The activities of the secret societies are well known.

With regard to the surname organizations, investigation in Singapore in 1964 has indicated that they too still play a role—in differing degrees among various groups—in settling domestic disputes. They tend however to bemoan their lack of authority in this area. The mutual benefit organizations are part of some of the surname associations and they provide insurance and death benefits for members. The wealthy still play a predominant role in the leadership of these organizations for reasons of prestige. Some of the mutual benefit organizations are growing in size by providing insurance schemes and provisions for an appropriate funeral, thus combining traditional and modern attributes. Youths also join the surname organizations (which generally do not require that one emanate from a specific geographical district in China, although the tendency of persons from the same geographical area to group together is quite pronounced) for social purposes, among other reasons. For example, there is a Lan surname organization, *Lan-shih tsung-hui*, composed primarily of Hakka people, which is moderately active in social matters. The primary purpose of the association is said in its literature to be to promote friendship among members of the clan. The leaders of the association, primarily composed of wealthier members, perform social services and functions befitting their prestige. Their hall, which contains the records of the association, is used for weddings and social functions, as well as an occasional place for the poor to sleep. The association does provide conciliation services in case of domestic or other problems, but the leadership feels a want of authority in this area.

The *Lan-shih Hu-chu Hui*, or Lan Surname Mutual Benefit Association, provides its members with a small book of credentials containing the by-laws of the society. Its members pledge to honor and observe the charter and rules of the society, as well as protect the collective welfare and promote the spirit of mutual assistance of the association. There is an insurance scheme, which encompasses financial provisions for funerals, as well as insuring the participation of the members in the funeral procession of a co-member. While the Lan association is only at best moderately active in family matters, other associations are much more active in both family and commercial matters. Thus even in Singapore—the most cosmopolitan area in Malaysia—the surname associations still retain some vitality.

In family matters, as Freedman has noted, new types of marriage ceremonies have developed. However, a more recent survey of a street in the poorer Chinese section of Singapore has indicated that seventy percent of the Chinese marriages were still of the old type, while twenty-two percent were of the new type; and that sixty-eight percent of the marriages were arranged in traditional fashion, twenty percent were arranged with the consent of the parties and only twelve percent self-arranged.[1] So that while there has been substantial social change, much of the traditional system retains some viability. Therefore traditional attitudes towards law are of significance, and there still exist alternatives (albeit somewhat weakened) to the use of the formal court system.

3. *Transition from the Capitan China System to Formal British Rule in Singapore and Malaysia and the Institutionalization of the Court System*

> The history of the government of the Chinese by the British in Malaya may be described as a transition from indirect to direct rule. This is made clear in the legal history of the Straits Settlements. The process was from rule by Chinese custom administered by Chinese headmen, to rule by English law side by side with Chinese custom administered by British judges, then as the law was interpreted, to rule by the law of England, taking account of Chinese custom. The interpretation of the law meant progressive restriction on the operation of the custom of the Chinese. At the same time a body of statute law was growing up in the Colony itself which was further to restrict this custom.[2]

The first major step in this regard was the granting of the First Charter of Justice in 1807, establishing "The Court of Judicature of Prince of Wales' Island." The court was to have "...the... jurisdiction and powers of the Superior Courts in England... 'so far as circumstances will admit' and... as an Ecclesiastical Court 'so far as the several religions, manners and customs of the inhabitants will admit.'" "The Judges of the Colony have, without exception, held that the Charter of

[1] Barrington Kaye, *Upper Nankin Street, Singapore: A Sociological Study of Chinese Households Living in a Densely Populated Area* (Singapore, 1960) at p. 176.
[2] Purcell, at p. 143.

1807 introduced the English law as it then existed into Penang."[1] The Second Charter of 1826 extended the jurisdiction of the Court of Judicature of Prince of Wales' Island to the new British colonies, i.e., Malacca and Singapore. This Charter was similarly deemed to have introduced English law into the new colonies.[2] A third Charter was issued in 1855 reorganizing the Court.

In 1946 the British protected states of Sarawak and North Borneo became Crown colonies and until the formation of Malaysia in 1963, they retained that status. In 1951 the Supreme Court of Judicature was established for the two territories (and Brunei); this court was later incorporated into the Malaysia Act, 1963.[3] English law was introduced into Sarawak and North Borneo "... so far only as the circumstances of Sarawak and of its inhabitants permit and subject to such qualifications as local circumstances and native customs render necessary."[4] The

[1] "Letters of Patent" (1855), R. Braddell, *The Law of the Straits Settlements, A Commentary*, II (2nd edition, Singapore, 1931) p. 232 at p. 249 and p. 13. The "customary" family law of the inhabitants of Malaya and Singapore was given expression within the ambit of these restrictions upon the scope of the applicability of common law. This unfortunate negative definition of the role of "customary" law and hence of Chinese "customary" law has placed a restrictive judicial interpretation on the scope of customary Chinese law in both Malaya and Singapore. Thus, for example, although secondary wives have been given recognition by the courts, they have been permitted to inherit equally with the principal wife under the Statutes of Distribution (*Six Widows Case* 12 S.S.L.R. 120). This has rightfully been designated a "most curious result," Report of a Committee Appointed by the Governor in October, 1948, *Chinese Law and Custom in Hong Kong* (Hong Kong, 1950) at p. 89. In part this interpretation as Braddell notes was probably the result of the fact that Muslim wives are regarded as having equal status unlike Chinese wives and the courts tended to analogize these two separate legal situations.

See also *Ong Cheng Neo* v. *Yeap Chia Neo* 1 Ky. 326; L.R. 6 P.C. 381. It was held in *Regina* v. *Williams* (1858) 3 Ky. 16 that :"...the prescribed adaptation to native opinions and usages shall go only 'as far as the same can consist with the due execution of the law and the attainment of substantial justice.'" It was further noted that "...nothing is said about applying native law to native cases, but it is merely required that the 'Administration of Justice' shall be adapted, so far as circumstances permit, to 'the Religions, Manners, and Customs' of the native inhabitants, while the rules of Practice are to conform, as nearly as may be, to the Rules of the English Courts of Request." See also *Fatimah* v. *Logan* (1871) 1 Ky. 255.

[2] Braddell at pp. 26–27. See *Regina* v. *Williams* (1858) 3 Ky. 16.

[3] The High Court in Malaya, the High Court in Singapore and the High Court in Borneo were vested with the judicial power of the Federation of Malaysia (Cap. 4, 13, [1], [a], [b], [c] Malaysia Act 1963; Article 121, Constitution). A Federal Court in Kuala Lumpur has jurisdiction to hear appeals from decisions of the High Courts ([2] [a]), as well as original and consultative jurisdiction in specific cases (Article 128, Constitution).

[4] North Borneo: Application of Laws Ordinance (Cap. 6), Ordinance No. 15, 1960; Sarawak: Application of Laws Ordinance (Cap. 2). See also February 1928 Ordinance, Revised Laws of Sarawak, 1947 (Cap. 1, Sec. 2); "The Law of England, in so far as it is not modified by Ordinances enacted by the Governor with the advice and consent of the Council Negri, and in so far as it is applicable to Sarawak having regard to native custom and local conditions shall be the Law of Sarawak." The actual introduction of English law, however, was a slow process and is still only gradually being effectuated. In part this is due to questions of political power, in part the result of the rural nature of the territory and in part reflects a difference in colonial policy. The early Letters of Patent of the Court of Judicature in the Straits Settlements do not use the word "*only*," nor "...and subject to such qualification as

provisions of the Sarawak Ordinance are somewhat stronger with regard to the role of custom than those of the early Charters. The introduction of English law into the Malay states was a somewhat complicated process, but in general the courts filled many "gaps" in the existing law through use of English law when a state became subject to English rule.[1]

The establishment of English courts that were to administer law to the Chinese was obviously meant to usurp the function of the Capitan China. The restricted role provided for the administration of Chinese customary law, the alien nature of British legal institutions, and the fact that the Chinese had already developed and adapted institutions of self government over a considerable period of time, prevented the early effectuation of this English policy. The Capitan China provided a connection between the British colonial government and the Chinese community; the establishment of the court destroyed this relationship while failing to provide a realistic alternative to legitimate rule of Chinese society. Whereas previously secret society leaders had legitimately played an important role as the recognized headmen of their communities, the legitimization was now removed,[2] and the secret societies (over the objection of some of the more enlightened officials) were proscribed.[3] The result has been that, while the secret societies

local circumstances and native customs *render necessary*." [Emphasis supplied.] This is perhaps another reason for the Borneo court's somewhat broader interpretation of the role of customary law. Finally the Borneo states were not thoroughly integrated into the colonial administration until a later period, being subject to Chartered Company rule.

1826 is the generally accepted date for the reception of common law. It is of interest to note that the early Charters proceeded on the rather humorous assumption that the island of Penang was uninhabited in 1786 when Light occupied the island. Since there was therefore no existing *lex loci*, and the Chinese, Malays and Chulias could not establish their laws in a British possession, English law could be applied at the discretion of the colonial government. *Regina* v. *Williams* (1858) 3 Ky. 16; *Re Loh Toh Met* (1961) 28 M.L.J. 234 at p. 237.

[1] See L. A. Sheridan, *Malaya and Singapore, the Borneo Territories, the Development of Their Laws and Constitutions* (London, 1961) at pp. 14–23.

[2] As Freedman notes with reference to Singapore: "...it is necessary to point out here that, historically, it is probably only since the last quarter of the nineteenth century that government intervention in Chinese affairs has had any great influence. With the disappearance of the Capitans China the internal affairs of the Chinese community largely passed out of the purview of the British administration. Legally and politically the Chinese contrived to maintain their own world. The few civil cases which came up for judgment before the courts had only a limited significance for the Chinese community as a whole. During the half-century before the growth of a system of direct control of Chinese affairs the codes by which the Chinese regulated their family affairs and the bodies to which they resorted in cases of dispute were beyond the reach of the government. It was during this period that the secret societies flourished as instruments of political control and courts of law within a closed Chinese society." Maurice Freedman, "Colonial Law and Chinese Society," LXXX *Journal of the Royal Anthropological Institute of Great Britain and Ireland* (London, 1950) at p. 98.

[3] W. A. Pickering, "Chinese Secret Societies," *J.S.B.R.A.S.*, Vol. III, pp. 1–18, as quoted in R. N. Jackson, *Immigrant Labour and the Development of Malaya*, 1786–1920 (Malaya, 1961) at pp. 49–50.

still exist, their activities have taken a more anti-social direction. For example, in Singapore the Criminal Law (Temporary Provisions) Ordinance of 1955[1] was amended in 1958 (and thereafter) to permit police supervision and detention without trial of persons "associated with activities of a criminal nature..." because of a crime wave in 1958 attributed to the secret societies.

II. THE SUBSTANTIVE LAW

The intrusion of English law was first attempted in the Straits Settlements (including Labuan prior to 1946), thereafter in the Malay states, and only more recently in the Borneo territories. In part because of this, Singapore has been the first state virtually to eliminate judicial recognition of Chinese family law for future marriages by passage of the Women's Charter, 1961; while in areas of marriage and divorce "Chinese family law" is still applied by the courts of Malaya. The Borneo states apply "customary Chinese law" to more extensive judicial areas, including inheritance.

Before dealing with Chinese law in Malaysia and Singapore, some general historical notes are relevant.

A. Traditional Chinese family law: some general notes. The law code, the *Ta-Ch'ing Lü-Li*, and portions of the *Ta-ch'ing Hui-tien*, contained the broad general provisions of family law, and when supplemented by *li*, provincial regulations, law cases, and the rules of customary law, it provided the legal basis for family law in Manchu China.

In general, family law was administered by the clan institutions and other informal organs of control. While the law code and case material dealt with family law, there were substantial areas of family law untouched by the code. Furthermore the code was national in scope, and local legal customs varied significantly in the areas of marriage, divorce, etc.[2]

[1] No. 26 of 1955; amended, No. 25 of 1958; No. 36 of 1958; No. 34 of 1959; No. 56 of 1959; No. 43 of 1960 and No. 56 of 1960. This should be differentiated from the Preservation of Public Security Ordinance, No. 25, 1955, as amended, which permits detention without trial of individuals "...with a view to preventing that person from acting in any manner prejudicial to the security... or maintenance of public order..."

[2] For example the procedure for establishing a betrothal, *ting-hun*, a condition precedent to a legal marriage, varied substantially among the provinces, *hsien*, and in fact among different classes and groups within the same local community. The forwarding of a bottle of wine to the girl's house by the go-between was an essential part of the betrothal procedure in Hungshui and Ting-hsi *hsiens* in Kansu. Receiving tobacco and smoking was an

Interestingly enough, legal secretaries and local officials were exhorted in settling disputes or dealing with legal cases: "If you never act on a penal law or an edict without first seeing that it does not conflict with what local custom values, then there will be harmony between *yamen* and people... whereas applying the law rigidly on every occasion would probably give rise to much dissatisfaction and complaint."[1] Caution was suggested in quoting precedents too readily as a standard. The arbitrators and local officials were concerned with restoring harmony and not merely with adjudicating rights and duties. The village leaders in particular were concerned with local customs and local precedents in solving disputes.

Alongside the common law and customary law of the Malays, Dyaks and other peoples of Malaysia and Singapore, Chinese law was given recognition by the courts and legislature, primarily in family matters. While the courts have attempted to recognize Chinese "customary" law,[2] Chinese customs in Singapore and Malaysia were undergoing changes under the impact of new social circumstances, and thereby certain aspects of family customs were altered. Once the courts and legislature intruded sufficiently into the Chinese society the legal rules themselves had some slight impact upon Chinese custom of either a positive or negative sort, and the Chinese attitudes toward the law courts were undoubtedly affected in part by their decisions in these areas of family law.

B. Some problems in the development of substantive Chinese law in Singapore and Malaysia. The courts have had particular difficulty with certain aspects of Chinese law which were alien to the jurist trained in the English common law system. In particular, the question of the status of secondary wives and questions of adoption have disturbed the courts and provided the large majority of cases on Chinese law in Singapore and Malaysia.

essential part of the procedure in parts of what was then Feng-tien (Liaoning) and failure to receive tobacco at the girl's home by the potential bridegroom's family meant that there would be no marriage. Somewhat more relevant to the Chinese of Singapore and Malaysia, the betrothal money, *p'in-chin*, was an essential element of the marriage procedure in parts of Fukien. *Chung-kuo Hsien-tai Shih-liao Tzu-shu* No. 6 (Taiwan, 1962) at p. 121f. These procedures were given sanction during and even for some time after the fall of the Ch'ing dynasty by the code and law courts, as well as by the informal legal organs. See for example *Ta-li-yüan P'an-chüeh-li Ch'uan-shu* (1933 ed.) case no. 596, 1913, where it was deemed essential to pass through the established customary betrothal procedures (or ceremonies), "hsi-kuan shang, i-ting i-shih" as well as the marriage ceremony in order to constitute a valid marriage.

[1] Van der Sprenkel, at p. 150, quoting from a book for legal officials by a Manchu gentry member and long-time legal secretary, Wang Hui-tsu.

[2] See Braddell, I at p. 80–88.

a. The status of secondary wives, t'sips.[1]

(*1*) *Traditional Chinese law.* In that the English common law concept of marriage is rather specific (see *infra*), and has for a long period of time excluded even potentially polygamous relationships, the status of Chinese secondary wives has been one of the most difficult problems for the courts.

The *ch'ieh* (or *t'sip*) in traditional Chinese law was of lower status than the primary wife. The birth of a son elevated the position of the *ch'ieh* within the household. The ideological justification for taking a secondary wife was to provide heirs for posterity.[2] The secondary wife like the primary wife had to be of a different surname and could not be within the prohibited degrees of relationship.

Ch'ing law provided punishment of 100 blows of the bamboo to those who degraded the principal wife to the position of secondary wife; or 90 blows to those who during the life of the primary wife raised the secondary wife to an equivalent rank. Similarly those having a living primary wife who purported to enter into marriage with another woman as primary wife were to be punished with 90 blows of the bamboo and the marriage declared null and void.[3]

(*2*) *Singapore and Malaysia.* While in Southeastern China the secondary wife was probably confined to the wealthier citizens, in Singapore for example Freedman notes that "...[n]obody can measure the extent of polygamy in the Colony, but there is the impression among Chinese themselves that it is widespread from the clerk and small shopkeeper upwards in the social scale, and that it increases as wealth increases."[4] At the same time he cautions it is not as common as popular conceptions hold, although rather common among the wealthy Chinese (at least at the time of his study). An excellent

[1] Cantonese pronunciation more properly romanized *ts'ip*, i.e., *ch'ieh* in *Kuo-yü*. In that the courts in Singapore and Malaysia use the spelling *t'sip* it will be used in the text. *Tsai* is the Cantonese romanization for primary wife, i.e., *ch'i* in *Kuo-yü*.

[2] Tai Yen-hui, *Chung-kuo Shen-fen Fa-Shih* (Taipei, 1959) p. 73, 74. As Meng-tzu noted, "Of the three unfilial [acts], not having a posterity is the worst."

[3] There is evidence that custom modified the severity of this provision under certain circumstances as will be noted below. There is even a little evidence, although it is rather weak, that punishment could be avoided by the officials regarding the second woman as a *ch'ieh* or secondary wife. See *T'ai-wan Kuan-hsi Chi-shih*, Vol. 2, No. 12, p. 943ff. Nevertheless as noted in the code and *Ta-Ch'ing Hui-tien* at p. 14762, if you have a living primary wife and again purport to marry a primary wife you will be punished by ninety strokes and the second marriage will be severed by divorce. There was however an earlier provision in the *Hui-tien* which indicates that the second marriage is to be regarded as the taking of a *ch'ieh* and no divorce is to result (apparently not indicating that there shall be no punishment). This provision was expunged in 1741. There was however a revival of this provision under special modified circumstances in 1821, as will be noted below on p. 163, footnote 1.

[4] Maurice Freedman, *Chinese Family and Marriage in Singapore* (London, 1957) at p. 121.

1954–1956 study of one of the poorest streets in the Chinese residential area in Singapore—and thus one where people are least likely to be able to afford secondary wives—indicates that of the married women on the street, four to five percent admitted to being secondary wives. The author cautions that two important factors are relevant to these statistics: viz., to admit to being a secondary wife is to suffer a loss of face; and some women, believing themselves to be the only wives, are in fact secondary wives.[1] Even if the practice of polygamy is declining with the impact of Western ideology (although this must be balanced against the Chinese population's rise in economic status), it is nevertheless a problem of some importance.

Recognition of the polygamous nature of Chinese marriage is of long standing in Malaya and Singapore. In the early cases, the requirements of proof were rather strict, and the threefold test included proof of: (a) long continued cohabitation, (b) an intention to form a permanent union, and (c) repute of marriage.[2]

In a series of later decisions, the requirements for attaining the status of a *t'sip* were modified and standards for attainment of such status became less stringent. In 1920 it was decided that the traditional need for a ceremony (although perhaps usual) was not required in order to become a lawful secondary wife.[3] In addition the courts did not emphasize the question of long-continued cohabitation in their judgments. Thereafter the courts reduced the requirements of attaining the status of a *t'sip* to proof of mutual consent to marry, "...and [held] that the requirements of a ceremony, of a formal contract and of repute of marriage were

[1] Kaye, at p. 174. See also W. A. Hanna, *The Formation of Malaysia* (New York, 1964) p. 206 f.

[2] See, e.g., *Re Lee Choon Guan, decd.* (1935) 1 *M.L.J.* 78; *Lew Ah Lui* v. *Choa Eng Wan* (1935) IV *S.S.L.R.* 78 (Singapore); *Woon Ngee Yew* v. *Ng Yoon Thai* (1941) 7 *M.L.J.* 32 (Perak); *Tan Ah Bee* v. *Foo Koon Thye* (1947) 13 *M.L.J.* 169; *Yap Kwee Ying* v. *Law Kiai Foh* (1951) 17 *M.L.J.* 21 (Johore Bahru).

[3] The doctrine of presumption of marriage was applied to the Chinese in *Ong Cheng Neo* v. *Yeap Chia Neo* (1872) 1 Ky. 326. See also *Cheang Thy Phin* v. *Tan Ah Loy* (1920) 14 S.S.L.R. 79; *Khoo Hooi Leong* v. *Khoo Hean Kwee*, L.R. (1926) A.C. 529.

Traditional Chinese custom required the *t'sip* to be introduced to, and accepted by, the primary wife (if any) at a tea ceremony. The *Li-chi* said it was not necessary to prepare the six ceremonies of marriage in order to marry a *ch'ieh*: "P'in yüeh ch'i, pen yüeh ch'ieh; liu li pu pei, wei chih pen." Nevertheless certain elements of the formal marriage rites were also likely to be undertaken, including the calling of the go-between, and undoubtedly the use of *p'in-chin* or *p'in-li* and possibly the marriage contract. See Shih Yi-yun, "Kuan-yu Wu Kuo Chin-tai Fa-shih Shang di Ch'ieh Chih Yen-chiu," *T'ai-wan ta-hsüeh Fa-hsueh-yüan K'an-hsing* (September, 1956) p. 137 at p. 145ff. See also *T'ai-wan Szu-fa Jen-shih Pien*, p. 630ff., for examples of certain marriage contracts used to marry a *ch'ieh*. It has also been held that family recognition of the marriage is not required as evidence of a valid marriage. *Lee Siew Neo* v. *Gan Eng Neo* (1952) 18 *M.L.J.* 184 (Singapore). Remarriage of widows is tolerated by the courts of Malaya and Singapore. *Chan Lam Keong* v. *Tan Saw Keow* (1951) 17 *M.L.J.* 21 (Kedah).

evidentiary only and not essential to the acquisition of a status of a *t'sip*." In *Chu Geok Keow* v. *Chong Meng Sze* it was held that the dismissal of the appellant's claim (in the lower court) for maintenance on the basis of being a secondary wife of the respondent was erroneous. The lower court had given judgment on the grounds that in order to prove this status, one must prove: a) long cohabitation, b) intention to form a permanent union, and c) repute of marriage. The court held however:

> With this view of the Magistrate I am unable to agree ... for the legal requirements of a marriage with a *t'sip* ... the law merely required a consensual marriage or mutual consent to marry and that the requirements of a ceremony, of a formal contract and of repute of marriage were evidentiary only and not essential to the acquisition of a status of a *t'sip*.[1]

Despite this legal ruling, the court in a surprising decision held that the appellant was not entitled to the status of a secondary wife, although there was some evidence of the couple having adopted a child as husband and wife, and the appellant had known the respondent for ten years. The magistrate felt that the appellant's evidence of a ceremony (a photograph) and the birth of a child were not substantiated and felt that even if there was adoption of children "...it is my opinion not by itself sufficient proof of marriage and although in Exhibit P-3 the words 'husband and wife' are mentioned, to my mind, they are merely intended to induce the parents to part with the child."[2] The onus placed on the appellant in this case appears to be fairly heavy.

The burden of proving this consensual marriage was placed upon the party who alleged it. Although it has been held that a formal contract of marriage would be conclusive evidence of acquisition of this status:

> The legal requirements for marriage with a *tsai* or a *tsip* are, I think, the same. This means that the law of this Colony merely requires a consensual marriage, i.e., an agreement to form a relationship that comes within the English definition of marriage. It is no longer any part of that conception that such a relationship must be life-long. It merely means one of indefinite duration as distinct from one for a definite period ....

Mere cohabitation for a considerable period was held insufficient. Living together publicly "...so as to acquire the reputation of being man and *tsip* ...would be evidence that the status had been acquired."[3]

[1] (1961) 27 *M.L.J.* 10 at p. 10 (Alor Star).
[2] *Ibid.*, at pp. 10, 11.
[3] *Er Gek Cheng* v. *Ho Ying Seng* (1949) 15 *M.L.J.* 171 per Murray-Aynsley, C. J. (Singapore). Although a tea ceremony and recognition of the marriage by the husband's family was expected in most cases, the court held it was evidentiary only and not essential to the acquisition of the status of a secondary wife. See also *Lee Siew Kow, decd.*, (1952) 18 *M.L.J.* 184.

These cases not only reduced the legal requirements for acquisition of the status of a *t'sip*, but also analogized the status of a *tsai* to that of a *t'sip*, despite the fact that the principal wife or *tsai* was of a substantially higher social and legal position in traditional Chinese law.[1] To some extent the judgment reflected the fact that in Singapore and Malaya plural marriages tended not to be coresidential and therefore the secondary wife was generally not subject to the supervision of the primary wife, as she was in traditional Chinese circumstances.[2] The decision also reflected the growing body of case law which was developing independently of Chinese society. The courts in Malaya and Singapore noted that the Chinese law is now a fusion of English law and Chinese custom, and experts are no longer required to testify on Chinese custom. As one judge noted: "In my judgment I had to determine the issues not by Chinese custom exclusively but by the relevant portion of the Law of Singapore applicable at the material time."[3] Therefore the courts in Malaya and Singapore would be unable to reflect changes in Chinese customary law that conflicted with established precedent.

The reductions in the requirements for attaining the status of a *t'sip* were reinforced by other decisions which held that where a man who had a living primary wife thereafter went through a second ceremony appropriate to the acquisition of a primary wife, the latter marriage would be deemed a secondary relationship.[4] These opinions were at

[1] H. McAleavy, "Chinese Law in Hong Kong: the Choice of Sources," *Changing Law in Developing Countries* (New York, 1963) (ed. J. N. D. Anderson), p. 258 at p. 264: "The essential difference between wife and concubine must be insisted upon, if Chinese law is to be understood at all. It was a difference not of degree, but of kind." The wife unlike the *t'sip* had the right to administer the family estate after the death of the husband until the son reached the legal age. The wife also "...shared her husband's status in the family and the clan." Secondary wives, "...who could be taken without restriction of number, enjoyed no comparable right, and as a rule were limited, and then only in the absence of a legitimate widow, to expressing their opinion in the family or clan council." This is rather a strong statement of the differences between the primary and secondary wife; nevertheless their status was undoubtedly different in law.

[2] See Freedman, "Colonial Law..." p. 102.

[3] *Re Ho Khian Cheong, decd.*, (1963) 29 *M.L.J.*, 316 at p. 317.

[4] "In my opinion, as the deceased had a principal wife living in Singapore at the time he went through a ceremony of marriage with Quek Boo Lat, he could only take her as a secondary wife. Considering the fact that the deceased and Quek Boo Lat had agreed to become man and wife, it seemed unfair to me to relegate her to a position of a concubine merely because the position of principal wife which she intended to fill had been taken by someone else. Both justice and common sense required that she be accorded the status of a secondary wife." Per Ambrose J. (1963) 29 *M.L.J.* 316 at p. 317. See also *Woon Kai Chiang* v. *Yoe Pak Yee* (1926) *S.S.L.R.* 27, where it was held that since there was a presumption against bigamy, the status of a secondary wife devolved upon the women who went through a ceremony appropriate for a principal wife with a man already married.

variance with traditional Chinese positive law, although permitted under certain specific circumstances by Chinese customary law.[1]

Another unusual interpretation of the status of a *t'sip* has been the fact that these secondary wives are entitled to the same share in the estate of the deceased husband as the primary wife under the British Statutes of Distribution.[2] While this has not necessarily modified the requirements for attaining this status, it has put a premium upon obtaining such a relationship in view of the financial rewards involved. Such an interpretation has given rise to cases where after the death of a wealthy gentleman some women will claim to have been his secondary wives on the basis of some minor or tangential association with the decedent in the hope of sharing his estate with his wife or wives of long

[1] "From the earliest ages Chinese law allowed a man to have only one [primary] wife at a time." McAleavy, "Chinese Law in Hong Kong..." at p. 264. *Chien t'iao*, or *Kim Tiu* in Cantonese, however, was a method of dual succession whereby for example a younger brother's son was permitted to succeed to both his own line and his father's elder brother's line if the latter had no sons. This was accomplished by the taking of two wives, one as the adopted child of his uncle - his father's elder brother, and the other in his own right. Although the law code prohibited the keeping of two wives, a case in 1821 declared that punishment in the case of *chien t'iao* would not be the same as if bigamy had been committed, but the second woman was to be treated as a secondary wife if a case were taken before the court. McAleavy at pp. 264–266. See also Case No. 852 (1917) decided in the early Republic. There it was held under the revised laws of the later Ch'ing period, *Hsien-hsing Hsing-lü*, that in the *chien t'iao* situation, during the life of the first wife, the second would not be regarded as having the legal status of a primary wife. The courts in Malaysia have not recognized the specific circumstances in which taking a second primary wife was permitted by Chinese customary and positive law. Generally the courts have given recognition to what could be deemed bigamy and potentially receive severe punishment in traditional China. It is also likely that in Chinese society in Malaysia these primary marriages which were given recognition (at least as secondary relationships) by the court would be regarded by social custom at least as bigamous in nature. Indeed there is little question that a person having a primary wife who is going through a second ceremony appropriate to the taking of a primary wife realizes that he is doing wrong unless involved in a *Kim Tiu* situation.

[2] *In the Goods of Lao Leong An* [1867] Leic. 418, (1867) 1 *S.S.L.R.* 1. The court seems in part to be influenced by the fact that the English Statutes of Distribution were previously applied to Muslim wives although it does indicate recognition of the differences in status. In Perak, Order in Council No. 23, 1893 did not permit inferior wives to share in the husband's estate; however this was repealed in 1930 and the Distributions Ordinance was applied to all Chinese wives. The *Lao Leong An* case, the first case upholding the status of a *t'sip* and applying the English Statutes of Distribution, was supported by numerous subsequent decisions, including: *Lee Joo Neo* v. *Lee Eng Swee* (1887) 4 Ky. 325; *In the Goods of Ing Ah Mit* (1888) 4 Ky. 380. *The Six Widows Case, Choo Ang Chee* v. *Neo Chan Neo and Others* (1908) 12 *S.S.L.R.* 120, is regarded as establishing finally the polygamous nature of Chinese marriages and parenthetically seeming to require a ceremony for marriage of primary wives. Despite the wording of the Charter, a dissenting opinion on this issue was registered by Sercombe Smith J., who felt that only English common law could be applied by the courts. "We cannot import into this Colony a marriage of such a nature as that it is capable of being followed by or subsisting with another, polygamy there being the essence of the contract." In *Ngai Lau Shia* v. *Low Ch'u Neo* (1915) 14 *S.S.L.R.* 35, it was held that the courts will take judicial notice of the polygamous nature of Chinese marriage. The Privy Council affirmed the question of the validity of secondary marriages raised in *Cheong Thye Phin* v. *Tan Ah Loy* (1916) 14 *S.S.L.R.* 79 in *Khoo Hooi Leong* v. *Khoo Hean Kwee* (1926) L.R. [1926] A.C. 529 and also indicated that since no ceremony was needed, secondary marriage with a Christian woman could be permitted.

standing.[1] Thus, while in effect raising the status of these women—and in fact the status of all wives—by permitting them to inherit a portion of the estate of the deceased contrary to Chinese law,[2] these decisions have also helped indirectly to promote the frequency of such relationships (i.e. the *t'sip*)[3] by offering this substantial financial inducement. These cases have also served to lower the status of the primary wife in relation to that of the secondary wife. If the object of these decisions was to protect potential offspring, rather than merely an uncritical imposition of English law upon an alien population, a more reasonable approach might have been to allow all sons to inherit as they do under traditional Chinese law.

(*3*) *Sabah and Sarawak.* Sabah and Sarawak have, as noted supra, differed in their interpretation of the scope of Chinese "customary law," as well as in their handling of individual cases.[4] It has been held for example that "...any proved or accepted Chinese custom [when dealing with administration of a Chinese estate] should prevail over English law."[5] In accordance with traditional Chinese law, sons inherit equally where there is intestacy, being responsible thereafter for the support of their mother,[6] thereby not putting a premium upon acquisition of

[1] See *Straits Times*, April 10, 1964 at p. 4, for a recent discussion of this problem in the case of the estate of Lee Gee Chong, "biscuit king." In this case it was alleged that a woman who apparently had had an on-and-off relationship of approximately 16 months' duration with the decedent—a wealthy heir—without the knowledge of his family, had acquired the status of a secondary wife. Therefore she would be entitled to the same portion of the widows' share as the decedent's primary wife and other lawful secondary wife. While this problem is somewhat moot, or will be in several decades in Singapore with the passage of the Women's Charter, No. 18 of 1961, it is still of significance in the states of Malaya. Sabah and Sarawak, having interpreted the scope of Chinese law somewhat more broadly, do not have this problem (as will be noted).

[2] *Ta-Ch'ing Lü-Li*, Chüan 8. The sons generally inherit equally with the minor exception of certain hereditary rank which devolves upon the oldest son and "...articles of pure personal adornment...." brought by the wife to the family; see H. McAleavy, "Certain Aspects of Chinese Customary Law in the Light of Japanese Scholarship," XVII *B.S.O.A.S.* (1955) at p. 546. Note *Chinese Law and Custom in Hong Kong* at p. 89: "The main difference between the Straits Settlements and Hong Kong is that in Hong Kong the courts have held that the Statutes of Distribution are totally inapplicable to the distribution of the estate of a Chinese intestate...."

[3] Which, as noted supra, are generally no longer coresidential in Malaysia. There has also been an inference in recent decisions and obiter dicta in other cases indicating a possible tendency to permit Christians to become secondary wives, thus tending to universalize this status. See David C. Buxbaum, "Freedom of Marriage in a Pluralistic Society" (1963) 5 *Malaya Law Review* 383.

[4] In part this difference has been fortified by statute. See North Borneo, Procedure Ordinance, 1926 (No. 1) which provides that matters of inheritance upon intestacy shall be determined by the communal laws of the people. See also *Matasin bin Simbi* v. *Kawang binti Adullah* [1953] S.C.R. 106 and R. H. Hickling, "The Borneo Territories"; *Malaya and Singapore, The Borneo Territories...*, pp. 115 ff.

[5] *Tay Sok Ann* v. *Tay Sok Hiong* [1955] S.C.R. 17 at p. 20. But cf. *Chan Bee Neo* v. *Ee Siok Choo* [1947] S.C.R. 1.

[6] [1955] S.C.R. 17; see also *Chan Bee Neo* v. *Ee Siok Choo* [1947] S.C.R. 1; and *Ko Jin Moi*

the status of a secondary wife such as exists in Malaya and Singapore.

The courts in the Borneo states have also differentiated customs of the various Chinese groups (e.g., Hakka, Foochow and Henghua) and have thereby upheld certain ancient customs.[1] The criteria upon which the court determines Chinese "customary law" however seem to be the customs of the Chinese people living in the Borneo states at the time of the decision. For example, the courts have upheld as "within the Hakka custom, the modern custom" a divorce by a wife where the wife has left the husband of her own free will, the husband has failed to get her back, there is no hope of reconciliation and the husband cannot support the children adequately.[2] This decision is clearly contrary to traditional Chinese positive law which gave the wife almost no opportunity for divorce. While the court has thus assumed a substantial burden, i.e., determining what modern custom is, it has retained a flexible position so as to permit itself to be responsive to social change. The courts in the Borneo states have also favored settling differences by arbitration and informal conciliation.[3]

While in general the courts in the Borneo territories are willing to look more carefully at Chinese customary law and to give it emphasis in conflict with English law, statutory changes have altered some of this. The Chinese Marriage Ordinance, 1933,[4] defines Chinese

v. *Siow Chong Koo* [1956] S.C.R. 48 which held a Hakka wife has no right to the real property of the husband, which devolves upon the sons, and who in turn must support her.

[1] In *Loh Chai Ing* v. *Law Ing Ai* [1959] S.C.R. 13, the court upheld a *T'ung Yang-hsi* marriage where a girl was given to the father of the respondent at the age of seven so that she might become the future wife of the respondent, as she did at age 18.

[2] *Lo Siew Ying* v. *Chong Fay* [1959] S.C.R. 1. The courts in the Borneo territories have jurisdiction over questions of divorce of a customary marriage, *Liu Kui Tze* v. *Lee Shah Lian* [1953] S.C.R. 55, and unlike the Malay states and Singapore (until recently) a court procedure is required to effectuate such a divorce although apparently a mutual petition for divorce will suffice. *Wong Chu Ming* v. *Kho Liang Hiong* [1952] S.C.R. 1. Cf. *Re Soo Hai San* and *Wong Sue Foong* (1961) 27 *M.L.J.* 221 (Kuala Lumpur) which indicates Chinese customary marriages can only be dissolved by Chinese custom and not under the Divorce Ordinance, 1952. Divorce of a *t'sai* under traditional Chinese law was restricted to specific circumstances (see Freedman, "Colonial Law and Chinese Society" at p. 109); however a *t'sip* could be disposed of rather easily although as noted divorce was not much practiced in Chinese society. The courts in Malaya and Singapore seem to permit divorce of a secondary wife providing there is the necessary intent and repute, e.g., by informing clansmen and relatives. See *In the Estate of Sim Siew Guan, decd.* (1924) 1 *M.L.J.* 95; [1933] S.S.L.R. 539. See also *Khoo Hooi Leong* v. *Khoo Chong Yeok* [1930] A.C. 346 for the possibility (which seems remote) of divorcing a secondary wife who had given birth to a son. Divorce of primary wives by mutual consent is accepted practice in Singapore and Malaya. See B. L. Chua, "Domestic Relations," *Malaya and Singapore...*, p. 364 at 373 f. See also *Lew Ah Lui* v. *Choo Eng Wan* [1935] S.S.L.R. 177; *Six Widows Case* (see *supra*).

[3] See *Siaw Moi Jea* v. *Lu Ing Hui* [1959] S.C.R. 16, pp. 18, 19. The court refused to reopen questions relating to possible grounds for divorce that had been previously settled in "arbitration" by influential community members.

[4] Revised Laws, 1946. Cap. 74. Relevant Sections are: Sec. 4, (1) (2) (3) (4) (5).

marriage as "...a marriage contracted according to established Chinese law or custom and includes a marriage constituted by the marital intercourse of persons betrothed according to such law or custom." The Ordinance requires registration with a Registrar of Chinese marriages of the marriage one month after it is contracted and provides: "No such marriage shall be valid unless so registered..." unless a Resident's Court declares that it is satisfied the marriage is valid upon application of husband or wife or any interested party.[1] Registration of the marriage gives it a presumption of validity and therefore the party alleging the marriage does not have the same burden of proving its existence as in Malaya and Singapore. Only the court can determine whether an unregistered Chinese marriage is valid.[2]

The Borneo states have thus attempted to gradually integrate Chinese custom into the contemporary legal system by requiring registration of marriages, unlike Malaya and Singapore until the promulgation of the Women's Charter, with minor penalties stipulated for failure to register. Chinese custom has been permitted a larger role including the application of traditional Chinese law to questions of inheritance. Divorce—an institution which has more serious social consequences, although not much practiced by the Chinese[3]—is regulated by requiring a court procedure before it can be effectuated, in contrast to Singapore (prior to 1961) and Malaya.

b. Adoption.

(*1*) *Traditional Chinese law.* Adoption—a significant institution in China, Singapore and Malaysia—was of particular importance traditionally as a means (upon failure of male issue) to provide someone to support people in their old age, continue the lineage branch, and to maintain the sacrifices to the ancestral spirits. In that the ancestors were thought not to accept sacrifices from other than related individuals, adoption of persons of a different surname for purposes of inheritance and thus for conducting the sacrifices was strict-

[1] In which case it is to be registered forthwith. Sec. 5 requires that: "The Registrar shall not register any marriage until he is satisfied that the ceremonies required by established Chinese law or custom have been duly performed and that the marriage is valid according to such custom." Some registration of marriages takes place prior to the filing of an action, or as an attempt to prevent a party from dissolving the marriage. In *Lo Siew Ying* v. *Chong Fay* (1959) S.C.R. 1, a 1945 marriage was registered in 1958 "...so as to tie her to him."

[2] *Chiew Boon Tong* v. *Goh Ah Pei* [1956] S.C.R. 58.

[3] "There is, indeed, a very strong emotional resistance among Chinese in Singapore today to the idea of divorce (and Malays and Europeans are derided for their recourse to this practice), despite the fact that a process of separation tantamount to divorce is generally recognized." Freedman, "Colonial Law...," p. 109.

ly prohibited. Those of the same surname were thought to be of the same ancestry.[1] Those who attempted to adopt and gave for adoption someone of a different surname (as the legitimate heir) could be punished with sixty strokes of the bamboo and the child would be returned to his family of birth.[2]

In order to consummate the adoption it was expected that one would pay a sum of money as recompense for the initial suckling and nourishing of the child.[3] Nevertheless this *ju-pu-yin* was conceived of as a kind of gift and possibly not one of the essential legal elements necessary to establish the adoption.

The Ch'ing code prohibited adoption of a child as the legal heir unless the primary wife had passed her fiftieth year without bearing a son.[4] Thereafter the eldest son of the secondary relationship, or, if none, relatives in descending order of proximity and age could be chosen and adopted as the lawful heir. In the absence of eligible relatives, someone of the same surname could be adopted as the heir.

While an abandoned child under three years of age could be adopted and possibly given the family name, he could not become the heir. It was also possible under customary law for a family having legitimate heirs to adopt other relatives or children of the same surname as insurance for their posterity and a sign of the bountifulness of their family.[5] This type of adoption permitted by customary law was common among wealthy citizens in both China and Singapore-Malaysia. Adoption of the only son of another family however was forbidden by the Ch'ing code. Generally speaking adoption for the purposes of establishing an heir had to be within the proper generation.[6] The adopted child, in particular the child adopted for purposes of providing for the ancestral sacrifices and thus the legitimate heir, was entitled to the same powers and status as an eldest son.

(2) *Singapore and Malaysia.* The situation in Malaya and Singapore was affected by the passage of legislation and the refusal by the courts to recognize the traditional forms of adoption. As Freedman noted, "...the disinheritance of adopted children has certainly been looked upon by the Chinese as an injustice."[7]

[1] Tai Yen-hui, at p. 88, 89, 90.
[2] *Ta-Ch'ing Lü-Li,* Chüan 8.
[3] Tai Yen-hui, at pp. 88–90.
[4] *Ta-Ch'ing Lü-Li,* Chüan 8.
[5] Tai also suggests (p. 90) that custom sanctioned the adoption of a child of a different surname as the legitimate heir.
[6] T'ai-wan Wen Hsien Yeh-k'an, *T'ai-wan Szu-fa Jen-shih Pien,* p. 640, 643 ff.
[7] Freedman, "Colonial Law..." p. 112. He also notes that: "In Singapore at the present time adoption of one kind or another is very common."

The Adoption of Children Ordinance in Singapore[1] was interpreted as prohibiting adopted sons from sharing in the estate of a Chinese intestate, unless they had been adopted under the provisions of the ordinance.[2] The situation in Malaya was unclear for a considerable period of time; however the Adoption Ordinance,[3] and the Distribution Ordinance,[4] defined a "child" for purposes of inheritance as "...a legitimate child and where the deceased is permitted by his personal law a plurality of wives includes a child by any such wives, but does not include an adopted child other than a child adopted under the provisions of the Adoption Ordinance, 1952."[5] Because of the expense, differentiation from traditional Chinese custom and general lack of relationship to the legal organs, there was little recourse to use of the ordinance. In Singapore for example between 1940 and 1949, only twenty-one children were adopted under the ordinance. Thus while the situation in Singapore has improved somewhat in recent years, in the Malay states the number of adoptions registered under the ordinance by all groups in the population including Malays, Indians, etc., in 1961 was 1,852 in a population of 7,136,804[6]—the entire population of the Malay states. There is undoubtedly a large number of customary adoptions not being registered.[7]

[1] No. 18 of 1939, Revised Laws of Singapore, 1955, Cap. 36 is modeled after the English Adoption of Children Act (1926) (16 and 17 Geo 5, c. 29) as amended 1950, as is the Malayan Ordinance.

[2] *Khoo Tiong Bee* v. *Tan Ben Gwat* (1877) 1 Ky. 473.

[3] No. 41 of 1952.

[4] No. 1, 1958.

[5] *Ibid.*, Sec. 3.

[6] The latest date for which statistics were available at the time of the writing of this article. Ibrahim bin Ali, *Report of the Registrar-General on Population, Births, Deaths, Marriages and Adoptions for the Year 1961* (Malaya, 1963) p. 12. The comparative figures of registration of adoptions for previous years include: 1955: 225; 1956: 460; 1957: (population 6,278,763) 526; 1958: (pop. 6,515,385) 740; 1959: (pop. 6,697,827) 982; 1960: (pop. 6,909,009) 922; 1961: (pop. 7,136,804) 1,852. While the increase from 1960 to 1961 was 100.9 percent, the 1960 figure showed a decrease of 6.1 percent as compared with the 1959 figure. Trends therefore are somewhat difficult to ascertain.

[7] While, as noted earlier, traditional Chinese adoption generally involved the payment of a specific sum of money, Section 10 of the Singapore Adoption of Children Ordinance, 1939, prohibited parent or guardian from receiving payment or reward without the court's sanction. In *Re Sim Thong Lai* (1955) 21 *M.L.J.* 25 (Singapore) p.27, the Secretary for Chinese Affairs, Mr. R. N. Broome, testified: "But in my opinion a genuine Chinese adoption is rarely considered correctly completed except where the adopters are near relatives of the maternal parents unless there is a payment of money by the adopters to the natural parents. It is not sufficient that there be a token payment in the sense of a small coin wrapped in red paper. The payment is normally substantial, and may be up to $200 or more. I do not think this payment is regarded as a purchase price. It is rather a token of compensation to the parents for the expenses incurred in bearing and rearing the child up to the time of adoption." This so-called "ginger and cake" money of $200 was held not to be a reward for the transfer of the child in this case, but is merely compensation for care. The court in a wise decision upheld the adoption. Sale of a child has been deemed illegal in the Borneo territories, which

This is another area of the law where unnecessary hardship has been imposed upon innocent parties, i.e., adopted children, by a rather unimaginative application of English law to the Chinese population of Singapore and Malaya, without consideration of existing social custom. The adverse effects of this imposition will be felt most severely by the poorer members of the community. The broader recognition of traditional Chinese adoption in the Borneo states seems more humane and just and more likely to promote use of law courts as a means of resolving disputes.

c. Recent statutory innovations in Singapore.

Singapore has been the first state in Malaysia to virtually abolish Chinese law, at least within the next several decades, with passage of the Women's Charter, 1961.[1] As a piece of legislative drafting, this ordinance has been soundly and deservedly criticized[2]; nevertheless its social significance is of substantial importance.

The Charter at one stroke exorcised the remaining facets of substantive Chinese "customary law" which were sanctioned by the judiciary for the future generations of Chinese citizens in the State of Singapore. The Charter provides exclusively for monogamous marriage (Part II), requires that these marriages be registered (Part IV), and prohibits customary divorce (Part IX).

After many years of sanctioning the status of the *t'sip* or secondary wife, and inadvertently putting a premium upon such relationships by a series of decisions, the legislature provided:

therefore refuse to permit a civil action for recovery of the sum—*Pang Chin* v. *Pang Chow Pee* [1952] S.C.R. 18. The courts have also construed Chinese wills rather strictly, giving primary consideration to the English concept of legitimate birth, rather than to the Chinese concept wherein paternal recognition was sufficient to confer the status of a legitimate child. E.g., see *Re Tan Tong, decd.* (1962) 28 *M.L.J.* 355 (Kuala Lumpur) where specific references to sons were made by the testator (who did not differentiate between adopted and natural sons) including references to sons who were adopted. The testator permitted his grandchildren to take his children's share of the estate if one of his children were to die within twelve years of the death of the testator. Adoption was widely practised in the testator's family and the adopted grandchildren were adopted while the testator was still alive. Under Section 10 of the Evidence Ordinance, No. 11 of 1950, which says wills are to be construed as they would be in a court in England, and despite the court's recognition of Chinese custom, it held that the testator meant natural children when he referred to children. This is a remarkable decision in that the testator specifically referred to his own adopted children as his sons, had knowledge that his sons' children were adopted, but nevertheless the court refused to uphold the rights of the adopted grandchildren to inherit their father's share. Cf. *Cham Lam Keong* v. *Tan Saw Keow* (1951) 17 *M.L.J.* 21 (Malaya).

[1] No. 18 of 1961.

[2] G. W. Bartholomew; L. W. Athulithmudali, "The Women's Charter (1961)" 3 *Malaya Law Review* 316. The criticism is not confined to the drafting but includes other external factors.

> Every person who on the 2nd day of March, 1961, is lawfully married under any law, religion, custom or usage to one or more spouses shall be incapable, during the continuance of such marriage or marriages of contracting a valid marriage under any law, religion, custom or usage with any person other than such spouse or spouses.[1]

Any person who married after March 2, 1961, was similarly prohibited "during the continuance of such marriage" from contracting a valid concurrent marriage. Not only was a marriage contracted in violation of this section deemed invalid and the children born of such a relationship deemed illegitimate and prohibited from rights of succession in the father's estate,[2] but anyone "lawfully married under any law, religion,[3] custom or usage who during the continuance of such marriage purports to contract a marriage under any law, religion, custom or usage" shall be held to have committed an offense under section 494 of the penal code. Thus enforcement of this law was to be effectuated by criminal punishment.

In summation: now, after a prolonged period of time when customary marriages were not registered, all marriages must be registered to receive judicial sanction; after prolonged recognition of the status of secondary wives, their status is now prohibited; and after holding for a prolonged period of time that the children of these secondary relationships were legitimate, these children are now deemed illegitimate and barred from a share in the estate of an intestate father.

Polygamy is probably reasonably widespread, at least among the middle and upper class Chinese in Singapore. Is it desirable therefore to legislate it out of existence for all future marriages? Even if many of the Western-oriented members of the younger generation associate monogamy with modernization and social justice (the logic of which is not self-evident), because of long-standing acceptance there will undoubtedly be those who will enter into polygamous unions despite the law.[4] The primary result of such relationships will be—not that the penal aspects of the law will be applied, in that people are not likely to present such

[1] Part II (4) (1). It should be emphasized that the Charter is prospective in its effects and therefore does not render plural marriages in existence at the time of its passage invalid.

[2] As was the purported wife. The relevant sections are: Part II 4 (2) (3); Part II 5 (1) (2).

[3] But see Part I, 3 (2): "Parts II to VI and Part IX and section 166 of this Ordinance shall not apply to any person who is married under, or to any marriage solemnized or registered under the provisions of Muslim law or of any written law in Singapore or in the Federation of Malaya providing for the registration of Muslim marriages."

[4] To a random sample questionnaire circulated among college students and adults in Singapore in 1964, 100% of the 183 persons who responded said they knew of or had heard of people who had entered into "non-legal" secondary relationships despite the passage of the Women's Charter. Of course such a survey is not very meaningful, but seems to indicate that there is general belief that the provisions of the Charter re secondary wives are not being obeyed.

matters to the law enforcement authorities—but rather that the children of these marriages will not only be unable to inherit but will also be stigmatized as illegitimate. The social desirability of such a result is questionable. A more gradual approach could have been found, even assuming the desirability of enforcing English common law on all the Chinese people in Singapore. A first step might have been to require registration of all marriages in Singapore, after which penalties could have been assessed for failure to register. This would perhaps have given some small indication of the number of polygamous unions to be dealt with. Thereafter either traditional Chinese concepts,[1] or others, could have been enforced to restrict the quantity of these marriages. The early Charters, for all their defects, recognized that, especially in family matters, different groups have different customs and habits. It is unlikely that the customs and habits of the Englishman will be directly applicable to the people of Malaysia.

If one is of the opinion that all customary law should be abolished and supplanted by the "modern common law," the Charter fails to meet that standard. For example, Section 82 (1) (6) provides for the future that:

> Nothing herein shall authorize the court to make any decree of divorce[2] except (b) where the marriage between the parties was contracted under a law providing that, or in contemplation of which, marriage is monogamous; (c) where the domicile of the parties to the marriage at the time when the petition is presented is in Singapore.

This section determines the jurisdiction of the court to make divorce decrees, and subsequent sections in effect abolish traditional Chinese divorce by mutual consent and require the institutionalization of an adversary proceeding to effectuate divorce.[3]

Thus the court's jurisdiction under the ordinance in questions of

[1] The need to introduce the secondary wife to the primary wife—who was almost always taken first—and thus have her accepted at a tea ceremony is one traditional aspect that could have been utilized as a preliminary basis for the reform of Chinese law. The underlying basis for the taking of a secondary wife was to continue the family line, and this could have been the ideological basis for further restrictions, etc. For example, emphasis upon the fact that to "...the Prophet Mohammed divorce is the most detestable of all permitted things..." has provided an ideological basis for reform of divorce under the Muslim Ordinance, 1957, in Singapore. See Ahmad Ibrahim, State Advocate-General, Singapore, "Muslim Marriage and Divorce in Singapore," XXVIII *M.L.J.* (1962) p. xi at p. xiv.

[2] See also 82 (2) and (3) which provide that the court will similarly have no authorization to make decrees of nullity or judicial separation and restoration of conjugal rights unless the marriage was contracted under a monogamous marriage law, in addition to which in the case of nullity the "marriage to which the decree relates" must have been celebrated in Singapore. In the case of judicial separation or restitution of conjugal rights, the parties to the marriage must in addition reside in Singapore at the time of the commencement of proceedings.

[3] Part IX, 81 provides that, subject to exceptions contained in the ordinance, "...the court shall in all suits and proceedings hereunder act and give relief on principles which in

divorce is limited to either (a) marriages registered or deemed registered under the ordinance,[1] or (b) cases where the original marriage was contracted under a law providing for monogamous marriages, and where the parties' domicile at the time of the petition is Singapore. Subsection (b) above is undoubtedly a statutory re-enactment of *Hyde* v. *Hyde* (1866) L.R. 1 D and D 130, which is said to have defined marriage at common law. In this ancient case, the court refused to grant a divorce to the petitioner, a Mormon, who had been married by a lawful ceremony and had never practiced polygamy. The court defined marriage "...in Christendom... as the voluntary union for life of one man and one woman, to the exclusion of all others." Since the court felt that a Mormon marriage was potentially polygamous[2] it did not fit within the English definition of marriage and therefore the court was unable to grant judicial relief. The judges apparently failed to realize that the Mormons, at least, considered themselves Christians. This case has been the cause of much hardship and bad law; so much so that it has recently been said by an eminent legal scholar: "Almost any proposal which would rid the law of the rule that matrimonial jurisdiction is not available in the cases of marriages which are potentially polygamous, ought to be viewed sympathetically."[3]

This archaic relic of the common law is being whittled away by the English courts and those of Commonwealth countries[4]; however, the

the opinion of the court are, as nearly as may be, conformable to the principles on which the High Court of Justice in England acts and gives relief in matrimonial proceedings."

[1] 82 (1) (a). See also Part XI, S. 166, which may be construed tI deem all legal "customary" marriages to be registered under the ordinance if contracted prior to its enactment.

[2] But see G. W. Bartholomew, "Recognition of Polygamous Marriages in America" 13 *I.C.L.Q.* (1964) which purports to show that Mormon marriages were never potentially polygamous in Utah because the law prohibited such polygamous unions at the time *Hyde* v. *Hyde* was decided. Bartholomew feels that the American courts have dealt with the problem of polygamous marriages "...far more neatly... logically and consistently than the English courts." The American courts define polygamy as de facto polygamy and even in such cases may be willing to give legal affects to some incidents of such unions. These cases, the author holds, "...demonstrate very clearly that there exists an acceptable alternative to the policy of marital apartheid followed by the English courts." p. 1075.

Potentially polygamous marriages are given some indirect recognition by English courts, e.g., *Baindal* v. *Baindal* [1946] P. 122; *Sinha Peerage Claim* (1939) 171 Lords Jo. 350 [1946] 1 *All E.R.* 348; see also 48 *L.Q.R.* 341; 66 *Harvard Law Review* 961; 31 *B.Y.B.I.L.* 248; and 19 *M.L. R.* 690.

[3] Zelman Cowen, "A Note on Potentially Polygamous Marriages," 12 *I.C.L.Q.*, p. 1407 (1963).

[4] E.g., *Sara* v. *Sara* (1962) 31 *D.L.R.* (2 cd) 566; *Cheni* v. *Cheni* [1963] 2 *W.L.R.* 17. The court held in *Cheni* v. *Cheni* that where a marriage, potentially polygamous at its inception, becomes monogamous by the *lex loci celebrationis* at the date of suit, the court would have jurisdiction. In *Sara* v. *Sara*, a Hindu form of marriage was consummated in India, which permitted polygamy at the time of celebration. The husband thereafter acquired a domicile of choice in British Columbia and the Hindu law was changed to make polygamous marriages illegal in India. The court retained jurisdiction over the marriage.

legislature in a jurisdiction which has long sanctioned polygamous marriages has seen fit to perpetuate the English past in the Malaysian present.[1] Similarly the desirability of an adversary divorce proceeding has been questioned in many common law jurisdictions; nevertheless it has been institutionalized at this late date in a jurisdiction that has long sanctioned divorce by consent.[2]

CONCLUSION

The development of Chinese family law in Malaysia and Singapore, from its historical base in China to self-administration by the Chinese community in Malaysia and finally to incorporation into a common law framework has been a prolonged and complicated process. The difficulties of incorporating a foreign body of law into an alien judicial system having rules of evidence and matters of procedure totally alien to the imported system are evident. The problem involved in importing a substantive code which originally served as a rather strict model used in large part to encourage formal and informal settlements of disputes and giving wide latitude to local custom, into a judicial system that is designed to serve as a major arena for resolving social problems according to fixed, "universal" standards, is enormous. The contrast between traditional Chinese legal institutions and contemporary common

[1] See *Lee Wah Fui* v. *Law*, *Times*, March 4, 1964, Cairns J. In this recent English case the parties were married in Hong Kong by Chinese traditional custom in 1942. In 1959 they entered a contract of mutual divorce and the husband returned to England where he is domiciled, and wishing to remarry there wanted first to ascertain the validity of his divorce. In view of the importance of this case, the Queen's proctor was called in and he requested that the court avoid the difficulty of jurisdiction in view of the fact that the marriage was originally potentially polygamous, by deciding that "the divorce was valid to dissolve *any* marriage in fact celebrated." He cited *Russ* v. *Russ* [1962] 3 W.L.R. 930, and *Merker* v. *Merker* [1963] P. 283. The final decision has been rendered in *Lee* v. *Law* [1964] 2 *All E.R.* 248. The court held that, although the marriage was potentially polygamous, the divorce validly dissolved *any* marriage between the husband and wife. The court did not determine whether or not a valid marriage was celebrated, but avoided that question by narrowing the issue to whether or not the husband was free to marry. The court said that cognizance can be taken of a potentially polygamous marriage for some circumstances, including the facts in this case, without necessarily determining whether the marriage was valid in the first place. The court's reasoning is somewhat specious, in that unlike the legitimacy of offspring or questions of property rights, in determining the question of the legitimacy of a divorce the validity of the original marriage is more directly at issue. Nevertheless this is some indication of the lengths courts are willing to go to avoid the consequences of *Hyde* v. *Hyde*. See also *Shahnaz* v. *Rizwan* [1964] 2 *All E.R.* 993 enforcing a contract for deferred *mehar* or dower in an English court, arising out of a potentially polygamous marriage. See P. R. H. Webb, "Polygamy and the Eddying Winds," 14 *I.C.L.Q.* 273 (1965).

[2] There have been recent discussions in Malaysia about the possibility of eliminating this adversary divorce proceeding from the Singapore statute in view of the premium it puts upon perjury and in view of its undesirable social effects.

law institutions in Singapore and Malaysia is perhaps too graphic to warrant further elaboration. The necessity of differentiating the traditional Chinese context from the circumstances of the Chinese society in Malaysia, however, must be carefully noted. It is certainly conceivable for example that certain aspects of secret society organization and Capitan China administration could have been beneficially incorporated into the existing legal framework. However, the failure of the colonial administration either to understand or to sympathize with the local population was in part responsible for the maintenance of the cleavage between Chinese society and the law courts. The Borneo territories in part because of the facts noted above and partially as a result of the progressive charter granted by the Liberal government of Mr. Gladstone to the North Borneo Chartered Company, requiring that justice be administered with care and "due regard to native customs and laws" have evolved a much more rational program for judicial development.

There is however a danger in the approach of the Borneo courts: by applying local custom in the light of modern conditions, there may arise certain local customs which are of an anti-social nature; or on the other hand, the court by gradual recognition of evolving social custom could ratify certain social trends that may not be desirable.[1] It also puts a rather heavy burden on the courts: i.e., to determine just what contemporary customary practice is.[2] The courts may also have a function of leadership as well as one of applying the law in accordance with customary change, i.e., the courts can reflect what social behavior should be, and not only what it is. This does not mean that strong

[1] See *Lo Siew Ying* v. *Chong Fay* (1959) S.C.R. 1 at p. 3, where Mr. Kong Fen Fatt, former Registrar of Chinese Marriages for the Hakka community testified that according to modern Hakka custom "...if the parties were incompatible the wife could get a divorce even if the husband refused to agree." Query as to whether legal ratification of such custom, if it exists, is desirable? See *Tang Sui Ing* v. *Goh Tiew Liong* (1964) 30 *M.L.J.* 406 (Siba) where the Foochow Chinese headman testified as to customary divorce among the Foochow community. He claimed a marriage contracted under Foochow Chinese custom may be dissolved if there is a complete and absolute desertion by either party, or absolute failure on the part of the husband to maintain the wife and children, for at least two years; or if the parties are completely out of sympathy with one another. Serious questions arise about both the reality of such customs and the desirability of giving them judicial sanction, if they exist.

[2] For example in *Yong Mong Yung* v. *Chai Shang* (1964) 30 *M.L.J.* 424 (Kuching). The court, while calling for evidence of Hakka custom on divorce merely found "...there is no custom governing divorce among [the] ...community, the modern practice being to leave it to the courts." There is substantial doubt as to this being modern practice and doubt whether the community lacks custom regarding divorce, but in that the court feels it must rely upon experts when dealing with this question, if the experts are inadequate such a result is possible. The court thereupon examined the question of cruelty and finding none, disallowed the divorce. This decision by Williams, C. J., is one of the poorer judgments in this area, arising from lack of information about the people, area and prior cases in Sarawak. See for example (1959) S.C.R. 1, cited in preceding footnote.

recognition of social change should not be reflected in the law, but only that the law may have an ideal function as well as being a reflector of society's mores. On the other hand the strong customary orientation of the Borneo courts is highly preferable to the strange mixture of English and Chinese law that the courts and legislature of the Malay states and Singapore have developed. The legislative and judicial decisions regarding Chinese family law have stimulated neither justice, social progress, nor respect among the Chinese for the legal organs. If the local community is to be encouraged to avail itself of the judicial organs for resolution of its disputes, then the decisions of the courts will have to be comprehensible to the people. This will probably require an understanding of traditional Chinese law and custom, in conjunction with a comprehension of the extent to which contemporary Chinese society in Singapore and Malaysia reflects traditional law and custom.[1] The unfortunate consequences of the misinterpretation of the role of Chinese law in traditional society, the failure to comprehend the socio-legal structure of the Chinese community in Singapore and Malaysia,[2] and the misinterpretation of traditional law as well as the harsh results caused by the somewhat arbitrary imposition of alien law upon the citizens of Malaysia and Singapore, have of course failed to bolster confidence in the judicial system.

At the same time care must be taken that recognition of traditional customs and their existence in present-day Singapore and Malaysia does not become an excuse for fostering those customs which impede the ability to modernize and to enable these societies to master their own economic and political problems. This is especially complicated in states like Sabah and Sarawak where many of the higher administrative positions are under the control of the English expatriates, who of necessity enjoy their present position of authority; and in other states where judicial officers are remnants of the colonial system of government. If English law is to be used as one source of the development of law, then it must be used with care. The Lord President of the Federal Court in Malaysia, Dato Sir James Thomson, has noted:

[1] See Freedman, *Chinese Family and Marriage...*, at pp. 155–177 for an interesting study of modern forms of marriage among groups of Chinese in Singapore. It should be emphasized that the social structure of various Chinese communities differs and that this should be considered in evaluating Chinese law.

[2] See David C. Buxbaum, "Preliminary Trends in the Development of the Legal Institutions of Communist China and the Nature of the Criminal Law," *I.C.L.Q.* (1962), 1, at p. 1, for some information on the attempt by the government on the Chinese mainland to foster formal and informal institutions to handle legal matters. See also David C. Buxbaum, *Osteuropa Recht*, No. 1, 1964, for some notes regarding possible traditional influences upon legal development in mainland China.

In the law of England, however there are no codes. There is much that is good. There are, however, anomalies, anachronisms, and peculiarities dating back to long forgotten pages in the history of England and which have now become a burden and an obstacle to justice in modern England itself far more so in countries like this, with far different historical background and social organization.

The time has come now, however, for each of the new nations, each now master in its own house, to consider how much of its [English] legal inheritance is altogether suitable to the changed circumstances of today, how much of it should be retained and how much of it should be discarded.[1]

This can only be ascertained by an historical evaluation of the traditional law of the people of Malaysia in the light of the present social and political conditions.

The courts in Singapore and Malaya have never fully recognized the importance of either *li* or customary law in China, which could override provisions of the positive law in the formal legal system itself, and which were of major significance in the administration of justice by the clans, the guilds and other informal organs. The paramount role of conciliation and arbitration and informal means of settling disputes was generally ignored by the Singapore and Malaya judiciary. In fact in interpreting Chinese law the courts often relied solely upon Staunton's English translation of the *Ta-Ch'ing Lü-Li*, some text books, or expert testimony which was at times of dubious value.

The role of *stare decisis* in an English model judiciary is particularly conservative in that the Supreme Court is bound by its own decisions and cannot overturn its own result; and while some may consider this of value in a relatively small homogeneous English society, it is of questionable utility in a multi-ethnic society in a state of relatively rapid social change. To this difficulty must be added the fact that the highest court of appeal in Singapore and Malaysia was, and still is, the Judicial Committee of the Privy Council, which sits in far off England, and whose members have little real knowledge of the social and legal situation in Malaysia and Singapore (despite the ostensible assistance of experts).[2] The results have been to strengthen the role of the already

[1] *Straits Times*, October 2, 1963, at p. 7.

[2] See H. H. Marshall, "The Judicial Committee of the Privy Council: A Waning Jurisdiction" 13 *International and Comparative Law Quarterly* 697 (1964). The original right to hear appeals from colonial and dominion courts was a prerogative of the King and it was in 1833 that the King's power was delegated to the Judicial Committee of the Privy Council. In the debate which resulted in elimination of the Privy Council's jurisdiction over appeals from the courts of the Irish Free State in 1933, Senator Conally noted: "A State, from the decisions of whose court an appeal lies to any court or tribunal or authority outside itself cannot be said to possess judicial sovereignty in the fullest sense." In Canadian debates it was noted that appeals to the Privy Council were often decided upon grounds of Imperial political policy, as some of the members of the Council had admitted. All appeals from Canadian courts were abolished in 1949, from Burmese courts in 1947, from Israel in 1948, from India

weakened informal social organs and undermine the role of the formal judiciary as the major arena for settling family disputes as well as to inadvertently create social problems and cause injustice, perhaps thereby also weakening the fabric of unity in Malaysia and Singapore by failing to ameliorate such social strife and at times exacerbating social tensions.[1]

in 1949, from Pakistan in 1950, from South Africa in 1950, from Somalia in 1960, from Ghana in 1960, from Cyprus in 1960, from Cameroon Republic in 1961, from Tanganyika in 1962, from Nigeria in 1963, and from Zanzibar in 1963. A factor in abolishment of the Privy Council's appeal jurisdiction has often been their lack of intimate knowledge of local conditions or of the local legal system. (p. 708) Limited appeal lies from the High Court of Australia and appeal lies from the courts of New Zealand. Kenya has continued to permit appeals as have Northern Rhodesia, Nyasaland and Ceylon.

[1] As has been noted: "A society can be forced to modernize under the impact of external forces, and indeed in the 19th and 20th century modernization has meant, to a very large extent, the impingement of Western European institutions on new countries in the Americas, in Eastern and Southern Europe, and in Asia and Africa. Some of these societies have never—or not yet—gone beyond adaptation to these external impingements. Lacking a high degree of internal adaptability, many become stagnant after having started on the road to modernity, or their modern frameworks have tended to break down," S. N. Eisenstadt, "Transformation of Social, Political and Cultural Orders in Modernization," *American Sociological Review* (October, 1965) p. 659, 660.

PART III

CUSTOMARY LAW AND THE FAMILY IN MODERNIZING SOCIETY

X. MALAY CUSTOMARY LAW AND THE FAMILY

The term Malay custom or "*adat Melayu*" is often confused or misunderstood to mean merely the habit, usage and the tradition of the Malay people. This is largely untrue. Custom in the days gone by was the institution whose laws and usage regulated the social, political and constitutional pattern of the government of the day. Those laws were expressed in hallowed maxims of great antiquity.

Foremost among the Malay customary institutions were the *adat temenggong* and the *adat perpateh*. The two systems differ diametrically in that one is patriarchal and the other matriarchal in their character and application. However they have evidently come from one original stock and in fact one is the offshoot of the other.[1]

Of the two systems which affected the Malay society the *adat perpateh* is the more characteristic and rigid while the *adat temenggong*, being patriarchal in character, has in later years identified itself with the Islamic social-political system since the advent of Islam in this part of the world about the 14th century. Thus in the matter of land inheritance, Malay property which is not inherited through tail female in accordance with the *adat perpateh* is taken to be inherited through the *adat temenggong* which is in fact the same as the Islamic law of Feraid.[2] In this paper, therefore, any reference to customary law largely refers to the system of *adat perpateh* which is still being followed in the state of Negri Sembilan and parts of Malacca in Malaya. The rest of the States of Perlis, Kedah, Perak, Selangor, Johore, Pahang, Trengganu and Kelantan represent the Islamic cum *temenggong* system of customary law.

Basic Family Customary Rule

In the *perpateh* tradition the rules of custom begin to close in upon a married couple from the moment the child is born, when custom impresses upon the father and mother six customary duties. It is ruled by custom:

[1] Taylor, E. N., "Malay Family Law" 5 *J.M.B.R.A.S.*, May, 1937.
[2] Islamic law of inheritance.

The day he is born, the day he is named,
And the day the parents inherit the customary debts.
The debts are six in number:
Firstly the fee for severing the umbilical cord,
Secondly the payment of the midwife's fee,
Thirdly the holding of the ceremony of circumcision
Fourthly the holding of the ear-piercing ceremony (for a girl)
Fifthly to send him to a teacher to learn the Koran
Sixthly to find a spouse for the child, a debt of custom and Muhammadan Law

Sahari ada sahari bernama
Sahari berhutang pada ibu bapa
Hutang di-atas enam sharat:
Pertama kerat pusat
Kedua upah bidan
Ketiga sunat rasul
Keempat tindek daing
Kelima di-serahkan mengaji,
Keenam nikah, hutang adat dengan hukum.

Thus the Malay child is taught to read and write and learn the Koran or the words of God from about 6 years of age. As the child grows up, the girl is taught the extra vocation of weaving and sewing and a boy is taught the arts of seafaring and self-defense to fit himself for his manly life. Thus the saying goes:

For the girl:
She is sent to learn to weave and to sew
She completed a mat and a pillow
This delights her parents
For the boy he is sent to read the Koran
He learned a verse or two to counter gambling and cock-fighting
Then for the boy:
When he reaches the age of maturity
If at sea he is taught to handle the oar
If on land he learns the art of sword play.

Bagi anak perempuan di-serahkan mengayam dan menjahit,
Dapat tikar sahelai bantal sabuah,
Suka-lah emak dengan bapa-nya,
Bagi si-laki2 di-serahkan mengaji
Dapat ayat sapatah nan dua
Tangkal judi dengan sabong

Kemudian anak si-laki2
Sampai ukor dengan jangka-nya
Kalau ka-laut belajar chinchang dayong
Kalau darat belajar chinchang pedang.[1]

The training of the Malay children conformed very much to this pattern until very recent times when, of course, it began to follow the modern system of school education. While the children are sent to read the Koran or learn weaving and sewing, custom imposes the duty on the father to see to their welfare and safety:

If a son send him to read the Koran,
If a daughter send her to learn to sew,
From that moment the tribal groom inherits a debt,
In the evening to gather them back to the fold,
In the morning to let them off
At night to keep them watched
During the day to keep them supervised
The chicken is protected
From the ravages of the fox
The buffalo prevented from destroying the fence

Kalau laki2 di-serahkan mengaji
Kalau perempuan di-serahkan menjahit
Masa itu terhutanglah orang semenda
Petang mengandangkan
Pagi melepaskan
Malam mendengarkan
Siang memandangkan
Di-jaga ayam

[1] Mohamed Din bin Ali, *Sambaan Chakap dan Perpateh Adat Melayu*, 1957, p. 41.

Jangan di-makan musang
Kerbau jangan merompak.[1]

Character training for both boys and girls thus begins at an early age and is more severe for girls, who are expected to help the mother with the family duties and chores and who begin to learn to cook the family dinner early in life starting with the boiling of rice and then the cooking of the curry. She learns to do the family laundry and at times to help her parents even in the rice fields. For development of her character and behaviour she must observe the rules of custom: to sit properly among adults, and not speak unless she is spoken to. She is not expected to enter into men's conversation, nor to speak to men out of her own family circle, especially not to strangers. She must respect her elders and some of her tom-foolery must cease at an early age. A young girl usually goes about only among lasses of her own age. With the observance of partial seclusion, the girl cultivates a sense of reserve, mystery and dignity. This is reflected on the occasion of the *bersanding* ceremony,[2] when the bride is expected to stoop down with patience and dignity and bear the brunt of the slanted and pointed remarks directed at the couple by well-meaning friends at such an occasion.

For a boy the training is not as strict nor severe. His religious education usually ends with the *Khatam Koran*[3] which generally precedes the circumcision ceremony.[4] Once out of the thraldom of the *guru* or teacher, the Malay boy often runs wild and does a great deal of mischief, which is regarded as a tolerable exhibition of spirit, and it is at this period that they often resort to gambling, petty pilfering, love-making and quarrelling. It is inevitable that the parents are concerned about his reformation and the logical step is to find him a wife. Marriage in the majority of cases succeeds in reforming him into a good member of society, especially with the advent of his children.

Relationship of Parent-Child

In the Malay family the children are nurtured in the spirit of close relationship of father to child. The child, especially a boy, often partakes of food and sleeps with the father; he is taken often to small feasts, festivals and sporting meets, and he normally has great attachment to

[1] Mohamed Din bin Ali, *op. cit.*, p. 65.
[2] Sitting in state of marriage ceremony.
[3] Koran graduation ceremony.
[4] Clitoridotomy for a girl.

the father. Swettenham writing in his *British Malaya*, 1948, notes: "The Malay child wears no clothes, and does as it pleases. When the parents are well-to-do there are always several people running about to attend to the child's wishes. I never saw a Malay child slapped, and they never seem to cry unless they are ill. They eat when they are hungry and sleep when they feel inclined." (p. 135) Perhaps this was true some fifty years ago, however, now that Malay children are receiving a Westernized education, these observations have been modified to a large extent.

The Family is a Member of a Tribe

The followers of the *adat perpateh* are divided into twelve tribes,[1] each taking its descent through the female line[2] so that, excepting male grooms who marry into the tribe, the females and their children form one large tribal community. Males married into the tribe are collectively called "*orang semenda*"[3] and the male and female members of the tribe are together called the "*orang tempat semenda.*"[4]

In a society where the female and male belong to a common tribe, the males assume the role of guardians of their females. They regard themselves as related through the female blood which engenders a common feeling for social security and protection. Within the tribe, members move freely without any real suspicion of sexual proximity as the idea of an immediate family circle of some six to seven houses is enlarged to embrace a tribe of 100 to 200 families. It is stated by custom:

Live they in homesteads
Neighbour to each other
Allowed to ask and to give
During illness encouraged to visit and be visited
The same closet they can visit in turn
The same well they can bathe in turn
The front yard they can play in together.

Dudok berpelarasan
Dekat rumah, dekat kampong,
Boleh pinta meminta,

[1] Mohamed Din bin Ali, *op. cit.*, p. 14. The tribes are as follows: Biduanda (Waris dan/atau Dagang); Batu Hampar; Seri Melenggang; Tanah Datar; Mungkal; Seri Lemak; Tiga Batu; Tiga Nenek; Paiah Kumboh; Anak Melaka; Anak Acheh; Batu Belang.
[2] Matriarchy or *soko*, as opposed to patriarchy or *baka*.
[3] The in-laws of the tribe.
[4] The bride-giving members of the tribe.

Sakit pening jengok menjengok
Sajamban saperulangan
Saperigi sapermandian
Sahalaman sapermainan.[1]

The *orang semenda* must comply with the social pattern of their wives' tribe, as a condition of every customary marriage.

Although permitting the members of the tribe to mix somewhat freely, custom nevertheless lays down very strict rules of *sumbang*, or acts of impropriety. Thus it is improper for a man and a girl to enter into a conversation on too familiar terms,[2] or to sit down together in a manner permitted to husband and wife[3] or to walk together or to gaze at one another in a passionate fashion. It is of course forbidden for a girl and a boy to be found together in a secluded place, whether or not they are in a compromising position. Thus custom lays down five improprieties of conduct:

Impropriety as to conversation
Impropriety as to movement
Impropriety as to gaze
Impropriety as to situation
Impropriety as to walking.[4]

Land Tenure

The female of the family, like the female of the tribe, is by custom vested with the customary property, which normally comprises of a piece of *kampong* (part of the usufruct), a piece of *sawah* (rice field), and a customary house. By law, a female must be identified with a piece of land. Land proprietorship is, in other words, made a personal law to the female of the tribe in the same sense that as:

Life reposes in the body
The body reposes in the (customary) property.

Nyawa terletak di-atas badan
Badan terletak di-atas harta.

[1] Mohamed Din bin Ali, *op. cit.*, p. 20.
[2] Especially one with whom they are within the potential marital relationship.
[3] This is even disallowed between brother and sister.
[4] Sumbang perchakapan / Sumbang kelakuan / Sumbang pemandangan / Sumbang kedudokan / Sumbang perjalanan.

To deprive a tribal female of her customary inheritance is tantamount to reducing her to the status of a foreigner (*dagang*) in her own tribe; therefore it is the duty of every *lembaga* (chieftain) to see that no female member of the tribe is so deprived.

This right to her customary entail matures on her marriage, when it is incumbent to settle upon her and her husband a customary house, a portion of *kampong*, and a piece of *sawah*. Normally the couple start off their married life with these few assets. It is the practice in *perpateh* society that on the marriage of the daughter, the parents and the rest of the family move to another house on another part of the family land, which is usually ready by the time each daughter marries. Thus in a family property there may be as many houses as there are married daughters. It is normal for the parents to live finally with their youngest daughter until their deaths, and whatever property the surviving mother has will be inherited by the youngest daughter. This is called *kapan* or the shroud and it thus becomes the duty of the youngest daughter to see to the funeral needs of the mother.

This system of gift *inter vivos* is sometimes attended with difficulties, especially when the daughters receive unequal shares of the customary entail. Also this system of land fragmentation has some obvious social defects, in that when parents give up the family house on the marriage of a daughter, they are often forced to live in a less satisfactory abode and condition. This is evidenced by the fact that many old women are poorly accommodated, either in a less conspicuous part of the family house, or in small huts separately built for them.

Such a system too tends to encourage a disinclination on the part of the husband to work the family usufruct. Thus it is very common to find women at work in the rice fields in Negri Sembilan and Malacca, where the *perpateh* system is being followed.

Marriage Properties

Marriage or conjugal properties are divided into three kinds:

1. Those brought by the husband called "*harta pembawa.*"
2. Those which are the property of the wife, called "*harta dapatan.*"
3. Those which the couple acquire during their wedlock, called "*harta sapencharian.*"

The extent of the *harta pembawa* and *harta dapatan* is recited soon after the marriage, in the presence of witnesses who are relatives of the parties of the marriage. This procedure is useful and practical for, in the event of a divorce, the conjugal properties can easily be determined and divided according to custom. The *harta pembawa* can be an heirloom weapon, such as a *kris* (Malay dagger) or gun, or even ordinary livestock such as a buffalo, and so on. The *harta dapatan* usually takes the form of gold ornaments belonging to the wife, or such property as may be given her by her parents. The *harta sapencharian* is the property acquired jointly by the parties. On divorce the conjugal properties are divided in accordance with the rules of custom expressed as:

Destiny maketh a marriage
Destiny endeth a marriage
Joint earnings are shared
Wife's property remains
Husband's effects revert
Union is dissolved
Settlement permits a gift.[1]

As to the effect of divorce in the *perpateh* society, it is not as severe as one might find in a patriarchal society where the wife must leave the husband's house with her children. The tribal wife will still keep the house, the family usufruct and her rice field. Her family is still intact. If her position as a wife in the family has suffered a decline, her position as a tribal woman is still unaffected: she is still vested by custom with the tribal heritage; she is still the guardian of the customary laws, the repository of the customary titles and the owner/trustee of her customary entails. Thus it is said in custom: "Customary offices are based in the female (*Jejak pesaka di-atas soko*)." Thus, on the demise of a Chieftain (*lembaga*) or *Undang* (law giver), the position reverts to the females of the tribe, and it is they who are most concerned to find the rightful successor to fill the office. This is effected through popular vote, and nomination of candidates should be made from the eligible leaders of the *perut* of the branch family whose turn it is to supply the candidate. It is surprising to note that democratic election of a sort was known to these followers of custom long ago. Custom has ruled that in the election of a candidate the better man must win. This is expressed as:

The hard core shine
The soft wood scattered.

Teras bermangun
Gubal melayang.

[1] Ada pertemuan di-nikahi / Habis pertemuan di-cheraii / Chari bagi / Dapatan tinggal / Pembawa kembali / Sekutu belah / Sa-orang berageh.

There is also a system for an election campaign for the candidate.

Whoever seeks to have horns, he will chisel his head
Whoever seeks to be the lucky one, he will carry the spear
Whoever seeks to be the Chieftain, he will scatter the gold dust.

Siapa nak bertandok, dia memahat kepala
Siapa nak bertuah, dia mengandar tombak
Siapa nak menjadi Lembaga, dia bertabor urai.

Voting is done by show of hands, and both women and men have the franchise.[1]

The Role of the Woman

The role of the woman in the customary family seems paramount. By her proprietorship of the tribal land, the *padi* field and the customary house, it is logical to expect that she will occupy a position of dominance in her own family. But this is not entirely so. It is ruled by custom:

The *Raja* rules the country
The *Penghulu* rules the shire
The *Lembaga* rules the *suku*
The *Buapak* rules the *anak buah* and
The husband rules the wife.

Kunchi alam Raja
Kunchi luak Penghulu
Kunchi suku Lembaga
Kunchi anak buah Buapak dan
Kunchi bini laki.

If there was a tendency in the past for the woman to assert her dominance, the teaching of Islam has emphatically placed the male in a superior position; thus it is the father who gives the daughter in marriage, and patriarchal consanguinity is paramount in all relationships of the family in matters other than those determined by custom.

[1] On the death of either spouse joint earnings, or *harta sapencharian*, are left totally to the surviving spouse.

The Preference for Daughters

The female inherits the customary entail by female tail; custom makes her the permanent member of the tribal society (which often occupies a whole valley in any particular area).

Thus when a family has no natural daughters, the mother will adopt a girl to inherit her property at death. In the choice of an adopted daughter, the adoption of the nearest niece in the family would be ideal according to custom, but this is often impractical since the girl so adopted tends to return to her natural mother when she reaches the age of discretion. The adoption of an indirect heir or close relative within the tribe is informally effected and so, should the girl return to her natural mother subsequently, there is no institutional remedy. It is thus usual for a mother to adopt from outside the tribe, or even outside the Malay race. A girl of Chinese origin is often preferred. In such an event, the child must be formally adopted and the adoption is announced to the whole tribe at a formal ceremony in the presence of the tribal chief. Custom clearly states that such an adopted child steps fully and effectively into the position of a natural child in matters of inheritance.[1] The ceremony of adoption is called "*Berkedim.*"[2]

To adopt a non-tribal female, it is incumbent upon the adopter mother to hold a feast and to slaughter a buffalo. The tribal chief, the minor *adat* officials, and those indirect heirs to the adopter's customary entail will be invited to the feast, which is followed by the performance of the rituals of adoption before the customary officials. If the feast represents the more mundane side of the adoption, the ritual ceremony provides the spiritual and legal link sanctioning the initiation of the "stranger" into family and tribe with rights of inheritance to the customary entail. The ritual of adoption is:

The touching of blood
The supplication of doa or prayer
The affirmation of an oath
The bearing of witness by the Koran.

Darah di-chechah
Doa di-tampong
Sumpah di-laboh
Koran di-junjong.

[1] Except that she does not bar the natural brother to be registered as life occupant of her mother's land.

[2] An adopted child does not inherit the parents' property in Islamic law.

The touching of the blood by the adopter mother and adoptee daughter symbolizes the initiation of the similarity of the adopter's and adoptee's blood which thereby acts to render the adoptee almost a natural child. After this there will be the supplication for the blessing and grace of God, His prophets and the messenger spirits. Subscribing to the Koran is designed to strengthen the effect of the initiation by bearing witness on the word of God. The purpose of the ceremony, ritual, and feast is that those present will bear witness, and see that other members of the adopter's family and indirect heirs shall in no manner detract from the rights of the adoptee to inherit the customary entail. Thereafter it is the adoptee and no longer the indirect customary heir who should be responsible for the customary duties incumbent upon the person or family of the adopter.

In the customary arrangement, the sons do not inherit the customary entail. The male members of the family, and indeed the tribe, are by custom altogether excluded from the customary inheritance. But they are not otherwise dissatisfied with the state of affairs, as they are compensated through the system of the tribal exogamous marriage. When a tribal man marries into another tribe his wife is apportioned the family usufruct including a house, *kampong* and *sawah*. The male thus need only "hang his hat" as the expression goes.

As for the unmarried males, it is the duty of the mother to provide for them until they get married. If the mother fails, the duty falls on her sisters, or nieces or grandmother or whoever inherits the mother's customary entail. Thus an adoptee sister will step into the shoes of the customary heir to be responsible for the brother. The customary obligation includes and extends to giving sustenance and shelter to them while single, the payment of their marriage fee or making good their customary debts on appropriate occasions,[1] and being responsible for their funeral expenses in the event of their death.

A male heir is entitled to be registered as a *life occupant* of his mother's customary land on her death if she leaves no natural daughter. This has now been made into a legal provision[2] which enables the male heir to be registered as a life occupant of the mother's customary land even if the mother has adopted a daughter in the family. In other words, an adopted sister does not preclude or bar the male heir from having a registered interest in the mother's customary land.

[1] Including payment for misdemeanour or even gambling debts.
[2] Section 13 of the Customary Tenure Enactment Cap. 215.

The Modifying Influence of Islam

The coming of Islam has had a modifying influence upon the effect of customary law. First Islam with its patrilineal system requires the wife to recognise the supremacy of the husband as head of the family. The Islamic rules of predominance of males over females in matters of inheritance correct the otherwise anomalous position of custom, which makes women the sole proprietresses of customary holdings. With the passage of time and the development of the rubber industry, vast areas of fringe forest land gave way to small holdings planted with rubber. This new alienation effected under the Australian Torrens System of survey and registration becomes ordinary non-customary land holding when registered in the District Record. The customary lands—those originating from the old occupational titles, were subsequently registered in the District roll but endorsed with the words "Customary Land" which ensure and perpetuate the succession of these lands through female tail. Thus while customary lands are divided among the females per capita the non-customary lands are divided according to Islamic law, whereby the share of a male is equivalent to twice that of the female. The ratio of land holdings is therefore maintained at some semblance of equality and fairness between the male and female.

In the early customary period male members of the tribe were satisfied that their mothers and sisters were well provided for while they held the position of unregistered heir over the customary property, and that their mothers and sisters could only occupy but not sell the land. Of late, however, due to the statutory registration of the interests of their female relatives under the Land Code Cap. 138,[1] and the increasing assertion of proprietary rights, the male relatives are becoming less content with their supervisory position. Many male heirs have attempted to lay claim to the customary property under Islamic law, in that as Muslims, they argue, they should abide by the law as expounded in the Koran. Here orthodox Muslims join together to frown at the existence of the customary inheritance. Thus in a family without female members to inherit the family usufruct, the son will often use every means in his attempt to claim the mother's customary property. Such a situation often results in suits and counter-petitions, often ending before the highest tribunal in the land, that of *Majlis Keadilan Negeri*.[2]

[1] Section 13 of the Land Code Cap. 138.
[2] See "Custom as seen in Land Inheritance", Inche Lokman bin Yusof, *op. cit.* p. 11.

The Marriage System

Through the rules and rituals of the *perpateh* tradition, marriage has been made into an institution which more than merely brings individual parties into a lawful union. It binds the host of relations and tribal organizations into a complete cohesive whole.

It is to be remembered that *perpateh* society begins at the tribal level. One may suppose that the tribes would dissipate themselves in tribal feuds, as is often the case with tribal society. Here, the *perpateh* system by its exogamous marriage ties makes one tribe biologically and racially dependent upon another. A marriage is therefore a factor of unity between the individual family and members of the exogamous tribes, just as divorce is a factor of disunity. Between the frequencies of marriage and divorce there is a fairly peaceful equilibrium of society. As marriages occur between any two of the twelve tribes, we find that they are responsible for unity and cohesion at inter-tribal as well as the state level.

Before a marriage takes place there are different steps and rituals to be observed for the proposed union. A marriage is first preceded by a discreet enquiry by the matchmaker (*duai*), usually the female relative of the interested groom. If this enquiry has a hope of success, then a seeker ring (*chinchin tanya*) is presented to the prospective bride's family. The ring should be returned within 3 days if the proposal is not accepted. In the likely event that it is accepted, the bride's parents will hold a simple ceremony of showing the ring to the bride's relatives, usually the immediate members of the bride's family. If the proposal is again accepted, then another ceremony is held called the "*mengembang chinchin*" announcing the ring to the relatives of both the bride and bridegroom. When all is well the engagement of the parties will follow. It is symbolized by the bride's parent placing another ring beside the first, in the presence of the guests assembled. The appearance of a double ring signifies unanimous consent. Thus it is said by custom:

> One ring to sound the parents.
> Double ring unanimous agreement.
> Unanimous agreement warrants a reply
> Disagreement the ring is returned.
> Unanimous agreement the pact is sealed
> Agreement made is honour-bound
> Meanwhile keep in mind
> On due date the pact is executed

Repudiation by the male he forfeits the token
Repudiation by the bride she repays two fold
Insanity and lunacy are outside the pact.[1]

After the engagement a wedding date is fixed. At this ceremony it is usual to invite the headman of each tribe. If the ceremony is a big one, even royalty is invited, as this tends to raise the status of the marriage.

The marriage of a spinster daughter, especially the eldest, requires the slaughter of full grown cattle as a symbol of status. In this context the feast of the day should not be supplemented by other than meat dishes.

Marriage without fulfilling the several rituals as demanded by custom is regarded as a blemish on the parties, and carries with it the aspersion that the parties have had access to each other, thus causing disrepute to the family and shame to the tribal relatives. Runaway marriages are unknown to custom.

Divorce

Customary divorce, like customary marriage, has its own laws and rituals. Custom rules that before a divorce is possible there should be proper attempt at reconciliation. A husband contemplating divorce will hold a feast to which he will invite his own and the wife's relatives. Such a reconciliation is called *Bersuarang*. Here, the husband will air his grievances for the consideration of the parties. In the majority of cases the misunderstanding can be mended. The presence of elders has often been beneficial in patching up what may prove to have been a hasty decision or an irrelevant quarrel. Divorce is consented to only upon cogent and sufficient reasons; the failure of love alone does not always suffice. Should good counsel not prevail, however, divorce is permitted after settling the marriage debt and property.

The Death of Either Spouse

The death of the husband does not call for any special ritual. It is only necessary that the husband should be buried with honour and in a manner befitting his service to the wife's community. He is normally buried at the burial ground of the wife's tribe and there should be performed the ceremony of the 3rd-day and the 100th-day feast. At this feast it is usual as a last act of rememberance of the deceased to his rela-

[1] Chinchin sa-bentok menanya ibu bapa-nya / Chinchin dua bentok oso sekata / Oso sekata kata di-balekkan / Ta'oso sekata chinchin di-balekkan / Oso sekata janji di-ikat / Janji di-buat di-muliakan / Dalam janji di-gadohkan / Sampai janji di-tepati / Elah si-laki2 lonchor tanda / Elah si-perempuan ganda tanda / Sawan gila luar janji.

tives to return to them at a simple ceremony a complete suit of wearing apparel used by him during his lifetime. This is symbolic of returning his tribal entity to the members of his tribe. The suit normally consists of trousers and coat, shoes and headgear plus a weapon, normally a kris.

The death of a wife, however, does call for a definite customary ceremony. At a suitable date, usually the 100th day, the husband is fetched by his blood relatives back into his mother's tribe. This ceremony can be quite elaborate and often attended by pathos as the father has to leave the family house and separate from his children. This is an occasion for making appropriate excuses and reciting verses and similies with hidden meaning.[1]

The Customary Tribal Obligations

In a society where marriage is exogamous the children belong to the tribe of the mother. The father, in a sense, is the patriarch of the family only until the children come of age. Thus it is said:

When young they are your siblings
When grown up they are your wife's relatives.

Kechil2 anak
Sudah besar tempat semenda.

[1] Then the marriage fee fulfilled the marriage solemnised, / If his luck together we pray, / If his fortune together we supplicate, / If during the day together we look after, / If at night together we listen.

Then within the month and a half / In-laws are begotten / Within one year or two / Children are begotten.

In the meanwhile, / As luck would have it, / Misfortune befalls the parties, / Like in the sea the ship has floundered / Like on land the rice pot is broken / Your tribal female meets with untimely death / The spouse of my tribal member / It is natural that both / Relatives of the wife and the husband should be concerned about it / I have invited those who are far away / And fetched those who are near / Now those who are far away have come / And those near have assembled / If water together we bale / If twigs together we break them / The dead we must inter / The living we must give sustenance /

Then:

To take an example from the prophet / A precedent from our forebears / To hold a ceremony is a must / Thus a handful of rice / A piece of bamboo shoot / An egg boiled / A sip of water / As a token that / Our pact is not broken / Our fidelity is not shaken / What is planted to be digged / What is buried to be uncovered / What is missing to be found / Like the betel leaf to return to its stalk, / Like the arecanut to find its corolla / Like the eel to return to the mud / Like the crows to return to the continent / The quadrupeds to gather back to the fold / Those that fly to return to the mountain / The tribal member to return to his tribe / Tribal office to vest in the female.

The significance of the fetching or menjemput of the bride is to enable him to regain his status in his tribe which is useful if he is a contender of the tribal Chieftain or the tribal office.

In matters of *adat* the children are regarded as in the mother's line. Thus in the betrothal ceremony of a daughter, the father plays a less important role than the mother, brothers, uncles and aunts of the family. However on the solemnization of marriage, the father assumes the patriarchal authority as a result of the influence of Islam.

In the matter of crime, especially blood crime like murder, the father cannot draw upon the blood of his children. In *perpateh* tradition, murder or slaying is avenged not by retribution but by restitution of the life lost. There is no "eye for an eye" or "tooth for a tooth" principle in *Perpateh* justice. They believe that "two wrongs cannot make one right" and are adverse to unnecessary loss of life. Thus the *perpateh* saying goes:

> Compensate damage
> The slain restitute.
>
> Chinchang pampas
> Bunoh beri balas.

Thus if a man, who is a father, slays a person—for example the son of another family—he has to restitute a life for this crime. The restituted life cannot be that of his son but can be his nephew from his own tribe.

Here the justice of the *adat temenggong* in common with the justice of most of the world, is diametrically opposed to the sense of justice of *perpateh*. The *temenggong* concept is:

> Whoever casts the net must jump (into the water to drag it out)
> Whoever owes must pay
> Whoever slays must be slain.
>
> Siapa menjala siapa terjun
> Siapa berhutang siapa berbayar
> Siapa membunoh siapa kena bunoh.

There is always a sense of difference running through the family between the wife's side, including the children when grown, and the father. Thus the "*tempat semenda*"[1] are differentiated from the "*orang semenda*" or the males related by marriage into the tribe. The collective custom as applied to the wife-giving tribe is called the *adat* and the

[1] Members of the bride-giving tribe.

collective custom as applied to the male in-laws is called the *resam*. Thus it is said:

Orang semenda sa-Resam
Orang tempat semenda sa-Adat.

Sometimes they are referred to as *orang sa-adat*, meaning the bride's tribe, and *orang sa-resam*, *i.e.*, the male married into the tribe. This classification is necessary to determine the different rights, duties, and obligations to and by the tribe. The *orang semenda* is expected to give his services to the wife's family and improve the customary property. The rule is:

If religious, ask for his prayer
If rich, ask for his dollars
If clever, ask for his wise counsel
If bushy, to get his shelter.

Kalau alim minta do'a-nya
Kalau kaya minta ringgit-nya
Kalau cherdek minta akal-nya
Kalau rimbun tempat bertedoh.

The *orang semenda*, however humble, should not be underestimated or looked upon with disfavour, for all are useful members of the tribal society. Even the physically handicapped are assigned their task:

The blind to blow the pound mortar
The deaf to fire the cannon
The skin-afflicted[1] to carry the bamboo
The physically handicapped to watch the drying of padi.

Yang buta mengembus lesong
Yang pekak membakar bedil
Yang kurap mengandar buloh
Yang patah menunggu jemoran.

Nevertheless, the *orang semenda* is subservient to the wife's tribe and must respect her near relatives. Of his duties it is said:

To go when bidden
To come when called[2]

[1] *Kurap* or itches or ring-worm.
[2] Largely applied to the fetching of a bridegroom on a marriage by the existing *orang semenda*.

If clever to seek his counsel
If dull to carry the errand.

Di-suroh pergi
Di-panggil datang
Kalau cherdek teman berunding
Kalau bingong di-suroh arah.

To all intents and purposes the *orang semenda* become members of and identify with the wife's tribal society upon marriage. To keep equanimity and peace, custom has laid two opposing taboos or prohibitions over which neither the wife's tribe nor the married male members may transgress:

It is taboo:

To take two when one is given
To have one tree with two ladders
One ship with two captains
An evil spirit with two haunts.

Satu di-beri dua di-tarek
Satu enau dua sigai
Satu kepal nakhoda dua
Pelesit dua sajenjang.

This means that a groom is forbidden to give undue attention to other female members of his household nor to marry another woman within the members of the tribe. In this sense the *adat* encourages monogamous marriage. A man is forbidden to let another man share his wife's love, or to have any illicit or clandestine affair within the tribe himself. These are acts of ignominy and shame to the bride's tribe, which may be punished by severe sanctions.

In favour of the groom, the wife's side must observe the opposing prohibition. It is taboo:

To retract a gift after it has been given
To pull the tail when the animal is strained
To keep watch when the property is bailed
To keep on reminding what has already been requested.

Sudah di-beri di-tarek balek
Sudah di-uja di-tegang ekor

Sudah di-pertaroh di-pemalami
Sudah di-pesan di-turuti.

Any property once given to the couple may not be recovered. Further, after her marriage the parents may not bar the husband from taking the wife away from the family house, *e.g.*, to his place of work. It is a great family offence to retract anything once it has been agreed or made firm. It is also a species of impertinence on the part of the wife's relatives to distrust the groom. Thus if property is bailed to him for his keep, it is not necessary and is even highly impolite for the bailer to go to his house to watch the property already subject to bailment. It is also apparently impolite to remind the groom repeatedly of what he has been asked to do.

The Prohibition of Marriage Relationship

While most patriarchal social systems prohibit marriage within the consanguinity of agnates, the *perpateh* system prohibits marriage not only within the relationship of cognates but also within the entire tribal group claiming ancestry through a single female line.

Before a marriage takes place the rules of custom as well as the laws of Islam have to be observed. Islam forbids marriage within the blood relationship of agnates. The Koran states:

Forbidden to you are:
Your mothers
And your daughters
And your sisters
And your paternal aunts
And your maternal aunts
And the daughters of a brother
And the daughters of a sister
And the mothers who have given you suck
And your foster sisters
And the mothers of your wives
And your step-daughters who are being brought up under your care
From wives with whom you had intercourse
And the wives of your sons who are from your own loins
And (it is forbidden to you) to have two sisters (as wives together).[1]

[1] Al-Koran, An-Nisa, Verse 23.

In custom the above patriarchal relationship[1] is more or less reversed following the matriarchal dilution of the tribal female blood. Thus while the children of brothers of the same father may intermarry in Islam,[2] marriage between parallel cousins through the same grandmother is not allowed in custom. Thus the degree of marriage prohibition apart from the prohibition of Islam is enlarged by prohibiting marriage intra-tribe because ancestral female blood runs through members of the tribal society.

On the death of the wife custom allows the husband to marry the sister[3] of the deceased wife. This is called in custom "*ganti-tikar*"—changing the mat. This is allowed by custom and is also a practical step in the interest of the children. The story of cruelty of step-mothers is well known, and in a bereaved family where the young children lose their mother the maternal aunt can effectively step into the family pattern.

Custom is insistent that the parties of the marriage should be of the same generation status. Thus marriage is arranged preferably between cross cousins of the first or second degree. It is most common between mother's-brother's children for this relationship is free from the prohibition of custom and Muhamadan law.[4] While *ganti-tikar* is permitted it is only occasionally resorted to. *Sororate*, or marrying a deceased brother's wife, is highly disapproved by custom, having a stigma in custom although legal in Muhamadan law. Both the bridegroom and the issue thereof would be barred from succession to tribal chieftain.

Succession of Property

Mention was made earlier that on marriage a tribal woman inherits her customary entail. It is often the case that in this era of legal registration of customary interest such legal requirements are left unattended, sometimes for years and even for generations, so that it is not uncommon to find that the usufruct has been fragmented into multiple holdings with multiplicity of ownership while the registered proprietress still remains in one single name. Here custom and Islamic law ensure that each female will inherit her mother's usufruct on a per capita basis and her portion is not forfeited by a system of eclipse. Thus a grand-

[1] As well as lego-social relationship.

[2] Subject to the renouncement of the position of *wali* or guardian on the part of the groom over his wife.

[3] Usually the younger sister.

[4] The male of a tribe marries into another tribe so that the cousins are in exogamous relationship.

daughter inherits the property of her deceased mother even though the mother predeceased *her* own mother, which ensures that every member of the female tribe will inherit tribal land. The system of land tenure is successful in attaching the females to their homes and children and ensures their income and livelihood, which gives women a sense of dignity and status and helps to save them from being driven by economic factors into becoming women of easy virtue.

XI. CODIFICATION OF HINDU LAW

(1) *General*

Hindu law has the oldest pedigree of any known system of jurisprudence,[1] for which the Vedas of the Srutis[2] are the primary source although they contain very little law, as such. According to the needs and progress of Hindu society, new customs evolved and were recognized in Smritis, Nibhandas, and Puranas and were incorporated into the law. Thus law was amended by great sages like Manu, Yajnavalkya and others, but these men attempted to support their amendments with the text of Sruti in order to derive sanction from divine authority. While professing to interpret the law laid down in the Smritis,[3] they introduced changes to harmonize the law with the usages of those governed.[4] This form of codification was known even in ancient times, and exists today.

Gajendragadkar J. observed:

> Since the said commentaries were written, several centuries have passed by and during this long period, the Hindu mode of life has not remained still or static. Notions of good social behaviour and the general ideology of the Hindu society have been changing; with the growth of modern sources and as a result of the impact of new ideas based on a strictly rational outlook of life, Hindu customs and usages have changed.[5]

Traditionally law lags behind social opinion and the function of

[1] Mayne's *Hindu Law and Usage*, preface to First Edition, (1935).

[2] "Sruti" literally means what is heard. It is in theory the primary and paramount source of Hindu law and is supposed to be a divine revelation. Srutis include the four Vedas, Six Vedangas and the Upanishads. These contain very little of law properly so called, although they contain facts from which these rules of law may be inferred.

[3] The Smritis (what is recollected or remembered) are of human origin and refer to what is supposed to have been in the memory of the sages who were the repositories of the Revelation. As the Vedas were orally transmitted from generation to generation, their subject matter was classified and put into writing. They are the Dharmasastras. They contain rules, as distinct from instances of conduct. The principal Smritis or Codes are of Manu, Yajnavalkya and Narada. The Smritis do not agree with each other in all respects. The conflict between the Smritis gave rise to commentaries which are called Nibandhas.

[4] *Atmaram* v. *Bajirao* (1935) 62 I.A. 139. See D. H. Chaudhari, *The Hindu Marriage Act*, (1955), 23.

[5] *Madhavrao Raghavendra* v. *Raghavendrarao* (1946) 48 *Bom. L.R.* 196 at 224.

social legislation is continually to adjust the legal system to a society which is constantly outgrowing that system.[1]

According to Dr. Derrett,

Hindus were by no means inexperienced of codification before 1955. It is not generally appreciated that the first Hindu Code was that enacted for the Portuguese possessions in Goa during the 16th Century. Comparables Codes were enacted for Damao and Dui in the 19th Century. The French did not attempt to codify Hindu Law and it remained throughout a customary system, enjoying the indirect assistance of Sanskrit text-books and modified slightly by statutes.[2]

The Hindu law in recent years has been considerably modified by (i) The Hindu Marriage Act (1955), (ii) the Hindu Succession Act (1956), (iii) the Hindu Minority and Guardianship Act (1956), and (iv) the Hindu Adoptions and Maintenance Act (1956). Before we consider these changes, it is necessary to understand the historical development of Hindu law before and during the British rule in India.

(2) *Historical Development of Hindu Law*

The Hindu law is derived from the customary laws of India. Thus, Ganapathy Iyer notes,

It will be seen that the Hindu Law as ascertained in the Code and other Sanskrit writings is not a myth but it is based on immemorial usage and that the Brahmanical writers never could have supplanted and none did supplant these usages by laws of their own fancy although they might have been instrumental in developing the law to suit the growing needs of the society of their time.[3]

Mayne also said,[4]

I think it is impossible to imagine that any body of usage could have obtained general acceptance throughout India merely because it was included by Brahman writers or even because it was held by the Aryan tribes. In Southern India, at all events, it seems clear that neither Aryans nor Brahmans ever settled in sufficient numbers to produce any such result.

In support of his statement he takes these distinctive features of Hindu law, viz. the undivided family system, the law of inheritance and the practice of adoption, and shows that their early history and their main features did not derive from Brahmanism.

[1] Social Legislation, (Publication Division) 1; L. S. Mehta, *Some Implications of the Hindu Code Bill* (1948); (1950) *A.I.R.* Jr. Sec. 26.
[2] "The Codification of Personal Law in India: Hindu Law," *Indian Year Book of International Affairs* (1957) 188, 193.
[3] Ganapathy Iyer, *Hindu Law*, 36.
[4] *Mayne's Hindu Law* (9th Edn.), 4.

The oldest sources of Hindu law are the Vedas (1500–800 B.C.), and the most recent are details of caste or tribal customs collected in the nineteenth and early twentieth centuries. Between these lie the *Dharmasastra* (consisting of the *mula*, or root, which is the collection of Srutis and Smritis, and of the commentatory body, partly in the form of straightforward *Vrtti* and *Tika* on the text chosen for the purpose and partly in the forms of digests of selected smrtiaphorisons, or commentaries nominally upon a single continuous Smriti-treatise but in reality in the shape of legal digests) and other[1] evidence of law in practice, such as inscriptions, collections or individual examples of legal documents. The age of the commentaries and digests is from 600 A.D. to 1795 A.D. There are inscriptions from the time of Asoka Maurya, but more substantial numbers date from about the fifth century A.D. Legal documents other than inscriptions are available from the 17th century.

The Institute of Manu is the earliest attempt among the Hindus to fix ancient customs and traditions in systematic form. The Code is, at best, only a large collection of the "usages of a peculiar tribe of the country," and a compendium of "moral and religious duties and precepts to pious Hindus." The original compilation of Manu must have suffered mutilations and interpolations, modifications and alterations at the hands of the glossators and the later School of Brahmanism, as the needs of the growing communities demanded.[2]

Sir Henry Maine observes:

> The Hindu Code, called the Laws of Manu, which is certainly a Brahmin compilation, undoubtedly enshrines many genuine observances of the Hindu race, but the opinion of the best contemporary Orientalists is, that it does not, as a whole, represent a set of rules ever actually administered in Hindustan. It is in great part an ideal picture of that which, in the view of a Brahmin, ought to be law.[3]

It is important to consider the influence of Brahmanism, which is of later development, on the then existing customs. History tells us that the first country in which the Aryans settled was the tract of land drained by the great river Indus and its tributaries. The holy land of Brahmavarla, as described by Manu (Laws of Manu, Chap. 11, 17) was situated between the two ancient rivers, Sarasvati and Drisadvale in the Punjab, and was the land where the custom handed down in regular succession among the (four chief) castes of that country was

[1] J. D. M. Derrett, "The Origins of the Laws of the Kandyans," *University of Ceylon Review*, July-October, 1956, 102.

[2] S. Ray, *Customs and Customary Law in British India*, 28.

[3] H. Maine, *Ancient Law* 17; see also S. Ray, *Customs and Customary Law in British India*, 14.

called the "conduct of the virtuous men" (Manu, Chap. 11, 18). Manu further says, "from a Brahmin in that country let all men on earth bear their several usages." (Chap. 11, 20). It is worth noting that Manu has throughout his treatise enjoined unqualified reverence for, and implicit obedience to, the Brahmans, and placed them, as a class, above all other human beings. The Brahmans, armed with shastic injunctions, assured for themselves the position of sole interpreters of the Vedas and shastras, and became the expositors of usages and customs both secular and religious and ultimately attained an ascendency even higher than that of the rulers of the soil. Through their influence, ancient customs and usages became clothed with all sorts of religious rites and superstitions. However, there exists a large body of customs and usages, absolutely pure and untouched, amongst the indigenous population of India who were unaffected by Brahmanism. Even in the Punjab, the birthplace and cradle of Brahmanism, the ancient customs and usages did not suffer much change because soon after the Aryans began to move further east, the hold of Brahmanism slackened to a considerable extent. In Southern India, the Brahmans never settled in sufficient numbers to produce a lasting effect on existing customs and usages. Consequently, in Malabar, Canara, and among the Tamil inhabitants of the South of India, and the Nambudri Brahmans on the West Coast of the Madras Presidency, certain peculiar usages and customs are noticed which remained uninfluenced by Brahmanism.[1]

Nevertheless, the origin and nature of the Hindu law were naturally affected by Brahmanism, and Indian society was wholly dominated by sacrifices and rituals and remained so throughout the last century.[2] The Hindu law as propounded by Brahmanism of a later period assumes the joint family as the unit of society. The law of the joint family is the basis of Hindu personal law; the law of marriage, of adoption, of inheritance all have to serve the purposes of the joint family and accommodate themselves to the rules governing the joint family.

(3) *Influence of Hindu Law in South East Asia*

Furnivall said,

> when the Pilgrim Fathers left the shores of Europe to found a new world in the West, they took with them their supreme Code of Law, the Bible. In like manner, a thousand or more years earlier, the emigrants from India, Hindu and Buddhist, who laid the foundations of a new world in the Tropical Far East, took with them

[1] S. Ray, *Customs and Customary Law in British India*, 18.
[2] *Hindu Law and Usage*, *op. cit.*, 9.

their new law book, the Code of Manu. Everywhere throughout this region Manu has left his mark; in Burma both among Mon and Burman, in Siam, Cambodia, Java and Bali. To follow him through his various incarnations, Hindu and Buddhist, in these various countries would be a fascinating problem and should throw much light upon the cause of Indian influence in Further Asia.[1]

It is generally recognized that Hindu law as presented in the Dharmasastras has exercised a deep influence on the development of indigenous law in Burma, Siam, Cambodia and Laos, and is still visible in their present legal systems. In all these countries, the name of Manu is associated, as in India, with the origin of the law.[2]

According to the Kinwun Mingyi, the compiler of the Digest of Burmese Buddhist Law, a Dhammathat is "a collection of rules which are in accordance with custom and usage, and which are referred to in the settlement of disputes relating to person and property."[3] The word Dhammathat is a corruption of the Sanskrit word "Dharmasastra"[4] meaning a law book. By law, we mean not the sacred law preached by the Buddha, but the customary law of the Burmese. In *Kirkwood* v. *Maung Sin*[5] their Lordships of the Privy Council said that "'Burmese Buddhist Law' is contained in a series of books entitled 'Dhammathats' which have been composed from time to time by the expounders of that law ever since the thirteenth century if not before." This does not, however, justify the view that customs and usages contained in those Dhammathats are still current. Burmese customary law is not a codified law and the Dhammathats contained not only the ancient customary law of the people but also practices which were prevalent at the time of their compilation, and which at times conflict with the ancient law.

In *Min Lan* v. *Maung Shwe Daing*[6] the learned Judicial Commissioner remarked,

> The Hindu Law has been borrowed though we do not know exactly when and from what source, and has been modified by the requirements of a non-Indian race which had adopted the religion of Buddha. In applying Hindu Law essential differences of conditions, racial and religious, must have been found in two important particulars, the position of the wife and the constitution of the joint property.

It may be said that the debt of the Burmese jurists to the Dharmasastras lies in method of expression rather than in substance. They

[1] J. S. Furnivall, "Manu in Burma, (Some Burmese Dhammathats)," *The Journal of the Burma Research Society* (1930–31), Vol. XXX 351.
[2] R. Lingat, "The Buddhist Manu," *Annals of Bhandarka Oriental Research Institute*, Vol. 30 (1949) 284.
[3] Digest 1, Sec. 2.
[4] S. C. Lahiri, *Burmese Buddhist Law*, 1.
[5] (1924) 2 Ran. 693 at 773.
[6] Chan Toon's *Leading Cases*, 308.

borrowed the magic name of Manu, and to claim authority for the customary law they were writing, they began their work by assigning, as the Hindu writers had done, a divine origin for it. The original Dhammathats writers must have been acquainted with Dharmasastra texts and adopted such portions of them as were applicable to the Burmese system.

(4) *Distinction Between Hindu Religion and Hindu Law*

The religious element in Hindu law has been greatly exaggerated. The method adopted by the Smritis in dealing with topics of secular law in the light of metaphysical and religious considerations has several times caused difficulties even to the Privy Council in deciding questions of Hindu law.[1] In *Rao Balwant Singh* v. *Rani Kishore*[2] their Lordships observed: "All those old text-books and commentaries are apt to mingle religious and moral considerations, not being positive laws, with rules intended for positive laws."

In a later case, *Sri Balusu Gurulingaswami* v. *Sri Balusu Ramalakshmamma*,[3] their Lordships cited those observations and said:

> ...They now add that the further study of the subject necessary for the decisions of these appeals has still more impressed them with the necessity of great caution in interpreting books of mixed religion, morality and law, lest foreign lawyers accustomed to treat as law what they find in authoritative books, and to administer a fixed legal system, should too hastily take for strict law precepts which are meant to appeal to the moral sense, and should thus fetter individual judgments in private affairs, should introduce restrictions into Hindu Society, and impart to it an inflexible rigidity, never contemplated by the original law-givers.

Rules of inheritance were probably based upon a religious doctrine and were probably closely connected with the rules relating to the offering of funeral oblations in early times. It has often been said that he inherits who offers the pinda. It is truer to say that he offers the pinda who inherits.[4] The duty to offer pindas is primarily a religious one, the discharge of which is believed to confer spiritual benefit on the ancestors as well as on the giver. In its true origin, it had little to do with the dead man's estate or the inheritance, though in later times some correlation between the two was sought.[5]

[1] Justice P. B. Gajendragadkar, "The Hindu Code Bill", (1951) 53 *Bom. L.R.* 77 at 83.
[2] (1898) 251 A. 54 at 69.
[3] (1898) 22 Mad. 398 P.C. at 415.
[4] Vishnu XV, 40; "Pinda follows the family name and the estate": *Manu IX*, 142.
[5] *Hindu Law and Usage*, *op. cit.*, 15.

Now however, it is admitted that according to the Mitakshara school of law, which prevails over the greater part of India, the factor of religious benefit is irrelevant except in order to solve a conflict of claims amongst very remote heirs, one of whom is a male and one a female, whereas according to the Dayabhaga school, which largely applies in Bengal and Assam, spiritual benefit dictates the order of succession. A close inspection of the Dayabhaga position on its authorities however, suggests that the spiritual benefit theory was applied with the object of inserting into the list of heirs, which then included only agnates, certain near relations who were cognates. By this means remote agnates were on the whole excluded by comparatively near cognates, and the final effect was to bring near relations through female links upon a more nearly equal plane with agnatic kindred. This was most sorely needed, since the existing law of succession excluded large numbers of kindred who had a moral claim on the "propositus" simply because they did not belong to the patri-lineal clan which from the most ancient times had monopolized succession. Artificial distinctions as to the relative quality of the apparently identical offerings themselves depending upon the sex and relationship of the offerer had to be invented in order to erect a workable order of preference in the succession. In fact the spiritual benefit theory is but an example of the notion commonly encountered that property should pass to those who would be grateful to the "propositus" and who can remember him after his death. It serves the more useful purpose of providing an intellegible reason why one relative should be preferred to another. The author of the ingenious theory, Jimutavahana, could not find a more appropriate manner of assessing nearness to the "propositus".[1]

(5) *Hindu Law During the British Rule*

It was a fundamental principle of British policy that the particular habits and customs of the various communities under British rule should be recognized and respected. In 1858 Queen Victoria declared that in framing and administering the law, due regard would be paid to the ancient rites, usages and customs of Hindus. Successive Government of India Acts have emphasized that policy.[2] Thus Hindu law is applied only as a personal law to Hindus in all matters relating to succession, inheritance, marriage, religion, usage and institutions except in so far as they may have been altered by legislation. It is applied in certain other matters also, such as adoption, guardianship, family

[1] J. D. M. Derrett, "Religion and Law in Hindu Jurisprudence," (1954) *A.I.R.* Jr. Sc. 79 at 84.

[2] E.g., the Madras Civil Courts Act III of 1873, S. 16; Bengal, Agra and Assam (vi) Courts Act, 1887, S. 37; The Punjab Laws Act, 1872, S. 5; Bombay Reg. iv of 1827, S. 26; The C.P. Laws Act, 1875, S. 5; The Oudh Laws Act, 1878, S. 3; Government of India Act, 1915. Section 112; Government of India Act, 1935, Section 223. See also The Burma Act (XIII of 1898), S. 17; Section 13 of the Burma Laws Act exports the principle laid down in Warren Hasting's Ordinance of 1772 prescribing the law to be administered in the East India Company's then recently established Muffasal Civil Court in Bengal, and subsequently embodied in similar legislation for all parts of British India; *Tan Ma Shwe Zin* v. *Koo Soo Chong*, (1939) Ran. 548 (P.C.); Article 372 of the Constitution of India continues the law in force at its commencement until altered or amended, but subject to the other provisions of the Constitution. See also Article 225; personal laws are always subject to alteration by legislation and they have been altered from time to time. Under the Indian Constitution too, personal laws are placed in Entry 5 of the Concurrent Legislative List.

relations, wills, gifts and partitions, either by virtue of express legislation or in principles of justice, equity and good conscience. Similarly, Mohammedan law is made applicable to the Mohammedans,[1] although until the Shariat Act of 1937, custom had precedence over law, in some areas.

Not all Hindus are governed by Hindu law, for there are classes who are governed by their customary laws; for instance, those who follow the Marumakkattayam law in Malabar and the Alyasantana[2] law in Kanara and those Hindu communities in the Punjab who are governed by their customary law. On the other hand, some Mohammedan communities, descended from an original Hindu ancestry, like the Khojahs, the Cutchi Memons, the Borahs, and the Halai Memons, who are subject to the Shariat Application Act, 1937, are still governed by Hindu law in matters of succession and inheritance. Subject to the above exceptions, Hindu law applies to Hindus by birth as well as to Hindus by religion.[3] It is applied to Jains, Sikhs, Nambudri Brahmans[4] and Lingayats.[5] It is also applied to sons of Hindu dancing girls of the Naik caste converted to Islam where such sons are taken into the family of the grandparents and brought up as Hindus; and also to Brahmo and Arya samajists, etc.; as well as to Hindus who have made a declaration that they are not Hindus for the purpose of the Special Marriage Act. Mere departure from orthodoxy in matters of diet and ceremonial observances or denunciation of the caste system does not affect its application.

After the establishment of the British rule, no new commentator has been able to modify the law by engrafting his own views on it; for the power of effecting changes in the existing law was vested exclusively in the legislature.[6]

The British legislature, in pursuance of the policy of religious non-interference, declined to legislate on the personal laws of the Hindus, except in a few cases. Hence, the growth and development of Hindu

[1] *Social Legislation*, (Issued by the Planning Commission, Government of India) (1956), 20.

[2] The Marumakkattayam Law is founded on the matriarchate while all the schools of Hindu law are founded on the agnate family. In South Kanara, the system is known as Alyasantana; the people governed by that law are Hindus in the fullest sense. Marumakattayam Law, however, has been materially modified by the Madras Marumakkattayam Act, 1932 (Act XXII of 1939). Their customary marriages are made legally valid and binding and strictly monogamous, though dissoluble.

[3] *Hindu Law and Usage, op. cit.*, 82.

[4] Nambudri Brahmans are settled on the West Coast of India; they recognized the authority of the Vedas and Smritis like all other Brahmans of South India.

[5] A body of dissenters from Hinduism, who deny the supremacy of the Brahmans and the validity of caste-distinctions.

[6] Report of the Hindu Committee, 1941, Paras. 15 & 16; D. H. Chaudhari, *The Hindu Marriage Act*, 1955, 23.

law in accordance with changing customs was checked. However, a few acts, such as the Hindu Widow's Remarriage Act, Child Restraint Act, and the Hindu Women's Right to Property Act, were passed at the instance of the members of the legislature.

(6) *Hindu Law as Applied by Courts*

(i) *Marriage*

In the Vedic period, the sacredness of the marriage tie was repeatedly declared. According to Manu:

> Women must be honoured and adorned by their fathers, brothers, husbands, and brothers-in-law who desire their own welfare. Where women are honoured, there the gods are pleased; but where they are not honoured, no sacred rite yields rewards.... The husband receives his wife from the gods; he must always support her while she is faithful.... Let mutual fidelity continue until death. This may be considered as the summary of the highest law for husband and wife.[1]

A marriage according to Hindu law is a sacrament and is not considered a contract, but is one of the necessary religious rites for all Hindus. According to Hindu Shastras, marriage is a holy sacrament and the gift of a girl to a suitable person is a sacred duty enjoined upon the father which, if duly performed, is held to confer upon him great spiritual benefit.[2] The Indian Majority Act 1875 does not apply to Hindus in matters of marriage. Marriages contracted for minors by their parents are valid. The Child Marriage Restraint Act (XIX of 1929) as amended by the (Amendment) Act No. XLI of 1949, constitutes the contracting, performance and facilitating of marriages of boys under 18 years of age and girls under 15 years of age an offence, but leaves the marriage itself valid.

A man could have any number of living wives, but a woman could not have more than one husband except through divorce. In Madras, the Hindu (Bigamy Prevention and Divorce) Act, VI of 1949, and in Bombay, the Bombay Prevention of Bigamous Marriages Act, 1946, however made bigamous marriages void.

According to Manu: "A widow who from a wish to bear children slights her deceased husband by marrying again brings disgrace on herself here below, and she [will] be excluded from the seat of her Lord." Previously, a Hindu widow could not remarry under Hindu law, except where sanctioned by custom; however, the Hindu Widow's Remarriage Act (XV of 1856) legalises re-marriage and declares the

[1] Manu, III, 55–76; IX, 95, 101, 102; Yajn., 1. 82; *Kamani Devi* v. *Sir Kameshwar Singh*, (1946) 25 Pat., 58 at 63.

[2] *Velayutha Pandaram* v. *Suryamurthi*, (1942) Madras 219 at 220.

issue to be legitimate. But on remarriage her rights in the properties of her deceased husband and of his family are cut off.

The parties to every marriage must not be within the prohibited degree of relationship; Sapindas who have descended from a common ancestor cannot inter-marry. No such marriage is valid unless it is sanctioned by custom. The Hindu Marriage Disabilities Removal Act of 1946 has, however, validated marriages between persons belonging to the same Gotra or Pravara (agnatic groups). The parties must belong to the same caste or different sects or sub-divisions of the same caste to make such marriage valid. The Hindu Marriages Validity Act, XXI of 1949 on the other hand validates retrospectively marriages between parties belonging to different religions, castes, sub-castes, or sects. The Act applies to Hindus, Jains and Sikhs but does not validate marriage between a Hindu and a Mohammedan.

According to the Mitakshara school, the duty of giving a girl in marriage is laid on certain persons in the following order: "The father, the paternal grandfather, the brother, kinsmen (sakulyas) and the mother." According to the Dayabhaga school, the father, paternal grandfather, brother, sakulyas, maternal grandfather, grand-uncle and mother, are entitled in succession to give the girl in marriage. A marriage otherwise valid is not invalidated because the girl is not given in marriage by the paternal relations. The consent of the paternal relations is not an essential condition of a valid marriage and the doctrine of *factum valet* would apply. The marriage will be treated as valid in such circumstances, for according to the doctrine of Hindu law "a fact cannot be altered by a hundred texts."

A Hindu marriage is not a contract and therefore a consenting mind is not necessary, and its absence, whether from infancy or incapacity, is immaterial. It is undoubtedly abhorrent to a modern mind that a congenital idiot should be allowed to marry, but the Hindu law undoubtedly does not regard such a marriage as being impossible.[1] It has been held by the High Courts of Madras and Allahabad that under the Hindu law, marriage of a lunatic or an idiot or an impotent person is valid[2] unless invalidated on the ground that the capacity for performance of the essential ceremony of marriage is lacking in the bridegroom.[3]

Marriage ceremonies vary from one place and community to an-

[1] *Amirthammal* v. *Vallimayil Ammal*, (1942) Mad. 698; D. H. Chaudhari, *The Hindu Marriage Act*, *op. cit.* 1955, 83.

[2] *Kaura Devi* v. *Indra Devi*, (1943) All. 711 & 712; *Bhagwati Saran Singh* v. *Parmeshwari Nandan*, (1912) All. 518.

[3] *Ratneshwari Nandan* v. *Bhagwati Sanan*, 1950, F.C. 142.

other. The usual essential ceremonies are the performance of the homam, the panigrahana or taking hold of the bride's hand and going round the fire with Vedic mantras, the treading on the stone, and the seven steps or Saptapadi. The marriage becomes complete and irrevocable on the completion of the Saptapadi and from that moment, the wife passes into her husband's gotra. Till then, the marriage is imperfect and revocable.[1] The actual performance ceremonies of the marriage are subject to custom or usage. The Special Marriage Act (III) of 1872, as amended by Act XXX of 1923, provides that a civil marriage between persons who profess the Hindu, Buddhist, Sikh or Jain religion may be celebrated before a Registrar. Succession to the property of a person married under the Act is regulated by the provisions of the Indian Succession Act, 1925. Such person has no right of adoption but his father has a right to adopt another person as a son if he has no other son living.

(ii) Divorce

The indissolubility of marriage has been a distinguishing feature of Hindu law except where divorce and remarriage were permitted by customs among the lower castes[2] and in certain states in India where it was permitted by legislation.[3] There are divergent views on the question of divorce in ancient texts. According to Narada, "there are five cases in which a woman may take another husband, her first husband having perished, or died naturally, or gone abroad, or if he is impotent, or has lost his estate."[4] Manu declares that a man may only marry a virgin and that a widow may not marry again.[5] On the other hand, Manu appears to recognize and sanction the second marriage, either of a widow, or of a wife forsaken by her husband.[6] However, the commentators have laid down that the conception of marriage in Hindu law is a sacrament and, having been performed with the accompaniment of religious rites and ceremonies, it is intended to be an indissoluble life long union.

When a Hindu is converted to Christianity, the Native Converts Marriage Dissolution Act XXI of 1866 enables the convert to petition

[1] *Hindu Law and Usage, op. cit.*, 161.

[2] *Jiva Magan* v. *Bai Jetthi*, (1941) *Bom. L.R.* 538; *Thangamonat* v. *Gangay Ammal*, (1946), 1 *M.L.J.* 279.

[3] The Bombay Hindu Divorce Act (1947); The Madras Hindu (Bigamy Prevention and Divorce) Act (1949).

[4] Narada, XII, 97–101.

[5] Manu, VIII, 226, V. 161–163.

[6] Manu, IX, 175–176.

for a dissolution of marriage if he is deserted by the spouse. If a marriage between Hindus is solemnized under the Special Marriage Act, 1869, it can be dissolved under the Indian Divorce Act, 1872, which also applies to cases where one of the parties professes the Christian religion; or (under the amendment by Act X of 1912) if both the parties become converts to Christianity. Previous to this amendment, there was a difference of opinion between the Calcutta and Madras High Courts.[1] The Hindu Married Women's Right to Separate Residence and Maintenance Act (XIX of 1946) gives a Hindu married woman the right of separate residence and maintenance from her husband on one or more of the following grounds: (1) if he is suffering from any loathsome disease not contracted from her; (2) if he is guilty of such cruelty towards her as renders it unsafe or undesirable for her to live with him; (3) if he is guilty of desertion, that is to say, of abandoning her without her consent or against her wish; (4) if he marries again; (5) if he ceases to be a Hindu by conversion to another religion; (6) if he keeps a concubine in the house or habitually resides with a concubine; (7) for any other justifiable cause. She loses such right if she is unchaste, or ceases to be a Hindu by conversion to another religion, or fails without sufficient cause to comply with a decree of a competent court for the restitution of conjugal rights.

It is necessary to reform Hindu law because cases decided by the courts in India have gone so far as to hold that neither change of religion, nor loss of caste, nor adultery of either party, nor even the fact that the wife had deserted her husband and become a prostitute gives the right to have Hindu marriage dissolved[2]; and such a law of marriage is intolerable in the social conditions prevailing in India today. To retain it would not be conducive to upholding the sacredness of the marriage ties but would perpetuate unhappiness and suffering, and encourage anti-social elements to cut into the very vitals of Hindu society.

(iii) *Joint Family*

The majority of the Hindu population, (except in West Bengal and in certain tribal areas and among the agricultural communities of the

[1] *Gobardhan Dass* v. *Jasadomoni Dassi*, (1891) 18 Calcutta 252; *Thapita Peter* v. *Thapita Lakshmi*, (1894) 17 Mad. 235.

[2] *Govt. of Bombay* v. *Ganga*, (1880) 4 Bom. 330; *A.G. of Madras* v. *Anandachari*, (1886), 9 Mad. 766; *In the matter of Ram Kumari*, (1891) Cal. 264; *Subbarava* v. *Ramasami*, (1900) 23 Mad. 171; *Narain* v. *Tirlok* (1907) 29 All. 4; *Pakkian* v. *Chettiah Pillai*, (1923) 46 Mad. 839 (F.B.). *Gopal Krishna* v. *Mst. Jaggs.*, (1936) 63 I.A. 295; *Banarai Das* v. *Sumat Prasad*, (1936) A.I.R. All 641; *Gul Muhammad* v. *King Emperor*, (1947) Mad. 205.

East Punjab) is governed by the Mitakshara school, the chief characteristics of which are the coparcenary form of joint family system and the rule of survivorship. The joint and undivided family system is the normal condition of Hindu society. An undivided Hindu family is ordinarily joint not only in estate but in food and worship. A Hindu undivided family usually consists of all the descendants in the male line from a common ancestor, their wives and unmarried daughters; a female passes into her husband's family on marriage. A Hindu coparcenary is a much narrower body than the joint family. It includes only those persons who acquire by birth an interest in the joint or coparcenary property. They are the sons, grandsons and great-grandsons of the holder of the property for the time being, and the undivided colaterals, who are descendants in the male line, of one who was a coparcener with the ancestor of the last possessor. Widows or unmarried daughters or disabled persons do not form the coparcenary, but they have a right to maintenance out of the joint family property. A coparcenary is purely a creation of law and cannot be created by act of parties except insofar as a stranger may be introduced into it by adoption. There is community of interest and unity of possession in property between all the members of the family, and upon the death of any one of them, the others take by survivorship. Each coparcener has a right to claim a partition, if he likes; but until he elects to do so, the joint family property continues to devolve upon the members of the joint family for the time being by survivorship and not by succession. He therefore has no power to devise it by will, nor is there any question of succession to it. In no part of the coparcenary property has he left an "estate" of his own. In the classical words of Lord Westbury: "According to the true notion of an undivided family in Hindu Law, no individual member of that family whilst it remains undivided, can predicate of the joint and undivided property, that he, that particular member, has a certain definite share."[1] It is liable to fluctuations; it increases with every death in the family and decreases with every birth. The management of the family and its property are in the hands of the manager, who as a general rule is the father, if alive, or in his absence the senior member of the family. The manager can alienate the joint family property for value so as to bind the interests of both adult and minor coparceners in the property, provided the alienation is made for a legal necessity or for the benefit of the estate. The undivided interest of a coparcener is liable to be taken in his lifetime in execution of a decree against him for his separate

[1] *Appovier* v. *Rama Subbayyan*, (1866) 11 *M.I.A.* 75.

debts. Where a Hindu father is adjudicated an insolvent, his power to sell or mortgage the joint family property for payment of his antecedent debts, not incurred for immoral or illegal purposes, vests in the Official Assignee under the Presidency Towns Insolvency Act 1909,[1] or the Official Recoverer under the Provincial Insolvency (Amendment) Act, 1948.

Under the Dayabhaga system of law, the sons do not acquire any interest by birth in ancestral property. The father is the absolute owner of the property and he can dispose of the property by sale, gift, will, etc. The sons cannot claim partition so long as the father is alive and on his death, his property devolves by succession to his heirs, both male and female. The Dayabhaga school recognizes unity of possession and not unity of ownership.

The Hindu Women's Rights to Property Act (XVIII of 1937) was passed to amend the Hindu law of all the schools so as materially to confer greater rights on women. The Act effects revolutionary changes in Hindu law, more particularly on the Mitakshara law. It affects the law of the coparcenary, partition and alienation. It also affects the topics of inheritance and adoption. It confers upon the widow, whether governed by the Mitakshara or the Dayabhaga law, rights of inheritance to her husband's property even when he leaves male issue. Similar rights are conferred upon the widows of his predeceased son and of *his* predeceased son. In a Mitakshara undivided family, the widow of a deceased coparcener takes his interest. In all cases, the widows are entitled to claim partition, a right which had been denied before, but they take only the limited interest of a Hindu woman. Where a coparcener leaves a widow, the rule of survivorship no longer takes effect.[2] Unfortunately the Act is not happily worded and defective in many respects; it has given rise to complicated questions in the courts.

Under the Hindu law, the gains of science or valour were held to be joint property, if the learning had been imparted at the expense of the joint family, and therefore it is possible to call upon an undivided Hindu family to bring all his acquisitions into hotchpotch, but the Hindu Gains of Learning Act, 1930 makes the property acquired by a coparcener by means of learning in all cases his separate property.

Thus it may be seen that the judicial decisions and legislative enactments have considerably modified the characteristic feature of the joint

[1] *Sat Narain* v. *Das*, (1936) *I.A.* 384; *Official Receiver of Rammad* v. *Devarayam*, (1948) 2 *M.L.J.* 415.

[2] *Hindu Law and Usage*, *op. cit.*, 79.

Hindu family. It cannot be disputed that the present Mitakshara joint family system has given rise in some cases to injustice and inconsistency. The case of a Mitakshara joint family, consisting of a father, brother and a daughter may be used as an example. When the father dies, his interest in the coparcenary property goes to the brother by survivorship and if the brother dies leaving a daughter, the interest goes to the brother's daughter, the original owner's daughter being thus ousted.[1]

Many learned persons gave evidence before the Hindu Law Committee and the evidence of one of them may in short be adverted to. The Rt. Hon. V.S. Srinivasa Shastri said:[2]

> I confess, having grown up under the old ideas of the joint family, I was a little shocked at first at the right by birth being abrogated. There is some point in the objection that the joint family system is being disrupted. But the joint family is already crumbling; many inroads have been made into it; the modern spirit does not favour its continuance any longer. The choice is between maintenance of big estates and recognition of the independence of individual members of the joint family. The latter, in my opinion, is a more important aim as it affords greater scope for individual initiative and prosperity.

Some may, therefore, conclude that the Hindu law of joint family needs to be modified so that it may be adapted to meet the modern circumstances, exigencies and expediencies.

(*iv*) *Woman's Right of Inheritance*

Under the Dayabhaga law, the widow, daughter, mother, father's mother and father's father's mother are the only females who are recognized as heirs to all the property of a male, whether separate or family property, and whether divided or undivided. Son, grandson and great-grandson are the first three ranks and the five females mentioned above are ranked as 4, 5, 14, 18 and 20 in the list of heirs. The unmarried daughter succeeds first; the next preference is to the married daughter who has or is likely to have male issues, and lastly, the barren or widow without any male issue. Under the Mitakshara law, the widow, daughter, mother, father's mother and the father's father's mother are the only females who inherit the property of a male. The inheritance first goes to the unmarried daughters, then to the married and unprovided for, and finally to the married and provided for. The Hindu Law of Inheritance (Amendment) Act, 11 of 1929 has added other females as heirs. They are the son's daughter, daughter's daughter,

[1] R. K. Ranade, "Hindu Law and Mitakshara Joint Family, (1950) 52 *Bom. L.R.* 65 at 66–67.
[2] *Ibid.*

and sister. In the Bombay states, the right of several other females to succession has long been recognized. They are the daughters of descendants and ascendants and collaterals within five degrees and the widows of gotraja sapindas. According to all the schools, the female heir takes a limited estate, except in Bombay where she is a full owner of the property.

The explanation of this state of affairs is that all females were thought in ancient times sufficiently well provided for by their comprehensive right to maintenance, a right which was secured by their right to a share in severalty if the male owner partitioned his property; that joint family property was managed and worked principally by males and that if it were broken up by rights to shares on the part of females who would take them away to other families, the result would be great loss and inconvenience to all concerned; and finally that agnates and males in particular had always enjoyed preferential treatment since the days of pure Aryan custom, according to which the gotra or patrilineal clan, was the residual owner of all unowned property.[1]

The Constitution of India accorded to Indian women equal rights with men and no distinction was sought to be made between men and women in respect of political rights. Discrimination of any kind in the enjoyment of political, social and economic rights and privileges on the grounds of sex is clearly prohibited. The Law of Inheritance is not consistent with modern notions of equality between the sexes. Therefore it seems necessary to remove this inequality which exists in the Law of Inheritance.

(7) *History of Codification*

Mr. Iyengar, who edited Mayne's *Hindu Law* said,[2]

While many parts of Hindu Law require reform and legislation may be welcome, it is essential that Hindu Law should be in a form readily accessible to the Indian ministers, politicians, legislators, the Press and the Public. A codification of Hindu Law of property and succession is very desirable. In future, the legislators will be frequently called upon to consider measures of reform. And any legislation will be most unsatisfactory if reform is undertaken at one point without envisaging its consequence throughout the whole field of Hindu Law. The time has certainly come to cheapen the ascertainment of law, to make it, if only in its broad outline, a common possession of all literate citizens and to minimize the inconveniences and complications of a personal law, intermixed as it is with local or family customs which have long outlived the needs of an earlier day, by the enactment of a code of Hindu Law applicable to the whole of Hindu India which is governed by the two schools.

He said further,

[1] J. D. M. Derrett, "The Legal Status of woman in India from the most Ancient times to the Present day," (1956) *A.I.R. Journal* 73 at 82.

[2] *Hindu Law and Usage, op. cit.*, 11th Edition, Preface X.

Whether the personal law is Hindu or Mohammedan, a reasonable degree of uniformity and certainty is necessary throughout India and it should not vary from province to province or, it may be, almost from district to district as in Bombay or in the Punjab.

After the passing of the Hindu Women's Rights to Property Act, 1937, the Government of India by its resolution dated 25th January, 1941 appointed a committee, which is known as Rau Committee, with the following terms of reference:

(a) To examine the Hindu Women's Right to Property Act 1937, and to suggest such amendments to the Act as would (i) resolve the doubt felt as to construction of that Act; (ii) clarify the nature of the right conferred by the Act upon the widow, and (iii) to remove any injustice that may have been done by the Act to the daughter; and

(b) to examine and advise upon (i) the Law of Inheritance Bill and (ii) the Hindu Women's Right to Separate Residence and Maintenance Bill.

The committee found "that Hindu Law is a complicated organic structure, the various parts of which are interconnected so that an alteration of one part may involve the alteration of the others." In the report the committee pointed out how the question of adoption, validity or otherwise of anuloma marriage, or intercaste marriage, will making power, succession to agricultural land and other property, maintenance, etc. were affected while considering the amendment of the Hindu Women's Property Act, 1937. The committee observed,

Defects of this kind are inevitable in piece-meal legislation effecting fundamental changes in the Hindu Law. The only safe course is not to make any fundamental changes by brief, isolated Acts; if fundamental changes are to be made, it is wisest to survey the whole field and enact a Code; if not of the whole Hindu Law, at least of those branches of it which are necessarily affected by the contemplated legislation.

The committee therefore in its report suggested,

we ourselves think that the time has now arrived to attempt a Code of Hindu Law. We do not suggest that all parts of the law should be taken in hand at once. The most urgent part, namely, the law of succession may be taken up first; then the law of marriage, and so on. After the law relating to each part has thus been reduced to statutory form, the various Acts may be consolidated into a single Code. We suggest this as reasonable compromise between piece-meal legislation and the whole-sale codification.

The committee did not regard the existence of various schools of

Hindu law in the several states as an insurmountable obstacle to codification.[1]

The government of India by its resolution of 29th January 1944 entrusted the Hindu Law Committee with the work of "formulating a Code of Hindu Law which should be complete as far as possible." The committee prepared a Draft Hindu Code, and circulated it for public opinion. The following are some of the more important recommendations of the majority of the committee: (1) The right by birth and the principle of survivorship are to be abolished and the "Dayabhaga" substituted for the "Mitakshara" throughout the country. (2) The next recommendation is that in intestate succession to the father's property a daughter should have half the share of a son. The cases of the married and of the unmarried daughter are considered separately. (3) Monogamy is to be introduced as a rule of law. Such a rule of law would, according to the committee, prevent the husband from deserting the wife at will and contracting a second marriage. (4) The Hindu women's present limited estate is to be converted into an absolute estate. The committee does not accept the argument that Hindu women, any more than others, are incapable of managing property and that they are likely to be duped by designing male relatives. (5) Divorce is to be permitted under certain specified conditions. Among them are: where either party to a marriage (i) has without just cause deserted the other for a period of not less than five years; or (ii) is incurably of unsound mind and has been continuously under care and treatment for a period of not less than five years; or (iii) has been guilty of such cruelty as to render it unsafe for either party to live with the other.

There are a number of other minor changes which the committee has proposed in the existing law. The provisions regarding civil marriages have been included in the Draft Code. The restrictions relating to inter-caste marriages are to be removed. Caste restrictions in regard to adoption are to be abolished and the Bombay rule, giving authority to a Hindu widow to adopt a son to her husband where he has not prohibited an adoption by her, is to be extended.

The committee visited important cities in India and heard the views of representative persons and then made necessary changes in the draft. The government then introduced the Hindu Code Bill in the Central Legislative Assembly on 11th April 1947,[2] where it raised an un-

[1] Report of the Hindu Law Committee, 1941; D. H. Chaudhari, *The Hindu Marriage Act*, *op. cit.*, 25.

[2] D. H. Chaudhari, *The Hindu Marriage Act*, *op. cit.*, 25.

paralleled storm of controversy. At one extreme were the rigidly orthodox persons who vehemently opposed it and denounced it as a highly retrograde measure bound to sap the very vitals of Hindu society, while at the other stood the ultra progressive persons who keenly maintained that one uniform territorial law should govern not only Hindus but also Muslims, Christians, Parsis and all others in the land. The bulk of the Hindu community occupied the middle position, some leaning to the right and some to the left. When introduced in the Legislative Assembly, it was found that the Code had not yet received any departmental scrutiny and hence the Ministry of Law examined the bill and produced a revised draft which is more satisfactory in several respects. This was considered by the Select Committee which reported to the Constituent Assembly of India on 12th August 1948. The Hindu Code (as amended by the Select Committee) was published consisting of 9 parts, as follows:[1]

(1) Preliminary.
(2) Marriage and Divorce.
(3) Adoption.
(4) Minority and Guardianship.
(5) Joint Family Property.
(6) Women's Property.
(7) Succession.
(8) Maintenance.
(9) Miscellaneous.

The most important points on which there is a difference of opinion are:

(1) It was said that the time had now come to remove a long standing grievance and do justice to the mothers of the race by presenting monogamy as a rule of law. There are some persons who say that monogamy is even now the rule in practice and consequently no law is necessary on the point. If monogamy is already the rule in practice there can be no hardship in translating it into a rule of law. The Right Hon. Srinivasa Shastri says: "I thought that the pride of Hinduism was that although polygamy was permitted in theory it was monogamy which was actually practised. It is, therefore, surprising that when monogamy is sought to be enacted as a rule of law hands should be raised in horror."

(2) Orthodox view is vigorously opposed to any provisions of divorce. It is, however, to be noted that the text of Narada, Parshara and Devala permit divorce in certain circumstances. It is also to be noted that amongst various Hindu communities divorce does prevail

[1] R. K. Ranade, "The Hindu Code, 1948" *A.I.R.* (1949) *Jr. Sc.* 12.

as a custom. The evidence before the committee showed that where divorce was not allowed by law or custom the parties concerned managed to obtain written release from the former husband of a woman and to get remarried. Public opinion is now in favour of allowing divorce in certain cases and hence it is proper to make a provision for divorce in certain cases. The Select Committee after considering the provision of the Indian Divorce Act and the Bombay Prevention of Hindu Bigamous Marriages Act set out in detail the circumstances in which relief by way of dissolution of marriage could be had in respect of marriages solemnized before and after the commencement of the Hindu Code.[1]

Prolonged debates on the Select Committee took place in the Constituent Assembly (Legislative). Finally in December 19, 1949, the House formally adopted the motion that the bill as referred to by the Select Committee be taken into consideration. The Hindu Code Bill remained for consideration before the Constituent Assembly (Legislative) and the provisional Parliament till September 1951, but it could not be passed before the dissolution of the provisional Parliament. When the Parliament was elected in 1952 for the first time under the Constitution, the matter of the Hindu Code Bill was again taken up. In view of the fact that considerable time would be required for the passing of the whole Hindu Code, it was thought that it would be better to split the Hindu Code Bill into certain parts and place each part separately before the Parliament. It may be mentioned that when the Hindu Code Bill was debated before the provincial Parliament, it was argued by many prominent members in the Ruling Congress Party and the opponents of the Code that in respect of such a revolutionary measure of social reform, vitally affecting the religion, culture and traditions of the Hindus, who formed the bulk of the population, the provisional Parliament had no mandate to pass such a bill in the absence of a referendum or approval by the majority of the people. When the provisional Parliament was dissolved at the time of the election of the first new Parliament under the Constitution, Pandit Nehru, as the leader of the Congress Party, made it a part of the Congress Manifesto that if returned to power, the party would enact the Hindu Code Bill. After its return to power in 1952, the party has introduced and passed four separate pieces of legislation relating to various topics of Hindu law:[2]

[1] *Ibid.*
[2] H. K. Shah, "History of the Hindu Code," (1958) *Bom. L.R.* 81.

1. The Hindu Marriage Act No. XXV of 1955.
2. The Hindu Succession Act No. XXX of 1956.
3. The Hindu Minority and Guardianship Act No. XXXII of 1956.
4. The Hindu Adoption and Maintenance Act No. LXXVIII of 1956.

(8) *Changes Made in Hindu Law*

(i) *Marriage*

The Hindu Marriage Act, 1955, has made drastic changes in the old Hindu Law of Marriage. It gives all Hindus, married before or after the commencement of the Act, the right, in specified circumstances, to obtain a decree of nullity, or of dissolution of marriage. This is a revolutionary change in the Hindu law but Hindu marriage does not, like Muslim marriage, become contractual. It is still an act-in-law performed by the observance of certain rites and ceremonies creating a new status which cannot be changed by agreement of the parties. Such an act may be void or voidable, and the resulting status may be dissolved by a decree of a court in the same way as a Christian marriage, but a Hindu marriage is a sacrament even under this Act and the sacramental character of the marriage has not been lost. The Brahmanical ceremony of Saptapadi (the taking of seven steps by the bridegroom and bride jointly before the sacred fire) is specially mentioned in the Act,[1] but a Hindu marriage may be solemnized in accordance with the customary rites and ceremonies of either party.[2] A marriage between two Hindus may be solemnized either under this Act or under the Special Marriage Act, 1954 before a Registrar (which may be regarded as an amendment of the Special Marriage Act 1872.) Under this Act, it is no longer necessary for parties to a marriage to declare either that they do not belong to any religion or that both of them belong to the same religion. Previously they had to make a declaration that both of them belonged to the same faith, namely, the Hindu, Sikh, Buddhist or Jain religion.[3] Marriage under the Special Marriage Act is deemed to effect his severance from such joint family.[4]

If the Hindus desire to marry in the sacramental form, then their marriage is governed by the Hindu Marriage Act, 1955, with the following necessary conditions:[5]

[1] Hindu Marriage Act, (1955) Sec. 7 (2).
[2] *Ibid.* Sec. 7(1).
[3] The Special Marriage Amendment Act, 1923.
[4] The Special Marriage Act. Sec. 19.
[5] Sec. 5. The rule of sapinda relationship is based on blood relationship.

(1) Neither party has a spouse living.
(2) Neither party is an idiot or lunatic.
(3) The bridegroom must have completed 18 years of age and the bride 15 years of age.
(4) The parties should not be within the degree of prohibited relationship, unless custom or usage governing each of them permits a marriage between the two.
(5) The parties should not be sapindas[1] of each other, unless custom or usage governing each of them permits a marriage between the two.
(6) Where the bride is under 18 years of age the consent of her guardian in marriage must be obtained.

The father, mother, paternal grandfather, paternal grandmother, brother, paternal uncle, maternal grandfather, maternal grandmother and maternal uncle is the preferential order of persons consenting to the marriage of a girl under 18. No consent is required in the absence of these relations. The intended marriage can be prohibited by the court by injunction if (1) the bride is below 18 years of age and (2) the intended marriage is injurious to the interest of the bride.

The marriage must be monogamous; a specific provision has been made applying sections 494 and 495 of the Indian Penal Code to Hindus who might be guilty of bigamous marriage.[2] Where a marriage is contracted between parties who are under age the parties will be liable to simple imprisonment for 15 days or fine of up to Rs. 1,000 or both; where a marriage is contracted within the prohibited degrees of re-

[1] The expression "Sapinda" is defined in sec. 3(f); two persons are said to be "sapindas" of each other if one is a lineal ascendent of the other within the limits of sapinda relationship, or if they have a common lineal ascendant who is within the limits of sapinda relationship with reference to each of them.

[2] Sec: 17; Sections 494 and 495 of the Indian Penal Code, 1860 run as follows: "494. Whoever, having a husband or wife living, marries in any case in which such marriage is void by reason of its taking place during the life of such husband or wife, shall be punished with imprisonment of either description for a term which may extend to seven years, and shall also be liable to a fine.

Exception – This section does not extend to any person whose marriage with such husband or wife has been declared void by a Court of competent jurisdiction.

Nor to any person who contracts a marriage during the life of a former husband or wife, if such husband or wife, at the time of the subsequent marriage, shall have been continually absent from such person for the space of seven years, and shall not have been heard of by such person as being alive within that time provided the person contracting such subsequent marriage shall, before such marriage takes place, inform the person with whom such marriage is contracted of the real state of facts so far as the same are within his or her knowledge."

"495. Whoever commits the offence defined in the last preceding section having concealed from the person with whom the subsequent marriage is contracted, the fact of the former marriage, shall be punished with imprisonment of either description for a term which may extend to ten years, and shall also be liable to a fine."

lationship or between sapindas, the parties will be liable to imprisonment for one month or fine which may extend up to Rs. 7,000 or both, and where a marriage with a girl under 18 years of age is contracted without obtaining the consent of the guardian for her marriage the person so marrying would be liable to a fine up to Rs. 1,000 (section 18).

The question of registration of Hindu marriage is left entirely to the state governments.

(ii) Void and Voidable Marriages

A Hindu marriage may be declared null and void by the court at the instance of "either party" to the marriage where either party has a spouse living at the time of the marriage, or the parties are within the prohibited degrees of relationship or the marriage is between sapindas. (Section 11).

A Hindu marriage solemnized, whether before or after the commencement of the Act, is voidable and may be annulled by the court on any one of the following grounds:

1. Impotency of the respondent from the date of the marriage till the time of the petition.
2. Either party to the marriage is an idiot or a lunatic at the time of marriage.
3. Consent of the petitioner or the guardian in marriage is obtained by force or fraud, provided that a petition presented more than one year after the force had ceased to operate or the fraud had been discovered shall not be entertained and provided further that the spouse has not lived with the other spouse after the force has ceased to operate or the fraud has been discovered.
4. Pregnancy of the respondent from other person, at the time of the marriage, provided that the petitioner did not know the facts alleged at the time of marriage and the proceeding is commenced within one year of the solemnization of marriage and that the petitioner had no marital intercourse voluntarily after the discovery of the ground entitling him to a decree of nullity. (Section 12).

(iii) Restitution of Conjugal Rights

This remedy is available to either party to marriage if the other has without reasonable excuse withdrawn from the petitioners' society. Only those grounds which entitle a party to claim judicial separation or nullity of marriage or divorce alone may be pleaded in defence to such a petition. (Section 9).

(*iv*) *Grounds for Judicial Separation*

Under the Special Marriage Act, 1954, the grounds of judicial separation and divorce are identical. But under this Act, they are separate for the following reasons:

...In considering this and the following clauses, the Joint Committee have taken into account the language employed and the scheme adopted in the Special Marriage Act, 1954, recently passed by the Parliament. In view, however, of the fact that Hindu Law has so far recognized polygamy, the Joint Committee feels that the approach to the problems of judicial separation and divorce need not necessarily be the same in both the cases and that it is neither necessary nor desirable in the present case that grounds for judicial separation and grounds for divorce should be identical as in the Special Marriage Act, 1954. Moreover, having regard to the high ideals which the Hindu Community has always lived up to, divorce should not be made easy and the law should be so framed as to provide the maximum opportunities for mutual adjustment. The scheme of this Bill is therefore slightly different.[1]

Either party to a marriage, whether solemnized before or after the Act, may seek judicial separation by petition on any one or more of the following grounds:

(1) Desertion by the respondent for a continuous period of two years immediately preceding the presentation of the petition.

(2) Cruelty on the part of the respondent.

(3) The other party has been suffering from a virulent form of leprosy for not less than one year immediately preceding the presentation of the petition.

(4) The other party has been suffering for three years from venereal disease in a communicable form, not contracted from the petitioner.

(5) The other party has been continuously of unsound mind for two years.

(6) The other party has after the solemnization of marriage had sexual intercourse with any person other than his or her spouse. (Section 10).

The wife is entitled to claim judicial separation under the Hindu Marriage Act, 1955, or maintenance under the Hindu Adoption and Maintenance Act, 1954, on the same grounds. The two reliefs are separate and provided by different Acts. It seems, therefore, that if a wife obtains a decree for maintenance, she does not forfeit her right to claim judicial separation on the same ground. Where, however, the period of desertion is less than two years or duration of leprosy is less

[1] See Report of the Joint Committee, 25th Nov. dated 1954, P. iv. Gaz. of India, Extra, Part II. dated 4-12-1954; Chaudhari's Special Marriage Act, 1954, 91; D. H. Chaudhari, *The Hindu Marriage Act*, *op. cit.*, 146.

than one year, the wife can only claim maintenance under the Hindu Adoption and Maintenance Act, 1954.[1]

(v) Dissolution of Marriage

Either party to a marriage whether solemnized before or after the commencement of the Act may seek a dissolution of marriage by decree of divorce on any one of the following grounds; that the other party—

(1) is living in adultery;
(2) has ceased to be a Hindu, by conversion to another religion;
(3) has been incurably of unsound mind for a continuous period of not less than three years immediately preceding the presentation of the petition;
(4) has for the above period been suffering from a virulent and incurable form of leprosy;
(5) has for the above period been suffering from a venereal disease in a communicable form;
(6) has renounced the world by entering a religious order;
(7) has not been heard of as being alive for seven years;
(8) has not resumed cohabitation for two years or more after the passing of a decree for judicial separation;
(9) has for the above period failed to comply with a decree for restitution of conjugal rights.

The following two additional grounds are available to the wife:

(1) That the husband has since the solemnization of marriage been guilty of rape, sodomy, or bestiality.
(2) In the case of any marriage solemnized before the commencement of this Act, that the husband had married again before such commencement or that any other wife of the husband married before such commencement was alive at the time of the solemnization of the marriage of the petitioner: provided that in either case the other wife is alive at the time of the presentation of the petition. (Section 13(2)(i).

It is open to the court to entertain a petition for dissolution of a marriage within the first 3 years of marriage in any case of exceptional hardship to the petitioner or of exceptional depravity on the part of the respondent and in such cases the court has to take into consideration the interests of the children of the marriage, if any, and the possibility of reconciliation between the parties. (Section 14). When a marriage

[1] Sec: 18(2).

has been dissolved by a decree of divorce and either there is no right of appeal against the decree or, if there is such a right of appeal, the time for appealing has expired without an appeal having been presented, or an appeal has been presented but has been dismissed, divorced persons are free to marry provided one year has elapsed since the date of the decree for divorce in the court of the first instance. (Section 15). The period of one year does not apply to a decree of nullity of marriage and either party is free to marry again immediately. (Section 12). Any child conceived or begotten before the decree of nullity is made shall be deemed to be the legitimate child of the parties, notwithstanding the decree of nullity, and shall have a right to inherit the property of either parent. (Section 16).

(*vi*) *Maintenance, Alimony, etc.*

The court is empowered to make an order in favour of either the husband or the wife for maintenance and expenses of the proceedings. The court also has jurisdiction to grant permanent alimony and maintenance to either party to the marriage for life or while the applicant remains unmarried. This order may be made, varied, rescinded, or modified at any time. Under the Special Marriage Act, 1954, the wife alone is entitled to claim alimony from her husband. (Section 25 & 26). Under the present Hindu law, such right is also given to the husband against his wife.

The old Hindu law did not permit divorce, and where customary divorce was allowed, the custom of payment or maintenance after the divorce by one party to the other was never in force. The only custom recognized was the payment of cash amount, either by the wife or the husband whoever wanted the divorce.[1] The Joint Committee for the first time recognized the husband's right to claim alimony. "Where the husband has no independent income but the wife is possessed of means, she shall be as much answerable for the payment of 'alimony' as the husband normally is." This amendment was strongly opposed. It was pointed out that in no other country alimony is payable by the woman. It is only when the women are given the right to inherit equal shares of property that the question of making man and woman equally responsible for the payment of alimony can be reasonably considered. The provision, apart from being sensational, is also a disgrace to Hindu manhood. The right may be conceded in favour of husbands who are physically unable to work or support themselves, or when the divorce is sought on the ground of leprosy, lunacy, idiocy, etc. The Council of

[1] D. H. Chaudhari, *The Hindu Marriage Act*, *op. cit.*, 326.

State and the Parliament nevertheless retained the amendment.[1]

The court has the jurisdiction to make necessary orders from time to time with respect to the custody, maintenance, and education of minor children of the marriage. (Section 26). The court may also make such provisions in the decree as it deems just and proper with respect to any property presented, at or about the time of marriage, which may belong jointly to both the husband and wife. (Section 27).

It is the duty of the court to be satisfied on the evidence produced by the petition and to see whether the petitioner has fully established his case or not and to see that a petitioner is not taking advantage of his or her own wrong or disability; in particular that the petitioner has not been guilty of connivance, condonation or collusion. Before proceeding to grant any relief the court must make every endeavour to bring a reconciliation between the parties. (Section 23). A proceeding under this Act shall be conducted in camera if either party so desires or if the court thinks fit to do so, and it shall not be lawful for any person to print or publish any matter in relation to any such proceeding except with the previous permission of the court. (Section 22).

(*vii*) *General and Suggestions*

A Hindu marriage under this Act does not cease to be a sacrament. Even if it is treated as a contract it is not a contract for limited duration, but for the life of the parties and terminates by the death of either party. If during the continuance of the marriage, marital offence is committed by either party to the marriage, such act gives the other party the right to seek its dissolution by a decree of divorce. Customary divorces are, however, preserved in the Act itself (Section 29). Divorce according to a valid caste custom has its advantages. It is very cheap and speedy. Divorce being a new remedy granted by this Act, in the absence of Indian decisions the principles of the law of divorce as understood in England may be applied; but their application must be consistent with Indian notions and ideas of the rights and duties of the spouses to one another and also, the parties being Hindus, with the notions of a Hindu marriage being a sacrament and not a contract.[2]

The grounds for divorce in the Act are somewhat reminiscent of English law and practice before 1950 and elsewhere of the English Act of 1950 itself. The principal difference between these parts of the two statutes are (i) adultery alone is no ground: the respondent must be "living in adultery"; (ii) conversion from Hinduism is a

[1] *Ibid.*

[2] *Kuppanna* v. *Palanaimal* (1955) Mad. 471; D. H. Chaudhari, *The Hindu Marriage Act*, *op. cit.*, 218–9, 377.

ground for divorce; (iii) so is suffering from virulent leprosy or from venereal disease; (iv) so is renunciation of the world (in a characteristic Hindu form); (v) there is no Queen's Proctor; (vi) both spouses may be liable in a proper case to pay interim or normal alimony; (vii) there are no decrees nisi; (viii) a party cannot take advantage of his own disability, and matrimonial offences by the petitioner are not (presumably) a hindrance to obtaining relief; (ix) there is no provision for the court to settle or otherwise dispose of the property of the spouses other than wedding-presents; (x) proceedings are in camera. A critical and comparative study of the Act's provisions relating to nullity and divorce would find many borrowings from English law, some of which are perhaps now of questionable value e.g. the right to a divorce when the respondent has failed for 2 years or more to comply with a decree for restitution; whereas desertion, as such, gives a right to separation, not divorce.[1]

The English law of nullity maintains a distinction between void and voidable marriages.[2]

The Hindu Marriage Act, like English law, has maintained the distinction between void and voidable marriages and hence the same results follow. It may be suggested that the distinction between the void and voidable marriages should be abolished; nullity of marriage, divorce and judicial separation only should be maintained.

It appears doubtful whether the provisions relating to the nullity, dissolution of marriage and judicial separation would conform with the modern needs of society. Many a ground, which could rightly have been, and which are considered in many countries sufficient for divorce proceedings, has been considered in the Act as giving cause for the

[1] J. D. M. Derrett, Hindu Law at the Cambridge Colloquium on the co-existence and inter-action of different Laws of Marriage and Divorce in the Commonwealth, A.I.R. (1958) Jr. Section 65 at 68.

[2] *De Reneville* v. *De Reneville* (1948) 1 *All E.R.* 56, 60 C.A.; Professor Newark considers that historically this distinction is incorrect. The Operation of Nullity Decrees, 8 *M.L.R.* 203 (1945); see P. M. Bromley, *Family Law*, (1962) 55.

The distinction has been thus judicially explained by Lord Greene:

A void marriage is one that will be regarded by every court in any case in which the existence of the marriage is in issue as never having taken place and can be so treated by both parties to it without the necessity of any decree annulling it; a voidable marriage is one that will be regarded by every court as a valid subsisting marriage until a decree annulling it has been pronounced by a court of competent jurisdiction.

It is the retrospective effect of the decree that distinguishes the annulment of a voidable marriage from a divorce. The latter brings an existing marriage to an end but it does not in any way alter the previous status of the parties; they are still regarded in law as having been husband and wife before the decree was made absolute. But like a decree of divorce, a decree of nullity of a voidable marriage effects a change of status, and it has therefore been argued that voidable marriages are today anomalous and that the grounds for annulling a voidable marriage should now be made grounds for divorce. The reason for the anomaly is basically historical. Decrees of nullity could originally be pronounced only by the ecclesiastical courts which, before the Reformation, applied the common law of the Roman Catholic Church. The Roman Catholic Church doctrine of the indissolubility of marriage prevented them from pronouncing that there had ever been a marriage at all, and the concept of the voidable marriage was retained by the English ecclesiastical courts after the breach with Rome. But retrospective effect of the decree is none the less artificial and confusing and in truth perpetuates a canonical fiction.

proceedings for judicial separation only. (E.g. desertion or cruelty).[1] It may be suggested that a single act of adultery, cruelty which is now a ground for judicial separation only, and desertion for three years, should also be additional grounds for divorce.[2] The Act should leave the choice between divorce and judicial separation to the individual who desires relief to decide which form of remedy he should seek.

(*viii*) *The Hindu Succession Act* (*No. 30 of 1956*)

In the matter of succession to property, Hindu women were subjected to various limitations on their power to hold, alienate, or transmit property. The Hindu Succession Act, 1956, has been enacted with the express object of amending and codifying the Hindu law of succession and enlarging the rights of the woman thus freeing her from the limitations imposed by the Hindu law. It lays down new rules of intestate succession, consistent, according to the legislators, with modern notions of equality between the sexes. The Mitakshara joint family is left undisturbed except where a coparener dies intastate leaving a female relative or male relatives claiming through such female relatives as are mentioned in class 1 of the Schedule to the Act (i.e. mother, wife, daughter, etc.); when his share ascertained by a notional partition on the date of his death will devolve by intestate succession as per the Act. On intestacy, these very relatives succeed as heirs, along with the sons, as class 1 of the Schedule. In the absence of the female heirs, the sons take by survivorship. Previously, the husband had a low place in succession to his wife's property but the Act has allowed him to share with his issue. The right of illegitimate children to succeed to their mother's property is established, but not their rights in competition with legitimate children.

The wife's or widow's legal rights in respect of the guardianship of her children are improved by the Hindu Minority and Guardianship Act, 1956,[3] her right to adopt has been improved by the Hindu Adoptions and Maintenance Act, 1956, which statute also places her right to be maintained upon a firmer foundation; and her right of inheritance has been revised but, in becoming somewhat more like that of the English spouse, perhaps not improved—in the Hindu Succession Act, 1956.[4]

[1] P. Diwan, "Divorce Law of Hindus, etc." *A.I.R.* (1953) Jr. sec., 6, 10.

[2] Sri S. Easwara Iyer, M.P. has introduced in the Lok Sabha Bill No. 36 of 1958 (Hindu Marriage Amendment Bill 1958) similar lines.

[3] The Hindu Minority and Guardianship Act (1956) aims at the reform of Hindu law relating to minority and guardianship, so as to fit in with the other Hindu law statutes. It applies to all the Indian citizens, including the Hindus. Under the old Hindu law, minority terminated at the age of 16, but for the purposes of the Act of 1956, it terminates at 18. It has abolished *de facto* guardians, a peculiar feature of the Hindu customary law, and now deals with natural guardians and testamentary guardians.

[4] J. D. M. Derrett, Hindu Law at the Cambridge Colloquium, *op. cit.*, at 66.

It may be pointed out that the Act requires clarifications in many places to avoid absurd and anomalous consequences, which need not be discussed here. These anomalies and difficulties could have been avoided if legislation with respect to joint family, adoption and intestate succession were taken up together, illustrating the dangers and shortcomings of a piece-meal legislation.[1]

(9) *The Validity of the Act*

In quite a few cases the question considered has been whether the Legislature could make a provision for Hindus specifically (on matters within Hindu law) without at the same time treating the other religious groups on the same basis. The consensus of the judicial opinions has been that it can be done. The Madras Hindu (Bigamy Prevention and Divorce) Act, 1949 applies to Hindus and prohibits polygamy amongst them. The objection raised was that the Act discriminates between Hindus and Muslims only on the ground of religion, the latter being still free to take more than one wife according to their personal law, and thus offends the provisions of Article 15(1) of the Constitution. The Madras High Court held that the discrimination was not based on the ground of religion only. The Hindus had been enjoying their own indigenous system of law which was based on Hindu Scriptures in the same way as the Mohammedans were subject to their own personal law.[2] Similar results were reached by the Bombay High Court when the Bombay Prevention of Hindu Bigamous Marriages Act, 1946 was challenged as discriminatory.[3]

[1] See, S. E. Aiyer, "The Hindu Succession Act of 1956. *A.I.R.* (1957) Jr. Sec. 3; see" further discussion, P. Chandrasekhar Iyer, "The Hindu Succession Act, Some Anomalies," *A.I.R.* (1957) 12.

[2] *Srinivasa Aiyer* v. *Saraswati, A.I.R.* (1952) Mad. 193.

[3] *State of Bombay* v. *Narasu Appa, A.I.R.* (1952) Bom. 84 at 87.

In deciding that question, the learned Chief Justice of the Bombay High Court observed:

The question that we have to consider is whether there is any reasonable basis for treating the Muslims as a separate class to which the laws prohibiting polygamy should not apply. Now it is an historic fact that both the Muslims and the Hindus in this country have their own personal laws which are based upon the respective religious texts and which embody their own distinctive evolution and which are coloured by their own distinctive backgrounds. Article 44 itself recognizes separate and distinctive personal laws because it lays down as a directive to be achieved that within a measurable time India should enjoy the privilege of a common uniform Civil Code applicable to all its citizens irrespective of race or religion. Therefore, what the Legislature has attempted to do by the Hindu Bigamous Marriages Act is to introduce social reform in respect of a particular community having its own personal law. The institution of marriage is differently looked upon by the Hindus and the Muslims. Whereas to the former it is sacrament, to the latter it is a matter of contract. That is also the reason why the question of the dissolution of marriage is differently tackled by the two religions. While the Muslim law admits of easy divorce, Hindu marriage is considered

On the basis of these decisions, it has been held that the Hindu Marriage Act, 1955, is a valid piece of legislation under article 15(1) of the Constitution of India.[1]

(*10*) *Hindu Law Outside India*

The Hindu Marriage Act, 1955, applies to all Hindus, whether they are domiciled in India or not, residing in any part of India, excepting the State of Jammu and Kashmir. It applies also to Hindus domiciled in the territories of India, who may, for the time being, be outside the said territories or outside India altogether. The Act does not extend to Kashmir and Jammu, but by virtue of the Jammu and Kashmir Act 8 of 1955, the provisions of this Act are now applicable subject to the modifications specified in the Schedule of that Act.[2] Article 245(2) of the Indian Constitution provides that no law made by the Parliament shall be deemed to be invalid on the ground that it would have extra-territorial operation.

Hindus in South East Asian countries such as Burma, Pakistan, Malaysia (except Singapore) still enjoy the privilege of their personal law. The Hindu Marriage Act, 1955, being a statute law enacted by the Indian legislatures, could not per se have any effect on the Hindus in these countries. The Indian legislature is not a competent authority to pass acts relating to Hindu law for these countries. The Hindu law as recognized by the courts in these countries is the customary law relating to Hindus and the law laid down by the decision of the courts.[3] It is left to the leaders of the Hindu community in these countries to press the legislature to reform the Hindu law along the lines achieved in India, if they so desire.

indissoluble and it is only recently that the State passed legislation permitting divorce among Hindus. The State was also entitled to consider the educational development of the two communities. One community might be prepared to accept and work social reform; another may not yet be prepared for it; and article 14 does not lay down that any legislation that the State may embark upon must necessarily be of an all-embracing character. The State may rightly decide to bring about social reform by stages and the stages may be territorial or they may be communitywise. From these considerations it follows that if there is a discrimination against the Hindus in the applicability of the Hindu Bigamous Marriages Act, that discrimination is not based only upon ground of religion. Equally so, if the law with regard to bigamous marriages is not uniform, the difference and distinction is not arbitrary or capricious, but is based upon reasonable grounds.

[1] *Singh* v. *Bhani Devi*, *A.I.R.* (1959) Manipur, 20.

[2] Jammu and Kashmir, Government Gaz. dated 5-11-15, 1; D. H. Chaudhari, *The Hindu Marriage Act*, *op. cit.*, 32, 33.

[3] *Union of Burma* v. *M.V. Gadhia*, Cr. Misc. Apl. 18, 1960.

Conclusion

Hindu laws have had to be gathered from the vast number of judicial decisions and,

> they have to be ascertained from a mass of case-law along with a few fragmentary statutes, some ill-understood books, many of which have either never been closely and comparatively studied, or have been subject to such a process only recently and with no certainty that the results will weigh heavily in the courts, and in default of these unsatisfactory materials from evidence of custom, which may seldom be agreed, and which even if it is agreed may not lead to reliable or consistent inference [only creates a] happy hunting ground for the lawyers.[1]

The codification has made Hindu law certain. When the law has been codified, any specific point should be sought for in the codified enactment and ascertained by interpreting the language used instead of, as before, roaming over a vast number of authorities to discover what the law was, and extracting it by a minute critical examination of the prior decisions.[2] The essence of a code no doubt is to be exhaustive on the matters in respect of which it declares the law. On any point specially dealt with by it the law must be ascertained by interpretation of the language used by the legislature. In respect of such matters the court cannot disregard or go outside the letter of the enactment according to rules of construction. The code therefore binds all courts so far as it goes.[3] The codification of Hindu law constitutes a big step forward towards attainment of the directive principle recognized by the Indian Constitution that the state shall endeavour to secure for the citizens a uniform civil code throughout the territory of India. The civil code, which will replace all the existing personal laws, appears to be essential in the interest of unification of the country; and building up a single nation with one single set of laws applicable to each and every person resident in India.

[1] J. D. M. Derrett, "The Codification of Personal Law in India," *The Indian Yearbook of International Affairs*, (1957), 189, 191.

[2] *Norendra Nath* v. *V. Kamalbasini Dasi*, (1896) 23 I.A. 18, 26.

[3] *Hukum Chand* v. *Kamalanand Singh* (1906) 33 Cal. 1923, 927 at 931; D. H. Chaudhari, *The Hindu Marriage Act*, *op. cit.*, 25–26.

XII. CUSTOMARY LAW IN VILLAGE INDIA

Like every other Indian village, Shivapur is a bi-legal village. When it suits them, individually and collectively, the villagers make use of customary law as well as the "modern" Westernized law established by the state. Being very close to the city of Dharwar, the headquarters of the district court and the judicial machinery, they are aware of some of the implications of modern law which are different from that which they have been used to for generations. They have resorted to the new law in litigations pertaining to land tenure and partition of family property. At present, two cases of partition and eight cases of land tenure are pending in the law court, besides a criminal complaint in connection with a fight that occurred a year ago during the Holi festival, the festival of the sprinkling of coloured water.

Recently, several disputes have been resolved by the traditional method of settling them on the basis of customary law. In fact, the villagers are even more sensitive to the presence of the traditional law than to the existence of a court in the city, which is, in a way, foreign to them. They remember many instances in recent times of punishment being meted out by the caste council (Jāti Panchāyati) even after the offender had undergone punishment by the court of law. My Jain informant, Mr. Nabhanna, owner of the Chandrasheela tea-shop, once told me how his father-in-law had mortgaged his land to the bank and then mortgaged it again to another person, and, being taken to court, was imprisoned for a month and fined 250 rupees. But on returning home the elders of the Jain community met and decided that he should pay a penalty of 50 rupees to the community and undergo expiation (prāyaschitta) in the Jain temple, as his conduct had been a disgrace to it. The Jains imposed this punishment in order to restore the good name of their community. The imposition was carried out by the offender without much resentment. This resembles what Radcliffe-Brown[1] calls the euphoria of society.

The inhabitants of the village think it proper to settle their disputes amicably in accordance with the customs and usage of the community. They consider it to be disgraceful to "climb the steps of the court" to

[1] Radcliffe-Brown, A. R., *Structure and Function in Primitive Society*, (London, 1964), p. 213.

resolve their litigations. A person appearing frequently in court as witness is regarded by them as unreliable and of questionable character. An instance of an old respectable person was once told me by one of my informants in order to illustrate how seriously he took to heart the fact that he was summoned by the court to give evidence in a family dispute. Within two weeks of giving evidence in the court much against his will, he suddenly died. The cause of his death was attributed by the villagers to the shock he received.

Whereas settling disputes in court is considered unworthy, litigants willing to resolve their conflicts in the village itself by decision of the elders in accordance with custom and usage are greatly appreciated. In their opinion, going to the court involves loss of money as well as prestige, so why not conserve both and be happy? In such a characteristic reaction by the villagers one can observe their anxiety to preserve and perpetuate the traditional legal institution.

Customary law as found in the village is an integral part of the normative system which is deeply rooted in the concept of "Dharma," which cannot be easily explained. The wider concept of Dharma comprises rules of morality, conduct and good behaviour, religious principles, legal precepts and all that supports a harmonious functioning of human relationships. Customary law as practiced in Shivapur must be viewed in the light of Dharma. Any attempt to explain fully the customary law cannot ignore its different dimensions and its interrelatedness with various other spheres of life. Law, religion, politics, commerce, administration, etc., are like different threads woven into the single fabric of society, and therefore have to be viewed in their entirety.

Jurists and anthropologists have in the past tried to reconstruct the growt hoflaw on the basis of scanty evidence. Henry Maine, Henry Paul Vinogradoff and others have attempted to formulate a theory of the origin and development of law amongst all the peoples of the world. As expressed by Maine, law is derived from pre-existing rules of conduct which are at the same time legal, moral and religious in nature. The severance of law from morality and of religion from law belong only to the later stages of mental progress.[1] According to him, the modern secular law has evolved from early religious law but has lost its religious basis.

In rural Indian society customary law, religion and morality are not separated but are found closely related forming an organic whole.

Again, early anthropologists like Elliot Smith, S. Hartland, W. H.

[1] Maine, H., *Ancient Law*, pp. 14, 16, (London, 1961, ed.).

Rivers and Hobhouse, who were comparative historians and moral philosophers, viewed law merely in terms of procedure, crime and punishment. Influenced by the outlook of the modern lawyer and the formally organized judicial machinery, they have ventured in vain to comprehend the legal system of simpler societies. Their study therefore resulted in misleading interpretations of law in simpler societies. Man in these societies appeared to them either as a savage devoid of law and order or as a kind and peace-loving man bound by custom. The following remarks by Elliot Smith and P. H. Buck serve as typical illustrations of such interpretations:

> Envy, malice and all uncharitableness usually have for the object of their expression some artificial aim, from the pursuit of which primitive man is exempt...
> So long as he is free from the disturbing influence of civilization, the nomad is by nature a happy and well-behaved child, full of generous impulses and free from vice.[1]
> ...Customs act automatically, and there is no need for Government control... What constituted right and wrong conduct had been defined by custom. Custom was obeyed without thought of opposition, and there was little need of courts of law with police to hale malefactors to justice. Prohibitions by tabus were observed out of fear and ingrained obedience.[2]

Unlike these writers, the anthropologist of today looks at law as an element embedded in the cultural matrix of a given society. In the study of customary law he undertakes to investigate a whole body of norms and beliefs covering the moral, religious and aesthetic behaviour of the people.

The moral standards of Shivapur are respected and protected by the people. Such norms of morality are jealously guarded since any breach, it is believed, would bring calamity to the society. Everyone knows what is morally right and what is morally wrong. When a guilty person is detected, he must make an open confession and repent his act, failing which he will be looked upon with contempt by the people. He is often ridiculed, and sarcastic remarks are frequently made about him. Such social censure will in itself restrain the individual and act as a deterrent for others. Institutions exist to support such social censure. There is the council of elders, for example, charged with the responsibility of dispensing justice. This body has to take every care to see that it discharges its duty impartially; otherwise, according to the belief of the people, it will become the object of divine wrath.

Let me give an illustration. Shepherd Ningappa's flock of sheep stole into the paddy field of Parappa and ate up the sproutlings. This news

[1] Smith, E. G., *Human History*, pp. 189, 199.
[2] Buck, P. H., *Ethnology of Tongareva*, pp. 52–53.

was communicated to the owner of the land, who also happens to be one of the village elders. In the evening Ningappa was summoned to appear before a committee of village elders representing the Kurub, Lingayat, Maratha and Muslim castes. The committee held its session in cooperative society No. 1. The plaintiff who is also a chairman of the cooperative society, accused Ningappa of gross negligence in not keeping proper watch over his sheep. Pleading with much emotion, the plaintiff told the gathering:

> I would not have cared if the flock had eaten the whole stock of fodder stored in the backyard of my house. Destroying the sproutlings is nothing less than murdering an infant. This is a serious offence.

The plaintiff claimed heavy damages which were out of proportion to the loss incurred and also beyond the capacity of the defendant. As the plaintiff was well-to-do and a leader of his caste as well as a member of the council of elders, besides being a chairman of the said society, his claim was unanimously approved and imposed on the defendant. The shepherd paid the penalty as decided by the council. A few days after this incident one of the plaintiff's best she-buffalos died suddenly. This invited the expected criticism from the members of the rival cooperative society, No. 2, composed mostly of landless labourers, shepherds and village artisans who form the bulk of the village community. In their opinion:

> The she-buffalo had died because of the unlawful punishment meted out by the partisan decision of the council. Since law had been misused, God rightly punished him.

The death of the she-buffalo has since become a precedent which has reinforced a part of the customary law in the village.

Misfortunes are often attributed to a breach of moral codes of the community. Illness, death, poor crops, drought, barrenness of women, physical deformities, etc., are alleged to be the consequences of immoral acts in the past and present life. I was once busy looking into the records of cooperative society No. 1, when the next-door neighbor, Mr. Gadigeyya, an old man of sixty, narrated an unfortunate incident that had occurred in his family just a month before. His youngest son, ten years of age, had died after suffering four years of constant agony as a result of a car accident near his house. Gadigeyya is a priest-astrologer and dispenses indigenous medicines to the villagers. He did his best to save his son. But all his efforts failed. In a reminiscent mood he repented the death of his son and said:

> I must confess I must have something wrong in my previous, if not in my present, life. And God punished me for it. Why else should my son die?

It is important to note that the people believe that calamities are the result of one's wrong deeds in the past and present life. A sinful act, known as "Adharma," produces an undesirable ritual condition for the wrongdoer and he accepts the onus of his suffering with resignation. The force of negative religious sanction compelling one to accept the responsibility for his wrong action underlies the existence of an effective customary law in Shivapur.

The aesthetic and other standards of the community are fairly well known to the people. These are noticeable during sports and wrestling, open-air plays, the procession of bullocks on festive days and on religious festivals like the Holi, the worship of snakes (Nāga Panchami) and the festival of Ganapati. One knows exactly how to conduct oneself on these occasions. On these social and religious occasions a good deal of fun and frolic takes place; young and old, men and women, mix freely and enthusiastically, forgetting their differences. It is usual to steal dried dung, fodder and fuel stored by the householders for the ceremonial burning of the God of Love (Kama) on "Holi" day. This kind of theft is morally approved and aesthetically appreciated, thus there are no customary law sanctions against this though many people keep a watch over their fuel storage a week in advance of the festival so that the young in their festive mood will not steal it.

People know that such thefts on Holi day must be taken in the proper spirit. Otherwise it would lead to disturbance in the village. Only two years ago, however, the police had to intervene and prevent a potential conflict between Lingayats and Marathas, the two powerful caste groups in Shivapur. Recently, it has become common in Indian villages, and certainly in cities too, to keep regular police vigilance on such festivals. The government prohibits some of the recreational aspects of some festivals like "Holi" and Moharrum in order to maintain communal harmony.

In the realm of economy, too, customary law exerts its influence. The traditional economic relations have largely been governed by the moral and social life of the community. As far back as the memories of the people go, they know that the village watch and ward was strictly maintained by the servants of the village, who were given fixed landed property in return for their services. This customary mode of remuneration continued until recently. Recent legislation concerning land-tenure and religious endowment has considerably affected the traditional relationships between the landlord and his tenant, which were those of parent and child.

For generations the relations between artisans and farmers were regulated by the traditional mode of payment in return for service. The farmers paid their artisans in kind with all kinds of grains all through the year during various important domestic rituals, and during many events related to the religious and agricultural calendars. The farmer and artisan both knew that, though the services and the payment were not measured, there was an implicit understanding as to the nature of services rendered and the payment made. The inter-personal relationships reinforced by economic dependencies had knit the people together as a whole, and influenced their behaviour in all spheres of life. This economic system which united them is known as the Āya system in Shivapur village. It is an institution of great strength comprising the economic, religious, moral and political values which still dominate the village scene.

Customs continue to influence family life, marriage, inheritance of property and adoption, and modern law has adjusted itself to the prevailing conditions of society. Social pressures and religious sanctions outlaw divorce for high-caste Hindus. But in the case of low-caste Hindus, divorce is customarily allowed and is known as "Sodachiti." Amongst the Lingayats of this village, the priestly caste (Jangam), Panchamasalis and Banajigas, who stand next in rank to Jangamas, are not permitted divorce by their religious heads, whereas the Sādars below them are permitted to do so.

The differential customary law prevalent among the different subcastes of Lingayats reflects the social structure of the Lingayats. The Jangamas, Panchamasalis, and Banajigas consider themselves to be higher than the Sadars because divorce is a phenomenon associated with lower castes and is also a social stigma which lowers one's status in the eyes of the people. The marriage of widows, widowers and divorcees (Udiki), though customarily allowed among certain castes, is forbidden by the Banajigas. Castes like Kurub, Maratha and untouchables practising "udiki" are held in low esteem. These castes are ranked below the Brahmana, Jain and Lingayat.

Customary law's predominant influence is seen in the practice of rules of primogeniture and ultimogeniture. In the inheritance of movable and immovable property, an extra share is given to the eldest brother. The term "Dastpāl," found current in the language of the people, refers to the usage of primogeniture. Recently, two brothers divided their parental property. The eldest brother got the bullock-cart as Dastpāl, besides an equal share of land. In a similar case the eldest brother got a big copper vessel meant for storage of water. This

Dastpāl is not merely viewed as an economic concession to the eldest brother. He is respected as the father, teacher and the custodian of the family traditions and values. This extra gift is a recognition of his services to the family and a tribute to the supporter of Dharma.

In addition to primogeniture, the practice of allowing the youngest brother to have the first choice in the selection of his share of family property at the time of partition also obtains in Shivapur village. A preferential treatment is given to him in relation to his elder siblings. These preferences of primogeniture and ultimogeniture are regarded by the people as based on justice, equity and good conscience. Any practice contrary to this usage is not appreciated by them. I have heard people say that even amongst the rich the eldest brother must get his Dastpāl and the youngest his preferential choice. It is Dharma to accept it and Adharma not to give it. This sense of duty and right conduct as expressed in Dharma is so rooted in conscience that there is no appeal against its binding force. Herein lies the distinctive and unique nature of customs and usages in Indian villages.

In a familistic society like that of Shivapur, the continuity of the family name and the burning of the fire in the hearth are a matter of great spiritual significance. The attainment of final salvation (*Moksha*) in this world and in the life after death depends on one's having a son, natural or adopted. Custom has provided very useful machinery here. The customary jurisprudence allows adoption, even ignoring certain kinship norms and values. The following diagrams illustrate customary law where the process of adoption has violated modern Hindu law which prohibits the adoption of individuals so related:

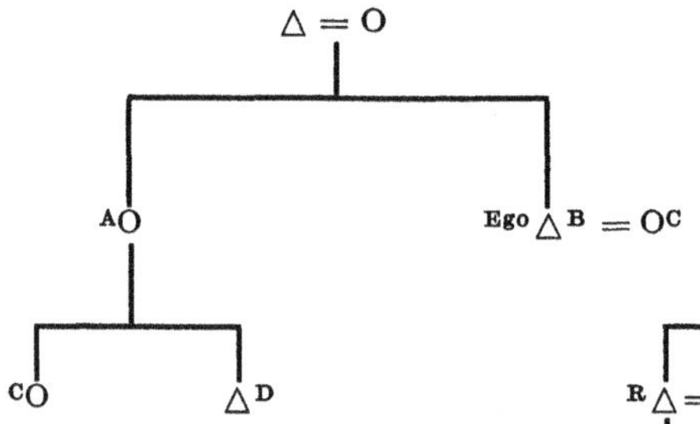

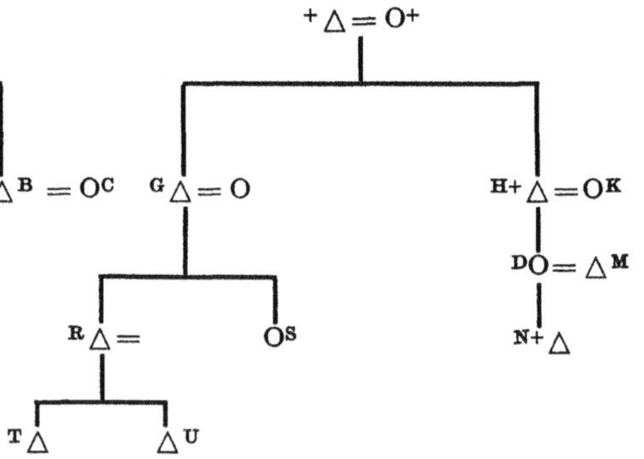

Key: △ = Male; O = Female; + = Dead

Fig. 1

Fig. 2

In Fig. No. 1, Ego married C, his sister's daughter, and later adopted his sister's son D. According to modern law, a sister's son cannot be adopted because adoptee's mother, A, would become Ego's wife whereas in reality she is Ego's own elder sister. Since customary law approves such adoption, the modern law accedes to it. In Fig. No. 2, G and H divided their family property and lived separately. After the death of H, widow K adopted her daughter D's son N who died unmarried. Thereafter, K adopted her daughter's husband M, the father of the deceased grandson. G's grandchildren T and U filed a suit in court to invalidate the adoption of M by K. In the court of law this adoption was considered legally valid because of the prevalence of custom. In cases like these, law always acts rightly as a supplement to custom, so that it can keep its hold on the people by cooperating with their customs rather than by differing with, or challenging, them.

From this illustrative account one can understand that customary law is a bundle of various rules related to morality, economy, religion, family, marriage, property, etc., all denoted by a single term Dharma. All that is opposed to Dharma is Adharma, sin, crime, and other wrong actions forbidden by society. It is, therefore, necessary to point out that those concerned with the administration of justice and law in Hindu society must take into account the fact that customary law still largely governs the lives of the people, and that justice must be dispensed in accordance with custom and usage. Any attempt at establishing and implementing a new uniform secular code contrary to custom and usage would lead to serious consequences. A scientific approach is therefore necessary at this moment when the Indian legislators are busy enacting a uniform civil code throughout the country.

The Indian villages like Shivapur are plural societies in miniature. Caste and sub-caste, religion, economy and to some extent language too have contributed to this plurality. Though traditional and archaic in nature, Shivapur reflects a highly stratified community. Its people, numbering about 3,809, are hierarchically arranged into 13 castes and 40 sub-castes, four religious groups, practising all forms of economy ranging from barter to international money economy, using at least four languages in their daily life.

To a casual visitor the social life of Shivapur appears to be very simple, closed, homogeneous and far away from the vicissitudes of urban life. A close look will, however, convince one that life here is heterogeneous and highly institutionalized. Customary law in this society is an outstanding example of this differentiation.

Every society has its own procedure and method of dealing with its problems. It may be a highly kin-oriented society, a chiefless society, a society governed by a highly centralized machinery, a caste-ridden or a classless society. In all types of societies peace and order are maintained in such a way that norms and values inherent in its social structure are preserved. In a caste-bound society like Shivapur, the administration of justice has its own complicated machinery; it has its own judicial personnel, arbitrators, juries, judges, advocates, publicity officers and people to carry out the decisions, in addition to the state-owned machinery which looks after modern law and its implementation. Although the goals of customary and modern law are the same, the languages of these two legal systems, as well as the manner and method of their handling disputes are quite dissimilar.

Village disputes, as the people themselves see them, may be classified into two categories, private and public. Private disputes and public disputes are sometimes wrongly identified by students of law in terms of civil and criminal or tort and crime respectively. As already pointed out, the villagers do not conceive of right and wrong in terms of modern law but see it in terms of Dharma and Adharma affecting the private and public life of the individual. They do make a distinction between private and public delict, and this is made while taking into account the nature and magnitude of the offence of the persons involved in the dispute, their status and position in the community, etc. The procedures adopted in the settlement of a private delict differ in many ways from the procedures adopted to decide a public delict. The following remarks by Radcliffe-Brown[1] regarding the nature of public delicts is relevant to Shivapur:

> In any society a deed is a public delict if its occurrence normally leads to an organized and regular procedure by the whole community or by the constituted representatives of social authority which results in the fixing of responsibility upon some person within the community and the infliction by the community or by its representatives, of some hurt or punishment upon the responsible person. This procedure, which may be called the penal sanction, is in its basic form a reaction by the community against an action of one of its members which produces a condition of social dysphoria. The immediate function of the reaction is to give expression to a collective feeling of moral indignation and so to restore the social euphoria. The ultimate function is to maintain the moral sentiment in question at the requisite degree of strength in the individuals who constitute the community.

A private delict may be concerned with family quarrels among womenfolk, partition of property, disobedience to elders, marital dis-

[1] Radcliffe-Brown, *op. cit.*, p. 212.

cord and other such delicate affairs. People say that such disputes should not be discussed in public and should be settled within the precincts of the family. Though much secrecy is attached to the nature of the dispute and the procedure in handling it, everybody in the village often knows something about it. The disputes, especially those concerning division of a joint family into separate units and partition of family property, may go on for years until it becomes unbearable for the members of the family to live together under a common roof. The arbitrators or conciliators, normally, come from the lineage and clan of the disputants. If a dispute arises in a small lineage of the same clan, the elders of the dominant lineage who are held in high esteem will participate. The members outside the lineage and clan are not expected to interfere in the family disputes, which are considered very private. Such privacy is highly cherished though in reality it is often an open secret.

My Maratha informant, Lakshman, is a carpenter, a leader of his caste council, and a person reputed for his religious devotion and practice. He happened to mediate in a Maratha family conflict practically leading to the disruption of marital ties of two couples. This was an old quarrel of three years' standing and had often burst into violent conflict. The members of the Maratha caste became sensitive to the affairs of the family, which had become the talk of the entire village. Once, during my field visit, I happened to be near the house of the litigants and observed a large gathering there. Lakshman and other elders of the Maratha caste were also there. Some hours later I went to Lakshman and inquired about the incident in the Maratha family. He at once reacted, saying, "It is nothing, just a family quarrel." It took me some time to convince him of my interest in the dispute. Reluctantly, he began narrating the whole story since its inception to date. On hearing it, I made attempts to check the information with other members of the village. To my surprise, I found that everybody knew about the affairs of the Maratha family, presented as a great secret by Lakshman.

The settlement of private disputes is a long process involving a number of caste elders and a variety of trial procedures. In the event of a conflict the matter is referred to one who enjoys the confidence and regard of the family, and also one known for his sympathy and ability in handling delicate affairs of individual and family. If the man consulted finds the situation difficult to handle, he suggests the names of one or two other persons who also possess the confidence of the litigants. The arbitrators or conciliators resort to various methods, ranging from timely advice to admonition. In cases of serious offences, such as theft, accusation of black magic and breach of promise, the alleged offender is made to take an oath by touching sacred objects like fire, earth, water, bullock, cow, the string of black beads tied around his wife's neck, the leaf of the Bilva tree, a religious book, and the like. Swearing is also done in the name of sons or wife, saying, "If I have done this wrong may my son die or may my wife not live long." Swearing is also done imprecating oneself and often expressed as follows: "If I am really an offender let me become blind," "Let me die a miserable death." Ordeals and oracles are also made use of in the process of trial. Sacred stones in the temple, fire and sacred ashes are some of the objects used in the process. The belief in oracles is a great help in the process of finding out the culprit. The arbitrators may take the matter to specific religious centres to consult the oracle to find out the guilty. I know a recent case in Shivapur of a mother-in-law being accused of having used black magic to divert her son-in-law's loyalty and devotion from his parents to her daughter. This accusation was taken to a religious place 200 miles away. In this trial the mother-in-law was cleared of her guilt.

Customary law with reference to the mode of punishment must be studied in relation to the cultural pattern of a given society. It clearly reflects the principles of the wider concept of Dharma. The sanctions upholding Dharma are positive and negative and these are applicable to both private and public delicts. Positive sanctions are less pronounced than negative ones, while both are related to the value system.

Negative sanctions, on the other hand, are felt directly by the people and often avoided. Public opinion in this small community rigorously controls and guides the behaviour of individuals. A person hardly escapes public censure on violating the taboos of caste, community, religion, family, etc. High-caste Hindus are forbidden to dine with low-caste people. Using bullocks on Monday for agriculture is contrary to custom. Refusal to pay subscriptions for fairs and festivals of the village deities like Dyamavva (Goddess of Fertility), Durgavva (Goddess of Epidemics), Basava (Sacred Bull) is viewed as hostile and irreligious behaviour. Disrespect shown to parents, non-observance of the rules of ritual purity and pollution invite sarcastic remarks and strong social resentment. The social censure is commensurate with the nature of the offence. Nicknames, ridicule, and other forms of verbal censure are some of the deterrents for such deviation.

In this highly kin-oriented society, even when the offences are serious, the kin group often tries to underrate the offence in the eyes of outsiders and at the same time exerts its influence in reprimanding the wrong-doer. It is likely that one without relatives might even be a victim of public censure and other serious punishments, especially when an offence is done to a person having many relatives.

Public delicts are conditioned more by the character, status, role and personality of the offender, and also the social situations in which the offences are committed, than by specifically defined laws. Trials of public offenders are held in public places, like the courtyard of the village Panchāyati, or the verandahs of cooperative societies, in temples and under holy trees, and are announced to the public by the beat of the drum. A messenger is sent round to inform the elders of each caste. The presence of the village elders representing all castes is considered necessary since the offence impinges on community sentiments and interests and in order to restore the fair name of the village, its moral and social prestige and solidarity which are affected by the offence, there is a keen sense of duty on the part of the villagers to participate in the proceedings and administer justice. Such occasions of public trial also provide the onlookers with entertainment. The way the litigants put forth their case, the language they use, their oratory, all have their comic side, and are often repeated later during gossip in many quarters of the village to the enjoyment of listeners.

Offences affecting the sentiments of the community as a whole are viewed as public delicts. A characteristic feature of a private issue is that it does not injure the community sentiments to the extent a public offence does, and it is not brought before the public gathering usually held to deal with the latter. Although a public offence is dealt with by the elders of the village, everyone assembled has a right to express his opinion if he feels the need, and everyone's opinion is certainly considered. Another significant point characterizing public law is that the contention exists between the offender and the community. Even when an individual or a group of individuals supports the offender, they are supposed to argue for restoring the damage done to the interests of the community. The decision of the council of village elders taken at the meeting is final and is supported by the entire community. If the offender does not abide by the council, then the community stands against him and penalizes him by way of excommunication, which is no less than social death to the offender.

Instances are known to Shivapur villagers, and narrated by them, of offenders having sought voluntary exile, being unable to face the stigma of excommunication. In one case the temple lands were mortgaged by a tenant of Shivapur to a money-lender of the adjacent village without the knowledge of the villagers. On the death of the tenant the money-lender refused to surrender the rights to the land. The trustees (Daiva-davaru) of the temple property sent word to the money-lender several times. Unable to settle the matter on their own, they called a public meeting and made a decision that none in the village should cultivate the temple land until it was surrendered back. A cultivator known for his notorious behaviour, however, dared to be the tenant of the land under dispute. He was given sufficient warning not to undertake the risk of cultivating the land and incur the displeasure of the village. Despite strong public opinion, he ventured to cultivate the land. In revenge, there was an organized effort by the people to destroy the crop when it was nearly ready for harvesting. Singlehanded he could neither go to court nor face social boycott. Being helpless he finally left the village to make his living elsewhere. The money-lender, too, had incurred the displeasure of the people in his own village and had suffered material loss. Ultimately he chose to surrender the rights to the land for the price fixed by the trustees of the Shivapur temple.

Another case offending the moral sentiments of the community occurred during the summer when it happened that the village washerman threw the carcass of a goat into the nearest pond of his neighborhood in the hope that high-caste Hindus would abandon using its water so that it would be made available for purposes of washing clothes. He was caught red-handed and brought before the council of village elders. People were enraged because of the pollution of the drinking water and imposed heavy punishment by withdrawing the traditional mode of payment for services rendered by him. He was thus paralysed economically and socially.

Other offences such as misappropriation of public funds, misuse of public authority and community lands, theft of images of village deities and their ornaments, pollution of sacred places, violation of communal taboos, etc., are recognized as public delicts. As mentioned above, the intensity of punishment varies according to the caste, personality and status of the offender. For instance, a high caste Hindu stealing the ornaments of the village deity would receive light punishment, whereas the same offence by an untouchable would end in severe corporal punishment.

The foregoing discussion indicates that the infringement of community interests and sentiments, the application of penal sanction, the organized collective responsibility of the people in administering justice and enforcing it, and the place of trial are some of the main characteristics of public wrongs which distinguish them from private wrongs. In case of private delicts, the interests of the individual or group are infringed upon, whereas in public delicts interests regarded as sacred by the community are in danger. That is why the community reacts with greater force against the person committing a public wrong.

The general sense of belonging and co-operative spirit among the members of the Indian village community induced some early writers to describe the village community as a little republic, self-sufficient, closed and having a worm's view of life. In this connection Charles Metcalfe[1] wrote:

> The village communities are little republics, having nearly everything that they want within themselves, and almost independent of any foreign relations. They seem to last within themselves where nothing else lasts. Dynasty after dynasty tumbles down; revolution succeeds revolution; Hindoo, Pathan, Mogal, Maharatha, Sikh, English, are all masters in turn; but the village communities remain the same. A generation may pass away, but the succeeding generation will return. The sons will take the places of their fathers; the same site for the village, the same position for the houses, the same lands will be occupied by the descendants of those who were driven out when the village was depopulated; and it is not a trifling matter that will drive them out, for they will often maintain their post through times of disturbance and convulsion, and acquire strength sufficient to resist pillage and oppression with success... all acting in union with a common interest as regards the Government, and adjusting their own separate interests among themselves according to established usage.

This conception of the little community gradually underwent change as intensive field studies of village communities started. It was soon realized that Indian villages, far from remaining in isolation and following a self-sufficient economy, were in fact a part of the network of the larger society. They had, long ago, established their economic, political, religious and legal relationships with the outside world.

The extra-territorial relations of Shivapur with the neighboring villages are found in many spheres of life. The carpenter, blacksmith, washerman, goldsmith, priests of various castes and marital ties are effective links connecting the village with those villages surrounding it. Besides, some of the lands belonging to the adjacent villages are within the territorial limits of Shivapur. This fact and other alliances have caused intercourse among the villagers so that they are obliged to mutually respect the customary law prevalent in the region. Thus village councils of two or more villages collaborate to decide inter-village disputes.

[1] Metcalfe, C., *Minutes of Evidence taken before the select committee on the affairs of the East India Company*, Vol. III (Revenue), 1832, pp. 331–2 (appendix 84).

Disputes concerning the use of river, tank and canal waters, engagements and divorces, celebration of religious festivals, using the services of artisans beyond their jurisdiction contrary to customary law, engage the attention of two or more villages. During the summer I came across a very interesting case which throws light upon the interrelationships between neighboring villages. The elders of Shivapur decided to celebrate the festival of Goddess Dyamavva and build a new chariot for the procession. This construction was dependent upon collection of large funds and the availability of a carpenter willing to render services at a cheap rate. The elders planned to collect contributions from the neighboring villages. In Sattur, a village situated at a distance of 3 miles from Shivapur, they faced a problem. The elders of Sattur asserted that their village is the natal home of the goddess and they would contribute on condition that the next festival be performed in Sattur. Otherwise, they would take the matter to the elders of the neighboring villages. Shivapur villagers feared loss of prestige and good-will in the villages, and therefore, they chose to decide the case by calling a meeting of the representative group of elders of both villages. It was there decided in favour of the wishes of the Sattur villagers.

Their next task was to search out a carpenter who would provide his services at a modest price. Finding that their own carpenter insisted on fixing the remuneration before undertaking the work, one member of the festival celebration committee retorted: "Being a carpenter of the village how can you demand fixing the remuneration in advance? I can get many carpenters from outside who would willingly take up the work without such a demand." The carpenter readily replied, to the surprise of all: "I challenge you to bring one." This challenge could not be met by the festival committee member. Since this news had already spread to the carpenters of the adjacent villages, none would come forth and accept the invitation to construct the chariot. Finally, the village elders, being helpless, indirectly persuaded the carpenter of their own village to undertake the construction of the chariot. This event illustrates that customary law recognized the common interests of neighboring villages and the social and economic obligations of artisans from those villages. Instances could be multiplied to demonstrate that the inter-village amity is reinforced by the mutual recognition of customary law and traditional procedures.

The foregoing description refers to some aspects of customary law as conceived of in terms of "Dharma," and "Adharma," manifested in different spheres of Indian village life. The rules of conduct expressed in Dharma and Adharma are closely related to the normative system of the larger society and are seen as such by the people themselves. The rights and wrongs, the positive and negative sanctions and the various social forces are, therefore, better understood and appreciated in their total context.

Customary law in Indian society is unique to the Hindu way of life. Its nature, mechanisms of social control, functional significance, areas and interests are all related to the entire social structure. It is a society hierarchically organized on the basis of caste, a very complex Hindu social institution. The traditional legal institutions govern the relationships between individuals and groups in the Hindu social system. The nature of customary law, and the way it is administered, point to a highly differentiated society.

In more than one way customary law overlaps the interests and areas of modern positive law. Both systems aim at safeguarding the interests of the society necessary for the survival of the members of both simple and complex societies. They are supported by similar sanctions, positive and negative, with functionaries to enforce the decision. These systems are differentiated into private and public delicts and take cognizance of kinship ties and collective sentiments. But at the same time these systems differ in many essential ways. Customary law is considered sacred whereas modern law is considered secular; customary law personal, modern law impersonal; customary law belongs to the people, modern law is alien. The attitudes of the people towards the two legal institutions are not the same. Modern law is formulated, controlled and enforced by those unfamiliar with them and, therefore, suspect, feared and often avoided. Customary law is respected, for it is from their forefathers. Its uniqueness lies in its final appeal to the conscience of the offender. In the transplantation of modern Westernized law, the element of conscience is omitted in the administration of justice and in the endurance of punishments by the wrongdoer. Customary law reflects the cultural diversity of society and contributes to the unity and colorfulness of social life, whereas modern law aims at uniformity and may ignore local customs and traditional institutions. The machinery used to enforce modern law is formal and organized, and there is no question of spontaneous mobilization of public opinion on the decision and enforcement of it. In the case of customary law, public opinion gathers momentum and strength when the offender becomes unbearable and dangerous to the interests of the community.

The existence of a variety of customary laws in India, and the various commentaries on them, are a testimony to its importance and continuity. Indian villagers have held customary law in high esteem and regarded it as essential for their survival. The binding force behind customary law is not merely its antiquity or sanctity or utility, but the will and desire to preserve the Dharma inherent in the Hindu social system. This has been made possible by the peculiar nature of the Indian village system based on the communal principle and the caste Panchayat. The relative isolation of Indian villages and the frequent changes in the head of the state induced collective leadership in the village, which took responsibility for the stability and orderly development of the community. The maintenance of the Dharma of the village was above the Dharma of the individual. The Dharma of the community was, therefore, Dharma *par excellence.* Inasmuch as Dharma is for the individual it is also for the community. In this sense it may be said that private law also contains germs of public law, but in the strictest sense of the word it does not appeal to the direct interests and conscience of the community as a whole, barring a few exceptions.

In pre-British India, the Indian rulers upheld customary law. They did not interfere in the local institutions of the people whose lives were regulated by diverse interests and values. The British rulers gave some recognition to the customs and usages of the people. But the growing complexity of the society soon made it necessary for them to modify the local legal institutions and their rights and privileges. In consequence, the British introduced for the first time a uniform criminal code throughout the country which dealt a serious blow to the importance of caste councils. In civil matters, too, such as marriage, family, divorce, property, etc., the role of custom and caste councils was effectively minimized by setting aside the customary authority of caste. Since then many efforts have been made in pre-independence and post-independence India to change the form and content of the Indian legal system. The recent attempts at the codification of Hindu law is a great set-back to the traditional legal institutions in India. The gradual disappearance of customary law from the social scene of the Indian village is evident in the steady decline of the powers of caste councils which enjoyed supreme authority in the past. The sanctions behind customary law are now affected by the organized machinery of the state. The Constitution of India does not recognize difference of religion, caste, creed, sex, etc., in the administration of justice. Obviously, this itself emphasizes the change brought about in the area of traditional legal institutions.

Despite the attempts made by the state to introduce a uniform civil code throughout India, it has given some regard to customary law prevalent in different parts of the country. Judges and lawyers have both given attention to the prevalence of customary law.

The Supreme Court has solemnly declared that "under the Hindu system of law clear proof of usages will outweigh the written text." The Indian legislators of different states have taken care to provide a necessary clause in the Acts passed by them to guard the customs and usages of the people, so that the officers entrusted with the task of administration of justice may decide the disputes in accordance with the ancient customs and usages of the people. Therefore, it is not quite true to say that customary law is not regarded as law by parliamentarians, and that the concentration on formal and written law has entirely distorted the perspective of Indian lawyers and intellectuals.[1]

The general reactions of the villagers in India, however, do not favour the changes that have been taking place in the legal system of the country. They express their dissatisfaction in this way. "The culprit goes without punishment in the modern court of law for lack of evidence, whereas it was not possible for him to escape punishment from the caste council." They feel that the modern law ignores the authority of caste, but nevertheless, continues to gain more strength and vigour. Yet while the modern law gives equal rights to both sexes in matters of property, people are systematically avoiding it by willing away the property to the eldest son or other member of the family.

In the countryside one often hears people talking about the increasing volume of litigation in the courts of law. "Every day a new law is made only to change it on the next day. How can one survive while there is so much legal confusion?"

From such responses one gets an impression of village India which is passing through a transitional period in the realm of law. If litigation is really on the increase in the Indian courts of law, as the people believe, then it points to the disintegration of the society of which increased litigation is a symptom.

[1] Srinivas, M. N., *Caste in Modern India*, p. 118 (Bombay, 1962).

XIII. THE WIDOW'S STATUTE IN VIETNAMESE CUSTOMARY LAW

Until recently, the men in Vietnam were granted the right to freely administer and dispose of family property. Moreover, if the wife predeceased her husband, he became the sole and absolute owner of the estate.[1]

It would however be erroneous to assume that the woman's role was of no importance in traditional custom. On the contrary, in the still recent past, she was called the "home secretary" (*noi tuong*) of the family, and it was not uncommon for her to provide the family's subsistence while her husband delicately praised the charms of nature or quietly prepared for his future by immersing himself in learned books hoping some day to pass the difficult imperial examinations.[2]

Should the woman survive her husband, her role increased considerably. By virtue of paragr. 113 of the Civil code of Tonkin and 111 of the Civil code of Anam which provides that in case of the husband's predecease, the conjugal community is continued as long as the widow remains in her condition. She replaces her husband as head of the family and in this capacity is entitled to his previous rights. She supplies the needs of the children and attends to their education. As a reward she is granted not only the enjoyment of her separate property but that of her husband, and upon this joint estate she possesses all her husband's previous rights of administration.

This same solution was adopted in Cochinchina where it derives from paragr. 82 of the Gia Long code which forbids the children to partition the inheritance as long as their parents live.[3]

The widow's rights appear to some authors as a tribute to her as a mother.[4] Unfortunately this opinion is not consistent with the situation where the couple lack offspring. The widow is not debarred on that account from her legal usufruct. Thus the latter provisions for the female are not due to her maternal capacity, but to her womanhood and widowship.

This right had been tentatively traced to the impact of Chinese

[1] Vu Van Hien, *Che do tai san trong gia dinh Viet Nam*, vol. 2, n. 390.
[2] Nguyn Manh Tuong, *L'individu dans la vieille cité annamite*.
[3] Lingat, *Les régimes matrimoniaux du Sud-Est de l'Asie*, vol. 2, p. 114.
[4] Lingat, *loc. cit.*

law[1] but this opinion is highly questionable because long before the promulgation of the Chinese-inspired Gia Long code, the widow's statute was already included in the Le legislation. As a matter of fact paragr. 373–375 of the Le Code originated from two laws promulgated by Le Thanh Ton in 1464, enabling the widow to keep and enjoy the inheritance, should her husband not leave any children at his death. A kind of usufruct is also recognized upon the joint property in other cases.[2] It is therefore clear that the widow's right in Vietnam has its origin in local customary law, of which the Le legislation is considered an accurate rflection.[3]

The question arises as to what extent customary law principles remain in force after the promulgation of the Family Code of January 2nd, 1959, since this code has not renewed the provisions devised by the earlier laws.

It is admitted that the ancient rule is not abrogated so far as it is not at variance or inconsistent with the new laws. Now, the new regulations, although they do not reiterate former solutions, contain no prescriptions that oppose them. Furthermore the new act is quite incomplete and merely promulgates general principles on several subjects.[4] It does not provide for the various cases of dissolution of joint property nor does it deal with the predecease of one spouse.[5] Inheritance law in the latter case is entirely omitted. Therefore, since the provisions adopted prior to the Family Code of 1959 remain in force, it may be interesting to examine the organization of the widow's statute and its legal foundation. We should then be able to see in what way it could influence potential future legislation.

It must be made clear that the widow's usufruct exists only in case she does not inherit from her husband. If the latter dies without leaving any relative entitled to inherit from him, the widow is granted the entire estate in her capacity as heiress. Nor is there any usufruct for her under the Anamese code, should the deceased have left an offspring of a first bed who is older than herself. The widow in this case would be entitled to an inheritance share equal to a child's, but be deprived of her usufruct.[6]

[1] Lingat, *op. et loc. cit.*
[2] *Quoc Trieu Hinh luat*, p. 150–153.
[3] *Quoc Trieu Hinh luat*, Foreword by Prof. Vu Van Mau, p. XX–XXII.
[4] Nguyen Xuan Chanh, *Luat gia dinh Gian yeu*, p. 7–15.
[5] Derrida, "Un Code de la famille au Sud-Vietnam," *Rev. intern. de dr. comp.* (1961), n. 1, p. 62.
[6] Paragr. 349, Anamese code.

In the other events the widow is granted legal enjoyment of the whole estate even against the decedent's will. According to most authors,[1] the husband cannot under any circumstances cut his widow off from the enjoyment of the family estate by virtue of paragr. 320 of the Tonkinese code which provides that his testamentary power cannot defeat the widow's right. The interpretation thus given of paragr. 320 has not met with unanimous approval,[2] but it is consistent with the court's doctrine which holds that the widow cannot be debarred from inheriting except by judicial disqualification.[3]

As a result of paragr. 346, Tonkinese code and 341, Anamese code, the widow is entitled to the administration of the whole estate. She collects and disposes of its income and revenue.[4] She is also the owner of such estate as is acquired during her widowship[5] by means of her savings and labor and retains this estate even if she marries again.[6] A decision of the court of appeal of Saigon once held that the law does not intend to give the widow the opportunity of making up a dower independently from and by means of the property upon which she is granted enjoyment,[7] but this view has not affected the courts' governing doctrine.[8]

As her husband's replacement and head of the family, the widow has the right to dispose of property. First she can dispose of movables in order to pay the decedent's and the community's debts and to provide for his parents, children, other ancestors, second rank wives and concubines.[9] The alienation of the widow's separate estate is permissible in these circumstances.

As for real property, the alienation is equally possible provided major children participate in the transfer.

In Cochinchina where the husband is the sole and absolute owner of the property, including the estate his wife brought with her upon

[1] Pompei, *Le droit patrimonial et familial au Vietnam*, p. 357; Vu Van Mau, *Les successions testamentaires en droit vietnamien*, p. 260–261.

[2] Lingat, *op. cit.*, vol. 2, p. 120.

[3] Hanoi Feb. 2, 1938, *Rev. Ind.* 1939, p. 804; Saigon Dec. 16, 1926, Dareste 1927.3.143, Penant 1927.1.195; Saigon Dec. 4, 1941, *Rev. Ind.* 1942, p. 173, commented by Camerlynck; contra: Saigon Jun. 18, 1897, *J.J.I.* 1897.3.909; Saigon March 1, 1923, Dareste 1923.3.78; Saigon Sept. 9, 1927, Dareste 1928.3.53; Saigon Nov. 1, 1929, Penant 1931.1.60.

[4] Saigon Oct. 19, 1916, *J.J.I.* 1918, p. 109.

[5] Paragr. 361, Tonkinese code and 360, Anamese code; add. Saigon Sept. 16, 1943, not published, in Lingat, *op. cit.*, vol. 1, p. 64, note 3.

[6] Hanoi Sept. 27, 1926, *J.J.I.* 1926, p. 378.

[7] Saigon Jun. 15, 1899, in Durwell, *Doctrine et jurisprudence annamites*, vol. 2, p. 114.

[8] Lingat, *op. cit.*, vol. 1, p. 64.

[9] Paragr. 347 1, Tonkinese code and 342 1, Anamese code.

marriage,[1] the widow has no right of disposition[2] unless she is compelled to do so out of absolute necessity: to pay her husband's debts for example or supply the needs of the children[3]: in that case the widow must be assisted by her major sons or if there are none by the eldest relative on the husband's side.[4]

It should be noted that the decree of July 21, 1925 demands a special authorization by the family council to be homologated by a court of justice to transfer a minor's estate. It has been decided that a widow must observe those requirements insofar as the estate is regulated by that decree.[5] This solution has been criticized by Camerlynck who holds that the decree should be relaxed in favor of the customary law and that a widow's right to enjoy and dispose of property is much stronger and wider than a guardian's prerogatives as provided for by law.[6] This view seems to have been adopted by recent doctrine.[7]

A similar question arises and is solved in a different way in Anam. If the children left by the predeceased husband are all minors, the Anamese code then applies the tutelage regulations. An authorization from the council of the family is then necessary for disposition of property.[8] In the same situation the Tonkinese code only requires the guardian's assistance.[9] Since the widow is the legal guardian her right of disposition is not limited. The preceding rules do not apply to such estate subject to the land regulations provided for by the decree of 1925. The widow's enjoyment, as a matter of fact, is then considered a usufruct[10]: transfers in those circumstances are valid only with the participation of those who are mentioned in the land registers as *bare* owners. Consequently the formalities required for the transfer of minors' property must be complied with if there are such minors among the children.[11]

The sanction against unlawful transfers is annulment of the transfer irrespective of whether they did or did not observe legal formalities[12] or

[1] Saigon March 7, 1946, not published, in Lingat, *op. cit.*, vol. 1, p. 65, note 1.
[2] C. Cass. Jan. 14, 1919, *J.J.I.* 1920, p. 54.
[3] C. Ind. Jul. 7, 1910, Dareste 1911.3.26; Saigon, April 21, 1939, *Rev. Ind.* 1939, p. 613; Saigon Dec. 4, 1941, *Rev. Ind.* 1942, p. 174.
[4] Saigon April 7, and 14, 1927, *J.J.I.* 1927, p. 156 and 159, Dareste 1928.3.14.
[5] Hanoi Dec. 28, 1934, Penant 1936.1.147; Hanoi March 31, 1939, *Rev. Ind.* 1939, p. 395.
[6] Comment under Hanoi March 31, 1939, *supra.*
[7] Saigon Sept. 1941 and April 13, 1944, not published, in Lingat, *op. cit.*, vol. 1, p. 67, note 1.
[8] Paragr. 342 2, Anamese code.
[9] Paragr. 347 2, Tonkinese code.
[10] Paragr. 184, decree of July 21, 1925.
[11] Hanoi Dec. 28, 1934, Penant 1936.1.147; Hanoi March 31, 1939, *Rev. Ind.* 1939, p. 395, commented by Camerlynck.
[12] Hanoi March 8, 1933, *J.J.I.* 1933, p. 377.

were unjustified.[1] Nevertheless the annulment cannot be requested by the children, whom filial reverence prohibits from bringing action against their parents.[2] Exception is made for the second rank wife's children, whom a transfer would defraud of their advantages.[3] Otherwise the action is open exclusively to the nearest relatives of the deceased husband or the eldest and nearest relative on his father's side.[4]

In Anam, even when legal formalities are not complied with, the annulment cannot be pronounced unless the transfer is proven not to be made in the family's interest.[5]

As a counterpart to her prerogatives the widow must assume the duties of a real head of the family. She must supply subsistence and see to the education of the children.[6] She is also charged with the debts of the property. In Tonkin and Anam this is so even if the debts exceed the value of the inheritance.[7] In Cochinchina, on the other hand, the widow cannot be charged beyond the assets of the inheritance.[8]

The widow's right is for her life. Nevertheless it can be ended before her death by her own action or as a consequence of certain events. First, she can release her enjoyment if she chooses, by partition (which she cannot be compelled to make).[9] In Tonkin and Anam the partition must be certified and signed by the decedent's heirs like any other amicable partition[10] and is permissible only when the widow has not yet begun the administration of the estate. In Cochinchina, mere consent from the children is required[11]; and a partition executed by the latter is valid provided that the widow has not objected.[12]

The widow can retain for her old age a portion of the inheritance[13] which she can dispose of,[14] at least if it does not exceed the property brought by her upon marriage.[15]

The partition cannot be revoked in Tonkin and Anam once the children are effectively in possession of their share.[16] In Cochinchina, on

[1] Saigon Oct. 1, 1896, *J.J.I.* 1897, p. 68; *C. Ind.* Jan. 7, 1910, Penant 1910.327.
[2] Paragr. 348 1, Tonkinese code and 344 1, Anamese code.
[3] Paragr. 348 3, Tonkinese code and 344 2, Anamese code.
[4] Paragr. 348 3, Tonkinese code and 344 3, Anamese code.
[5] Paragr. 344, *in fine*.
[6] Lingat, *op. cit.*, vol. 1, p. 63.
[7] Paragr. 345, Tonkinese code and 352, Anamese code.
[8] Trib. sup. Ind. Jan. 8, 1880, *Recueil Lasserre*, p. 13.
[9] Saigon Jun. 13, 1914, *J.J.I.* 1915, p. 79.
[10] Paragr. 382 2, Tonkinese code and 388 2, Anamese code.
[11] C. Ind. Jul. 6, 1882, *Recueil Lasserre*, p. 117; C. Cass. Jan. 14, 1919, *J.J.I.* 1920, p. 54.
[12] Saigon Dec. 30, 1943, not published, in Lingat, *op. cit.*, vol. 1, p. 63, note 3.
[13] Paragr. 351, Tonkinese code and 347, Anamese code.
[14] Paragr. 393, Tonkinese code.
[15] Paragr. 347, Anamese code.
[16] Paragr. 391, Tonkinese code and 397, Anamese code.

the contrary, children cannot have separate property as long as their parents are alive. The partition therefore, is not definitive and is revocable at any moment, as is any liberality made by parents. Nevertheless, revocation is permitted only if not too prejudicial to a third person or to the heirs themselves.[1]

The widow's usufruct can end by mere renunciation on her part before the major children and the Ly Truong.[2] In Anam, renunciation is permissible only before the widow has begun the administration of the estate.[3] If she makes such a renunciation, the widow keeps her separate property, but as a "compulsory heiress" she is still charged with her husband's previous debts and those owed jointly.[4] Nevertheless, it is likely that she will be no longer obliged ultra vires. As a matter of fact, paragr. 360, Tonkinese code and 359, Anamese code provide that renunciation does not exempt the widow from payment of her debts with her own property in case of insufficiency of the community's estate and of her husband's. It thus seems that the widow is chargeable within her separate estate.[5]

The rights of the widow can terminate by circumstances independent of her will, such as her disqualification or remarriage.

The widow who marries again definitively breaks all ties with her former husband's family[6] and automatically[7] loses rights associated with it. In Cochinchina, she retains only the property she brought upon marriage. In Tonkin and Anam she is entitled to her separate property and one-half of the joint property if the decedent left no children.[8] If there are offspring she loses all her rights upon the joint property (although she retains no separate share) unless she has contributed to the increase of the family estate by her savings and labor.[9]

The causes most frequently invoked for disqualification are notorious misconduct and squandering of fortune.[10] Other causes are forsaking of the widow's children or the parents or ancestors on the husband's side; condemnation for an attempt on the life or the person of one of the

[1] C. Ind. Nov. 6, 1913, *J.J.I.* 1915, p. 68; Saigon Sept. 16, 1919, *J.J.I.* 1920, p. 178; Saigon April 21, 1927, *J.J.I.* 1927, p. 162.

[2] Paragr. 363, Tonkinese code.

[3] Paragr. 363 1, Anamese code.

[4] *Recueil des avis du Comité consultatif de jurisprudence annamite*, Question 253.

[5] Lingat, *op. cit.*, vol. 2, p. 129.

[6] Paragr. 360, Tonkinese code and 359 Anamese code.

[7] Saigon April 16 and Jun. 4, 1942, not published, in Lingat, *op. cit.*, vol. 1, p. 70, note 9.

[8] Paragr. 360, Tonkinese code and 359, Anamese code.

[9] Paragr. 359, Anamese code.

[10] Saigon Dec. 4, 1941, *Rev. Ind.* 1942, p. 174; paragr. 357 2, Tonkinese code and 355 2, Anamese code.

deceased's near relatives; and failure to be in mourning for the decedent for twenty-seven months.[1] The enumeration is restrictive.[2]

Disqualification must be pronounced by the court.[3] In Cochinchina deliberation by an assembly of the family is required before submission to the court.[4] The action in any case is open to only a few members of the family,[5] to the exclusion of the other persons.[6]

The disqualified widow loses all her rights on the joint property and her husband's property. The estate is distributed to the decedent's heirs.[7] The widow merely resumes her separate estate. Nevertheless, if she has no such estate or if the latter is not sufficient to supply her needs then she has right to alimony which is deducted from the joint estate.[8]

Such is the widow's statute under the civil codes and according to the traditional doctrine. To what extent it is still in force depends on the legal nature and foundation of widowhood. The widow's statute has puzzled prominent authors who have endeavored to discover its legal nature.[9]

A first opinion, echoed by numerous decisions, held that the widow's enjoyment upon the family estate is a mere usufruct.[10] The assimilation to a usufruct was made by the Decree of 21 July, 1925. The widow, insofar as the estate she enjoys falls within the scope of the bill, ought to fulfill the duties of an ordinary usufructuary and in compensation be permitted to either transfer her right or to mortgage it.[11] It is now generally believed that this view is erroneous. Since it was early noted that the institution of usufruct in French law did not exist in Vietnam, it would be all the more peculiar to liken the widow's rights to such an institution.[12] Furthermore, the widow's prerogatives are at variance with the idea of a mere usufruct, as has been previously pointed out by the Commission of Jurisprudence of North Vietnam.[13] As a matter of

[1] Paragr. 357 2, Tonkinese code and 355 2, Anamese code.
[2] Hanoi Nov. 29, 1933, *Recueil de jurisprudence*, p. 170.
[3] Hanoi Jan. 13, 1932, *Recueil de jurisprudence*, p. 408.
[4] Cas. Req. March 2, 1931, *J.J.I.* 1932, p. 263.
[5] Paragr. 358, Tonkinese code and 356, Anamese code.
[6] Hanoi Oct. 19, 1932, *Recueil de jurisprudence*, p. 413; contra: C. Ind. Jan. 22, 1903, Penant 1905.1.28.
[7] Paragr. 357, Tonkinese code and 355, Anamese code.
[8] Paragr. 360, Tonkinese code and 359, Anamese code.
[9] Bui Van Thinh, *L'usufruit de la veuve en droit vietnamien*; Nguyen Phu Duc, *Le droit de la veuve en droit vietnamien*; Lingat, *op. cit.*; Vu Van Mau, *op. cit.*
[10] Cf. Bui Van Thinh, *op. cit.*
[11] Hanoi Jun. 30, 1939, *Rev. Ind.* 1939, p. 625.
[12] Saigon May 28, 1891, Penant 1891.1.140; add. Camerlynck, comment under Saigon April 21, 1939, *Rev. Ind.* 1939, p. 613.
[13] *Recueil des avis du Comité consultatif de jurisprudence*, Question 223.

fact, she has the right to dispose of the family property while a usufructuary ordinarily cannot alienate the estate he enjoys. On the other hand, there is no dismembering of family property which neither changes structure nor destination at the husband's death. The estate is assigned to the subsistence of the family and the education of the children and the widow has no right to alienate or hypothecate her enjoyment nor can the children transfer their would-be ownership.[1]

The foundation of the widow's statute has been as much discussed as its legal nature. Certain authors hold that the widow is granted her rights to offset the loss she incurred by bringing her separate property into her husband's family.[2] But there can be no doubt that the suggestion of a dower as allotted to the widow's subsistence is inconsistent with the responsibilities with which she is invested in the management of the whole estate.

According to a few decisions, the widow's right is a right of inheritance.[3] It applies indeed to the whole property and entails for its holder the duty to discharge the debts of the inheritance. But if this view is correct, then since the family property includes her own estate, the widow inherits from herself, which is impossible. Moreover, if the widow holds her rights as an heir of her predeceased husband, then the latter should be able to debar her from her enjoyment by testamentary dispositions. This is not possible according to the prevailing doctrine.[4]

The real foundation of the widow's statute has been perceived by the authors of the civil codes of Tonkin and Anam when they decreed that "in case of the husband's predecease the community is prorogated as long as the surviving spouse remains in widowhood."[5]

However, the idea of a continued community is rejected by most authors. It has been observed in particular that "the origin of the legal solution is independent of the community" and "the same situation is provided for in South Vietnam (Cochinchina) although community does not exist here."[6] Moreover, according to the Tonkinese and Anamese codes the spouses have the right freely to appoint their matrimonial arrangements and should they choose a regime excluding community, the widow would still be called upon to succeed her husband as

[1] Lingat, *op. cit.*, vol. 1, p. 60.
[2] Bui Ban Thinh, *op. cit.*, p. 13.
[3] Saigon Oct. 25, 1929, Penant 1930.1.198, Dareste 1931.1.152; Saigon Jul. 17, 1938, *J.J.I.* 1938.3.37.
[4] Cf. *supra*.
[5] Paragr. 113 1, Tonkinese code and 111 1, Anamese code.
[6] Lingat, *op. cit.*, vol. 2, p. 116.

the head of the family although there can be no question of a would-be continued community.[1]

The objection raised above becomes irrelevant if one does not mean by community the technical matrimonial system, but rather the conjugal society in its widest accepted connotation. As a matter of fact, the widow who replaces her deceased husband is bound by the same conditions to provide for the children and other members of the family. She has in compensation "all the rights of administration of her deceased spouse."[2] Is not this obvious proof of the continuity of the family despite the husband's death? Certainly, the widow's prerogatives are not exactly identical with her husband's previous ones, but the conjugal society survives all the same. Certain rules of management are merely modified because of the personality of the person invested with the manager's role.

Another criticism concerns the inconsistency of the functioning of a so-called continued community. Ordinarily, indeed, this community should have applied to each spouse. Should the wife predecease the husband, however, the community is not continued and the husband becomes the sole owner of her property.[3] It may be answered that this criticism fails to consider paragr. 368 3, Tonkinese code and 269 3, Anamese code which provides that "in case the wife predeceases [the husband], her estate is assigned to her husband who remains in possession of the family property, and administers and enjoys it in the interest of the family." There is no doubt that the same rights and duties are recognized by these provisions for husband and wife.

It is true that these provisions are somewhat opposed to the general rules of family law and have been considered a "recommendation" rather than a legal imperative.[4] They reflect all the same the legislator's concern for establishing a certain reciprocity between the spouses's respective conditions. This concern harkens back to the provisions of the Le code which considered the surviving wife on absolute equality with the surviving husband.[5]

The solution provided for above deserves attention despite the promulgation of the Family law of January 2, 1959. This law, criticizable in many respects, has the merit of recognizing equality between spouses. In a "universal community" as wide as could be conceived, husband and wife are entitled to and subject to the same rights and

[1] Lingat, *op. cit.*, vol. 2, p. 117.
[2] Paragr. 346, Tonkinese code and 341, Anamese code.
[3] Lingat, *op. cit.*, vol. 2, p. 116.
[4] Hanoi April 29, 1936, *Recueil de jurisprudence*, p. 350.
[5] Cf. *supra*.

duties. Most certainly, the new act does not provide for the situation of the surviving spouse nor deal with inheritance. It therefore leaves to the courts the difficult task of reconciling the new dispositions and the ancient codes. But it is precisely the conflict between the new rules and the old ones that grant the judges the opportunity to deduce the best solution.

As to the surviving spouse's rights, the solution referred to by paragr. 368 3, Civil code of Tonkin and 369 3, Civil code of Anam is consistent with and respectful to both customary law and modern legislation. In pursuance of these provisions the author respectfully suggests that the husband should be considered the owner of the family estate neither at his wife's death nor during her life. Then the widower's rights will be no different from his wife's should she survive, and the community is continued at the decease of either spouse.

The solution thus suggested may seem revolutionary and is certainly at variance with paragr. 113, Civil code of Tonkin and 111, Civil code of Anam. Nor does it fit the inheritance law provided by the latter. But its inclusion would be a most suitable and desirable part of a future unified legislation in which the whole of family law would be reformed in accordance with the habits of the people and modern insights. Customary law would then have actively and directly contributed to the re-establishment of an original Vietnamese institution from which the recent legislator, although aware of its merits, has failed to deduce its essential consequences.

XIV. CUSTOMARY LAW IN PAKISTAN

Pakistan, now hardly seventeen years old, cannot be said to have developed any new customary law. That part of customary law which was applicable before partition in the area now comprising Pakistan could be termed customary law in Pakistan. It is primarily the customary law in the Punjab regarding inheritance, succession, adoption and alienation, etc. which had overridden the personal law, and even the statutory law, in these matters.

(*A*) *Local Customary Law in the Punjab*

People in the Punjab adhered to customary law very strictly, and it is so various that the custom prevailing in one district differs from that in other districts. It is for this reason that even the English rulers did not dare to disturb customary law in the Punjab and were compelled to recognize it. In a Peshawar case their lordships of the High Court observed "In this part of the country it is a very strong habit of the people to adhere to their family usages." Keeping in view the great tenacity with which the people of this Illaqua follow their ancient usages, traditions and custom, the courts in prepartitioned India were compelled to hold repeatedly that the people carried their custom and usages wherever they went, even if they permanently left their original places of domicile and started living in a place where different customs and usages were in vogue.

It is for this reason that customary law in the Punjab received statutory recognition in the Punjab Act, 1872. When the English introduced their legal system into India, they allowed the Hindus and the Muslims to retain their own personal law relating to marriage, dower, gift, inheritance, etc. But certain sections in the Punjab declined to accept even personal law in these matters. They were rigidly governed by the customary law. Therefore under Section 5 of the Punjab Act, it was provided that the rule of decision shall be any custom of any class of persons which is not contrary to justice, equity and good conscience and has not been declared void by any competent authority, and that the personal law of the parties professing Islam or Hinduism will govern them, except insofar as such law has been altered or abolished by legislation or is contrary to the provisions of this act or modified by custom. It may be pointed out that this act did not provide that there was any presumption in favour of the existence of custom to the exclusion of personal law. The section prescribes that in certain matters personal law shall govern the parties in the first instance; but it is for the person relying upon the rule of custom, contrary to his personal law, to allege and to prove the existence of the custom. In a Privy Council case it was held in the Punjab that the burden lies upon those who assert that they are governed by custom to prove the fact, and to establish the particular custom, and if such evidence is not available the parties are governed by their personal law[1]. "There is, however a big jump from a custom which restricts gifts to one which restricts alienations for value. Unlike common law, customs do not grow and develop to meet the changing needs of Society and custom can not be extended by logical process, it can only be established by evidence. In the absence of any evidence to prove the existence of a custom against alienating ancestral property for value it can not be held that such a custom exists."[2]

Some examples of this customary law in the Punjab may be given. Among the members of the agricultural tribes there is a presumption in favour of the applicability of certain customs. For instance, among agriculturists living in a compact village of the Central Punjab, an agriculturist has no power to alienate his ancestral land save for necessity, and the onus lies on the vendor to rebut this presumption by proving a special custom of the family to the contrary. Similarly agricultural land held by a body of proprietors belonging to one tribe or descended from a common ancestor does not belong absolutely to the individual holder, but to the entire family or community.Likewise among agriculturalists, there is a general custom that a daughter's son or a sister's son cannot inherit and so also a widow of a male holder takes only a life interest when a proprietor dies leaving no male issue. In the matter of succession to non-ancestral property, daughters exclude collaterals, and so also daughters have preferential right to succeed to the ancestral land as against collaterals in the district of Abbottabad and some Tehsils of Lahore district. Further, a mother succeeding to a son does so as widow of her own husband. Certain

[1] 45 *I.A.P.* 20 relied on, Vol. 41 *P.R.* 390 referred to, p. 20.
[2] 12 Lah. 286, pp. 20–21.

agricultural customs governed a whole village community, e.g. one village had a right to cure wood from adjoining land.[1]

It has been decided that: "A right of pasturage arising from immemorial use resembles a right based upon custom and thus a right of pasturage can only be claimed on the basis of a customary right and the ordinary incidents of a customary right attached to it, including the manner and the methods of its proof and that even if after such proof the custom is found to have been established, it must still be shown that it is not unreasonable before it can be treated as a valid custom."[2] A custom observed in a particular district derives its force from the fact that it has, from long usage, obtained in that district the force of law. It must be ancient; but it is not of the essence of this rule that its antiquity must in every case be carried back to a period beyond the memory of man, still less that it is ancient in the technical English sense. It will depend upon the circumstances of each case as to what antiquity must be established before the custom can be accepted. What is necessary to be proved is that the usage has been acted upon in practice for such a long period and with such invariability as to show that it has common consent, being submitted to as the established governing rule of the particular district.[3]

Thus a custom must be proved by reliable evidence of repeated acts openly done, which have been assented to and submitted to in such a manner as to lead to the conclusion that the usage has by agreement or otherwise become the local law of the place.[4]

Recording and Proof of Custom

The British ordered a special record to be prepared of the prevalent custom in each district which was in regular settlement from 1845 to 1865 which is called Rewaj-e-Am. It is a public record prepared by a public officer in the discharge of his duties and is admissible in evidence to prove the relevant custom stated therein, and forms a strong piece of evidence in support of the custom.[5] Another method of proving custom is by the opinion of the persons likely to know of its existence, having

[1] PLD 1961, p. 131.

[2] PLD 1961 Dacca 79. See also, *Bholanath Hundi and others* v. *Midnapore Zamindary Company Ltd. and six others* 31 I A 75; *Lakshmidhar Miers and others* v. *Kiamatula Haji Chaudhry and others* AIR 1937 Cal. 248; *Syed Ali and others* v. *Vajaddin* ILR 63 Cal. 851; and *Asrabulla and others* v. *Kiamatulla Haji Chaudhry and others* AIR 1937 Cal. 245 ref.

[3] P. 84 C.

[4] P. 84 E.

[5] *Beg.* v. *Allahdita* 45 PR 1917, p. C.

special means of knowledge[1] or by statements of persons who are now dead but who when alive were aware of the existence of such custom (under clause (4) of the Evidence Act). It can also be proved by any transaction by which the custom in question was claimed, modified, recognized, asserted or denied.[2] It can be ascertained from village oral traditions, Rewaj-e-Am or Wajidul-arz.[3]

(B) *The Role of Custom in Islamic Law*

It is well established that *Sunnah* or tradition is one of the primary sources of Mohammaden law. It consists of the sayings of the Prophet and the precedents derived from his acts. In fact the Prophet himself during his lifetime recognized the source of law based on custom, as in many instances he either gave his express sanction to certain pre-Islamic usages or allowed such usages to continue without any expression of disapprobation.

As law paper was unknown in pre-Islamic Arabia, tribes and chieftains had only oral customs for their guidance. In his Mohammaden Jurisprudence, Abdur Rahim makes a mention of a number of such customs many of which were adopted wholly, or with modifications, by Muslim law. One of these customs was "Muta-" or temporary marriage which was a form of marriage during pre-Islamic times. It was tolerated for some time after the founding of Islam but the Prophet soon disallowed it. "*Mahr*" formed a part of the customarymarriage contract, but the guardian of the girl often received the amount, thus rendering marriage a sort of sale. Under Islamic law, *mahr* was regarded as a principal term of the marriage contract and the right of the bride. Again, under custom there was no restriction as to the number of wives, but Islam fixed the limit to four and that too under special conditions and circumstances. An Arab under custom could not marry his mother, grandmother, sister, daughter, or granddaughter. They are included amongst the prohibited degrees under Islamic law. Likewise, there were many forms of divorce and dissolution of marriage, some of which were adopted by Islamic law with modifications. The principle of agnacy or "Tasib" which is fundamental to the Sunnite law of inheritance owes its origin to pre-Islamic customs. Likewise, "Diyat" or blood money, the rule of evidence that the plaintiff must substantiate his

[1] Sections 48, 49 of the Evidence Act.
[2] Section 10 of the Evidence Act.
[3] Section 35 of the Evidence Act.

claim and the other party must take an oath, etc., owe their existence to pre-Islamic custom.

The customs and usages of the people of Arabia which were not expressly repealed by text are held to have a sanction. *Urf*, *adat* and *Ta'ammul*, *i.e.*, customs, have the force of *Ijma* and would be operative under the principles of Istehsan, even if they violate a rule by analogy. During later times, we get maxims like the following: Everything that is not prohibited is permissible; Custom is decisive.

Islamic law, besides sources of law like *Quran*, Traditions and Ijma, also recognizes the force of custom *(urf)* and usages *(adat)* in establishing rules of law. The validity of such laws as are founded on customs is based on principles which are somewhat similar to those which recognize the validity of laws based on *Ijma*; *e.g.*, the verse of the Holy *Quran* which says, "Whatever the people generally consider good for themselves, is good in the eyes of God." But in Islam customary law is an inferior authority to *Quran*, Hadies, *Sunnah* and *Ijma*, though superior to the law based on Qayas, Istehsan, Ijtehad and Muslehat inasmuch as it is based on the general practices of the people. While *Ijma* implies collective deliberations on the part of men well versed in the principles of law, customary law is superior authority to a rule based merely on analogy.

Again custom *(urf)* literally means an action or belief in which persons persist with the concurrence of reasoning, and which their natural dispositions agree to accept as right. It stands to represent unwritten custom as opposed to established law. It is sometimes held to be equivalent to case law or common law. In many tribal communities there are native "codes" of unwritten laws and traditions by which local life is regulated. Frequently, however, *urf* is simply the decision made in various cases by the sovereign or his agent.

In the case of those customs and practices which prevailed in the time of the Prophet and which were not abrogated by any text of the *Quran* or "Hadit," the silence of the Divine Books of Times is regarded as amounting to a recognition of their validity. Customs *(urf* and *adat)* as a source of law are generally spoken of as having the force of *Ijma*, as their validity is based on the same text as the validity of the latter. It is laid down in "Hidaya" by Hamilton that customs hold the same rank as an *Ijma* in the express text of the *Quran* or traditions; and at another place in the same book, custom is spoken of as the arbitrator of analogy. Though customs do not command any spiritual authority like *Ijma* of the learned, nevertheless, a transaction sanctioned by custom is equally operative even if it be in violation of a rule of law based on analogy. It must not, however, be opposed to the text of the *Quran* or authentic traditions.

(*C*) *Customary Law v. Personal Law*

Returning again to Pakistan, it may be said that the Muslims living in the undivided India always felt that Muslim personal law was being greatly affected by custom because the Hindus upon conversion to Islam, retained their customs. Therefore in 1937 after great agitation by the Muslims, the Shariat Act of that year was passed. It provided:

> Notwithstanding any custom or usage to the contrary, in all questions (save questions relating to agricultural land) regarding intestate succession, special property of females including personal property inherited or obtained under contract or gift or any other provision of Personal Law marriage, dissolution of marriage, including talaq, ila, zihar, lian, khula and mubarraat, maintenance, dower, guardianship, gifts, trusts and trust properties, and waqfs (other than charities and charitable institutions and charitable and religious endowments) the rule of decision in cases where the parties are Muslims shall be the Muslim Personal Law (Shariat).

The scope and purpose of section 2 is to abrogate custom and usage insofar as these have displaced the rules of Mohammadan law regarding matters specified therein. The effect of section 2, Shariat Act, is to make the Muslim law expressly applicable to matters which, under the terms of previous acts and regulations, had to be decided on principles of equity and good conscience. That this was the object of section 2 is made clear by the repeal of parts of the earlier acts and regulations.

Questions relating to agricultural land, charities, charitable institutions and charitable and religious endowments had been excluded from the subject matter specified in section 2 of the Act because, under the Government of India Act of 1935, these subjects were within the jurisdiction of the provincial legislaturc.

Therefore in 1948 the Punjab Muslim Personal Law (Shariat) Act was passed. Section 2 of this act is:

"2. Notwithstanding any rule of custom or usage, in all questions regarding succession (whether testate or intestate), special property of females, betrothal, marriage, divorce, dower, adoption, guardianship, minority, legitimacy or bastardy, family relations, wills, legacies, gifts, religious usages or institutions including waqfs, trusts and trust property, the rule of decision shall be the Muslim Personal Law (Shariat) in cases where the parties are Muslims."

The intention of the Shariat Act was merely to replace custom with personal law.[1] The plain meaning of section 2 is that after the 15th March, 1948, the property of a Muslim shall devolve according to Islamic law and not according to his custom. There could be no doubt as to the purpose and scope of the Act. Customary law, which has so long held the field to the detriment of females, is to yield place to the Shariat which recognizes their property right.[2]

[1] *Ghulam Bhik* v. *Mst. Hussain Begum*, PLD 1957 Lahore 998.
[2] *Muhammad Asghar Shah* v. *Muhammad Gul Sher Khan*, PLD 1949 116 FB.

TABLE OF IMPORTANT STATUTES, ETC.

MALAYSIA

TABLE OF IMPORTANT CASES

INDEX

GPSR Compliance

The European Union's (EU) General Product Safety Regulation (GPSR) is a set of rules that requires consumer products to be safe and our obligations to ensure this.

If you have any concerns about our products, you can contact us on ProductSafety@springernature.com

In case Publisher is established outside the EU, the EU authorized representative is:

Springer Nature Customer Service Center GmbH
Europaplatz 3
69115 Heidelberg, Germany

Batch number: 10830943

Printed by Printforce, the Netherlands